Between Two Worlds

Between Two Worlds

A CULTURAL HISTORY OF GERMAN-JEWISH WRITERS

• • • • •

by Lothar Kahn

with the assistance of Donald D. Hook

Iowa State University Press / Ames

Authorization to photocopy items for internal or personal use, or the internal or personal use of specific clients, is granted by Iowa State University Press, provided that the base fee of $.10 per copy is paid directly to the Copyright Clearance Center, 27 Congress Street, Salem, MA 01970. For those organizations that have been granted a photocopy license by CCC, a separate system of payments has been arranged. The fee code for users of the Transactional Reporting Service is 0-8138-1233-X/93 $.10.

♾ Printed on acid free paper in the United States of America

First edition, 1993

Library of Congress Cataloging-in-Publication Data

Kahn, Lothar.
    Between two worlds: a cultural history of German-Jewish writers / by Lothar Kahn with the assistance of Donald D. Hook.
        p.   cm.
    Includes bibliographical references and index.
    ISBN 0-8138-1233-X (acid-free paper)
    1. German literature—Jewish authors—History and criticism.
2. Jews—Germany—Biography. I. Hook, Donald D. II. Title.
PT169.K34 1993
830.9'8924—dc20   93-7676

This book is especially for

Lore

but also for

Liesel, Leslie, and Geoffrey

and their children.

CONTENTS

III

The War and Its Aftermath:
New Functions and Pressures

IV

Gathering Clouds:
Jews Exit from German Life

V

FOREWORD

orn in the Saar Territory on June 1, 1922, Lothar Kahn and his
family fled Hitler's Germany in 1937, first for Luxembourg, and
then New York City, where Lothar finished high school and
attended City College and Columbia University, earning his Ph.D. at
Columbia in 1954. Except for one year at Ohio State University, his entire
teaching career was spent at Central Connecticut State University in New
Britain. Upon his retirement in 1987, Dr. Kahn was named the first
University Professor in the history of the university and granted emeritus
status. He died suddenly and quite unexpectedly on January 23, 1990, not
long after being informed that he was to be awarded an honorary doctorate
in humane letters by the Johann Wolfgang von Goethe-Universität,
Frankfurt am Main, in recognition of his outstanding scholarly treatment
of German-Jewish exile literature.

Professor Kahn was the author or co-author of many books and
learned articles, pamphlets, essays, book reviews, filmstrips, and newspaper
op-ed pieces. Knowledgeable in French and German literature, he wrote
extensively in both areas, and often with emphasis on the creative Jewish
literary element. His books included *Mirrors of the Jewish Mind,* an
anthology of portraits of Jewish writers between the two world wars, and
Insight and Action: The Life and Work of Lion Feuchtwanger, an exposition
of one of the world's most popular novelists of the 1930s and 1940s.

Between Two Worlds is a unique reference work for scholars in the field
of German-Jewish writers. Probably no combination of works already on
the market will yield the large number of lesser writers covered. The reader
will surely be impressed by the surprisingly high consistency of information
from author to author, considering the paucity of facts available on so
many of them. But this is also a book in which American Jews in general
can take pride, for it displays a segment of their intellectual legacy
inherited at personal cost.

His most ambitious undertaking, *Between Two Worlds* is a logical
conclusion to Dr. Kahn's concentrated scholarly concern—the depiction
of the German-Jewish writer in conflict with his soul and his society. In the
production over the years of article after article on the Jew in literature,

Dr. Kahn collected and cataloged a huge corpus of facts and opinions—many his own—on writers great and not so great, which were to form the basis for his book. I do not think the idea for a book was in his mind from the start but developed gradually and rather naturally as his material increased. I worked closely with him, almost daily, for more than a quarter of a century, but do not remember hearing much about his "Jewish history," as he called it, until perhaps ten years ago. He once described it to me as somewhat encyclopedic, as cultural as well as specifically literary, and, rather cryptically, as a kind of "service history."

Sometime in the middle 1980s Professor Kahn began to pass me parts of chapters to read and criticize, and before long there was a first draft of the entire manuscript, which I carefully edited, as did his colleague and friend in the English Department at Central Connecticut State University, Professor Robert Spiegel. Since acceptance of the book by Iowa State University Press and Dr. Kahn's untimely death shortly thereafter, I have been editor *qua* author. My duties have included going through the text two more times, making changes here and there, responding to changes and suggestions entered by several editors, and proofreading. I have researched and identified or confirmed all but a handful of missing sources, names, titles, and dates; translated all remaining German citations and expressions into English and reworked and retyped Bibliography C. Given the extent and nature of the bibliographies, Dr. Kahn did not think it necessary to cite page references in footnotes.

During the early stages of my work I co-authored, with the help of a sheaf of unorganized notes left by Dr. Kahn in his files, "The Impact of Heine on Nineteenth-Century German-Jewish Writers," thereby gaining a better insight into questions and relations discussed in *Between Two Worlds*. The article appeared in *The Jewish Reception of Heinrich Heine*, edited by Mark H. Gelber, and published by Max Niemeyer Verlag in 1992. A paper on this topic was to have been delivered by Dr. Kahn at the three-day Heine conference held at Ben-Gurion University of the Negev in Beersheva, Israel, in April 1990, for which he had received a travel grant from the American Council of Learned Societies.

I gratefully acknowledge the support of the Consulate General of the Federal Republic of Germany, in Boston, which provided financial assistance at the outset of this project.

The work I did to bring this book to completion is offered to the fond memory of a fine friend and scholar and to the many students, faculty, and administrators associated with Central Connecticut State University where, for forty-six years, Lothar Kahn skillfully taught, wisely counseled, and gently led.

Trinity College   DONALD D. HOOK
Hartford, Connecticut

AUTHOR'S PREFACE

There is not at present a history of German-Jewish writers. Biographies or adequate studies of most writers discussed in these pages do not exist. Much has been written, to be sure, about Heine and Kafka, Schnitzler and Döblin, Broch and Feuchtwanger. But for most of the nineteenth-century writers the material available is minuscule and often unreliable. This cultural history is designed as an introduction to the lives, roles, and achievements of writers of full or partial Jewish origin. If for no other purpose, this focus and analysis should justify the study.

Beyond its primary function, *Between Two Worlds: A Cultural History of German-Jewish Writers* tries to determine whether any common bonds united the writers who played a vital role in the last century and a half of German cultural life. Years before I began this study, I formed the impression that Jewish writers I then knew—whatever their attitude toward Germany, the extent of their Jewishness, or their general *Weltanschauung*—were at the mercy of the host society that ultimately governed their view of themselves, their sense of acceptance or rejection, the strength of their psyche, and the direction of their literary endeavors. It was then I decided on a larger project: to find out whether my observations of the few held true for the many. Thus, in a broader sense this book examines the effect of the dual identities of German-Jewish writers as they reacted to being both German and Jewish.

The genius of a Heine or Kafka clearly operates outside the frame of the more representative writers, for the modest talents of "second-raters" approach more closely the thoughts and sentiments of the majority. Thus I found I derived as much insight from the writers of the second rank as I did from the exceptional ones who dominated the scene.

Many years ago, when I undertook as my doctoral dissertation the work of the French literary historian Gustave Lanson, I was struck by the persistent criticism of the number of pages allotted to different writers. Why so many pages to Racine and so few to Corneille? Why the dichotomy between Voltaire and Rousseau? No two observers will quantify importance the same way, and this task becomes increasingly difficult when, as in this book, literary quality is not the main criterion.

This literary-cultural history straddles two cultures; unfortunately, not many models exist for historical summaries of cross-cultural interaction. This deficiency is especially troublesome in the case of German-Jewish writers, who are not allied fully with either the German or Jewish camp. Groupings and generalizations become hazardous indeed in such uncharted territory.

While most of the writers practiced the main genres of *belles-lettres,* I have occasionally included peripheral and adjunct genres. Where critics and editors have been discussed, emphasis has been given them as promoters of specific careers or of literary directions.

I have not tried to fit my findings into a broad synthesis. The time is not ripe; far more work needs to be done before a successful attempt at synthesis can be made.

Had the brief cultural togetherness of German and Jew been allowed to continue, I might have become a part of it. Since it was not, I must be content with recording it.

INTRODUCTION

Despite many satisfying and even triumphant moments in their 150 years of involvement in German literary life, Jews never achieved their dual goal: overall integration into German life with retention of a measure of Jewish individuality. While integration was also imperfect in other western societies, rejection was more sharply etched in Germany.*

Here the emancipation battle continued for eighty years. The Jew was frequently invited to become German, only to see that invitation withdrawn again and again. He could become German only if. . . . The price for citizenship was raised ever higher, and the question eventually involved how much the Jew was willing to pay. Like the frog in La Fontaine's fable, the Jew inflated the German in himself and eagerly inquired, "Am I German enough now?" "No," the German seemed to respond, "not yet!" The Jew would inflate his Germanness still further. "Am I there yet?" "No, not yet; it is not enough." In the end, the whole relationship burst.

On the German side certain complaints remained fixed. To the Germans, Jews were essentially foreigners who could speak only as Jews. They were purveyors of materialism, secularism, and rootless change, thereby undermining solid German Christian traditions. They threatened to dominate cultural life as, it was charged, they already controlled the world of commerce and finance. Alien in manner and attitudes, they had no business as guardians of German culture. They were accused of politicizing, intellectualizing, and radicalizing German life, all the while believing they were improving and humanizing society. But in effect, they were merely weakening and corroding Germany. Moreover, they had the temerity to mock quiet obedience, love of order, and sense of duty—the

---

*In this book, the terms are used as follows: A *Jew* is a person belonging to the worldwide religious and ethnic continuation through descent or conversion of the ancient Jewish people. A *German* has been—at least since the Confederation of 1871—a native or inhabitant of that political entity identified most often as Germany. A *German Jew* is an ethnic Jew whose first language is German. —*Donald D. Hook*

very qualities that epitomized German decency and stability. Jewish intensity, rationalism, idealism, and wit—once briefly viewed as charming—were turned into threats to be crushed before the Jews could demolish what was worthwhile in German life.

In their fear of Jewish qualities the Germans revealed several historic weaknesses. The German Enlightenment had failed to provide a secure, liberal middle class such as existed in France and England. The Germans had no genuine, deeply anchored, democratic political traditions. In the absence of a unified nation or authentic national sentiment, such feeling had to be artificially fostered. Eventually, Germans developed these attitudes to excess—often at the expense of foreigners. And the Jew was the nearest foreigner in their midst.

Meanwhile, Jews were in turmoil from the moment they were released from their prison-ghettoes, in which they were required to live as minority members of society for economic, legal, and a variety of social reasons. For the first time in centuries they were afforded a choice. They could remain loyal to a tradition that was often perceived as arid and intolerant, or they could leave the fold—an act Jews viewed as despicable and Christians did not always trust. Between the faithful and the apostates was a great majority that preferred a German political and cultural orientation with a Jewish religious option. As the German states in the nineteenth century increasingly proclaimed themselves Christian, even the religious residue of Jewishness sometimes became a bothersome inconvenience.

The "Mosaic Persuasion" of the many was, after all, the ancient Judaism, which, like Christianity, had come under critical review by the *philosophes* of the Enlightenment. Out of this reassessment, as well as from the tensions with German Christianity, there evolved on German soil some of the major innovative trends in modern Jewish history. Tensions, choices, and Kantian and Hegelian thought combined to give birth to the Reform movement, the science of Judaism, the seminal thought of Hermann Cohen, Franz Rosenzweig, and Martin Buber. Yet not even these major contributions could halt the slide of Judaism toward nominal observances. The decline, however, was probably no greater than the disinterest of Christians in their faith.

As attacks on Jews erupted, the reactions of Jews seemed to divide into three types. The first division, the large center group, accepted its Jewishness as another fact of existence to which its members needed to adjust. A second group gave up on full acceptance and converted its awareness into a defiant attitude toward Germans and Jews alike. A third group persisted in the patient attempt to persuade Germans that Jews were virtuous, and deserving, and eager to blend into the landscape and make a contribution. This group was intent on demonstrating that the Jew as

German was no different from a Rhinelander or a Bavarian. In this book the first group will be referred to as "centrists," the second as "defensive-aggressors," and the third as "defensive-apologists." At various times in the lives of many writers, group members crossed lines for varying periods, often for tactical reasons, sometimes as the result of a potent emotional response. With the exception of a few Jewish anti-Semites, all reacted vigorously toward flagrant expressions of anti-Semitism. This reaction was the common denominator linking them together—perhaps their sole unified response.

Yet none of the anti-Jewish episodes—those of the post-Napoleonic period, the late 1870s, or the 1890s—had as disillusioning an impact as World War I. Most Jews, writers included, hurled themselves into the fray with the same enthusiasm and abandon as their Christian brethren, though Jews seem to have entertained doubts earlier and withdrawn support sooner. While the main support for the national war effort derived from genuine patriotism, there was the additional motivation of becoming part of a brotherhood, even part of the nation itself. What better way of demonstrating their desire for oneness and their craving for community than through an offering of blood and life? Their dedication would show their desire for unity with the struggling German people and win them the very recognition that had been so long withheld.

It soon became clear that this expectation was unrealistic, that their sacrifice would be viewed neither as patriotic nor as an offering, that it would adduce neither integration nor friendship. Confronted by numerous hostile officers, many Jews had good reason to think they were fighting a two-front war.

Rejections notwithstanding, some Jewish writers did see themselves, as some anti-Semites charged, as co-guardians of the German spirit. Was it the belief in *Geist* itself, the supremacy of *Geist*—a secular equivalent of the ancient belief in Torah? Or was it a specially fervent attraction to German *Geist?* If so, why? Was it merely the proximity of German spirit, a form of gratitude and identification? Or was it that German *Geist,* at the moment of the Jew's entry into German life, was epitomized by Herder, Goethe, Schiller, Kant, or Hegel—and that Jews had not recognized a marked change in the direction of power and physical might that had taken place since?

Jews clung to the universalist perception of German spirit, even as Teutonism; medievally inspired Romanticism; militarism; and notions of blood, soil, and iron increasingly held sway. The ideals embodied in the works of Treitschke, Wagner, and Lagarde had little in common with those held by the culture heroes of old. Jews saw themselves as protectors of a mentality to which people were politely paying lip service but one that had long been replaced. The perception of German *Geist* was not the same for many Christian Germans as it still was for most Jews.

Because of this ever-widening gap—but surely for other reasons as well—Jews attempting to explain themselves in terms of desirable values were doomed to frustration and failure. Their respective points of departure were different, as were their stations of arrival. Jews as Jews became too uncomfortable to explain themselves without inhibitions and fears.

Why were they ineffective in stating their case forcefully? In one form or another they had always been on the defensive unnaturally. Perhaps they were excessively burdened by historical memory. They were aware of persecutions, humiliations, exile, the pattern of flight and resettlement that had taken place in the territory in which German was spoken. They were also aware that the same evils were still tormenting Jews in Eastern Europe. Though most German Jews saw themselves as unlikely victims of past events, the memory of those occurrences had left psychic scars. These manifested themselves through a seemingly inexhaustible vitality, an uncommon breadth of intellectual interests, and a dangerous determination to accept nothing as true merely because tradition presented it as such. Historical memory and dominated status joined to fashion a Jewish psychology and creativity that intermeshed. In some instances they brought about personal turmoil, but in others they formed a rich source of stimulation. Jewish energy, unwillingness to let the status quo prevail, high visibility in spite of a barely tolerated outsider position became in turn new sources for hate and distrust of the Jews.

Since Hitler's rise to power, it has become common practice to condemn the German Jews' advocacy of assimilation. Although assimilation was often foolish and dishonorable, a blanket condemnation does not make sense. What was the alternative for urban Jews, those truly "assimilated," not too long conditionally released from the ghetto? Was there a road other than the German one, however many obstructions there might be on it? Did the host governments make any alternate routes available, and would they have tolerated them? With roots severed from Torah and Talmud, it was not easy for Jewish intellectuals to find accents of their own in new and unaccustomed situations. The only recognizable road was the one that led through German language and culture.

Yet in the first third of the twentieth century, Jews came to use even German culture as both a means and an end. Increasingly, Jewish writers employed German culture and their own brand of residual Jewishness as vehicles for reaching the broader goal of a universal European culture. The assimilationist pressures of the post-Napoleonic decades made participation in German life appear as the only viable course to follow. Toward the end of German-Jewish coexistence the aspirations of Jewish writers and thinkers turned increasingly toward the transnational. Neither German nor Jewish values had lost their intrinsic merits, but the writers were trying to transcend both in search of a higher and nobler ideal.

I

Jews Establish Themselves

in German Literary Life

Mendelssohn: Figure at the Gate

The history of German-Jewish literary coexistence is not without its shining moments. The most brilliant may have occurred at the very establishment of the nexus: the personal amity and spiritual harmony between **Gotthold Ephraim Lessing** (1729–1781) and **Moses Mendelssohn** (1729–1786). It is doubtful that any other friendship of comparable intensity and significance developed in the ensuing 150 years.

Their relationship prospered at a time when the values of the Enlightenment held sway over the world of intellect. The keys to this epoch were rationality and universality, the notion that mankind was one and that tribal, national, and religious stresses were of secondary import. Superstitions, atavistic beliefs, and improbable notions of all kinds were to yield to the primacy of new values that were needed for worship in the temple of humankind.

Lessing was among the first Germans to believe that a Jew could possess *Bildung*—culture, education, and refinement—and could be converted into a constructive member of society. Similarly, Mendelssohn was convinced that once the Jews were free from outside oppression and irrational religious fetters, they would be able to demonstrate their true mettle. Lessing in his liberal Protestant fashion and Mendelssohn in his independent Jewish manner sought to cast aside mystical practices and beliefs. Both the circle of friends they formed about themselves jointly—and those Mendelssohn cultivated separately—were largely attuned to their objectives.

The *Maskilim* (enlightened ones) who congregated about Mendelssohn spread the word of Jewish Enlightenment in different parts of the decaying empire of the German nation. Across the border in France, earlier in the century, a Montesquieu and later, a Count Mirabeau and Abbé Gregoire had come to essentially similar visions of the common, Jewish future. Though some advocates of the Age of Reason—notably the exiled Voltaire at Ferney—kept attacking Jews, it was partly out of petulant personal animosities and partly because Voltaire held Judaism responsible for its detested offspring, Christianity. The Jewish Bible struck Voltaire as a receptacle of contradictions and superstitions. Submitted to critical

3

scrutiny, this holy book could not stand the test of reason. In time, Voltaire's personal greed led to unpleasant incidents with Jews similarly motivated, and the usually lucid *philosophe* linked superstitious adoration of Torah and Talmud to the worship of bank notes. Yet Voltaire's particular brand of Jew-hate barely retarded the efforts of fellow rationalists to liberate Jews in the name of reason and justice.

Neither Lessing nor Mendelssohn, and certainly not Christian Wilhelm von Dohm (who drafted a famous document on behalf of civic equality), believed that in their present condition the Jews met the standards for citizenship. All deplored the occupations of most Jews—peddling, money services, and the like. They were also unhappy with the alleged Jewish obsession with *parnose* (earning a living); they detested the "jargon," i.e., Yiddish, which until recently had been a unifying force between Eastern and Western Jewry. They found Jews generally oblivious to the culture surrounding them and seriously backward in outlook. Except for a handful of wealthy, sophisticated Jews, mostly in Berlin and Königsberg, the Jews as a group were deficient in *Bildung.*

Inside Judaism, the Enlightenment had wrought revolutionary changes, perhaps more revolutionary than those within Christianity. The latter, after all, had suffered many shocks in its second millennium. Heretical movements, secessions from the existing church, wars, and civil wars had led from bloody massacres to thirty years of war. The "house" of Judaism, by contrast, had remained essentially intact, the rabbinic authorities challenged only intellectually, with change limited to reinterpretations of old texts. Now in the middle of the eighteenth century, and vastly accentuated after the meteoric appearance of Mendelssohn, the fresh air invading the house of Judaism caused it to shake from the impact. At the end of the century, it was a miracle that so much of the house was left standing at all.

The changes wrought by the hunchback from Dessau were both direct and indirect. As Leo Baeck noted, Mendelssohn demanded that Jews rationalize their religion, purging it of its empirical mysticism. Second, he urged that they learn the German language and enter the stream of German culture. Third, he insisted that Jews secure equal rights that would put them on the same level of humanity as their Christian fellow citizens. Through these and other measures he breached the wall of cultural isolation, awakening Jews from centuries of slumber, acceptance, and resignation.

His influence did not end here. Through examples of personal rectitude and his remarkable autodidactic achievement, he helped recast far and wide the image of the Jew. His friendships and involvements in the intellectual community at large afforded splendid examples of cultural cross-fertilization and religious tolerance.

Equally important, he set the tone and established a framework for ensuing debates with Christians about the Jewish condition. He was probably personally responsible for the occurrence of these debates in Germany rather than in some other nation.

However, the limits of the debates were soon pushed beyond Mendelssohn's expectations. Under his disciples, they included issues that this devout Jew—despite all his reformist zeal in specified areas—would have abhorred. These disciples, as well as his children, bear frightening testimony to the gap that can exist between the visions of a master and the reality perceived by his pupils. Mendelssohn's delicate balances between tradition and change and his clearly-heard admonition to adhere to the ceremonial law (which was revealed only to the Jews and set them apart) were soon abandoned or forgotten.

While Mendelssohn's disciples sometimes made a mockery of his teaching, they were instrumental in converting the Prussian capital into a center of Jewish life. They spread over the length and breadth of the German-speaking states, but their spiritual home remained Berlin. Berlin became the prime site of the early agitation for civic rights. It was in the staid Prussian capital, only a few years after Mendelssohn's death, that Jewish hostesses invited the great luminaries of German culture into their salons. While Germany remained culturally diffuse, with Dresden, Leipzig, Stuttgart, and Munich vying for honors as center, Berlin towered above the others as a focus of belletristic endeavors, with the presence of Jews gradually adding to this eminence.

Mendelssohn's achievements and personality did not escape the attention of provincial and even village Jews. The hold he had on their imagination is suggested by countless anecdotes involving his person. Again and again, their deformed champion, Moses Mendelssohn, is depicted scoring points in meetings with Frederick the Great (whom he never met) through his wit and wisdom. Just as often, Mendelssohn's prowess secured a request on behalf of Jews. His physical handicap, unprivileged birth, widely recognized "virtue," and defeat of Lavater in their epistolary duel all contributed to the creation of the Mendelssohn legend.

The great man's first published work was essentially literary, although its contents even then spilled over into philosophy, his more natural home. Unbeknownst to the young Mendelssohn, then employed as a clerk, Lessing had his friend's *Philosophische Gespräche* (*Philosophic Discourses*) (1755) published anonymously. Soon it became known that a Jew had written a book in German revealing his deep love for German language and culture. This Jew had actually recommended that Germans shed the vestiges of French influence, despite the ironic fact that the Prussian king thought little of German letters and preferred the French to the German language. Frederick the Great had even been dismissive of Lessing, whom the Jew Mendelssohn had publicly championed.

Soon the two friends collaborated on a satiric treatise on Pope as a metaphysicist, and Mendelssohn alone wrote a letter on sensations and feelings. The two works jointly have been regarded as the foundation of esthetic criticism in German. Together with the distinguished book dealer Friedrich Nicolai, Mendelssohn also edited a literary journal, and his reviews could henceforth be found in the *Bibliothek der schönen Wissenschaften und der freien Kunst* (Library of Fine and Liberal Arts).

Within ten years of his initial appearance on the German cultural stage, Mendelssohn had made a name for himself. From the first, philosophy had been his favorite discipline."Über die Evidenz in den metaphysischen Wissenschaften" ("About Evidence in the Metaphysical Disciplines") won him the prize for philosophy over Thomas Abbot and Immanuel Kant. His *Phaedon* (1767), modeled after Plato's dialogue, netted him a European reputation, but it also embroiled him in a repugnant controversy with the Swiss theologian Johann Caspar Lavater. Lavater had challenged: Why would he, Mendelssohn, not take the final, logical step and embrace Christianity?

An exchange of letters ensued, and when it was all over, Mendelssohn felt emotionally and intellectually drained. It had been a difficult and hated task. On the one hand, he could ill afford to antagonize the Christian world; on the other, he would not be disloyal to himself and his Jewish convictions. During the prolonged nervous illness that befell him in the wake of the Lavater debates, he resolved to enlist his remaining strength in the service of oppressed Jews.

While Mendelssohn emphasized the need to learn the German language, he did not forget the importance of knowing the "Holy Tongue." He wanted to avoid any impression of placing one above the other. Thus he advocated, if not a fusion of cultures, then at least a coexistence on equal terms. German Jews were to learn German through the words of the Bible. To help achieve this, he set about translating the Bible into German, as Luther had done for his own purposes.

At the same time, Mendelssohn called for a more nearly perfect and grammatical Hebrew, better religious training, and appropriate schools to achieve these goals. *Hameassef,* a Hebrew-language journal published by his disciples within the master's lifetime, responded to Mendelssohn's call. In his preface to the German edition-translation of Menasse ben Israel's *Rettung der Juden* (*Salvation of the Jews*) (1782), Mendelssohn produced the initial major document in the long literature to follow on the emancipation of the Jews. However, in one of this best-known works, *Jerusalem oder über religiöse Macht und Judentum (Jerusalem or about religious power and Judaism)* (1783), Mendelssohn may have committed the greatest single error of his career. Pronouncing the religious aspirations of all the faiths nearly identical—a tenet of the Age of Reason—he designated the ceremonial law alone as binding upon and distinctive to Jews.

If this were the sole differentiating feature of Judaism, what would be left in the ensuing decades that perceived transmitted ceremony and ritual as antiquated and, at best, merely symbolic in meaning? His formulation was to prove fragile and perilous. Mendelssohn's proclamation of freedom of religious belief was based on the assumption of the constancy and binding nature of ceremonial law. But to the ensuing generation, including his own children, only freedom of belief was appealing; the underlying assumptions were quickly forgotten. His proposals rested on what he believed to be firmly in place. He never suspected how much and how soon it would be considered outmoded.

After Mendelssohn's death in 1786, the delicate balance he espoused was lost, tilting in favor of German culture and away from Judaism. But Mendelssohn had forged powerful bonds between German and Jew, establishing a nexus that was to be dissolved only with the advent of Hitlerism. Though Mendelssohn refused to prove what a good German he was at the expense of his Jewish identity, those who assumed the mantle of leadership after him were willing to pay that price.

When conditions were calm, Mendelssohn could explain why Judaism was a valid, sound road to God and why Jews were entitled to equal rights. When he came under attack, foreshadowing nearly all Jewish writers in German, he became defensive and capable of striking back. He would let himself be nudged, not shoved; when sensing the latter, he could become a harsh judge of others.

Moses Mendelssohn, the remarkable figure at the gate of German-Jewish existence, was talented, restrained, dignified, and even (from a favorite expression of the time) "virtuous." In a way, this Jew seemed more than human at a time when most Jews had to settle for being less. Mendelssohn raised expectations for the quality and performance of Jews that could not possibly be fulfilled.

● ● ● ● ●

The Disciples

Most faithful to Mendelssohn's delicate balancing was **Naphtali (Hartwig) Wessely** (1725–1805), Moses's senior by four years who outlived him by nearly twenty. A progressive educator, in his writings he emphasized Hebrew grammar, comments on Hebrew texts, and translation into German.

In various essays in Hebrew, some of which vivified biblical history, Wessely clearly demanded secular knowledge for Jews in addition to the Hebrew texts he made available. Such knowledge was a requisite for the successful study of Torah and Talmud, and even the most observant Jew should respect it. Although his programs for youth were moderate, they garnered him the enmity of rabbis. Through his Hebrew epics, which influenced the likes of Herder and Klopstock, Wessely tightened the knot between Jewish and secular German culture.

The contribution of **David Friedländer** (1750–1834), born in Königsberg of a wealthy family, tipped the balance decidedly toward the German. During Mendelssohn's lifetime, this tendency was not manifest. When he became Mendelssohn's unofficial successor, he was expected to extend his teacher's work, though admittedly he was not Mendelssohn's equal as scholar or thinker. What tarnished Friedländer's reputation for posterity was his infamous letter on behalf of Jewish "fathers" of Berlin. To all intents and purposes, he offered the "sale" of Judaism in return for full German citizenship. His sole proviso: he could not accept any Christian dogma inconsistent with reason. This condition was insulting to Christians as well and was rejected by Probst Teller, to whom the letter was addressed.

It was the first major out-and-out assimilatory proposal made in the wake of the Mendelssohnian revolution. According to the letter, Jewish individuality and Jewish religion were to be integrated into Christianity. At the time Friedländer wrote his epistle, he thought the proposal was entirely honorable and in line with the changes of the previous twenty to thirty years. With the rejection of his offer, Friedländer had to accept the status quo. He remained a Jew, the epitome of the wealthy, businessman-intellectual Jew, the *Bildungsjude,* who was to become a standby of the German-Jewish scene. Unlike others who opted for baptism, Friedländer devoted himself to the Jewish Free School of Berlin, to writings pleading for Jewish rights, to charities both Jewish and Gentile. The poet Heinrich Heine referred to him in the 1820s, along with Lazarus Bendavid (see below), as a rock of Judaism whom his own generation was not likely to duplicate.

Though deeply immersed in the battle for emancipation, Friedländer failed to comprehend the nature of Judaism. He favored whatever in Judaism might be most attractive to Christians. He demanded war on rabbinism, narrowness, apartness; he urged vigorous reform and heightened interest in the external world. To achieve his ultimate goal, acceptance by others, he was prepared to lift prohibitions against intermarriage, suggesting dual ceremonies wherever such ceremonies occurred. To Friedländer—to paraphrase a quotation from *Henry IV*—being a full-fledged German was well worth a Chuppah or a Yom Kippur fast.

Lazarus Bendavid (1763–1832), who headed Friedländer's Jewish Free School for twenty years, is remembered as a mathematician, leading proponent of Kantianism, and Jewish educator. Just as Jews were soon to constitute the vanguard of Goethe admirers, so Bendavid, along with Marcus Herz and Salomon Maimon, noisily carried the banner of the Kantian system. Like many later Jewish writers, these men acted as pathfinders and publicists for German-Christian innovators.

Although Bendavid was a believing Jew, his modernism shocked the rabbis. They were appalled by his hostility to certain customs and his insistence that Jews shed external differences. Contrary to Mendelssohn's preaching, Bendavid suggested abolition of the ceremonial law, replacing it with the "pure Law of Moses." Ethical values—which Mendelssohn had judged the same for all faiths—represented for Bendavid the real significance of Judaism.

Bendavid could well be called the Luther of Judaism who asked for a rereading of original texts, in part to see how far the interpreters had strayed. His reverence for Torah was undiminished, and he prepared numerous commentaries. Talmudic emphasis and the general state of the contemporary synagogue did not, however, appeal to him. Nor was he concerned about the divisions his views might generate within the Jewish fold. The monolithic colossus of Judaism, he thought, could just possibly benefit from some moderate splintering. Bendavid enjoyed the respect of younger men like Heine, Zunz, and Moser. Mendelssohn would have been less pleased with him.

Herz Homberg (1749–1838), once the tutor of Mendelssohn's children, violated the Mendelssohnian balance more than other disciples. As Holy Roman Emperor Joseph II's inspector for Jewish schools, Homberg discarded the Mendelssohnian synthesis altogether, leaving the field free for total assimilation. When attacked by Jews for his policies, Homberg wrote the emperor slandering his coreligionists. He seemed determined to force his brand of *Haskalah* (Enlightenment) on the Jews of the empire. He went so far as to ask for the closing of Talmudic schools, lessening the importance of Hebrew (a total departure from early *Haskalah*), and doing away altogether with the "jargon." In his zeal, he seemed to demand virtual censorship of Hebrew books. It was only after lengthy infighting with the Jews of Prague—Homberg's headquarters—that Jews were able to secure his dismissal. Chastened by this action, Homberg wrote Hebrew texts more nearly consonant with tradition.

All the time that these educators, thinkers, and writers sought a rapprochement with German culture while trying to retain the essence of Judaism and gain in the battle for emancipation, most partisans of the *Haskalah* remained active in the field of Hebrew *belles-lettres*. These Hebrew works often showed the influence of Shakespeare, Racine, Goethe, or Herder. The members of the Enlightenment movement composed poetry, dramas, essays, and biblical exegeses. Much of this Hebrew literature appeared in *Hameassef* (*The Collector*), a journal that appeared with some interruptions and slightly altered titles between 1783 and 1829. At first some Königsberg *Maskilim* of the stature of **Isaak Euchel** (1756–1804) helped direct it; later, lesser figures from Berlin, Dessau, and Breslau had a hand in steering it.

It is not in the purview of this study to examine these writings, but merely to signify their purpose: to bring the literature of the non-Jewish world, from Orient to Occident, to the attention of German readers of the Hebrew language who were eager for *Bildung*.

• • • • •

Belletristic Beginnings in German

Considering the low esteem in which Polish Jewry was to be held in later years, it is ironic that the first Jewish poet in German, **Isaak Falkenson Behr** (1746–?), was born in Russian Poland (according to some, in Lithuania). Behr set out for Prussia at about the same time as the philosopher **Solomon Maimon** (1754–1800). Both told of the barrenness of their youth, the lack of refinement and *Bildung,* as well as disheartening experiences with crude religious teachers.

When Behr arrived in Germany he did not know a word of German and still wore the caftan. He rapidly acquired command of German and was admitted to the heady circle of Daniel Hitzig, possibly the wealthiest Jew of Berlin. Lessing ventured the prediction, unfortunately not to be realized, that the young man might go far.

His poems are interesting only because they were the first by a Jew in German. His subjects are routine for the time: the elegies of nature, the charms of maidens, the feats of Frederick the Great, special occasions in the royal household. What individuality exists manifests itself in a lightness of tone, a general merriment, a mock innocence.

Contemporaries appeared aware of the publication as an "event." Heinrich Christian Boie wrote to Karl Ludwig Knebel, a Goethe confidant, "The poems of the Lithuanian are said to be out now. You are right. The Jewish nation offers much promise, once it awakens from its slumber." Goethe himself reviewed *Gedichte eines polnischen Juden (Poems of a Polish Jew)* (1771), though he wrote more about his *Die Leiden des jungen Werthers (The Sorrows of Young Werther)* than about Behr's poems. He implied disappointment. He had hoped for a different voice; the one he heard was not very distinctive.

Although he had planned to return to his homeland, Behr settled in Germany as a medical doctor. His slim volume opened the door through which soon more talented men would enter. The connection between these poems of a Jew and German poetry was thin, but it was a connection.

Unlike Behr, who vanished into anonymity, **Moses Ephraim Kuh** (1731–1790) has been the subject of a biography and of fiction by Berthold

Auerbach. His life illustrates the dilemma of being an intellectually emancipated Jew in an age of transition.

Kuh's ill-concealed views led to confrontation with the rabbis of Breslau. The talented youngster preferred secular books to the study of Talmud. Common sense was not Kuh's strong point, and the lack of it, coupled with a deplorable sensitivity, brought him into conflict with his financier uncle in Berlin, the mint master Veitel Ephraim. During his stay in Berlin he also met Mendelssohn, but the two men had a falling-out. After extensive travels in Europe, he returned to Breslau. Hurt and reclusive, Kuh was summoned by a religious tribunal for not fasting. He was released without penalty only because his accuser would not come forward. Christians were equally demanding. When a clergyman asked in Kuh's own epigrammatic manner, "Kuh, why stay with the Father when you can have the Son?" Kuh severed his contacts with Christians as well. Bouts with mental illness were to plague him for the rest of his life; perhaps that is why he never married.

Kuh's religious beliefs were forged out of the Enlightenment and the Mendelssohnian formulations. He believed in God and thought all religions were valid ways of reaching Him. Conversion from one faith to another was hence unnecessary. "Ein Gebet" ("A Prayer") carries echoes of Lessing's *Nathan der Weisel* (*Nathan the Wise*). Neither religious nor ethnic identity, but human worth was of account:

Das gute Volk

Dies Volk ist recht nach Gottes Bilde;	These people are genuinely in God's image;
Ist gegen arme Brüder milde,	Kind toward their poor brothers,
Heilt Kranke, fordert keinen Lohn—	They heal the sick, demand no reward—
Wie heißt die seltne Nation?	What's the name of this rare nation?
Sind's Juden? Christen?—Es sind Wilde.	Is it the Jews? The Christians?—It's the savages.

A considerable bitterness often pierced the lightness of his verse, especially when he bemoaned the lack of Enlightenment about him. He was appalled that the Jew still had to pay a *Leibsteuer* (tax on his person) as he moved from one German state to another:

Zöllner: Du, Jude, mußt drei Taler erlegen.	**Publican**: Hey, Jew, you have to cough up three thalers.
Jude: Drei Thaler? So viel Geld? Mein Herr, weswegen?	**Jew**: Three thalers? All that money? Why, sir?
Zöllner: Das fragst du noch? Weil du Jude bist.	**Publican**: You have to ask? Because you are a Jew.
Wärst du ein Türk', ein Heid', ein Atheist,	If you were a Turk, a heathen, an atheist,
So würden wir noch einen Deut' begehren.	We'd ask just a trifle.

Als einen Juden müssen wir dich scheren.	As a Jew we have to fleece you.
Jude: *Hier ist das Geld. Lehrt euch dies euer Christ?*	**Jew**: Here's the money. Is this what your Christ teaches you?

Outbursts such as these are rare. Kuh's social awareness was limited, his religion private. Prayer, too, had to be personal, not prescribed, and he had little regard for memorized phrases without involvement of heart and soul: "God's good world becomes my altar, and the whole universe is my Temple."

This was not quite the religion of his one-time friend, Moses Mendelssohn. Ceremonial law played no role in this humanitarian faith, in which humanity has but one purpose: to elevate itself to a higher level of understanding and tolerance.

Kuh's life presaged the conflicts that beset many later writers. The title of Berthold Auerbach's novel on the life of Kuh, *Poet and Merchant,* reflects on the discord between businessman-fathers and poet-sons. Like Kuh, many later writers were devastated by the yearning for a world of human kindness and friendship and the real world they came to know. In Kuh's psyche the inner rift and unhealed wounds culminated in mental illness, foreshadowing that long list of writers from Daniel Lessmann to Stefan Zweig who evaded through suicide the conflicts that surrounded them.

The small volumes of lyrics left by the Alsatian **Mose Büschenthal** (1783–1818) are filled with verses as melancholic as most of Kuh's had been deceptively light. Büschenthal's lyrics suggested a religious disposition. He knew Hebrew, French, and German, and he translated into the third language cherished literary treasures from the other two. He also translated one of Mendelssohn's philosophical tracts into Hebrew. Büschenthal's *Sammlung witziger Einfälle der Juden als Beiträge der jüdischen Nation* (*Collection of Witty Ideas of the Jews as Contributions toward a Characterization of the Jewish People*) (date unknown) announced with Kuh's epigrams the lightness of tone that would soon be viewed as a characteristic of Jewish writing.

The aggressive stance of **Saul Ascher** (1767–1822) vis-à-vis developments within the German states marks a sharp departure from the calm, often pleading approach of Mendelssohn's disciples and the inoffensive banter of the early poets. While mentioned by Bendavid, Friedländer, Heine, and Zunz, Ascher has come into his own only recently. As a thinker and essayist—his novellas are of little import—he dared to question basic theories of the deified Mendelssohn, recognizing the brittleness of

Mendelssohn's formulation. Ascher was also among the first to realize the deadly threat to Jews and Germans alike of the nascent mystical and romantic nationalism sprouting around him. Since Romanticism was found especially often in aristocratic circles, Ascher was not a favorite among these elite. His boldness shows in 1810 in the treatise "Redemption of the National Debt" and in his criticizing of Karl von Altenstein, the Minister of Education and Culture. Ascher also suffered abuse for a defamatory article, wrongly attributed to him, in which the author "desecrated" the memory of the recently deceased Heinrich von Kleist.

Before Heine and Börne, Ascher fitted most closely the image of the naughty Jew who did not know his place and occasionally dared to fault the society about him. Ascher's defiant spirit first erupted when, barely twenty-one, he published his *Bemerkungen über die bürgerliche Verbesserung der Juden* (*Remarks Concerning the Improvement of the Civic Status of the Jews*). Here Ascher vetoed the idea of Jews becoming soldiers, on the grounds that they were psychologically unprepared for soldierhood and ignorant of their rights and obligations as citizens. They might become soldiers at a future time. Not only would they first have to discard their present ways and prejudices, but they would also have to replace them with a fearless wish to do battle for equality. Not much later, Ascher wrote *Eisenmenger der Zweite* (*Eisenmenger the Second*) (1974), a blistering attack on Fichte's nationalism, including his early destructive anti-Semitism.

In *Leviathan* (1792) he reassessed the doctrines of the recently deceased Mendelssohn. Ascher resolutely placed the ideal of humanity above any other. In Jews he no longer saw the representatives of a nation, but of a religion—one they had good reason to revere. Judaism did not have as its unique component the ceremonial law, but the vitality of Jewish spirit manifested through *Glaubenslehre,* or articles of faith. Ascher listed fourteen of these, which, in the view of many, bore a strong affinity for those of Maimonides. Their essence is the belief in the One God, God's conveyance to the Jews of the Torah, and His choice of Moses and the prophets as recipients of the gift of prophecy. With these concepts as their foundation, Jews could build on it the values of the Enlightenment and also become sensitized to the well-being of society as a whole. Ascher's reforms were modest; he even disapproved of organ music and choirs as imitative of Christianity.

Although Ascher clearly wanted a Jewry attached to German ways, while clinging to his concept of Judaism, he was the first to tangle with the so-called "Teutomania" then evolving under the aegis of Arnim, Jahn, and Müller, not to speak of the vehemently anti-Jewish professors Rühs and Fries. Ascher was not bashful about castigating the union of *Deutschtum,* Christianity, and Romanticism as an unsavory and frightening merger. The

Germanizing of nature, religion, and justice, and the labeling of dissenting religious thought as alien, struck him as ludicrous and regressive.

Where was yesterday's enlightened German, the "man of reason," the "reasonable man," the world citizen? Medievalism, clericalism, feudalism, and chivalry were all being exalted at the expense of those who had raised the German spirit to new heights in the closing decades of the eighteenth century. They impute to Germany and the Germans the noblest virtues and intoxicate themselves with these qualities. For these "Teutomaniacs" the Jews were doomed to remain undesirable strangers, a nation within a nation, unworthy of standing beside the noble German. Defiantly, Ascher reminded Teutomaniac pamphleteers like Rühs that German armies, whom Rühs had exalted at the expense of Jews, had lost battle upon battle to the French until Jews began participating in the war. (However, it is doubtful that Ascher was serious in believing that Jews were a major factor in the defeat of Napoleon.) Internal religious controversy continued as Jews entered the mainstream of German life and gave up centuries of apartness. The Germans were interested in them, some welcome signs were out, but already the favorable climate of the Enlightenment was yielding to the less auspicious one of Romanticism. For Jews this transitional period was one of heightened inner and outer struggle.

• • • • •

The Salons

The salons hosted by Jewish-born ladies for the benefit of writers, diplomats, and the "society of the mind" promoted the interchange of ideas and stimulated the arts. In spite of the hostesses' indifference to Judaism, they functioned unwittingly as a means of tightening the bonds between German and Jewish muses. In their salons the hostesses helped carve out for Schiller, and especially Goethe, the lofty niche the two were to occupy in German letters. The salons may have engendered in the German participants an increased awareness of the intellectual potential of Jews and of Jewish women as a significant cultural force. Finally, some of the drama inherent in the transition from the Enlightenment to Romanticism—the shifting emphasis from reason to feeling and mind to heart—was played out in the salons of the Berlin Jewish hostesses. As for the hostesses themselves, they were prepared to shed all vestiges of their Jewishness. All but one went one step further and accepted baptism.

Henriette Herz (1762–1847) was the daughter of a distinguished physician of Portuguese origin and the wife of Marcus Herz, Mendelssohn's personal physician and an eminent Kantian interpreter. Marcus initially hosted a salon of his own with a philosophic focus. Gradually, in an adjoining room, the attractive Henriette assembled her friends to discuss mainly literature. Among her devotees was Wilhelm von Humboldt who became infatuated with her. Before long, however, von Humboldt recognized that Henriette's sentimentalism, her *Schwärmerei* (rapturous enthusiasm), and her direction of the conversation only to topics with which she felt comfortable, barely concealed a shallowness he found less alluring. A deeper relationship, though platonic, linked Henriette to the theologian Friedrich Schleiermacher and, to a lesser extent, to the Schlegel brothers. A greater affinity for these Romantics than for the rational von Humboldt may explain the different quality of her relationships.

Schleiermacher more than others alienated Henriette from Judaism. His brand of religion, divorced from the rational notions of the Enlightenment, had an abiding influence not only on Henriette but on German

Protestantism. He was eager to discard the dry, intellectual components which the previous two generations had added. He redefined religion as an "emotion, feeling or disposition of the soul, a surrender of the self to the Infinite and the Eternal." Religion could grow out of the personal experience of the individual being. Schleiermacher also held that Judaism was no longer a vital force and, given the mass conversions of the time, predicted its early demise. As for Henriette, she waited for her mother's death before embracing Christianity. Her baptism was born of conviction, her romantic temperament, and Schleiermacher's power. While her salon strengthened some ties between Jews and the Christians who frequented it, it did even more for the spread of mystical Romanticism.

This direction was even more evident in the life and salon of **Dorothea (Brendel) Mendelssohn-Veit-Schlegel** (1763–1839), Moses Mendelssohn's daughter and Henriette Herz's childhood friend. Where Henriette was distinctly feminine (her sexuality, however, less developed than her "virtue" and prudery), Dorothea Mendelssohn was rather masculine—and neither virtuous nor prudish. Of her father's teachings she retained only the basic respect for religion, but from the first it was directed away from Judaism. She converted initially to Lutheranism, later to Catholicism. The influential figure in her life was Friedrich Schlegel, who cheapened their affair by describing it, at times insensitively, in his *Lucinda*. Schlegel remystified religion as Moses Mendelssohn had striven to demystify it. In the manner of the emancipated woman, Dorothea espoused the new and the different. She did not shy from scandal, and she dismissed all who "merely existed."

Her salon served as a vehicle for spreading the views of Friedrich Schlegel, who eventually married her. Toward her Jewish past, her views were sufficiently negative for some critics to label her the first self-hating Jewish woman. Dorothea did not serve as a bridge between German and Jew. Her feet were solidly planted in Christian Germany, with never a look backward. A devout Christian, she encouraged two of her Jewish-born children—from her first marriage to a Jew—to direct their considerable artistic gifts to the Nazarenist school of painting.

No salon of the time could match that of **Rahel Varnhagen**, née Levin (1771–1833). Homely, introspective, passionate, brilliant though undisciplined, she charmed her guests with her challenging mind and lively personality. In her first salon she received the likes of Count Mirabeau and Mme. de Staël on their trips to Berlin; the Germans she received included Jean Paul and Schiller. In her later salon, when she was already married to the diplomat Varnhagen, she hosted the Humboldts and the young Heine.

Royal princes frequented her salon. She was the prime confidante of both parties in the most celebrated love story of her time, that of Prince Ferdinand and the commoner Pauline Wiesel. Though Rahel was apolitical, the post-Napoleonic era was not. Leaders of the repressive Metternich regime were among her guests. At times, she commented freely on her negative perceptions of their activities.

From the first, Rahel fought two handicaps—her Jewish birth and her physical ugliness. She fretted over both and for a long time made her peace with neither. The salon enabled her to forget where she came from and what she looked like. Through her marriage to the aristocratic Varnhagen, her intellectual inferior and many years her junior, she lost the Jewish maiden name of Levin and perhaps even reduced the alleged disgrace of her homeliness.

Her comments about Jews ranged from neutral to unfavorable. She spoke up, however, against the persecutions of the Hep! Hep! riots of 1819, which led to beatings of many Jews, and toward the end of her life perceived a beauty in Judaism that had previously eluded her.

Rahel may not have felt at home in her salon established before the Napoleonic wars. Its cultural center was the new Romanticism, toward which she had reservations. Her second salon, after 1819, veered toward a Neoclassicism far more to her liking. What both had in common was an unqualified Goethe worship, Rahel being one of the foremost promoters of the Weimar sage.

There is an ironic quality to some of the later appraisals of Rahel. Her biographer Ellen Key called her "the greatest woman to come out of Jewry." Long after his wife's death, Varnhagen spoke of her as the "third light" (after Jesus and Spinoza) to shine forth from Israel. Kobler recognized in her a visionary, filled with the gift of prophecy. Margaret Susman, no mean thinker herself, identified in her the life force that issued from Hasidism. These assessments are not easy to reconcile with some of her rabidly assimilationist declarations. "The Jew in us must be extirpated," she wrote. "That is the sacred truth, and we do it even if life is uprooted in the process." Hannah Arendt remarks that having been born a Jew meant for Rahel "a slow bleeding to death." Every slight to her because she was a Jew opened a gaping wound that could be healed only by moving in the noblest circles of respectability. Everything Jewish was parochial, everything German and Christian universalizing. She had a more than casual relationship with the reactionary Friedrich von Gentz, who was no friend of Jews or their emancipation.

Although during the Hep! Hep! revolts she complained to brother Ludwig Robert that Jews seem to be preserved "only for torture, contumelies, insults, and brutal outrages," she did not break with some of her intellectual contacts who bore some indirect responsibility. Nor did she persuade the notables in her circle to speak out. Acceptance rated above justice and pity alike.

Rahel's salon welded together the upper strata of Berlin intellectual society. Sons of Junkers found relief from the confining atmosphere of their East Prussian estates. They found alluring the sophistication, wit, and thoughtfulness of the Jewish woman who invited them. They were grateful for the distance and shelter from the oppressive feudal order. Jews, on the other hand, found in the company of prestigious names the prestige they were eager to acquire.

While on diplomatic assignment in Vienna, Rahel's husband commented about **Fanny von Arnstein** (1757–1818) that Viennese Jews owed much of their "free and honored position to her." Her drawingroom raised a culturally retarded Viennese society to a higher *niveau* of conversation and cultural interest. Unlike Rahel, she employed her considerable reputation to improve the condition of the Jews of Vienna. Not only did she remain Jewish, but she never ceased to regard herself as a student of Moses Mendelssohn.

Born Vögele Itzig in Berlin, the daughter of a court-banker, Fanny felt a greater affinity for Berlin than Vienna. Unlike the Berlin hostesses, she knew wealth all of her life. Her continued belief in the moral equality of all religions enabled her to remain a Jew and associate with Christians on equal terms. The same conviction also enabled her to accept her daughter's baptism without serious inner conflict.

The Empress Maria Theresa wanted her Jews to convert to her own beloved Catholicism, and she was uncharitable to those clinging to the ancestral faith. She was cool to Fanny, who was both a Prussian and a Jew. Fanny was more fortunate in her dealings with Maria Theresa's successor, the Emperor Joseph II. She often discussed the "Jewish question" with him, and indirectly she may have played a part in the formulation of his Edict of Tolerance. During the Congress of Vienna, which strengthened the post-Napoleonic repressive regimes on the Continent, Fanny used her social and intellectual talents to improve the status of Jews in other countries. Toward this end, she invited Metternich, Hardenberg, and Wellington, along with other notables, to dine at her table.

Politically, she belonged in this company of stark conservatives. Fanatically anti-French, she was even more anti-Napoleon. She saw only the ruthless conqueror who had humiliated both her beloved Prussia and her beloved Joseph II. Fanny was blind to Napoleon's reforms, including those relating to Jews. For her, improvement in the civil status of Jews was feasible only through the goodwill of the powerful, crowned and un-crowned. Unlike Rahel, she broke with Gentz and his unique brand of cynical anti-intellectualism and anti-Semitism.

Although Fanny was knowledgeable and intelligent and her *Merkbuch* (journal) included interesting views of writers from Shakespeare to Voltaire, she was not capable of a consistent literary effort or of going beyond fragments. But except for her social views which disclosed little sympathy for democratic aspirations and the needs of the masses, Fanny von Arnstein, especially from a Jewish point of view, proved the most attractive of the salon hostesses.

To sum up: The salons facilitated socialization between German and Jewish intellectuals previously thought impossible. They served— sometimes to the dismay of the hostesses—the cause of a Christianizing German Romanticism and nationalism. Nor were they free of the *Deutschtümelei*—the "Teutomania"—about which Saul Ascher had justly complained. It is noteworthy that the guests often referred to their hostesses as "die Jüdin" ("the Jewish lady"), though all but Frau von Arnstein converted. They tended to look upon the ladies both as members of the tribe from which they issued and as members of the groups to which they wanted to belong. Like many writers and intellectuals to come after them, the women were extremely eager to belong—and to pay a price to do so.

•　•　•　•　•

Heinrich Heine

By 1800 Jewish writers had gained a foothold on German literary soil. Yet some talented writers still composed their dramas and poetry in Hebrew, while drafting their pleas for emancipation in German. They used both languages to plead for the enlightened regeneration of Jewish life. But the number of those who used German exclusively in whatever they wrote was rapidly growing.

By 1815 the use of language had shifted in favor of German. Young Jewish intellectuals were determined to become integral members of the "advanced society" that heretofore had been so near and yet so unattainable. Most Jewish writers who grew to maturity between 1815 and 1825 became Christians. Two basic reasons accounted for their conversions. First, without baptism it was virtually impossible to secure a public position, certainly not one commensurate with one's abilities. Second, why should the Jews continue to suffer for a religion that no longer seemed vibrant and enjoyed little respect in its present state of disarray? Often a meaningless baptism was delayed until the death of a surviving parent.

Many of the early writers imagined themselves more widely accepted by Christian colleagues than they actually were. While some Jews joined the Romantic movement that would relegate them once more to the periphery of society, their hearts often remained with the dying ideals of the Enlightenment. They associated with many Christians and sometimes, to their shame, with barely disguised Jew-haters. The optimism of postrevolutionary Europe that a new era might be dawning for Jews was repudiated by the events after Napoleon's defeat.

Different styles emerged for dealing with the new wave of Jew-haters. First came the attempt to explain patiently to real or imaginary anti-Semites that Jews were decent human beings, entitled to decent and humane treatment. Writers of this group assured Jew-haters that any undesirable traits in Jews would disappear, if only the present barriers to Jewish development would come down. These writers, in a different context, have already been called apologists. Then there were others who gave up on persuasion and resorted to angry, even noisy, challenges in

21

defiance of the enemy. As they saw it, anti-Semitism, a term not yet invented, had little or no relationship to any Jewish actions; it flourished independently. For want of a better term, I have already designated them as aggressors. The fact bears repeating that apologists and aggressors alike were *re*acting and that their stance was quintessentially defensive.

Jews settled down in German life rapidly and decisively, generating something akin to fear in the Christian majority. Warnings of a Jewish takeover and of a threat to traditional values were heard from now on, never to be quieted entirely in the 150 years of togetherness. The Germans portrayed themselves as victims with the Jews as their victimizers. The German view was that Jews were not humble and inconspicuous enough; they sat down at the German table, not as grateful guests, but as loud and noisy ones, far too conspicuous and eager to determine the menu. What Jews served up—wit, irony, satire, irreverence, social conscience, intensity, political and moral serious-ness—was not always tasty to the German palate.

The man who served up all these delicacies at once was the poet **Heinrich Heine** (1797–1856). Moses Mendelssohn, the individual most responsible for the German-Jewish connection, was a man of impeccable character. In contrast, Heinrich Heine, the first major poet to avail himself of the link, was a man of seriously flawed character. Within a decade after Heine's appearance on the German scene, he replaced Moses Mendelssohn as the epitome of the Jew in the German mind and was regarded as a less desirable successor.

Though Heine was capable of lying, deceiving, accepting bribes, and engaging in literary blackmail, he was not only supremely gifted, but also eminently likeable. Undoubtedly, Heine was the greatest Jewish-born poet in the German language; he was one of the most original lyricists and satirists that the German language has ever produced. Nevertheless, where there had once been a tendency to deify Mendelssohn, there now developed an equal trend to demonize Heine.

At first, in the early 1820s, there was only widespread admiration for the gentle new voice in German lyric poetry; it was a sweet, loving, mellifluous voice never heard before. Then came some satiric portraits that seemed neither gentle nor loving. Admiration rather quickly yielded to disgust. Skepticism increased about a man who could be both mild and vicious, caring and irreverent, worshipful and abusive. Clearly the turmoil to come in German-Jewish cultural relations cannot be placed at Heine's doorstep; at the same time, it cannot be explained entirely without him.

Yet, as Heine observed, Mendelssohn's formulations could not stand the test of time, and their weaknesses were already apparent by the time Heine reached maturity. The new era Mendelssohn had helped usher in paved the way for the cavalcade of baptisms that followed. On the other hand, Heine's lyrics and *bon mots,* his portraits of contemporaries, both good and bad, have survived to our time. They are remembered by Germans and Jews alike—quoted, anthologized, studied. His satirical travelogues have generated as much chuckling, laughter, amusement, and merriment in some as they have produced wrath and condemnation in others.

Bitter wrangling enveloped Heine's name from the time his satiric pen replaced the mildly erotic one of the *Buch der Lieder* (*Book of Songs*). For these lyrics he was, at worst, chided for sentimentality, repetitiveness, and a delicate eroticism. But once Heine responded to the anti-Semitic attacks of Count von Platen, a fellow poet, with a tasteless but not wholly unjustified attack on Platen's pederasty, he became fair game for all.

Controversy surrounding Heine has ranged from the date of his birth to the nature of his terminal illness, from his religious to his political oscillations, from his moral ambiguities to his literary feuds, from his craving for privacy to his pathological need for *Geltung* (validation) and the limelight. Different perceptions have followed him beyond the grave. To this day, attitudes toward Heine's work and Heine the man may offer clues to the political, religious, and moral makeup of the critic expressing them. Even hostile critics have had to concede the charms, beauty, and mellowness of Heine's verse. Unfortunately, only a handful have had the wisdom to divorce his exceptional gifts from his life and character, his politics and morals. More than that of any other writers, Heine criticism has been swayed by nonliterary factors.

On some points critics concurred. Heine existed between generations and systems. He himself viewed his time from the vantage point of another era and another place. He knew loyalty to no group and to no party, but seemed impelled—after some immersion in each—to mock them all. He built on his own intelligence, sensibility, imagination, mostly eschewing known models. His enemies justly commented on the discontinuity of his work, and his friends noted his sensitivity to outsider status. No Jewish writer of his century was such a bundle of contradictions or so divorced from the reigning biases of his or her time. S. S. Prawer spoke correctly of "Heine's Jewish Comedy" in referring to Heine's portrayals of Jews and non-Jews alike. Thus, Heine epitomized the Jew of the transitional period from the Enlightenment to Romanticism, from tentative acceptance of the Jew to renewed rejection, from those with one foot in the old to those with both feet squarely in the new.

Heine's main consistency lay in the predictable succession of contradictions. He converted to a Christianity he often reviled. But when it suited him, he could assert that he, Heine, was a Christian. He accepted baptism without conviction and at the very moment when he seemed most devoted to Jewish affairs. He scoffed at other liberals when their excessive faith forced the perennial skeptic to shine through. He was at once an heir of the Enlightenment and a Romantic. He wrote pro-Communist articles at the very time he accepted money from his wealthy relatives in Hamburg. His verses resound with nostalgic yearning for Germany and her language, but he pecked away at the German character and the retarded political regimes it fostered. He cultivated a private garden of sweet and gentle dreams, while simultaneously nurturing a ruthless irony that seemed to destroy them. Basically a republican, he was not beyond calling himself a royalist and accepting financial favors from the French king.

This often voiced change of opportunism is not without foundation. There is also the basic question of Heine's seriousness. Certainly his resentment of attacks he judged unfair sometimes drove him to untenable positions of contrariness. On the other hand, more than others of the time, Heine recognized the infinite complexity of modern existence and found no single position adequate to explain or resolve it.

Heine's Jewish history is as checkered as other facets of his being. Coming from a family that thought little of its Jewish heritage, in Berlin he came under the influence of both Rahel Varnhagen—who hardly steered him toward Jewishness—and a group of young men who did. They had formed a *Verein,* a Society for Jewish Culture and Learning. Among them were Eduard Gans, a noted jurist; Moses Moser, a businessman-scholar, and especially Leopold Zunz. All would become major names in Jewish history. Conscious of the apostasies all about them, the members of the society emphasized Jewishness in a cultural and existential sense. During his own membership, Heine observed from close up the conflicts of Jews who had at least a peripheral interest in remaining Jewish.

When it became clear in the winter of 1821–1822 that Gans, a brilliant if verbose legal scholar of Hegelian persuasion, would not obtain a lectureship at a Prussian university if he remained a Jew, a considerable gloom settled on the young intellectuals of the *Verein.* The Gans effort, supported by no less a personage than Chancellor von Hardenberg, made it painfully clear that no Jew could aspire to an official position in a state that regarded itself as increasingly Christian. Full acceptance of a Jew as a German proved less of a hope than it had been in the heady days of Enlightenment optimism.

In a course of Jewish history Heine taught for the *Verein,* Heine advised his teenaged class to emigrate to the New World, or at least to England, where no one would question them about their religion. Considering Heine's dislike of things British and, subsequently, his doubts about American values, his inner state must have approached despair. Of the three choices left open to intellectuals after the Gans Affair—emigration, conversion, suicide—none appealed to Heine in 1823. Emigration would be difficult for a poet severed from cultural roots; conversion was unappetizing in the light of his intense distaste for Christianity, though the Reform Judaism he saw sprouting up in Hamburg and Berlin was no more enticing. And suicide—no!

While his Jewish activities persisted, by 1825 he recognized the bankruptcy of contemporary Jewry and the failure of the *Verein* to bring about change. He was too much of a Romantic to appreciate the new emphasis on the scientific and historical study of Judaism. For Heine, the man of feeling, this approach neither sanctified nor enlivened Jewish life.

Between 1822 and 1824 he began his *The Rabbi of Bacharach,* a project to which he returned sporadically for fifteen years but never completed. In 1824 he converted to a religion he despised. It was an act over which he never lost his shame, and he sought, directly or indirectly, to devolve his own guilt upon others. Heine's failure to complete *The Rabbi of Bacharach* became emblematic of his Jewish problem. It remained close to his heart, but he could never resolve it.

After Heine's first sorties into satire, many critics and readers stamped the labels "non-German," "non-Christian," "pagan," or "Jew" on his work. He struck back hard at his enemies. To use his own words, toward his foes he maintained an "Old Testament attitude." From Platen to Pfizer, from Menzel to Hengstenberg, his enemies became targets of pitiless allies. His heaviest guns were trained at Wolfgang Menzel, once a Heine friend and admirer, now a *Deutschtümler* and crass Jew-hater. As a Christian, Heine could afford to indulge in what would have been off-limits for him as a Jew. When political conditions in Germany finally drove him into Parisian exile, Heine continued his feuds with undiminished vigor.

From his arrival in Paris to the end of his life, he wrote as often at the expense of Jews as in their defense. His real targets are often hidden: his "philistine" relatives in Hamburg who did not adequately support the great talent in their midst; financiers who had the power he would have liked to have; Christianity itself—though never Jesus, whom he revered. Samples of his remarks: "No Jew can ever believe in the divinity of any other Jews"; and "I have become a typical Christian—I sponge on the rich Jews"; or "Last Saturday I went to the Temple (in Hamburg) and was pleased to hear Dr. Salomon pillory the converted Jews and scorn those who had deserted the religion of their fathers for dubious benefits."

He could banter lightly about Jews and the evils they had brought into the world—Christianity, otherworldliness, the somber outlook of Nazarenism. But when Jews in France were under attack in the wake of the notorious Damascus Affair, in which a charge of ritual murder was brought against the Jews of Damascus in 1840, Heine became once more their staunch defender. During his middle years he appeared somewhat unconcerned about Jews, preferring the clever quip to a more meaningful statement of conviction.

In his Saint-Simonist period, in which he supported the ideals of the French Revolution, Heine appeared to be flirting with atheism. But he was unable to banish God permanently from his life. Later, he admitted to some dissatisfaction with the God-idea the Jews had given the world; nevertheless, it was "a creation worthy of praise." In the same vein: Was it not ironic that the people who invented this God should have been accused of killing Him? Heine's ambivalences are most patent in the *Denkschrift an Börne* (*Memorandum to Börne*):

> The Jews are made of that dough out of which gods are moulded; if you step on them today, you will kneel before them tomorrow; while some of them wallow in the filthiest mud of usury, others climb and attain the highest peaks of humanity, and Golgotha is not the only hill on which a Jewish god had bled for the salvation of mankind. The Jews are the people of the spirit and every time they return to their principle they are great and magnificent and overcome their shabby oppressor . . . a remarkable manifestation of the most glaring extremes. While among Jews one may find caricatures of meanness, one will also come upon specimens of pure humanity, and as they once led the world onto new paths of progress, so the world may yet expect from them other initiatives.

As anti-Semitism abated in the 1840s, Heine's interest in Jewish matters dwindled. The regional battles for emancipation fought by Gabriel Riesser bored him. Perhaps under the aegis of the Saint-Simonists and Marx, he became more aware of an economic base in anti-Jewish prejudice. In 1844, he could write that religion was no longer at the root of the anti-Semitism of the upper castes. As for the lower classes, it was a reaction against the smothering power of capitalism and the rich. But he also defended Jews from anti-capitalist agitation, now that greater wealth was concentrated in Christian hands. The Jews, Heine warned, were forced to become rich and were then hated for their riches. The solution of the Jewish problem became for him, as for socialists later, part of a larger problem: the realization that society as a whole cannot thrive while one of its segments suffers.

When Heine was finally restricted to his "mattress-grave," he turned once more to the Bible, by which he meant the Old Testament. He discovered that it offered him unexpected solace. The personal God he had so often scorned gained readmittance, though "outside of time and space." His return to religion and its new face are mentioned in his correspondence and in chats with visitors. They disclose a new warmth toward things Jewish. The rediscovered divinity bears a strong resemblance to the "old Jehovah." Yet even these comments that Heine uttered while under severe physical pain and mental anguish are not without their humor. God is a *Tierquäler* (someone cruel to animals) who should be denounced to the Humane Society. Heine's renewed dialogue with the divinity must not be viewed as the despair of a troubled, dying man. Anticipating this reaction, he kept repeating that his closeness was not merely in response to his need for divine support at a time of unbearable crisis.

Max Brod's biography of Heine clearly "overjudaized" the poet's final years. But Brod was right in claiming that the Heine of the "mattress-grave" recognized in the Bible infinite riches for the guiding of human lives. Even more than in his much earlier "Belshazzar," Heine saw in Judaism an especially strong ethical component. Now, as his life was patently drawing to a close, he dubbed the ethical dimension the unique Jewish contribution to civilization. The Greeks he had once so admired were merely handsome boys; the Jews had been strong and unbending men.

Heine's *Hebräische Melodien* (*Hebrew Melodies*) removed all doubt as to his renewed interest in Jewish themes. His "Sabbath Princess" and "Yehuda ben Halevi" enjoy universal regard as masterful poems inspired by Jewish sources. In the former poem, the Jew who has been persecuted all week, treated no better than an animal, turns into a man of dignity—a prince—as the Sabbath approaches. The holy day of rest stores up the psychic and spiritual energies that will enable him to endure the stresses of the week to come. In the second poem, the medieval poet Yehuda ben Halevi again represents the self-respect and dignity which for Heine represented the inner beauty of an observant and authentic Jew. With the *Hebrew Melodies* Heine achieves the status he had craved when, as a youthful member of the *Verein,* he had announced his desire to become a Jewish poet. While he is hardly, even in 1855, the perfect fusion of the national, religious, and cultural Jew, he has reacquired for himself a smattering of each. There is at least some truth to Heine's well-known assertion that he did not *return* to Judaism because he had never left it.

Heine's relationship to his German-ness was as ambiguous as his rapport with Germany. There was a strong and unmistakable love for the language and for many aspects of the culture and national character. But he was also immensely critical of this character and perceived weaknesses that others refused to see.

What was there in Heine's published views of Germany that made them so reprehensible in German eyes? In his early writings, he was unstinting in his praise of Napoleon, who had suspended anti-Jewish laws in Heine's native Düsseldorf. Later, he deployed his caustic wit at the expense of throne, altar, and hereditary privilege. He fought, without inhibition, the Teutomania that threatened to engulf German intellectual life. He thought Germans politically retarded, a people of hapless followers. He demolished the comfortable image that Mme. de Staël had painted of Germany as the land of idyllic Romanticism and *Gemütlichkeit* (atmosphere of comfort, smugness, informality). On a more personal level, he did not conceal his resentment at the many doors closed to him in Germany. After the July Revolution of 1830, Heine set out for the land of the "light-hearted people," as much for what he was trying to get away from as for what he was about to move to. In France his criticism of the sleepy nation across the Rhine intensified. His admiration for France continued, though his comments were interspersed with negative views that could only have come from a German.

At best a marginal member of the literary movement Young Germany, relabeled Young Palestine by Wolfgang Menzel, Heine was nevertheless among those whose writings were proscribed by law in 1835. In a remarkable melding of bitterness and wit he wrote:

> I had taken such pains with the German language, its datives and accusatives, and knew well how to string the words together—like pearls. I had experienced such pleasure doing this, for it shortened long, long winter evenings of my exile . . . and almost made me imagine I was home with my mother—and now I have been forbidden to write!

Then in characteristic fashion, a change of tone! "I accuse the authors of this decree and accuse them of having abused the people's trust; I accuse them of having insulted the majesty of the people; I accuse them of high treason against the nation. I accuse."

In "Deutschland, Ein Wintermärchen" ("Germany, A Winter's Tale") (1844), one of his more satiric verses, he placed love of Fatherland alongside scoffing and jeering thrusts:

Es ging mir äußerlich ziemlich gut,	On the surface things went pretty well,
Doch innerlich war ich beklommen,	But something within oppressed me,
Und die Beklemmnis täglich wuchs—	And day by day that oppression grew—
Ich hatte das Heimweh bekommen.	Homesickness possessed me.
Die sonst so leichte französiche Luft,	The air of France that had been so light
Sie fing mich an zu drücken;	Now smothered me with its weight;
Ich mußte Atem schöpfen hier	I had to breathe some German air
In Deutschland, um nicht zu ersticken.	or I would suffocate.

Then, a few pages later:

Ja, daß es uns früher so schrecklich ging	To say that things were hopeless here [in Germany]
In Deutschland ist Übertreibung.	Is gross exaggeration;
Man konnte entrinnen der Knechtschaft, wie einst	You could break your chains,
In Rom durch Selbstentleibung.	As they did in Rome, by self-extermination.
Gedankenfreiheit genoß das Volk,	The populace had freedom of thought,
Sie war für die großen Massen,	The greatest number possessed it;
Beschränkung traf nur die geringe Zahl	Only the few who published books
Derjen'gen, die drucken lassen.	Were ever really molested.

There is some evidence that Heine's once pure love for Germany turned into the same *Haßliebe*—love-hate relationship—that Germans developed toward Jews. The relationship between Heine and the Germans in microcosm contained the essence of the German-Jewish tensions to come.

Heine offered too drastic a contrast to the virtuous, deeply serious Mendelssohn, the only other German Jew to have received comparable attention. If Mendelssohn was a disturber, he disturbed within Jewry; if he was a revolutionary, he revolted within Judaism. The Germans, if anything, enjoyed the spectacle. The convert Heine, however, disturbed less the Jewish than the Christian world, and that was sinful. As Markgraff, an anti-Jewish critic commented, "Heine should have limited his criticism to Jews, their atavistic practices, the synagogue"—all of which required thorough overhauling. Christianity and Germany were unsuitable target practice for a Jewish satirist.

Because of the German reaction to Heine, many Jews began to regard him as a threat to their security. He gave the lie to the apologists who needed another virtuous Mendelssohn to explain what Jews were all about. Heine weakened the case of a Berthold Auerbach and Gabriel Riesser, both Heine foes who fought the good fight for emancipation. For them Heine was no longer a Jew and had lost the right to speak as a Jew. What one line did Heine write, asked Auerbach, that he could not also have written as a Christian? Auerbach's question was foolish. Without the Jew in him, few lines in Heine would have appeared as they did. There was no doubt that the towering figure of the witty, charming, somewhat demonic Heine affected the subsequent course of German and Jewish cultural relations.

•   •   •   •   •

Ludwig Börne

J uda Loeb Baruch, later known as **Ludwig Börne** (1786–1837), was the other major figure to become widely known. His mastery of the sharp, critical observation was only a notch below Heine's. There was in Börne something of both Mendelssohn and Heine. He disported himself with the rectitude and forthrightness of the former, while possessing the devastating wit and rebelliousness of the latter.

While Heine's positions fluctuated wildly and were not beyond suspicion of sale to the highest bidder, Börne's bore the stamp of firm and irrevocable commitment. A product of the Enlightenment, in his attachment to the political and human freedoms, he carried the fervor of religious devotion. Like Heine, his erstwhile friend and later foe, he frequently faulted his Jewish coreligionists but discovered an ever-mounting number of flaws in the Germans he loved with passion. His involvement with Jews was less deep and lasting than Heine's; Börne's baptism did not burden his conscience. Instead, it involved him all the more with the Germans, whom he tried to push forward into the era of modern human rights. To achieve this goal, he pointed out their shortcomings pitilessly in that domain. Germans disliked his criticism, often reacting abusively, but without some of the tumult with which they combated Heine.

Börne did not see in Judaism some of the grandeur which Heine recognized in his better hours. Throughout his life, however, Börne stood up for Jews when he suspected discrimination or unjust attack. As a young man in Frankfurt, long before his baptism, he denounced the ordinances that put restrictions on the number of Jews allowed to live in the city or to marry in a given year (twelve in all). But in the same essay he also assailed the orthodoxy of Frankfurt's Jews and the veneer of culture they assumed. In his famous portrait of the city's *Judengasse* (Jews' Street), he shows little love for Jews and their heritage, or respect or pity for their suffering.

Nevertheless, he demolished anti-Jewish pamphleteers and their assertion that Jewish rights would lead to Jewish dominance and control. In the Hep! Hep! riots which broke out in several cities, the police, according to Börne, displayed none of the hyperactivity and zeal that they were wont to show against dissidents. Jewish homes were left unprotected, the peaceful robbed of their peace. Worse, the riots offered encouragement to ever-busy Christian proselytes. Börne objected that a Jew was always referred to as a Jew, never as a citizen, subject, or human being.

Börne was not always serious about Jewish questions, anymore than Heine was. One of his rare love stories, which combines wit with Talmudic argument, twisted the logic of a Frankfurt senator who claimed that Jews could not be citizens of Frankfurt because Christians had built the city. Börne remarked: "If religion could confer or take away a right, Frankfurt Jews would be the only true citizens and the Christians only *Schutz-Christen* [safeguarded Christians] whom the Jews would lock into "Christ Street" at night, whom they would keep from marrying." In this same seventy-fourth Parisian letter, he continued: "When in 1818 the Jewish family Rothschild became all-powerful, I decided to convert to Christianity, for it had always been my inclination to side with the weak and the oppressed." Though Börne was facetious here, he was more consistently critical of the Rothschilds than was Heine, who softened his criticism when the Paris Rothschild offered him stock options, theater tickets, or other benefits.

Though he belonged to the defiant writers, Börne could never entirely shake off his Diaspora-defensive upbringing, in that he still had to prove Jewish worth as he saw it. In 1832, he wrote to his confidante Jeanette Wohl that "it was now up to the Jews to do something for the cause of the Fatherland," i.e., for the liberal-national cause. If Jews should show themselves fearful, the liberal leadership would not steer the people in a direction friendly to Jews. He was pleased that there were Jewish activists in Poland. Polish Jews realized that if the Poles gained their freedom, so would the Jews. His conclusion is simplistic and false in regard to Germany: "If the Jews fight for German freedom, they will also be fighting for their own."

The Jewish allies of reaction, especially the Jews of wealth, were repeatedly targets of his anger. Messrs. de Rothschild, von Haber, and von Hirsch would not take time out from conferences with ministers and mistresses to heed the appeal of Polish Jews. Jewish aristocrats had forgotten their ancestral origin, he felt. The Jews and the nobility, money and privilege, represented the remaining pillars of feudalism. Jews threatened by the masses sought the protection of noblemen, who, frightened by the specter of equality, turned for protection to Jewish money.

Nor was Börne sympathetic to Jewish eminence in the cultural world. Rahel Varnhagen had his approval, as did his former great love, Henriette Herz. Their salons merely filled a void left by Christians. But, like Heine, he was merciless toward the offspring of the banker Jakob Herz Beer, namely Giacomo Meyerbeer, the composer, and Michael Beer, a poet—neither a convert. Börne mocked the composer and poet and, indeed, all Jewish writers of the time.

He could also be socially cruel to Jews. While at a resort he would rather flee to "any uninhabited garden" than suffer the presence of some noisy and deferential Jews. He neglected to add that Jews sought out the famous author, whereas Christians preferred to fawn over other celebrities. Despite his love for Jewish freedom-fighters in Poland, Börne satirized Jewish businessmen's German speech patterns, which were filled with Yiddishisms. Jeanette Wohl, who remained a Jew—she may have refused to marry him because he was a "Goy" (Gentile, non-Jew)— asked him why he had suddenly taken to deriding Jews. Yet Börne was in no sense a self-hating Jew, only an indifferent one. Perhaps he merely objected to the lack of *Bildung* he observed in so many.

Börne carped even more at German than at Jewish characteristics. As Heine correctly remarked, Börne was truly a German patriot. He was a man in love and found the object of his love in distress. He depicted Germany as a dull, sleepy land filled with dull and sleepy people, made so by their docile spirit and willingness to follow arrogant, authoritarian leaders. Long ago, the Germans had obeyed these dukes out of reverence—now they did so merely out of habit. Their submissiveness to titled gentlemen and uniformed officials was their undoing. It had prevented freedom from prospering in German lands. With Prince Metternich and the *Bund* (federation) watching, the princes themselves had been stripped of their freedom; certainly, they now possessed less than under Napoleon, whom Börne, unlike Heine, had denounced as a foreign tyrant.

Börne's disparaging attitude toward Goethe must be viewed in the context of his perception of Germany's malaise. One of the first *écrivains engagés* (politically active writers), Börne had little tolerance for Olympian detachment. A man of Goethe's stature could not withhold his talent from the struggle for an emancipated society. The prince of

German letters was ruling like the other princes, outside the frame of societal concerns. While Börne's postulate on the social obligations of the writer left Goethe untouched, it impressed itself on the thinking of Friedrich Engels.

The *Parisian Letters* (*Briefe aus Paris*), Börne's most important collection of essays, also chided Germans for their base treatment of poets and people of intellect. Equally lamentable, Börne felt was their lack of wit. For Germans, authority stems from God; hence, wit at the expense of leaders is intolerable. The only joke the subjects of German princes permitted was at their own expense, not that of their leaders. Börne observed that the Jews poke fun at their oppressors as well as at themselves; Germans will laugh at their misfortune, not at those responsible for it.

Heine wrote of Börne that he loved Germany far more than France, "while loving humanity most." Yet Börne always held up French political life for emulation by Germans. The French press was free, and a free press was Börne's ultimate criterion for popular sovereignty. French authors did not need to worry about the wrath of the political censor. Moreover, Börne's reverence for 1789 was unbounded. Although his Jacobinism precluded an accommodation, while in Parisian exile with the *juste-milieu* (governmental policy characterized by moderation and compromise) of Louis-Philippe, Börne was aware of the advantages of the bourgeois monarchy over anything available in the Germanies. Even more than France, England and the new Republic across the ocean offered useful political models.

In Börne's eyes, liberalism and Jewish rights were indissolubly linked. In authoritarian states, Jews continued to be treated as second-class citizens, whereas libertarian countries, such as France, granted them equality. He was confident that with the eventual removal of princelings, aristocrats, their hired moneymen, and the Holy Alliance, Jews would come into their own. He was, therefore, not interested in special legislation for Jews, but all the more intent upon promoting liberal values. Thus, his advocacy of new political directions was indirectly linked to the Jews' acquisition of civil rights. Jewish emancipation as a specific issue receded ever more into the background, whereas it remained very much alive as part of the *general* political problem.

Though intensely patriotic in the liberal sense—his Parisian home became a center for Germans in exile—Börne was also one of the first universalist Jews. The "brotherhood of men" was more than a slogan for him. To the end, his mind remained open to new developments affecting his ideals. His worsening quarrel with Heine was not one of personal rivalries, rather, it showed Börne's disillusionment with Heine's skepticism, detachment, and unwillingness to walk side by side in the only cause that mattered.

• • • • •

Minor Contemporaries

B y about 1817, the writers then growing to maturity began to doubt, unlike Börne, that new ideas, secular education, and the participation of Jews in the Napoleonic Wars would enhance prospects for civic equality. The evolution of the concept of a Christian-German state, which excluded Jews from significant involvement in public affairs, shattered the optimism of the postrevolutionary years. With "liberty, equality, and fraternity" giving way to Metternich's reaction and exclusivism, even the most patriotic Jewish intellectual began to wonder whether they had not fought the wrong enemy and against their own interests.

Among Heine's and Börne's fellow writers who were approaching maturity, or had already achieved it, were **Ludwig Robert** (Liep Levin, b. 1778), **Michael Beer** (b. 1800), **Daniel Lessmann** (b. 1798), and **Moritz Gottlieb Saphir** (b. 1795). With the exception of Saphir, who died in 1858, all died between 1831 and 1833.

These writers had much in common. With the exception of Beer, they became Christians, a step they thought would help them realize their potential. They recognized too late, as one writer put it, that critics attacked not the *Parisian Letters* (*Briefe aus Paris*) but the Jew in Börne. All of these authors were to encounter hostile reminders of their Jewish origin, some suggesting an early racial component in hatred of Jews. Several died young, and only Heine and Robert married, though remaining childless. They made few if any references to Maimonides or even Moses Mendelssohn, but many to Goethe and Kant, Fichte and Hegel. They were all affected by the dominating presence and reputations of Heine and Börne and were labeled as radicals when actually several were conservative. They were drawn to German cultural achievements and deprecated foreign literature, especially that of France. Strangely, despite this fact, they spent much time in France, a phenomenon that suggests that they felt uncomfortable and uninspired in the

Fatherland whose praises they chanted in all sincerity. The anti-Semites of the time were right in commenting on the restlessness and haste of the Jewish writers and in complaining about their lack of a consistent production. (Of course, the anti-Semites were unaware that *they* were a contributing factor.) Finally, the star among them, Heinrich Heine, made his fellow writers a bit nervous as his quarrels, polemics, and public image reflected more and more negatively on them. Together with Heine, they possessed a strong *Geltungsgefühl,* an unwholesome craving for recognition, and they suffered deeply when it was denied.

Ludwig Robert, Rahel Varnhagen's brother, converted early to Christianity and appears to have had some genuine religious convictions. Though a friend of Heine's, he disapproved of Heine's jibes at Christianity. Like Heine, he was often castigated for "bad taste" in his epigrams and for a Heinean lack of restraint. On those occasions, even so-called friends remembered that he was one of "the children of Israel." Driven to a defensive stance, Robert may have agreed to head up the attack on Moritz Saphir, a Jew whose occasional lapses in taste bordered on the outrageous.

Robert's lack of success, a result of his paucity of talent, gnawed at him deeply. His failure to achieve recognition turned a once charming and witty conversationalist into an often embittered and excitable man. Of his many plays, only two are still of interest. *Die Überbildeten* (*Overly Educated Women*) is a takeoff on Molière's *Les Précieuses Ridicules,* which allowed him to vent his resentment at having been overshadowed first by his sister Rahel, whom he loved, and later by his wife Friederike, whom he loved still more. The play is also noteworthy for its moderation and balance. The other play, *Die Macht der Verhältnisse* (*The Power of Social Position*), protested the humiliation inflicted on one whom the accident of birth had permanently placed in an inferior position. Written as early as 1811, but not published until eight years later, the drama tells the story of the writer Weiss, son of a pastor, who believes his honor has been violated by an aristocratic officer. Weiss challenged the officer to a duel, but is denied the honor of fighting, dueling being the prerogative of the nobility. Thereupon Weiss shoots the officer in cold blood. It is easy to perceive in this drama the outcry of the erstwhile Jew, still conscious of his second-class status and the occasional thrusts of his enemies. However, there may be a more tangible linkage to a Jewish issue, an actual incident that had occurred earlier. Moritz Itzig, a Jew whom the poet Achim von Arnim refused to meet on the field of honor, publicly slapped Arnim as an expression of his contempt.

Robert was both a Prussian patriot and conservative thinker. *Die*

Kämpfe der Zeit (*Battles of Our Time*) is a slim volume of ultra-patriotic poems in which he calls a Frenchman "Franzmann," uses other pejorative terms, is intolerant of the *blöde Pöbel* ("rude mob"), and doubts the ability of the masses ever to govern themselves. He extols all things German, his "benevolent government's mildness and justice." In the 1820s, he moved gradually toward a neutral stance, in which he described himself as equally removed from the liberal Eduard Gans and from the advocates of hereditary privilege. Not too much should be made of his modest new liberalism. When the old and now deaf Börne visited a spa in which Robert was also staying, the latter refused to see him because of his alleged *sans-culottism*.

Like his whole family, **Michael Beer** (1800–1833) rejected baptism but did not fault those who accepted it. Of his various tragedies, *Der Paria* (*The Pariah*) merits special attention. Beer puts the pleas and complaints of a contemporary Jew into the mouth of an Indian untouchable. Gadhi, the hero, struggles for recognition of his dignity and humanity, his right to define himself and not to be defined on the basis of birth. "Stellt mich euch gleich," exclaims Gadhi, "und seht, ob ich euch gleiche." ("Put me on your level and see if I am your equal.") As for patriotism,

Ich hab' ein Vaterland, ich will's beschützen,	I have a Fatherland, I want to protect it,

Gebt mir ein Leben, und ich zahl's mit
    Wucher.
	Give me a life, and I'll pay it back with
	    interest.

Beer was a consistent advocate of political freedoms. Perhaps this explains why he spent many months at a time in neighboring France, whose 1830 July Revolution generated more enthusiasm in him than any other event of his time. Nevertheless, he considered himself an obedient subject in Bavaria, where he befriended the archconservative Minister Eduard von Schenck, who was to edit his collected works.

Beer was reverent in his discussion of the German people and their virtues. The Germans possessed *Innigkeit* (depth of feeling), a quality missing in the French. Beer detested Napoleon as a tyrant, and French letters inspired only his distaste. Again, why was he in France so often and so long? Why did he refer to French writers as "human beings"? Why did he advise his brother Wilhelm not to remain in the Prussian army, given the reaction that followed the Prussian victory?

Clearly, Beer wondered whether his anger at Napoleon had been misdirected. The Hep! Hep! riots gave him pause to reflect, and in 1830 he remarked in despair that "the canes of the citizens of Hamburg were descending once more on the backs of hapless Jews." Beer never lost his sensitivity to anti-Semitism. The apologists' notion that patient argument, as in *Der Paria* (*The Pariah*), would eventually triumph over darkness and stupidity had become suspect to this man of goodwill.

Beer had no use whatever for orthodox Judaism, whereas the convert Heine always retained his respect for it. Beer's father opened his home for reform worship. Beer's poem "Der fromme Rabbi" ("The Pious Rabbi") is a fierce attack on liberal Judaism untouched by the Enlightenment. Generally moderate in his likes and dislikes, in his denunciation of the pious rabbi, Beer was as extreme as he was capable of becoming. This restless man, who moved from city to city, from France to Germany and back again, often vain and ambitious, willing to curry favor with the powerful, but essentially honest, decent, and balanced, was as eager to act in harmony with German culture as this culture would allow.

Beer and Heine were opposites, and no love was lost between them. Heine admitted to having praised Beer's tragedy *Struensee* (*Lake Struen*) for practical purposes. He saw Michael Beer as the lucky but not overly gifted poet born with a silver spoon. He was envious of Michael's carefree existence, when his own struggle to stay afloat was so burdensome. Beer, in turn, recognized Heine's superb gifts but thought them ill-used and enlisted in questionable causes. After Heine's attack on Platen's homosexuality, Beer said that he felt indigestion and nausea. For Beer, Heine was something of an irresponsible rascal; for Heine, Beer touched everything with *Glacéhandschuhe* (kid gloves). Heine's aggressive and Beer's apologist stance were among the factors separating the two men.

Daniel Lessmann was the first German-Jewish writer to end his own life. None of the reasons given for the suicide is fully convincing. His Jewishness was an unlikely factor.

Although Lessmann served at the front in the Wars of Liberation and glorified the soldierly life in some novellas, he was disenchanted with the victorious Prussia. While he depicted Jews in some works, they were all old Jews, as though young and authentic Jews eluded both his experience and imagination. His old Jews were men of integrity and hard work; they believed in their God and were willing to abide by His revealed Will. On the whole, however, Lessmann's Jewish interests were minimal, as was his involvement in the struggle for emancipation. On the other hand, he participated, both before and after his conversion, in circles that consisted mainly of Jews and baptized Jews. Perhaps he encountered among them the *Schwermut* (melancholia) that constituted one of his main themes and may have presaged some of the inner turmoil to come.

Like Beer and Robert, Lessmann spent a great deal of time in foreign travel. It is conceivable that he merely needed to get away from Berlin, a city he thoroughly disliked. Yet there was little of the rebel in him, and his political consciousness—where it existed at all—led him to search in British institutions for a proper model for an underdeveloped Prussia to follow. Though some of his works, especially those portraying the Italian past, revealed a tendency toward Romanticism, in his later life he returned to the Enlightenment of his youth.

Moritz Gottlieb Saphir was almost as controversial as Heine, but infinitely less talented. His fame skyrocketed, having been based on scandalous writings, including unwarranted attacks, verbal tricks, and exercises in tortuous reasoning. According to contemporary accounts, this one-time rabbinic student was repeatedly beaten up and forced to leave various towns in the dark of night. After 1832, his reputation suffered when it became known that he was in Metternich's pay.

Saphir, a native of Hungary, did not know German until well into his teens. Then, in quick succession, he learned French, Italian, and English, and their literatures gradually displaced the Talmudic studies of his youth. His earliest published works dealt with stories of Jewish communal life and remained popular for decades. His greatest successes came in Berlin as an editor of humorous publications, which His Majesty avidly read.

It was in Berlin that he aroused the most lasting enmities. To attract attention, Saphir was willing to resort to almost any tactic. His vicious attacks, clothed in humor, invited strident counterinvectiveness. He had few illusions about himself, calling himself a humoristic Satan one day and a *gemütlicher Bösewicht* (benevolent or good-natured rogue) the next. Saphir reenforced the widely held view that wit was a Jewish trait. He was acutely aware of its novelty in German writing. Contrasting the police-authoritarian mentality of Prussia and the Jewish need for laughter, he observed that Germans failed to recognize Jewish laughter as a response to suffering, but instead thought it was motivated by revenge.

On one subject Saphir remained deadly serious, even after his baptism: anti-Semitism. He fought it earnestly and stubbornly as a major evil, regardless of which Jew or Jews were its intended victims.

Like Ludwig Robert, his enemy, Saphir held essentially conservative views, parting ways with Börne, whom he admired, and with Heine, whom he liked, except in the latter's dealing with Börne. His conservatism was less the result of deep conviction than of a skepticism he could never shed. Belief in change and perfectibility were a chimera. It took God six days to create the world, he snapped, and here were liberals trying to remake it in three. Perhaps Saphir had no politics at all because he could not believe. (Curiously, he accused Heine of exactly that, which supposedly accounted for Heine's lack of "godliness.") His skepticism extended to such diverse issues as German unification, hope of a better world in America, and the accomplishments of the French Revolution. Like Beer and Lessmann, Saphir also believed in the superiority of German over French letters—especially the French drama, which lacked the chastity Saphir demanded of theater.

Except for the violence of his mood swings and the seeming disintegration of his personality, **Joel Jacoby** (1807–1863) would fit the group of minor writers whose characteristics were outlined earlier. Born in Königsberg, Jacoby first came to public attention in 1833 with his *Zur Kenntnis der jüdischen Verhältnisse in Preußen* (*Toward a Knowledge of Jewish Conditions in Prussia*) in which he deplored the disadvantaged status of Jews and appeared to be involved in the struggle for emancipation. His *Stimmen aus Berlin* (*Voices from Berlin*) revealed his political opposition to the regime, and he was briefly jailed for his heroics.

Barely four years later, he had become both a reactionary and a Christian fanatic. *Klagen eines Juden* (*Complaints of a Jew*) (1837) explored in a strangely ambivalent manner the *Judenschmerz* (Jewish suffering) of his time. Jacoby expressed his reverence for the rocklike Judaism of old, while barely hiding his contempt for the new Jews, who tampered everywhere with the essence and cared only for acceptance. However, he noted, not even the true Jews he respected might have a role to play in the future, since Judaism had fulfilled its mission when it evolved into Christianity. If real Jews nevertheless wanted to attend their synagogues, let them! But what joy there would be if they could free themselves from the yoke of the Talmudic Law, join the mainstream of Prussian-Christian life, and involve themselves freely in the great events of the time. Jacoby realized that Jews were unlikely to do this, so it became the chief plaintive note in his book of laments.

Indeed, soon Joel Jacoby, the concerned Jew, had become the devout Christian Franz Carl Jacoby. He had also become a public official, a *Kanzleirath,* empowered to censor newspapers for the police. Was he corrupt, as charged by some, or deeply torn inside, as asserted by Karl Gutzkow?

Jacoby went on to chant paeans to German life, thought, discipline, and wisdom. He wanted devoutly to enter German-Christian temples, but doubted the feasibility of Jewish emancipation. Emancipation required assimilation, a process Germans might accept for individual Jews, but would they and could they assimilate a whole people? Would Jews ever willingly enter Christian-German churches and receive the sacrament of rebirth? Jacoby yearned for that sacred day when Judaism would be integrated with Christianity, its logical extension.

Jacoby entreated Christians not to begrudge Jews their bread or deprive them of security in exile, as Christians must not dishonor the holy creed that supplied the basis for their own belief. Nor should Christians disseminate absurd and monstrous fictions about Jews, seeding pogroms and murders. But if Jacoby was so aware of the crimes committed by Christians in the name of Christianity, why would he wish to impose upon Jews a religion that had permitted such crimes?

In later years, Jews impressed the ever more reactionary author as dangerous innovators. Fortunately, Prussian traditions served as an effective bulwark against experimenters and malcontents. Jacoby had now wholly aligned himself with those from whom he had once demanded equal rights for his people.

●   ●   ●   ●   ●

Assimilationists and Patient Explainers

Gabriel Riesser and Berthold Auerbach, whose literary works have little in common, nevertheless shared a belief in the desirability of integrating Jews into German life. They believed this to be wise from both a German and Jewish standpoint. They had no illusions that all Germans would agree; far too many persisted in seeing Jews as perennial aliens—and undesirable ones to boot. The Jews, too, would have to alter certain attitudes before assimilation could be realized. But it was the Germans they addressed in the main.

Gabriel Riesser (1806–1863) carried on a seemingly endless dialogue with anti-Semites who would deny Jews equal rights. He explained and argued, all with a view to persuading them. From the first, too, he begged Jews not to sit idly by and expect that with the passage of time their goals would be achieved. He emphasized that they were to assume personal responsibility and learn to work harmoniously in groups. In his rejoinder to H. E. G. Paulus's anti-Jewish tracts and to Eduard Meyer's attack on Börne, Riesser argued vehemently against their closed minds and hateful hearts. On the other hand, he warned Jews against notions of Jewish nationhood and called for clear affirmations of their German identity. Jewish apartness was not the Jews' doing, but the result of discriminatory legislation. Another constant in Riesser's basic argument was his view that Jewish *religious* distinctiveness, which he powerfully defended, did not set Jews apart from other Germans.

In praising Jewish attributes to the anti-Semite, Riesser at times transcended the apologist's approach. He proposed that the Jewish past was wholly deserving of admiration and that Jews manifested physical heroism in defense of their faith in ancient times and in stoic suffering over the past millennium. Furthermore, their sacrifices for the ideals of the spirit were awesome. He mocked Christian prophecy that Jews must remain wretched until they admit the divinity of Jesus. In his short-lived publication *Der Jude* (*The Jew*), itself a sign of courage as more timid Jews shed *Jude* for *Israelit,* Riesser courageously lashed out against injustice at home and persecutions abroad such as those produced by the ritual murder charge in the Damascus Affair.

Riesser's stature as a legal authority and political leader prompted some Jews to request his views on the internal religious battles of the time. Disclaiming sufficient theological knowledge, Riesser responded blandly. He observed that Judaism had the capacity for further development, that ritual law lacked binding power, that circumcision was not obligatory, and that the Talmud did not constitute ultimate wisdom. Messianism, he declared as he warmed to the subject, was only a perennial hope. Jews should never see themselves as bound by any strictures to return to the Holy Land.

Obviously his position was close to that of Reform, in spite of his initial reluctance to express himself. Certainly, he was horrified by the actions of Orthodox leaders who turned to German civil government to adjudicate internal Jewish disputes. But he was intolerant of those Reformists whose main goal was to make Judaism more acceptable to Christians. Christians had no right to judge Judaism or Jewishness in religious terms, he stated. Religion was a private matter to be divorced from interference by the state or religious authorities.

This patient explainer sometimes displayed the courage of the aggressors. Riesser became a champion of Börne, though he lacked understanding of Börne's wit and was too temperate to approve his politics. He refused to share Börne's gloom on political progress, yet he admired the true patriot in him, the lover of human freedoms, the opponent of all limitations on thought and print.

While Riesser greatly admired Börne, he thoroughly disliked Heine, especially after Heine's tasteless attack on his onetime friend. Riesser even offered to meet Heine in a duel to defend the deceased Börne. In Riesser's writings about Heine, it is evident that he underestimated Heine's immense poetic gifts and his deep loyalty to Judaism. He heard only Heine's abusive comments of Jews, while never coming close to understanding their source. But it was not literary blindness that was at the root of his contempt for Heine. It was the less-than-virtuous Heine, the man with the questionable reputation, whose many undignified feuds and public quarrels imperiled Riesser's campaign to achieve legal equality for Jews—chiefly on the ground that they were *decent* and deserving citizens.

Whereas Riesser's voluminous writings consist of treatises and tracts, commentaries and rejoinders, and very occasionally some literary criticism, the collected works of **Berthold Auerbach** (1812–1882) are almost entirely *belles-lettres*. It is curious that like Heine and Börne, who were both apostates, this Jewish writer kept returning to Jewish problems, while Auerbach, a loyal Jew, largely ignored them. Following his critical anti-Heine work, *Juden in der neuesten Literatur (Jews in Our Most Recent Literature)* (1836), and his historical novels on Spinoza (1837) and M. E. Kuh (1840), Auerbach turned his attention entirely to the village tales (*Dorfgeschichten*), a genre permanently linked to his name. In his novels of village life, as in his more numerous shorter works of fiction, Auerbach occasionally introduced Jewish characters. But on the whole, they were rare and peripheral.

For the apologist Auerbach, Jews served to demonstrate how coexistence of both German and Jew was not only possible, but beautiful and desirable. How useful Jews could be to their fellow citizens if given only half a chance! His Jewish characters led exemplary lives, were largely idealized, and were intended to disarm surviving prejudices. Fifty years after Mendelssohn's death, Auerbach was still intent on proving the virtue of Jews. His claim to emancipation was founded on the "virtue principle" much more than the Enlightenment ideal of the rights of all people.

The morality of his village tales was based on a psalm: "I was young once and have grown old and have never seen the world remain indebted to one doing his duty." Biblical sayings abounded in this writer whose initial career choice had been the rabbinate. These sayings were joined by an indissoluble faith in goodness, justice, and the sense of "oughtness." Though his own religious inclinations had diminished, he advocated more religion for the greater good of society. The Yom Kippur services moved him deeply because of their touching thoughts on life, death, and redemption.

Like all apologists, Auerbach rejected Jewish national ideas. Jews were integrated by culture and sentiment into the land they had inhabited for centuries. From the first they differed only in religion. French Jews had become fully French and German Jews fully German. They were Jews by their particular ethical legacy and the forms of their religious expression. Nationality had little to do with blood origin, all the more with *Geist*.

Auerbach's need to ask for the indulgence of the Germans was already evident in his tract on Jews in recent literature. No, Jews were not radical like Heine and his ilk, Auerbach said. (Auerbach himself had once been arrested for unallowable political activity, and his arrest precluded a rabbinic career forever.) Jews were simple and decent people, he wrote, not rabble-rousing poets without judgment or taste. It was Auerbach who denied any Jewish specificity in Heine's writing. Auerbach's failure to fathom Heine's ongoing quarrel with his Jewishness—especially his conversion—is harder to comprehend than Riesser's. Riesser was not a *Dichter* (poet); Auerbach was.

Perhaps it was the decline of anti-Semitism between 1840 and 1865 that prompted Auerbach to direct his attention to German national questions. He identified with those liberals who, like Riesser, spearheaded and then miscarried the Revolution of 1848. Later, he demanded a unified Germany in which the people's voice would be heard through parliamentary representatives. Moreover, his devotion to improved education was abiding. Auerbach was intrigued with the New World, and he exported to America those characters who had not made their peace with German life. Many of Auerbach's novels were suffused with an almost childlike faith in a more humane age from which immorality and evil would be permanently banished.

For one who believed German and Jewish goals to be nearly identical, the resurgent anti-Semitism of the 1870s proved to be a severe blow. He wrote to his rabbi cousin, Jakob Auerbach, that even intellectuals were "sniffing a Jew everywhere." He complained that Karl Gutzkow was negative about Jews; Gustav Freytag could not suppress his prejudices; even Julian Schmidt seemed to reject them. After reading Wagner's *Die Juden in der deutschen Musik* (*Jews in German Music*), he was deeply depressed. He sensed in the composer's anti-Semitic work a throwback to earlier times. He briefly contemplated a response to Wagner but feared for his nervous constitution under the pressure of lengthy polemics. Although as a young man he felt strong enough to attack the Jew Heine, he did not dare tackle the anti-Semite Wagner. He longed for a Börne to mount a courageous counterassault.

His anger at German historian Heinrich von Treitschke and disillusionment with the physician Theodor Billroth (1829–1896) were such that novelist Karl-Emil Franzos claimed a despondent Auerbach had lost interest in all other matters. Auerbach now publicly condemned the conditions he had at last come to recognize. The German spirit had become unclean; the nation had retrogressed; Germany was no longer a humane country. Christian clergymen, the representatives of the religion of love, were instilling hatred for Jews. In his final two years, when he thought everything he had fought for had been illusory, he became outspoken in his denunciation of mass fanaticism. Jews—not their enemies—could breathe the air of innocence and hold their heads high for having chosen integrity and love over sham and hatred.

Only a few years after Auerbach's death, Ludwig Geiger wondered what had happened to Auerbach's literary reputation. The answer was clear: The public had wearied of realism—of realism in general and the sweetened variety in particular. But the *Dorfgeschichten* (village tales) invited legions of imitators, and for Jewish writers they provided a model for the ghetto tale.

The Jewish attitudes of **Ludwig August Frankl** (1810–1894) remained constant throughout his life, which began thirteen years after Heine's birth and concluded eleven years after Kafka's. One of the few nineteenth-century Jewish writers to have embarked on the arduous trip to Palestine (1856), he drew on this experience for his remaining years.

In his lyric recollections of "the land of our fathers," Frankl evoked the sites of Mount Carmel, Mount Sinai, the Sea of Galilee, and numerous other biblical locales. The poet conjured up visions of a glorious past and compared it to a less glorious present. He can hear the prophets thundering against the sins of Frankl's contemporary Jewish world. Pagan potentates arrive at the gates of Jerusalem after victorious battles, but these stand-ins of earthly power are touched by the Jewish sages who plead with them to spare the Holy City. In another ballad Frankl imagined his idol, Yehuda ben Halevi, approaching the City of Spirit only to be cruelly deceived by an ironic and inscrutable fate.

Perhaps his proximity to Jewish problems as a lifelong employee of the Vienna Jewish community made him view anti-Semitism as a constant of the Jewish conditions. His Jews are often in flight, begging for admission to foreign lands but are coldly denied entrance. The Wandering Jew appears in a poem, meeting a gypsy who mocks his desire for a permanent home. Jews, Frankl said, are "holy nomads."

Frankl balked at a "lachrymose" view of the Jewish past that was far more than passive acceptance of unrelieved suffering. He revered the moral grandeur he found in Jewish history and the traditions that spawned it—the holy pages of text that served as moral guides. A rabbi, consigned to the flames, defies a fire nourished by the burning pages of the Talmud.

Frankl honored the memory of Yohanan ben Zakkai, who exhibited great courage in his escape from Jerusalem, but counseled abandonment of the struggle once resistance had become futile. Yohanan also intrigued him for his ingenuous vision of Jewish continuity through study and learning—the possibility of survival without the physical base of a land or state.

Though continuity was possible, life in exile was never easy. In "Der Primator" ("The Big Shot"), a lengthy poem, the Jews of Prague are desolate because one of their leaders, a court Jew revered in the ghetto for his power outside its walls, succumbs to the Cross. The Jews are unaware that the court Jew had often been the butt of jokes and an outcast in the castle he virtually owned.

Though Frankl kept both feet solidly on Jewish soil, he was also a conscious member of Austrian society. His poem "Die Universität" ("The University"), written in the revolutionary year 1848, sold half a million copies and was set to music by several composers. Wounded in street fighting during the 1848 Revolution, he was soon hailed as one of its heroes. But Frankl easily grasped the difference between courage and foolhardiness. Even as he wrote a "Marseillaise" dedicated to the French poet Rouget de Lisle, he pacified Metternich's police by touching on the horrors perpetrated by the fanatics of 1789. Frankl managed to leave little doubt that for him the "Marseillaise" was awe-inspiring.

Like other apologists and most liberals, Frankl counted on education to pave the way for better times. He deployed his literary talents to teach Jews and Gentiles alike about the Jewish condition—the unwanted status of perennial alien, the craving for the lost land of freedom and strength that in some way either in Palestine or in Austria they needed to affirm.

While **Fanny Lewald** (1811–1889) also belonged to the patient teachers who plead for Jewish acceptance, she was emotionally removed from those she was trying to help. She came from a liberal home from which all religion was banned, so the baptismal act carried neither conflict nor conviction for her.

Though dubbed the "German George Sand," she was neither a dreamer nor a romantic, but a hard-eyed realist and ardent champion of the liberal-bourgeois revolutions of her century. While she called herself a socialist, this meant little more than fraternal feeling between the religions and the sexes or the rich and the poor. She advocated equal rights for women in her *Frauenromane* (*Novels about Women*), although equal rights did not include the right to vote. She thought women were not well equipped educationally. The same applied to many of the Jews of her time. Their ignorance was not their fault, nor was the ignorance of women to be laid at their doorstep. Similarly, Christians were poorly instructed on

Jewish matters. If they could gain improved knowledge and insight, then the prejudices that harmed Jews and cheapened Christians would soon disappear.

Lewald began writing late, anonymously at first, and only her Jewish novel *Jenny* (1843) was published under her own name. *Jenny* recounts the story of a Jewish girl from a wealthy family who, out of love for a Christian clergyman, is willing to embrace his faith. Her liberated banker-father and physician-brother—the latter in love with a girl from a Jew-hating family—allow her to submit to religious tutoring by her fiancé. Unfortunately, his lessons distance her from Christianity. He breaks their engagement, and Jenny shies away from men until she meets an enlightened count who is killed in a duel over slurs to Jews.

Jenny may be one of the most reliable accounts in fiction of Jewish families' respect for education in the first half of the century. The accelerating assimilation of Jews was depicted neutrally, as matter-of-fact, and perhaps as inevitable. Decades later, Georg Hermann's *Jettchen Gebert* (1906), a more polished and sophisticated novel, would also deal with the Biedermeier Jewry of this time, but by then this period belonged to history. Hermann's knowledge was second-hand, based on research. Interestingly, anti-Semitism, a constant concern in *Jenny,* played virtually no role in *Jettchen Gebert.*

More than other liberals, Lewald was aware that there are common denominators linking the problems and psychologies of dominated groups, be they women, Jews, or the poor. Likewise, she was conscious that dominator groups were also linked by common interests and tactics. Moreover, Lewald identified with the interests of the enlightened bourgeoisie, although she was unaware of economic factors and motivation. She credited the bourgeoisie with many of the freedoms that had been acquired since the French Revolution. That revolution and the class that embodied it promised the emancipation of the individual and the brotherhood of all people. She kept working for an enlightened citizenry that would know how to be well represented in the parliaments of Europe. Peace also impressed her as a great good, and, for that reason, she initially opposed Bismarck's wars. But the advantages emanating from his victories became too seductive and outweighed other considerations.

While opposed, like other liberals, to privilege based on birth, she was a firm advocate of the recognition of merit. In this she differed drastically from her archenemy, countess Ida von Hahn-Hahn, with whom she carried on a lengthy feud and for whom both the claim to special privilege and anti-Jewish attitudes were second nature.

No overview of the liberal, assimilatory, and often apologist position would be complete without brief consideration of the Hungarian-born **Karl Beck** (1817–1879), the Bohemians **Moritz Hartmann** (1821–1872), and **Hieronymus Lorm** (Heinrich Landesmann) (1821–1902). Throughout their lives, Beck (until 1848, when he changed direction), Hartmann, and Lorm were committed to a free and progressive Germany, in which censorship, privileged birth, and authoritarianism would play an ever smaller role.

Of the three, Karl Beck manifested the greatest respect for the Jewish heritage, and this respect did not diminish even after his baptism in 1843. In poems such as "Die Juden auf der Messe" ("Jews at the Fair"), he expressed revulsion at the dehumanization of the Jews. This once-proud people, he contended, had lost courage and become doglike, fearful, submissive, and obsessed with an unwholesome love of gold. The Jews' situation, he said, continued to be unique in the world. Without a land of their own and clearly defined rights anywhere, they could at best hope for a modicum of tolerance. Rejected and despised, they remained objects of Christian derision.

In another poem Beck transported the reader to Frankfurt's Jew Street, home of a slave people that was then producing a Jewish *Wilhelm Tell.* The hero was Ludwig Börne, Beck's idol. In "David and Goliath" Beck aimed his arrow at the "Goliath" of prejudice. This Goliath simply would not die in spite of the wounds he sustained. Moreover, Jesus the Messiah, who had failed to improve the world, necessitated a search for other redeemers. Yet Beck was attracted from the first to the rich, emotive, colorful symbolism of the Catholic church.

In spite of his conversion, Beck admonished Jews to keep alive their love of Zion. In "Das neue Palästina" ("The New Palestine"), he urged them to rebuild the city of their ancient glory. "Land, Thou holiest of all/ Thou, the lovely bride of heaven," he wrote. He depicted the absence of Jewish pride in "Der jüdische Hausierer" ("The Jewish Pedlar"), a short story, the inner conflicts of individual Jews in "Der Spieler," a novella, and human dilemmas in biblical garb in *Saul,* a drama.

More than most writers, **Moritz Hartmann** was personally and artistically detached from Jewish issues. Only on one occasion, when the ghetto was stormed by Czechs, did he join those who protected the Jewish population. Because of his universalist outlook, he described this as a human duty, not an act of help to Jews in distress.

His universalism simply did not admit of special concern for any group. If he attacked Jews more than he praised them, it was because of their parochialism. Jews thought only of the welfare of other Jews, a notion repugnant to him. Watching Gabriel Riesser in St. Paul's Church as a fellow delegate in 1848, Hartmann was distressed that Riesser seemed to

fight exclusively for Jewish rights. And those of workers? Riesser appeared
not to care. Hartmann saw nothing distinctive in the Jewish past, nothing
that would set Jewish suffering apart from that of the laboring man. He
praised, in contrast, Johann Jacoby who also stood up for Jewish rights but
had found other groups equally worthy of his support. As for religion,
Hartmann was neither Jew nor Gentile; religion did not matter to him.
Only in one story, "Bei den Kunstreitern" ("With the Circus Riders"), was
there a glimmer of interest in things Jewish. A baptized Jew is moved by
a Yom Kippur service that resurrects a wave of nostalgic sentiment. Like
other writers of his time, Hartmann would have liked to see a Jew of
greater courage; the Jewish "fighter" held a distinct fascination for him.

The deaf and blind poet **Hieronymus Lorm**, his work suffused with
stark pessimism, also cared little about religion and was frequently critical
of Jewish behavior. In works of Jewish relevance, *Gabriel Solmar* (1885)
and *Der ehrliche Name* (*One's Good Name*) (1880), Lorm dealt harshly with
the bourgeoisie, but reserved strong sympathy for the lower classes. In the
former, he expressed his contempt for the crude ostentation of the
bourgeoisie; in the latter, he admired a basic simplicity of the lower classes.
He regarded conspicuous consumption in the Jewish upper middle class as
a form of compensation; given greater normalization of the Jewish
condition, he asserted, many current undesirable traits among Jews would
disappear. Jews would be as good and as bad as non-Jews. He claimed no
special virtue for them, but neither would he tolerate notions of inherent
Jewish vices. He remained sensitive to anti-Semitism and was annoyed
when Christians saw in the negative actions of a Jew only the Jewish—not
the human—element.

Not much should be made of Lorm's Jewish interests. The hero of
Gabriel Solmar, though once destined for the rabbinate, gradually
distanced himself from Judaism, immersing himself all the more in the
intrigues of a Christian court. In an external way, Solmar resembled
Berthold Auerbach, Lorm's brother-in-law and longtime moral mainstay.
When relations between them cooled, the critic Eduard Kuh, with whom
Lorm had once feuded, became his new friend and confidant.

Beck, Hartmann, and Lorm all looked upon Börne as their idol. Beck
called him his "God and guiding star," "the man capable of rewriting the
Bible, a Freedom Bible." Beck's passionate verses on behalf of Börnean
freedom evoked a more enthusiastic response than did Beck's subsequent
poems. Called the "leader of the *Sturm und Drang* (*Storm and Stress*) for
liberty," the young Beck clamored for freedom from foreign oppressors,
censors, clerics, the rule by One. Where Börne achieved his intensity
through irony and satire, Beck attained his effect through eloquence,

anger, and shameless yearning. His *Nächte* (*Nights*) (1838) garnered the enthusiastic approval of Georg Herwegh who put him beside Michael Creizenach (1749–1842) and poet and translator Ferdinand Freiligrath as one of the "three children of one mother"—Mother Freedom.

Beck could never see himself as belonging entirely to one nation. He sensed in himself a Jew, a Hungarian, a German—but none to the exclusion of the others. Soon after *Nächte* he wrote *Der fahrende Poet* (*The Itinerant Poet*) (1839), still pursuing Börne's enemies. Here the poet is transported to Weimar at the invitation of Goethe's family. While in the great man's room, the poet is filled with sentiments far more Börnean than Goethean.

Stille Lieder (*Silent Songs*) (1840) already marked a departure, the love of freedom yielding to contemplations on life, love, and sorrows. A new mood took hold of Beck. He was filled with sadness and resignation. His new preoccupation was with the poor and wretched of this world. But it was not through economic or social action he wished to help, but through charitable understanding. Christian kindness and gentleness moved ever more into the foreground as old ideals seemed to be gradually cast aside.

Earnest pro-German affirmations characterized the early poetry of Hartmann, freedom being generally equated with the German national idea. He exhorted his readers to turn to Prussia rather than multinational Austria as their champion. He was disturbed by the heavy presence of Slavs, who outnumbered Germans in the parliament in Vienna, an ill omen for Germans and Jews alike in his native Bohemia. Upon the outbreak of the Revolution of 1848, he sat with the radical left in the Paulskirche (St. Paul's Church), content to observe in silence. In his *Reimchronik des Pfaffen Maurizius* (*Rhymed Chronicle of the Preacher Maurizius*) (1848), Hartmann revealed his utter disenchantment with the ineffective and constantly jabbering parliamentarians. A further sobering experience was the unification of Germany: Bismarck's Reich included neither Austria nor Bohemia. Coupled with the new militarism, 1871 was only a notch lower in unfulfilled expectations than 1848. Ailing in his final years, Hartmann clung ever more desperately to his belief in human rights for all. By contrast, the increasingly pessimistic Hieronymus Lorm retained a measure of political optimism longer than either Beck or Hartmann did.

• • • • •

Narrators of Ghetto Life

The writers of ghetto fiction, popular between 1840 and 1890, addressed both Gentiles and Jews. To Gentiles they wanted to make clear that what was transpiring in the "Jew streets" of Europe was of a decidedly human and not demonic nature. To be sure, Jews had some distinctive traits, the result of their unique history. But these characteristics were harmless, certainly to the host people, if not always to themselves.

To Jews, the ghetto novelists made appeals of a different nature. The occupations of old—*Hausieren* (door-to-door peddling), endless studying, and mental activity to the exclusion of anything physical—needed to be replaced by more "normal" pursuits. The ghetto novelists believed that there should be neither shame nor danger in physical labor, in the trades of farmer, carpenter, shoemaker—whatever. They urged mothers and fathers to rid themselves of ancient prejudices and begin to live in a modern and balanced world. The writers knew that these changes in outlook could not be realized overnight, but they insisted on a beginning. Less interested in emancipation and political rights, they were more intent on internal reform that would lead to better health for Jews and broader recognition of Jewish humanity by Christians. Thus the ghetto writers, for the most part, were also apologists and patient explainers.

Other themes in ghetto fiction dealt with the young Jew's attitude toward military service and his desire to avoid it. The ghetto writers also evinced a yearning for the Holy Land or, at the very least, for holy earth. Finally, the peril of conversion, especially as the result of sexual attraction, was to be avoided.

Among the favorite characters of ghetto tales are the brave Jew—the soldier Jew who can teach physical courage to other Jews who look upon it as an alien characteristic. Common, too, are the *Schlemiel* (a bungler or one easily victimized) in search of a suitable wife and the less-than-well-endowed female fearing inspection by a prospective husband. Frequently portrayed is the wealthy Jewish innkeeper or the estate lease owner, who knows the village secrets and has some restraining power over hostile Christians. There is the autocratic rich Jew who needs to be reminded that man does not live by bread alone. There is the person afflicted by blindness or a serious physical defect who has been given special vision and compensating qualities. Other popular figures are the matchmaker, the stern rabbi—rarely lovable—or the Jewish clerk or scribe who, for a consideration, will manufacture documents that exempt a young Jew from fighting for a hostile government. The *Beschau* (inspection of the intended bride) and the customs surrounding a draft notice are among the common scenes in ghetto fiction.

Relatively few of these works originated in Germany. Far more stemmed from the Hapsburg Empire and featured many of the conflicts of Jews in Lithuania, Ruthenia, and Bohemia. Here the Jews were squeezed by existing nationality struggles and the ancient prejudices of groups about one another. Perhaps it was a comfort to both the authors and their characters that in this vast empire they were not the only oppressed group.

There were many practitioners of the ghetto tale, and nearly all were liberals. They demanded a streamlined Jewry that would easily blend into the existing landscape. Nearly all were in the Börne succession in that they protested against incursions upon the right to think and speak freely. Though some of the characters yearned for the lost Judea, they did not take seriously the resurrection of a Jewish state. They were Jews of the Diaspora, and it was in the Diaspora that they proposed to live, contribute, and die.

The most important writers of ghetto fiction were the Bohemian **Leopold Kompert** (1822–1886) and the Galicia-born **Karl-Emil Franzos** (1848–1904). Between them were many others, some of whom were well-known and talented in their time. Most of these were closer to the tradition of Kompert than of Franzos. It must be remembered that Kompert and Franzos had completely different perceptions of Jewish life.

Kompert depicted the ghetto in a mostly realistic vein, though occasionally with sentimental and romantic overtones. Franzos described the Ruthenian Jewish ways of his youth in harsh, naturalistic terms with few charming or redemptive features. Kompert was moved by the poetry of Jewish life; Franzos, with the possible exception of his final novel, discerned little of this poetry. Moreover, Franzos condemned existing Jewish ways as backward, antirational, and superstitious. He called this Eastern part of the empire "Half-Asia," which is also his title for his early tales. The differences between Kompert and Franzos reflect in part their differences in temperament but they also reveal the dissimilarities between the Bohemian and Ruthenian Jewish communities.

In Kompert's writings the conflict between businessman-father and poet-son was replayed. For the senior Kompert, commerce was the sole and proper domain for a young Jew. As so often happens, his more sensitive mother leaned toward beauty and the arts and fought vigorously for a secondary education for her son. Young Leopold was a student at the Piarist Gymnasium when his father lost his business and the family became familiar with the starkest poverty. In 1838, Leopold literally walked from Bohemia to Hungary and from Hungary to Vienna. Though his literary career started early, it never enabled him to ward off hunger. But his deprivation never motivated him to follow in his father's footsteps.

Kompert drew upon a legend within his own family for his first well-known tale. A rabbi—his maternal grandfather—appeared in town in beggar's garb, wishing to test the charity of the community he was to serve. The beggar-rabbi was invited to the home of a kind-hearted but struggling merchant for the Sabbath meal. During the dinner the beggar regaled the guests with his wit and learning and earned the admiration of his host's daughter (who, in real life, was to become Kompert's grandmother). It was on the day after his grandfather's death that Kompert sat down to write "Von meinem Großvater" ("About My Grandfather").

Of his numerous works, *Die Kinder des Randars* (*The Children of the Innkeeper-Farmer*) is one of the earliest and most representative. The innkeeper Reb Schmul entertains good relations with the Count, whose estate he administers, and with the peasants who work for Schmul in the daytime and drink at his inn in the evening. They listen to Schmul's prayers as he walks among them in the fields wearing *T'fillin* (phylacteries, i.e., leather prayer boxes) and chanting from the Siddur (Jewish prayer book containing the daily and Sabbath liturgy). They like the fact that he is praying to God, but they do not like Schmul's refusal to extend further credit after they run up a sizable drinking bill. They then turn abusive and blame it on his Jewishness.

Much is going on at the inn. Reb Schmul is reluctant to send the hero, young Moschele, to secondary school. Schmul's wife enlists the help of the powerful Count who, from a respectful distance, has always shown her his love and respect. Schmul can refuse her, but not the Count. To the inn, too, come many *Schnorrers* (beggars) many of whom fire Moschele's imagination, but none as much as Reb Mendel, who speaks of rebuilding Jerusalem and returning to the land Jews had left centuries ago. Mendel leaves for Palestine promising to bring back a vessel of holy earth.

Moschele becomes Mosche and attends a school run by Piarists (members of a religious teaching institute established in the early seventeenth century by St. Joseph of Calasanza). He rooms at the home of Reb Salme, who feels young Jews should hurl their Latin books into the fire. (The wrong type of reading, he says, causes intelligent young men to abandon their Judaism.) Kompert responded through Mosche: He, too, was concerned about young Jews leaving the fold. Nevertheless, Jews' particularity cannot be emphasized so much that they forget they are human beings and must live with other human beings who are not Jews. Again, Salme raises the question of a suitable occupation for a Jew, asserting that a Jew cannot be a mason or carpenter, for it is unimaginable that a Jew should be working on a church tower or the roof of a building, thereby imperiling his life. Salme can barely tolerate the thought of a Jewish wife eating bread that her husband has earned in this manner.

Mosche thinks that Salme was both right and wrong. Suddenly, across the street, he sees a Jewish butcher plying his trade. If a Jew cannot be a mason or carpenter, why can he be a butcher? Isn't blood worse than cement or wood? Salme responds that a human being has to eat, to which Mosche replies that man must also live in a house built by a mason or carpenter. (Kompert was firm throughout his fiction: Jewish occupations must be broadened. Whatever members of the general community could do, Jews could also do.)

Upon completion of his medical studies, Mosche returns home. His sister Hannele has fallen in love with Honza, a peasant's son, Mosche's former friend and now, as priest, his worst enemy. When Honza's father is refused further drinks because he has not paid the tab, he burns down the barn, and Reb Schmul has him imprisoned. Vindictively, the priest seeks Hannele's conversion. Mosche, now called Moritz, rushes to the priest's home and rescues his sister from the clutches of the proselytizer.

Kompert did not trust the clergy. After this incident, Moritz agrees that he had been naive to think he could befriend the peasants. They were congenial and friendly to Jews most of the time; but when crossed, they did not hesitate to ruin the Jew. While the peasants could be trusted to a point, the clergy could not, Kompert wrote. They would turn the peasants against the Jew whenever the whim struck them. They believed that fighting Jews was part of their religious mission, one they would not fail. In other novels, too, the clergy were the guilty party in demonstrations against Jews.

Bohemian nationalism causes Moritz to wonder about the feasibility of a land populated solely by Jews. How should a new Judea be ruled? By an anointed king, a republican leader? Would Jews become masons or carpenters, or would they continue to resist normal occupations? Would a Jewish state have to import Christian workers to build houses and government buildings? Would Jews cultivate the land, be willing to relearn what they had once known? And if there were again Jewish peasants, would they also take to drink?

Other novels and stories mirrored Kompert's occupational concerns. In "Am Pflug" ("Ploughing"), an urban Jewish family purchases a large farm but needs to adopt a new way of life. All is not well at first, but soon the new farmers achieve a robust physical health they have not previously enjoyed. "Trenderl" is about a Jewish boy who likes to work with his hands, only to be discouraged by a mother who cannot envision her offspring climbing a cathedral tower to affix a decorative object. Even Trenderl, the over-protected youngster, hesitates until his Christian friend, ominously named Nazi, deliberately flings a contemptuous "just a Jew" at him, whereupon in anger Trenderl completes the job.

Influenced by Rousseau, Kompert viewed natural life as the real one, while a life spent in musty chambers perusing holy books was both unreal and contrary to nature. Kompert's didactic streak led him to his oft-repeated observation that a healthy, more natural, body-related occupation would in no way represent a diminution of Jewishness. In a restored balance between body and mind—elsewhere Kompert admired aspects of a Jewish education—lay the true hope for psychological normalization, self-respect, and—equally important—the respect of others.

In Kompert's later years his literary production declined, along with his devotion to Jewish issues. Like most German-Jewish writers, he retained a great sensitivity to anti-Semitism. Above all, he objected to the notion that a whole community should be held accountable for the alleged malfeasance of one of its members. On the whole, however, he remained content to speak softly and to appeal to reason on all sides, although he believed sentiment to be important. In many ways he resembled Berthold Auerbach, the raconteur of German village tales. Kompert also disliked Heine, who reflected negatively on the positive image he tried to create. Temperamentally, too, Kompert was similar to Auerbach; his was a soft nature that avoided conflict and feuds.

Karl-Emil Franzos claimed that Kompert's ghetto novels, to which he owed a great deal, painted life in far brighter colors than reality warranted. Kompert, Franzos argued, could not be harsh; evil caused him too much pain. Perhaps this was overstated. There were occasional acts of violence in Kompert, and not all was rosy. It remained for Franzos to bring to life the darker features of the ghetto. He became its Zola, recording what he saw and heard, however bad and disheartening, though never with malicious intent. What Franzos described as he peered into the ghetto streets was a complex of narrowness, superstition, and irrationalism.

Hasidic and Zionist critics have denounced Franzos's portraits as unbalanced, and some have charged him with self-hate. Rationalists and liberal Jews, by contrast, recognized a measure of truth and applauded him as a man of progress. Franzos certainly did not limit himself to relating the prejudices and foibles in Galician Jewish life. He exposed with equal severity the atavistic beliefs and practices of Poles, Hungarians, and Ruthenians. If Jews bore the brunt, it was because he knew them best and was more involved in their destiny. With them he was more insistent on the need for quick and incisive change.

In later years Franzos suspected he had underestimated the cultures of peoples he had lumped together as "Half-Asians." He had overrated Western and German values as well as modernist and scientific currents that now struck him as less admirable than before. Yet a degree of scientific optimism survived and stamped him unmistakably as a man of the outgoing nineteenth century. It was only in *Der Pojaz* (*The Prankster*), his last novel, that his criticism mellowed. He was as intolerant as ever of intolerance—whether a rabbi's or a priest's—but he had begun to discover some admirable traits in Hasidism.

Born in 1848, Franzos was raised by Dominicans, but both by faith and culture he was different from Christian and Jewish classmates. Yet he felt that he was a Jew. In Czernowitz, a center of Jewish activity, he sought out *Hasidim* (Hasidic Jews), but the contact merely alienated him further. He became infatuated with a Christian girl whose attitude toward Jews he mocked in an early tale. Franzos conceded that he was an unlikely candidate in those years to develop into a portraitist of Jewish life. He spent the last twenty years of his life in Berlin, editing a journal and writing his many novels.

A persistent theme in his fiction is that of Jewish elders and rabbis stifling the natural impulses of healthy youngsters. They looked down upon the less-gifted Talmudic students and despised anyone leaning toward physical pursuits. But they also repressed the intellectually curious who found traditional Jewish education too restrictive. Several talented youngsters in his work gave up precious possessions to bribe a guard to let them into the library to read in damp attic chambers a play by Schiller, Lessing, or Shakespeare. For example, when Sender Glatteis, the hero of *Der Pojaz,* is discovered reading the forbidden books, he is punished severely and eventually dies from the consequences. Social disapproval of those unfortunate enough to fall in love with a non-Jew is even more stringent. Such young men and women suffer parental as well as communal rejection.

Franzos depicted Jewish education as narrowly focused, choking both individuality and normal instincts. It postulated, he said, a way of life that is suitable only for lazy men who justified not working productively by staying glued to dusty tomes and engaging in spurious argument. It neglected totally the physical development of the young and prescribed conduct within a small range of do's and don'ts, strangling natural emotions.

Moschko of Parma is probably not Franzos's best novel, but it may be his most representative. The son of a hapless synagogue servant, the character Moschko is inept at learning the Hebrew letters but compensates for his inadequacies by developing his physical strength. Unlike other Jewish children, he does not run when insulted or attacked and wonders if he is not a Christian child. He broods a great deal: What is to become of him, a Jew and yet like *goyim* (Gentiles) in so many ways? To the Jews' horror, he apprentices himself to the village blacksmith, the first Jew to be so employed. The way he handles his tools proves that a Jew can be as good a smith as a Gentile. Since Moschko observes the commandments, the Jews make their peace with his unusual occupation. In time, Moschko decides that he is a human being first and only secondly a Jew. He has trouble understanding why God should even permit different religions, and although he accepts the idea that a Jew should not marry a non-Jewish woman, he can never think of a really good reason why. At the circumcision ceremony for his brother's son, Moschko is pained over the high esteem in which the community holds his pale, arrogant brother. Moschko asked himself:

> Can it please God . . . that a man loafs? And displease him that I work? Our wise men say it is so, but maybe they don't understand what God ordered written as the Law. And if they understand it, maybe the Law is wrong.

If the Jews were God's people, Moschko wonders, why are they despised? Why had Polish Baron Starsky spat on Jews that very morning and used his whip on their backs? Moschko would have pulled him from his horse and thrashed him. Yet Moschko realizes that Jews are not the only ones with strange opinions and attitudes. For example, he knows that, while his master-blacksmith likes and respects him, he also has guilt feelings about having a Jew—an infidel—in his smithy. Havrilo, his fellow worker, has ideas about Jews that are even move primitive and ludicrous than Moschko's about Christians. Franzos humorously depicts their religious primitivism as they spout forth their inherited prejudices. Both conclude after their debates that neither religion practices what it teaches, and neither is worth fighting over.

Because Moschko has no powerful Jew to protect him from the draft, he is a natural subject for conscription. All nationality groups sought to avoid serving. Germans left the region; Ruthenians cut off their toes; Jews used the feigned extra heartbeat or, more often, the purse. Luckily, Moschko is the Jew most likely to withstand the rigors of military service. He participates in several battles and is severely wounded at the Battle of Parma in Italy. Crippled, he returns, after years, to Barnow (site of most of Franzos's works). In spite of his critical injuries, Christians regard him as "only a Jew." For Jews he is just a goy. Broken in body and spirit, a dupe of national and religious stupidities, Moschko is introduced to his illegitimate son, whom Havrilo's sister had borne without telling him. The son, anti-Semitic at first, comes to love the dying Moschko. The latter concludes in his final days that once he had thought it a misfortune to be born a Jew, but it is neither a fortune nor a misfortune—only a destiny like any other.

Franzos could tolerate neither the absence nor the desire for *Bildung*. Nor could he make his peace with the fact that the outside world should not exist for the Jews, that the only legitimate subject of inquiry should be ancient Hebrew texts. The "prankster" Sender Glatteis has a deep thirst for the German language as a vehicle for his chosen profession of acting; he can only learn it on the sly and at the risk of severe penalties. Any misstep by a young Jew was blamed on the dangers of a secular education.

The method of contracting marriages came in for equal criticism. Finding a life's mate should have neither business nor social respectability as a goal, said Franzos. The denizens of Barnow know nothing about love; Christians fall in love, and a Jew has no use for such an exotic emotion. One of Franzos's more enlightened characters ventures the hypothesis that the rejection of love is more the denial of feeling among Jews than any sense of superiority vis-à-vis Jewish or non-Jewish marriage partners. Franzos's marriage broker, Itzig Türkischgeld, is one of his most delightful characters. While he may embellish the assets or endowments of a marriage prospect, he desists when he suspects an aversion "for the most wonderful of catches."

The lack of *Bildung* is also mirrored in Franzos's treatment of women. A heroine asks, "Is a wife like any other property? . . . Is she more than other chattel, an ornament, a house? Has she not a will like every other human being?" Franzos attributed the low estate of women less to Jewish tradition than to their status as a by-product of all half-Asian cultures, most of whom behaved toward their women much less generously than did Jews. At least Jews treated their wives and daughters with benign domination, through playful yet condescending and patronizing kindness.

Rabbis generally fared poorly in Franzos's work, though far better than priests. They were authoritarian, but neither evil nor hateful. Their questionable decisions on marriage and human relations stemmed from an ossified tradition, less than from arbitrary, wilful actions on their part. Some Hasidic rabbis might be charlatans, but the priests were either exploiters or bigots. Franzos treated the "Misnagdim" (rabbinic orthodox) more tolerantly than he did the Hasidim, though both confuse profound religiosity with senseless acts of devotion. He rejected kabbala outright; he defended the Talmud as an elucidation of Torah, though it tended to degenerate into absurd argument. Why should former friends become enemies over whether an egg is unkosher if a blood spot is on one side rather than another?

Toward the end of his life Franzos recognized warmth and beauty in the Jews of Barnow. Reminiscent of Heine, he depicted with charm the preparations for the Sabbath. He admired the adoration of the one God and the poetry of the Song of Songs, with its hymns of love and tributes to womanhood. Few of his characters ever considered Christianity as an alternative to Judaism. Franzos himself would settle for reforms within Judaism, but never for an abandonment of it. The following passage summarizes his position on Judaism:

> What a peculiar history the Jews have had: Their strong religion, founded on a rock, was once a protection and saved them from the axes and clubs of their enemies. They would have been destroyed without the protection, for the blows aimed at them were heavy and hard to parry; and for that very reason, they clung to it all the more tenaciously, until, at last, instead of enlightening their hearts, they made of it a bandage for their eyes. At one time, they were not to be pitied even for this, for all the world went about with eyes bandaged. But now when the light of day is shining in the West and even dawn has broken in the East, Jews have not raised the bandage one inch. I do not want them to do it too quickly, nor do I want them to throw away their religion; I only want them to open their eyes to the light shining ever more brightly about them.

•　•　•　•　•

Writers of Historical Fiction

The boundary line separating the Jewish ghetto writers from those who wrote historical fiction is not always clearly drawn. At times only a reference to an historical figure enables the reader to place the work in its proper historical setting. Like most ghetto tales, historical fiction has its location outside of Germany itself, sometimes even beyond German-speaking territory. Whether the setting is medieval England or seventeenth-century Constantinople, the narrative unfolds against the backdrop of oppressed Jews. The authors, mostly liberal, assimilated, apologetic Jews, are determined to prove the virtues of the Jewish people. Provided with the opportunity, Jews would not only be as good, but also as brave and courageous as German Christians. These writers wanted to demonstrate that Jews are flesh and blood, rejoice and suffer, laugh and cry. The historical novelists gravitated toward those periods in which, for one reason or another, Jews could be soldiers and more nearly "normal"—that is, like the non-Jewish population.

The novels were written at a time when the scientific study of Jewish history was still in its infancy, and liberties with historical fact could easily escape notice. A favorite device is the invention of a fighter-hero and his assignment to a time that would tolerate his heroism. Elaborately plotted, these works have little regard for verisimilitude. Some of the fiction reflects the influence of Walter Scott or Alexandre Dumas, although without the element of the *boudoir*. If love exists at all, it is presented in the form of a Gentile maiden seeking to entice a noble Jewish male away from the ancestral faith. Or an heroic Christian knight obscures the moral vision of a chaste Jewish girl. Occasionally, the young Jews will withstand wiles, threats, and other inducements to approach the baptismal font. While one or two may die for their faith, more will convince bishops and sultans of their Jewish steadfastness and be freed without having to undergo conversion.

Several authors of historical fiction were rabbis whose didactic intentions far outweighed any literary considerations. The tales became many-pronged pedagogic weapons. First, they militated against conversion, which, for the rabbis, represented the bane of nineteenth-century Jewish existence. Second, the tales could teach moral principles that had guided earlier Jews through even more perilous times. Third, they could present the essence of Jewish history, although rabbis, like others, took many liberties with historical fact if it suited their broader objectives. Jewish history as lived through fictional characters brought within the average reader's range the scholarly findings of Isaac Marcus Jost (1793–1860), Leopold Zunz (1794–1886), and Heinrich Graetz (1817–1891). Yet the goal of historical fiction writers was less to vivify the past than to use it as a tool to instruct about the present.

Historical fiction evolved under the aegis of Romanticism, with its general historical orientation and its emphasis on discovering the "root-essence" of ethnic groups. Like the Christian Romantics, the Jewish writers cultivated sentimentalism, nostalgia, and the virtues of chaste romance. Jewish family life, customs, and folkways were all enveloped in a warm, romantic glow. While Christian Romantics turned to medieval religiosity (the fervor that led to the building of great cathedrals), Jewish novelists turned to the medieval era to depict their heroism in withstanding Christian fanatics. Most of the writers are forgotten as writers although some, like **Ludwig Philippson** (1811–1889) and **Marcus (Meyer) Lehmann** (1830–1899), had distinguished careers in the rabbinate. The plots of several novels indicate the concerns of the writers.

In *Die Kreuzfahrer und die Juden* (*The Crusader and the Jews*) (1843) Eugen Rispart, writing as **Dr. Isaac Ascher Frankolm** (1788–1849), ventured into the England of Richard the Lion-Hearted. A Spanish Jew arrived to fetch the bride chosen for him long ago. He is enlightened, well read, and courageous—which the Jews of England are not. He falls in love with Hadassah, the daughter of Benedict of York, though his bride was Malka, daughter of the court Jew Jossen. True love is allowed to triumph, especially since Malka has fallen in love with a knight who rescued her from a Jew-hating mob. The knight is none other than Richard the Lion-Hearted, whose identity she discovers only on the day of his coronation. Though the novel revolves about the motif of the beautiful Jewess, victim of a royal infatuation, it is also an attack on intellectual darkness, economic exploitation, base prejudice, and the cheap rationalization of criminal acts. Here the patient explainer has evolved into an aggressor, not toward the host state but toward the religion which increasingly holds sway over it. Religious and economic circumstances converge in the story to bring about mob violence during the weeks of Richard's coronation. Frankolm was surprisingly modern in his realization that religious and psychological biases often conceal economic motives. The mightiest noblemen of the kingdom seek loans from Jewish financiers. When the time comes to repay the loans, Christian dissatisfaction with the perfidious Jews suddenly mounts, a mob is quickly organized, eliminating the "usurious parasites."

The tone was often bitter in Frankolm's work. Christianity, the religion of love, knows neither love nor compassion. It punishes all who will not accept its monopoly on unprovable truths. Bishops and noblemen pretend to be protectors of the Jews, but on the days of Christian "vengeance," they absent themselves. Though economically sophisticated, Frankolm was primitive in blaming the lower classes for the murderous onslaught on the Jews of York.

The historical figure of Benedict of York (Cardinal Henry Benedict, 1725–1807, impoverished by the confiscation of his property by the French Revolution), knew that a Jew should always be prepared to flee at a moment's notice, possess sufficient cash in store, and have a ready-made place of refuge in another principality or country. In the novels Benedict's thinking is sound but fails in the application. He does not recognize the moment of danger and is killed. Hadassah and her bold Spanish admirer escaped to Iberia, for unlike the English Jews, he has the boldness to act. Frankolm deplored the impact on the Jewish psyche of fear, worry, and the consequent immobilization of the will.

Far less believable than Frankolm's novel is *Gabriel: Eine Geschichte der Juden von Prag* (*Gabriel: A History of the Jews of Prague*) (1869) by **Salomon Kohn** (1825–1904). The hero, Gabriel Suess, discovers through his mother's deathbed confession that he is a "bastard." Feeling abandoned by the whole Jewish community, he has himself baptized, attains the rank of general in the imperial army, and becomes a great war hero. But his soul craves revenge, above all against Blümele, the Jewish woman he thinks has abandoned him and whose husband he threatens to have killed. Only the appearance of the scholar Michael Glogau and his persuasive arguments against revenge and for a new life prevent Suess's descent into an ugly world of hate and retribution.

While the actions strain credulity, certain scenes are vividly depicted: the Sabbath customs of Prague Jewry, especially the kindness to strangers on the Sabbath; the practice of inviting guests to display their Talmudic virtuosity after the Sabbath meal; the encounter between the Jewish-born general and the Jewish scholar. Suess's physical courage and military prowess are in sharp contrast to the Jews' resignation in the face of flight and possible death. Kohn deplored the Jewish lack of interest in the politics of the outside world that can affect their lives so profoundly. Only one question intrigued the Jewish community as a new ruler was crowned: What could or would he do to the Jews?

Like the ghetto novelists, Kohn was no friend of excessive mental

activity. General Mar (Suess's Christian name and title) is an example of
the bravery that once was and could again belong to a Jew. Kohn regretted
that the fencing masters of Prague were not permitted to teach their art to
Jews, the people most in need of self-defense.

Others voiced similar concerns. **Moritz Wassermann** (1811–1892) had
recourse to the American past for his *Judah Touro: Eine biographische
Romanze (Judah Touro: A Biographical Romance)* (1871). This author felt
it essential to enlighten Christians about the sturdy morals of Jews. He
sympathized with the weak and oppressed, be they black, Jews, or servants.
America appealed to him, as it did to other liberals, as the promised land
of liberty and equality. He lauded bravery under fire, steadfastness in the
face of adversity; he had little use for Christian clergymen and their special
brand of hatred for Jews and miseducation. His Touro falls in love with
Christian women in isolated Louisiana, where there were few Jewish
women, but he decides against a union outside the faith.

Moritz Friedländer (1848–1919) resorted to the arch hater of
antiquity, Apion, to do his instructing. Jewish calm and reason defeated the
ugly demogogue. **Marcus Lehmann** (1833–1890) narrated the improbable
feats of the famed Tosaphist Rabbi Samson of Cousy in "Der Fürst von
Coucy," a story in his *Jüdische Erzählungen (Jewish Tales)*. Samson saves
the life of Richard the Lion-Hearted, is raised by him to prince status, and
is taken prisoner by Moslem pirates. The rabbi-prince manages to teach
the Sultan's daughter the virtues of Judaism. In "Die Marannen," the first
novella in **Ludwig Philippson's** *Sarom* (1843), the heroic older Abravanel
loses his battle for Jewish rights to the evil Torquemada; nevertheless, he
states his case for Jewish decency and clerical villainy.

There were many others. To sum up: German-Jewish historical fiction
was neither good literature nor good history. But it is essential to an
understanding of a segment of nineteenth-century Jews who were eager for
normalcy, craved recognition as human beings, and wished to be as like the
Germans as possible while retaining their religious individuality. An
idealized Jewishness was to make them acceptable to the outside world.
Liberals and apologists for the most part, the writers of historical fiction,
glorified an imaginary Jewish past more with loyalty and goodwill than with
conviction, talent, or judgment.

• • • • •

Pre-Zionists

A lthough Moses Hess's *Rom und Jerusalem* (*Rome and Jerusalem*) (1862) has been labeled the first Zionist classic, this work did not contain more than the rudiments of a Zionist philosophy. It went beyond the mere expression of longing for the lost Jerusalem. Characters in the work of ghetto novelists set out for the Holy Land and returned years later with particles of the soil of Judea. Poet Ludwig Frankl visited Palestine and wrote many poems about the sentiments this visit evoked.

Perhaps the first writer to devote a whole volume of poetry to Zion was **Ludwig Wihl** (1807–1882). In the "Jehovalieder," which form the early portions of his *West-Östliche Schwalben* (*Swallows of East and West*) (1847), Wihl reconstructed the Jerusalem of old—vigorous, powerful, revered, the princess of the Orient, the center from which radiated the most enduring and lofty ideals of mankind. Wistfully he compared former glory with present sorrow and shame. Jerusalem was no longer a living rose but only a dried-up flower. When would that hero emerge who would lift the Holy City to heights of power and world significance? He would appear only after Jews had rekindled the flame and their spirit was reignited by pride in their heritage.

Like Heine, who thoroughly detested Wihl, the poet resurrected the image of Yehuda ben Halevi at the gates of Jerusalem where a cruel fate struck him down. But with all his longing for the immortal city, Wihl could not forget his roots in German soil. If he stood in Judea before a palm and an oak, he would also have to embrace the oak as symbol of the land of his birth. He affirmed his attachment to Germany, but acknowledged—not without resentment—that this Germany reduced him to inferior status. Wihl now approximated the stance of the aggressor. He sharply rebuked those Jews who would lick the boots of their oppressors. How much more edifying the example of the Jews of Babylon who overcame the trials of exile by clinging to their people and its traditions while they eagerly awaited the return to Judea!

With equal passion Wihl lauded the ancient religion. He recalled nostalgically the legends on which he was nurtured that by themselves provided inadequate intellectual nourishment for today's times. The beliefs of old had to be in accord with the requirements of modern times. There could be no compromise, however, with the centrality of the one God. Nor could the current deities of skepticism and materialism occupy space in a rejuvenated Judaism. The beauty worshipped in Greece could not compare with the spirituality of Judea. Unlike Heine, Wihl never faltered: Jehovah over Zeus and Baal.

Many of this poet's favorite themes are summarized in his "Mittelalterliche Elegie" ("Medieval Elegy"):

Ohne Land und ohne Thron	Without country or throne
Irren seit zweitausend Jahren	For two thousand years we have wandered
Wir weitab vom Libanon	Far away from Lebanon
Unter Leiden und Gefahren.	Midst suffering and dangers.
Keine Palme wehet hier	Here wafts no palm tree
Duft'ge Kühlung, wenn wir beten,	Its aromatic cooling breeze, when we pray,
Kein Altar, kein Opfertier!	No altar, no sacrificial animal!
Priester fehlen und Propheten!	Both priests and prophets are missing.
Wo die Hütte Jacobs stand,	Where Jacob's hut once stood,
Lagern jetzt nur wilde Horden,	Are now camped about only wild hordes,
Und der Väter theures Land	And the precious land of the fathers
Ist den Söhnen fremd geworden.	Has become unknown to the sons.
Selbst der Sprache heil'ger Laut,	Even the sacred sound of the language,
Ach, er ist nun längst verklungen,	Oh, it has long since faded away,
Harfe, David, süß und traut!	Play on your harp, David, some sweet and
Deine Saiten sind zersprungen!	familiar tune!
	Your strings are broken!
Nur ein Schatten alter Pracht	Merely a shadow of old splendor
Schleppen wir uns mühsam bange,	We drag ourselves along laboriously and full
Um uns herrschet finstre Nacht,	of fear,
Juda's Stern, was bleibst du lange?	All around us lies dark night,
	Judah's star, why are you taking so long?

Julius Kossarski (1811–1879) voiced a similar longing for an heroic Jewish past in *Titus oder die Zerstörung Jerusalems* (*Titus or the Destruction of Jerusalem*). This long historic-dramatic poem demonstrates the author's awareness of the melding in Judaism of religious, cultural, and national elements. Kossarski injected the democratic issues of his time into ancient Judea. Echoes of the Revolution of 1848 could be heard in events of two thousand years earlier. John of Gishala and Simon Bar Goras, Jewish leaders, pled for freedom and national unity among their people as they rose against the tyrants of their time—the aristocracy at home, the Roman Empire abroad. Kossarski also discerned an economic basis for the Judean Wars, for Rome was greedy for the gold of Judea. Even vague feminist strains can be heard in this curiously modern but anachronistic play.

In his desire to depict the heroism of ancient Jews as they defended themselves and their interests, Kossarski sometimes stretched the boldness of his Jewish heroes. In indicating the need for qualities in which German Jews were allegedly deficient, the author did not neglect the spiritual genius of the Jews whose invisible God had triumphed over all heathen idols. As they contemplate the destruction of the Temple, the wise men of Jerusalem prophesy:

Diese Lehre [Jewish and Christian] *wird* *zerstümmern* [sic] (zertrümmern?) *Einstens in dem Capitol* *Eure Götter, welche schimmern* *Doch nicht lenken Menschenwohl.*	This doctrine will crush One day in the Capitol Your gods, who glisten, But do not direct the welfare of man.
Unser Tempel konnte fallen, *Aber nicht sein Glaubensgeist,* *Uns're Brüder werden wallen,* *Lehren, was er streng verheißt.*	Our temple could fall, But not its spirit of belief, Our brothers will go on a pilgrimage, Teach, what it rigorously promises.

Kossarski's interest in the homeland and its traditions is also manifest in long-forgotten prose works. Unfortunately, both his conceptual abilities and the vigor of his sentiments far outstripped his poetic and narrative talents.

Born the same year as his friend Berthold Auerbach, **Moses Hess** (1812–1875) reached conclusions opposed to those of this apologist. In fact, Hess's views represented a rupture with most previous writings on the German-Jewish relationship. In *Rom und Jerusalem* he stated categorically that Jews had gone to foolish lengths to prove their *Deutschtum* (German-ness) with exorbitant cost to their pride and dignity. When Hess declared that Jews were a people and represented a distinct culture as well as a religion, he seemed more attuned to the anti-Semites of his time than to Auerbach-Riesser liberals. Where the latter were addressing the imaginary anti-Jew, vainly expecting to convert him, Hess either ignored or defied them. To any and all he proclaimed that Jews were Jews, not *Israeliten,* or people of the Mosaic persuasion.

The polarity Rome-Jerusalem of Hess's title did not symbolize, as one might think, the conflict between worldly and spiritual power. It alluded to a liberal nationalist consciousness much like that of the nineteenth-century Italian patriot and revolutionist Giuseppe Mazzini that was flowing from Rome to Jerusalem, eventually reconstructing there a Jewish nation.

Rom und Jerusalem was not widely read. When it *was* read, it elicited mostly adverse comment. Even Theodor Herzl, the founder of

Zionism, had not read it at the time he wrote his *Judenstaat* (*Jewish State*) thirty years later. Herzl hinted that had he read it, he might not have needed to write his own book. Though the conclusions of the two men were sometimes similar, their points of departure were different. Herzl's interest originated in his preoccupation with anti-Semitism and its impact on the Jewish psyche; Hess's derived from his study and observations of liberal-nationalist movements everywhere.

Hess displayed an aggressor attitude more extreme than that of Heine and Börne. He could not be swayed by arguments that he was damaging a carefully nurtured image of Jewish goodness. Hess rejected Auerbach's contention that he had no right to speak publicly for Jews, only privately and as a personal statement. Auerbach feared that Hess's ideas were dangerously explosive, especially when misused by enemies. Hess was unimpressed with an argument built on fear. Long before he addressed the Jewish questions, Hess had established a considerable reputation as a socialist. Socialism and Zionism still seemed compatible, and subsequent developments would have irked Moses Hess. He managed instead to be attacked on both issues.

His writing career had begun with *The Sacred History of Humanity by a Young Spinozist* (1837), a philosophy of history described as a fusion of Jewish-Messianic, Spinozist, and Hegelian ideas, with a touch of the revolutionary added. *The European Triarchy* (1841) proposed the union of Europe's "civilized nations," namely France, England, and Germany. An essay, "The Philosophy of Action," advanced notions that attracted the unwanted attention of the authorities on one side and the charge of "betrayal of socialism" from Marx and Engels on the other. Here, as elsewhere, Hess had a problem in reconciling two conflicting tendencies in his being: extreme individualism on the one hand and the need for socialization on the other. The particular causes he espoused earned him Arnold Ruge's pejorative "the Communist Rabbi Moses," a title Marx found exhilarating.

Hess's relationship to Marx remained problematic. Marx's uncompromising temperament and Hess's volatility and humanitarian concerns were bound to clash sooner or later. From being Marx's mentor, Hess had to descend to the status of disciple. In the 1840s both were collaborating on the same publications. Marx was more selective than Hess in the causes he championed and often seemed repelled by Hess's good intentions and strong emotions. When Hess distanced himself from Marx's rigid conception of class warfare, Marx turned abusive, and Hess's gradual evolution along more human and ethical lines brought only strident and sardonic comment from London. In the 1860s Hess teamed up with Lassalle to establish what was eventually to become the German Social

Democratic Party. But then and later, when he joined the Bebel-Liebknecht wing of the emerging party, Hess never ceased to admire Marx and often defended his positions in internal socialist debate. Hess's socialist crusading extended into the 1870s but did not significantly diminish the Jewish concerns he had professed earlier. Living mostly in his beloved Paris—another German-Jewish exile in the French capital—he was instrumental in helping to establish the Alliance Isréalite Universelle.

Underlying the direction in *Rom und Jerusalem* was Hess's insistence that Jews represent more than religious and cultural entities: They are a people, a race. Germans perceived their differences from Jews not in religious belief or practice, but in the Jew's distinctive nose, his curly hair, his black eyes. They sensed a different temperament, a different inner life, different values. For this reason, the fact and perception of distinctive Jewish qualities are bound to make ineffective any attempt by Jews to declare themselves different only in their religion.

Jewish misfortunes resulted from the loss of nationality, of a home, and from the resulting substitution of alien—and thus exposed—status among peoples. Europeans never viewed the Jews among them as more than anomalies. Only a radical solution could make Jews respectable, said Hess: the restoration of a Jewish state to be initiated by the establishment of Jewish colonies in the land of their ancestors. Skeptical about philanthropic arrangements then being made, he urged instead the legal acquisition of land and the promotion of industry and commerce on "Mosaic" principles, that is, for both social and communal interest. For Hess, Judaism represented family and group, whereas Christianity stood for the religion of the individual.

Yet Hess believed that national and social principles alone could not support his Jewish state. A religious component was essential to being Jewish. Though his own private life was devoid of religious commitment, in his public program he even justified Orthodoxy, since for centuries it had provided a comprehensive way of life. Now neo-Orthodoxy had rejuvenated the old faith, providing it with a new and solid base. Like Heine, Hess preferred Orthodoxy to the bland Reform movement that he believed violated the indivisibility of Judaism.

In spite of these Jewish affirmations, Hess believed that religions, philosophy, politics, all amounted to little if they failed to end the caste system in society. The emancipation of Jews had meaning only as yet another vital aspect of the emancipation of the human race. Hess's Jewish nationalism was strong to the point of defying enemies without and within, but like Mazzini's brand, it worked for integration into a broad human history.

Hess was profoundly pessimistic about the German-Jewish future.

Hatred of Jews in the German states was more deeply anchored and more widespread than in England or France. The attraction-repulsion principle that operated between Germans and Jews resulted from both their similarities and their marked differences.

With all his personal flaws as a thinker, the nonsystematic, non-doctrinaire "Communist Rabbi Moses" stood with welcoming, out-stretched hands at the gatepost of the Zionist and socialist camps. In his mind there existed a bridge between these neighboring groups, a bridge that was not used much by later socialists and Zionists.

• • • • •

II

• • • • •

Attraction and Repulsion:

Jews Determine Their Function

Writers of Humor and Comedy

By 1840, although Jews had not achieved legal or social equality, they had come to feel at home. Between 1840 and 1865 anti-Semitism as a major issue had lost some of its significance. Writings against Jews diminished, and the debates about emancipation, while continuing, had lost some of their edge. Jews did not feel compelled to defend themselves as they had previously. It was as quiet a period as the history of German-Jewish existence had seen—or was to see.

Heine, Börne, Saphir, and Robert had all been known as practitioners of the art of humor. Even before 1840 it had come to be known as a Jewish property, and now it evolved further, turning into comedies in one direction and clever humorous pieces in the other. The relative quiet and the sense of belonging, whether real or imagined, was not the only source of the proliferating Jewish humor. Humor had always been part of Jewish life. Laughter was, after all, a defense against human misery; it had always been the solace of the oppressed, and its expression made life tolerable. Though life was better than before and not without hope, it was still an existence with minimal prospects.

Although tensions between Germans and Jews occasionally intruded themselves into the comic works, their main purpose was to create mirth and laughter. The devices employed were singularly unoriginal: mistaken identities, failed schemes in bringing males and females together, punishment of trickery and deceit, and rewarding of virtue. There was no Molière among the writers of comedy and no Voltaire or Heine among the satirists. Perhaps there were no worthy targets. The subjects of the comedies are, indeed, ordinary. Differences in social status are accentuated as men and women from different classes fall in love and are subjected to fierce societal pressures and prejudices. For instance, an impoverished nobleman is willing to offer his beautiful daughter to the highest financial bidder, who is really the man she has already fallen in love with when he was disguised as a butler or merchant or traveling salesman.

In the comedies, when a Jew appeared, he was usually the wealthy

Jew a notch below Rothschild who would like to marry into aristocracy, enhancing his prestige and filling the nobleman's coffers. More often than not, in actuality the Jew was not rich at all, but a petty merchant or peddler desperately trying to remain solvent. He was forever worried about his ability to earn his livelihood—or his ability to amass a dowry for his marriageable daughter. In the plays, this lowly Jew's pride has been destroyed by mockery and abuse, and he seems to have internalized many of the prejudices of the Christian world. The writers were not always charitable. They mocked his use of German, his tendency to speak Western Yiddish—his *mauscheln* (wheeling and dealing)—his social ineptness, his lack of *Bildung*. But more often than not, they left him a modicum of dignity. Even when he was laughable, he was never dangerous. The same Jew was frequently presented as a threat to Christians in dramas by Christian writers.

The writers of comedy translated and helped import the far more sophisticated and brilliant comedies that had excited Parisian theater-goers for over a century. While Ludwig Robert had given the German stage a feeble imitation of Molière's *Les Précieuses Ridicules,* more skillful dramatists were far more successful intermediaries between Parisian comedy and that needed on German stages. What Jewish writers admired in their perennial travels to Paris they eventually translated and supplied to German theater. Thus they helped introduce the Molièresque comedy of situation and manner, the psychological love comedies of Pierre Carlet de Chamblain de Marivaux, and later in the century, the works of Eugène Marin Labiche, Émile Augier, and Edouard Pailleron. Sometimes they did not translate, but rather imitated comedies in the vein of the newer French specimen. Although these writers were occasionally taken to task for bringing "immoral" French comedies to "pure" Germany, they did not encounter the hostility that the humor of Heine, Börne, or Saphir had engendered earlier.

Such writers as **Leopold Feldmann** (1802–188?), **Hermann Hersch** (1820–1870), and **Moritz Barach** (1818–1883) dealt with assorted human foibles, paradoxes, misunderstood intentions, and the peculiarities inherent in the relations between different social strata. A seventeenth-century duke married a commoner's daughter, proving that a love marriage can triumph over class prejudices. A Jew who is all business-man and is despised by the noblemen to whom he sells jewelry demonstrated his superiority.

Occasionally, a Jewish character was more than a walk-on with comic lines. **Eduard Jacobsohn** (1833–1897), physician-turned-dramatist, was interested in bringing Jewish second-class status to the attention of his audiences. He wanted to convince his audience that even a *Handelsjude* (Jewish tradesman) speaking the despised jargon demanded respect, possessed dignity, and need not be—as in many midcentury comedies—an object of ridicule or self-deprecation. One of his plays dealt with a rarity in life and fiction—a Christian girl converts to Judaism before she marries her Jewish lover.

Hugo Lubliner (also **Hans Burger**) (1846–1911) was often reproached for slavish imitation of the French. While the criticism is partly justified, Lubliner deserves credit for creating pleasant and recognizable characters that functioned well in a believable bourgeois setting. Lubliner, a successful businessman as well as writer, employed his knowledge of commerce to good advantage. But he was deficient in *Wortwitz* (word play) and inventiveness. **Oskar Justinus (Cohn)** (1839–1893) had also enjoyed some business successes before turning to the stage. His titles reflect his experience: *Die Getreidespekulanten (Commodity Speculators)* (1876) and *Öl und Petroleum (Oil and Petroleum)* (1877). But Justinus did not always see transactions through managerial eyes. *Ein Proletarienkind (Child of the Proletariat)* (1893) revealed great sympathy for the workers' plight.

In Vienna, **Karl Weiss**, who prospered as **Karlweiss** (1850–1901), became popular for his *Volksstücke* or folk plays, a variant of the Viennese farce. This one-time actor and railroad worker wrote amusing plays that illustrated the folk wisdom found in proverbs and popular sayings. He extolled those who followed their simple precepts and pitied others given to sophistication who had severed their roots. A conservative, he distrusted social action as in *Das grobe Hemd (The Rough Shirt)*, political sloganeering as in *Der kleine Mann (The Little Man)*, parliamentary shenanigans as in *Der neue Simson (The New Samson)*. He mocked artificiality and hypocrisy regardless of the social class in which they were found.

Unlike most satirists, Karl Weiss was gentle and almost naive. This *naïveté* proved immensely popular with the Viennese masses who loved their theater to be sentimental and mild. They sympathized with his goals and despised his targets. His plays fitted the age of Franz Joseph in which the old, the good, and the tired triumphed over the new and untested. There was little of the scoffer and disturber in him. He was content to express the spirit of Vienna, and Vienna identified with him.

More substance was found in the works of men who wrote humorous essays, short witty pieces, edited "lustige Blätter" (amusing writings), and frequently contributed to them. While their pen was rarely dipped in venom, its point was often soused with a substance only slightly less potent.

Ludwig Kalisch (1814–1882), the editor of *Narrhalle* ("Fools Hall"), showed throughout his life the influence of Ludwig Börne. He was exiled after the Revolution of 1848 and spent the last forty years of his life in Paris. Distance did not deter him from conducting his campaign against anachronistic monarchs, press censorship, and—unlike Börne—press irresponsibility. Some of Kalisch's clever definitions carried aphoristic force. "An aristocrat demands freedom only so as not to have to tolerate equality." Or: "Because aristocrats have only one head, but two legs, they understand little, but manage nevertheless to trample on others." A favorite device was the "examination question":

Examiner: What is the difference between Germany and Egypt?
Answer: Egypt suffered only ten plagues.

Examiner: Which animals resemble fish?
Answer: The Germans. Both remain dumb even if the wool is pulled over their eyes.

Kalisch rarely addressed Jewish themes. His humorous poem "Rabbi Pinchas und sein Esel" ("Rabbi Pinchas and His Donkey") was translated into Hebrew, and he was pleased that intellectuals in faraway Odessa should have read him "with echoes of the language of Moses when addressing the children of Israel." Kalisch accepted his Jewishness as a fact of life, to be neither hidden nor flaunted. In Judaism as in other religions he saw a once-potent force that had lost its power through the rationalism of modern times.

David Kalisch (not related to Ludwig) (1820–1872) enjoyed popular success in spite of his modest talents. Perhaps his most significant achievement was the establishment of the *Kladderadatsch,* a long-lasting humorous satirical journal. David Kalisch spent many of his early years in Paris, associating there with Heine, Marx, and Pierre Joseph Proudhon. His first farce, "Die Proleten" ("The Plebeians"), reflected their social influence. Back in Berlin, he began to experiment with the political-satiric couplet. Soon he became known for his "Berliner Lokalpossen" ("Berlin Farces") that abounded in couplets and featured recurring characters. His success grew rapidly, and soon he dominated the theater of farce. His couplets were collected under the title of

Berliner Leierkasten (*Berlin Organgrinder*), and his light comedies appeared as *Lustige Werke* (*Amusing Works*). Though most contributions to *Kladderadatsch* were unsigned, it is certain that the pieces about Müller and Schulze and Karlchen Miesnick derived from his pen. These characters gradually acquired families and friends and would outlive Kalisch by decades.

Police censors often confronted Kalisch with the choice of going to jail or moving to another city. Quite unheroic, he left. His absence from the management of the journal necessitated the addition of staff. A cousin, Ernst Dohm, joined him and later Rudolf Löwenstein. Both were converts. After Kalisch's marriage to a Christian woman, he converted as well.

His plays derived their humor from the usual plot situations, but also the inclusion of odd names such as Pieseke (someone who pesters?), Pausewolke (cloud that has been traced?), and so on. Another strategem relied on repeated phraseology ("*Ich bin kein Krakeler,*" or "I'm no scribbler"). He often made fun of the speech of the lower classes, which he gradually abandoned in favor of the more fashionable and comfortable bourgeoisie.

His Jewish characters, generally secondary, were mentally alert; they stereotypically bargained, sold, and were wheelers and dealers. He invented two stock-exchange Jews, Zwickauer und Zwittauer, who spoke Western Yiddish and were as ludicrous as they were ignorant. His portraits of Jews and his mocking disrespect of the jargon should not be seen as expressions of self-hate. Kalisch dealt similarly with Frenchified German, making it clear that he would extend himself in any direction for a chuckle.

However, his questionable seriousness, coupled with his weakness for forced rhymes, often obstructed his intentions. Is he arguing against anti-Jewish prejudice in the following lines, minimizing it, or both?

Obwohl heute unbestritten	Although undisputed today
Kein Religionshaß existirt,	That there is no religious hate,
Wird doch gegen Isrealiten	Yet many a joke is risked
Manches Scherzwort noch riskirt.	Against Israelites.
Neckereien pflegt zu üben	Many a Christian is accustomed
Gegen sie so mancher Christ,	To teasing them
Weil das Schweinefleisch sie nicht lieben	Because they don't like pork,
Was höchst abgesprochen ist.	Something that is highly disputed.
Denn der Jud' denkt: Mags sein,	For the Jew thinks: That may be.
Wir haben doch jetzt viel Schwein.	After all, we're very lucky right now
Daraus da muß man sich nichts machen.	[play on word "Schwein"].
	But one doesn't have to take it to heart.

The *Kladderadatsch* was not the first *Humorblatt* (humorous newsletter) by a Jew in German. Saphir had published several, as had Herlossohn and Oettinger. Only the French colony in Berlin offered as light a touch as some of the Jewish humorists.

A one-time collaborator of *Kladderadatsch*, **Julius Stettenheim** (1831–1916), later edited his own *Die Wespen* (*The Wasps*). A prime source of laughter were characters with totally predictable behavior. His Muckeenich, when tipsy, passed outrageous judgments on current events, which led to his eviction from every *Bierstube* (tavern) he visited. His "interviewer" questioned celebrities of his time and never found out much, but turned every failure into a splendid success. Stettenheim's most enduring character was Herr Wippchen, a war correspondent who reported gruesome battle scenes from the warmth and comfort of his German home. His despatches depicted bloodcurdling events in a style marked by mixed metaphors, misquoted and inapplicable proverbs, irrelevant mythological references, and countless other malapropisms.

Stettenheim's references to Jews disclosed sensitivity to anti-Semitism. "Im Konzert" was an often quoted poem comically resembling Heine's "Du bist wie eine Blume" ("You Are like a Flower"):

Du bist wie eine Blume	You are like a flower
Ein wundervoller Text.	A wonderful text.
Das ist das Lied der Lieder,	It's the song of songs,
Das hat mich ja behext.	That's what bewitched me.
Ich find auf dem Programme	I don't find on the program
Des Dichters Namen nicht,	The name of the poet.
Es ist gewiß von Goethe,	It [the poem] is surely by Goethe,
So deutsch, so tief, so schlicht.	So German, so profound, so unpretentious.
"Das Liedchen ist von Heine."	"The little song is by Heine."
Ein Jude machte das Lied?	A Jew composed the song?
Jetzt find' ich's ganz abscheulich.	Now I find it quite detestable.
Ich bin Antisemit.	I am an anti-Semite.

Daniel Spitzer wrote most of his witty commentaries on the events of the week for the magazine section of Vienna's *Neue Freie Presse*. His satire hit hard at lack of reason and moderation, the demagogic chauvinism of a Schönerer, and outmoded notions of privilege and exclusivity. Spitzer knew more clearly what he was against than what he was for.

But was he as detached as Egon Kisch, a doctrinaire leftist, would have us believe? Was there no significance in his choice of enemies on whom he applied a heavy dose of Voltairian satire? He hit hard, not only at the anti-Semitic Schönerer, but also at the racist Richard

Wagner. These and others he attacked as enemies of justice and obstructionists of the ideals of the Enlightenment. Spitzer, the satirist, was less effective in championing the building of schools, hospitals, and better roads—and he did agitate for all of those—than he was in militating against nationalist and war-mongering causes.

Many of Spitzer's barbs were at the expense of unenlightened, uneducated Jews. He was unkind, even hostile, to Polish Jews who had invaded Vienna. Some, he charged, were profiteering at a time of great wretchedness in the city. Here Spitzer lost his lightness of touch and descended to a level less than pleasant.

Known in early years as "Bloody Oskar" for his merciless theater criticism, **Oskar Blumenthal** subsequently developed into a well-known writer of light comedies. After the opening around 1900 of *Im weißen Rössel* (*At the White Horse Inn*), Blumenthal became for a time the most widely staged German dramatist, including Hauptmann and Sudermann.

Blumenthal, the critic, once feared as much as Saphir, became more compassionate after the production of his first play, *Der Probepfeil* (*The Probing Arrow*). Not satisfied with being a critic and playwright, he proceeded to found his own theater, the Lessing Theater, which he also directed. His name remained before the public, for he wrote at least one comedy a year. His work was cheerful, harmless, amusing, and—empty. His was a *Wortwitz* (play on words), accompanied by thin characterizations and action.

Against the backdrop of the renewed anti-Semitism of the 1870s new criticisms were aimed at Jewish writers. It was said that they preferred—apparently Christian writers never did—the lure of riches to quality. Indeed, Blumenthal preferred comfort to discomfort. He carried his need for *Behaglichkeit* (comfort) into literature itself, when he totally rejected the ugly subjects and pessimism of the naturalists. So strongly developed was his sense of the brevity of life that the stage could do without depressing topics. In shying from the wretched and the unpleasant, Blumenthal took after his models Labiche and Pailleron. He also avoided social and political themes. His Jewish origin mattered little. He seemed unaware of any invisible line that might exist between him and other Germans. He appeared impervious to anti-Jewish attacks, including those directed at himself. In this he differed from most assimilated writers, whose last vestige of Jewishness was sensitivity to anti-Semitism.

Blumenthal's huge success with comedies of light romance and eroticism was equaled for a time by that of **Ludwig Fulda** (1862–1939), who began his career with German translations of Molière, Beaumarchais, and Rostand. Like Blumenthal he was reproached for pandering to public taste, but Fulda took artistic aspirations more seriously. If he never achieved true *Dichtertum* (poetic greatness), it was because his production was too diffuse. Starting his creative work with light comedy, he changed over to social drama, then he returned to light comedy, only to try verse drama, and finally return to comedy.

Though Fulda supported Hauptmann and Ibsen in their drive to gain acceptance on the German stage, he was not able to move in a naturalistic direction. A man of his altruistic bent and goodwill could not see the world as Hauptmann perceived it. Fulda preferred the what-might-be to the what-was. His finest plays were written in the concluding decade of the century. *Unter vier Augen (Just the Two of Us)* related what happened to a couple who were scheduled to attend dinner but could not and were forced to spend the evening alone. They had never discussed their relationship, and the evening led to the decision to be together more often. *Die wilde Jagd (The Wild Hunt)* satirized ambition that did not allow one to have time to enjoy life.

When Fulda ventured into the field of social problems, he proved inept. In his novels and plays that dealt with management-worker relations, the emancipation of women, or the nature of political systems, the themes were beyond his ken. He looked at these as moral questions with no awareness of their economic base. There were few Jewish characters in his plays; if he recognized a Jewish problem, he thought it wise not to emphasize it. Fulda's literary fortunes declined in this century, though he kept writing diligently. Disheartened by his failures and an increasingly Nazified world, he took his own life in 1939.

On the whole, the writers of comedy and humor felt at home in the German cultural scene. The few who occasionally chose to create a Jewish character laughed at him with the Germans, though occasionally they imbued their Jews with some dignity. The writers regarded themselves as Germans. Perhaps they were not unduly proud of this fact, but it was a fact they would not allow anyone to take away from them.

•   •   •   •   •

Attraction to Modernity

As masters of the clever phrase, epigram, and quick repartee, the comic writers often suggested verbal agility transplanted to a new domain. As promoters of the French comedy and as practitioners of it on the German stage, they were strengthening their reputation as cultural intermediaries. Light, pleasant, and sentimental, the comedies purported to entertain. The French imports and imitations in the German theater were not penalty free. By offering love triangles, husbands or wives threatening to stray, and the foibles of married partners and lovers, the Jewish writers were often regarded as immoral purveyors of French decadence. The equation of Jews with immoral behavior was never far from the consciousness of critics and audiences who nevertheless thoroughly enjoyed the comic prose of Jewish writers.

As the comedy declined with the aging century, a new, influential, and far-reaching movement commenced its upward surge. This was the social realism represented by the problem dramas of Henrik Ibsen and the socialist naturalism of the early Gerhart Hauptmann. The Ibsen-Hauptmann conquest of the German stage was made possible by the bold support of German critics and by some early problem plays furnished by Jewish-born writers.

EARLY MODERNS: PROBLEM PLAYS

Though contemporaries treated them rudely, the plays of **Felix Philippi** (1851–1921) still read well today. Philippi himself was accused of using headline news as the basic element for his plays and of irresponsibly placing recently deceased statesmen on his stage.

He was one of the first to dramatize the growing conflict between the safety of society on the one hand and its economic needs on the other. Philippi clearly sided with the human concern, even as he sought to maintain an even-handed approach. In *Das dunkle Tor* (*The Dark Gate*), he placed himself behind his engineer-hero, who refused to go along with the scheme of his employer and benefactor. The engineer cannot bring himself to endanger the lives of men working in a tunnel known to be unsafe. While condemning the industrialist's greed, the engineer is equally incensed at the fiery labor leader who would have his men enter the mine to keep their jobs. In *Der Helfer* (*The Assistant*), a senator is nearly ruined by his hypochondriacal wife, ultranationalist son, and by his daughter, who literally enjoys playing with fire. In financial distress, the senator seeks the help of a stock market speculator, presumably a Jew, though not identified as such. Unlike the senator's family, which places bourgeois prejudices above all else, the speculator Steinharter ranks human considerations above monetary ones. Like all of Philippi's heroes, Steinharter is an outsider; he is a man of honor but one who, unlike the senator's family, never uses that word.

The Rumanian-born **Marco Brociner** (1852–1942?) wrote *Jonel Fortunat* (1890) and later collaborated with Ludwig Ganghofer in adapting it for the stage as *The Wedding at Valeni*. Fortunat's story unfolds against the backdrop of Rumanian serfs' struggle for liberation. Whereas in the novel the oppression of the Jews is linked to that of the peasants, in the drama gypsies assume the role of the Jews. For Brociner, domination by some humans over others was shown when the powerful hurled epithets at their victims, thereby maintaining their own superior status while keeping their victims permanently under control. Brociner did not romanticize the oppressed; they remained too ignorant and selfish to recognize the need for strong bonds with other dominated groups.

Brociner's novel delves into the pain and guilt of the Jewish jester whose daughter abandoned ancestral ways. She had forsaken Judaism because it had been unable to protect her from the physical and psychological hardships of Jewishness. Jonel Fortunat, who had persecuted Jews in his childhood, not knowing he also belonged to this despised race, grows into a champion of the oppressed; he is a nineteenth-century idealist who fails in his attempt to preserve his personal integrity while championing the downtrodden.

Max Bernstein (1854–1924) tackled the issues of women's emancipation, anti-Semitism, aristocratic arrogance, and destructive nationalism. All converged in *Hertha's Hochzeit* (*Hertha's Wedding*), in which Bernstein speaks through Rosenthal, the friend of Hertha's authoritarian father. Rosenthal repeatedly refers to his Jewishness and the omnipresence of anti-Semitism. He argues against all prejudice, be it against women, the poor, or Jews. He quoted his orthodox father who had continuously cautioned against the emphasis on money. For once it is a rich Gentile, not a Jew, who is made to say, "To money I attach no value—as long as I have it." The polarity of materialism-idealism also permeates other Bernstein plays. For this problem writer, as for Philippi and Brociner, "Man does not live by bread alone."

CRITICS

Though primarily a critic and theater director, **Otto Brahm** (1856–1912) played a unique role in promoting Ibsen, Hauptmann, and Schnitzler, whom he revered. His reputation as a critic has remained undiminished, and as a director he was surpassed only by Max Reinhardt. While Reinhardt strove consciously for innovation and experimentation, Brahm was content to give deeper meaning to works that caught his fancy. To these belonged the daring subjects of Ibsen, the controversial ones of Hauptmann, and the depth psychology of Schnitzler. He was strongly attracted by their bold realism and verisimilitude, their ability to replicate life's complexities. Brahm realized that these new idols would not come into their own until the old ones of French comedy were discarded.

Brahm was ruthless in his campaign against such fellow Jews (or half-Jews) as Blumenthal, Lindau, Lubliner, and others. On a German stage and in the German language, he asserted, these imitators of Augier, Victorien Sardou, and Labiche sounded false. In critical essays he denounced the empty, uncommitted literature that centered on erotic adventures and unconvincing, absurd situations. Why not present lifelike characters, credible situations, recognizable problems?

Loyalty to his idols nearly robbed Brahm of his critical independence. When on rare occasions he refused to produce one of their dramas, his decision was based on his certainty that the play did not measure up to the dramatist's reputation. Even after Hauptmann abandoned naturalism to try the neo-Romanticism of *Die versunkene Glocke* (*The Sunken Bell*), Brahm still followed him, persuaded that he deserved support in exploring uncharted terrain. Yet Brahm's devotion had unfortunate effects. Dramatists vying for his attention were neglected. Thus he turned a deaf ear to the likes of Strindberg, von Hofmannsthal, and Wedekind, whose achievements compared favorably with those of his protégés.

Brahm was hoping to breathe fresh air into the musty edifice of German drama—to replace stagnation with movement and artificiality with naturalness. Though not beyond polemics, he fell short of being the "fighting man" he fancied himself. More northern than southern in temperament, he disliked flamboyance, rhetoric, and display. Very sober, this Jew preferred cold, verified truth to anything freely generated by the imagination.

Though some called Brahm a German Protestant, Theodor Fontane saw in him mainly the Jew. Fontane noted that Brahm, like his co-religionists, was single-mindedly guided by principle. Others saw Jewish qualities that Brahm would have had difficulty recognizing as Jewish: eagerness to embrace the new, passion for social justice, the earnestness of moral vision. Brahm made little of his Jewish origin. He admitted it, frankly and without apology. If he did encounter anti-Semitism, he might not have recognized it.

This suspicion seems warranted by his refusal to produce Schnitzler's *Professor Bernhardi*. Brahm wrote that he liked the characterizations and structure of the play, but the milieu was "alien." "Berlin Jewish physicians," Brahm lectured, "are not being persecuted as was Viennese Dr. Bernhardi; on the contrary, they occupy a dominant position; we are not Catholic—I am not either [a joking reference to press reports that he had turned Catholic to assume the directorship of Vienna's Burg-theater]—and thus the situation of the play as well as its plot development will fascinate here less than in the country of Eucharist Congress." While Schnitzler did not entirely accept Brahm's explanation, he suspected no deeper Jewish connection in Brahm's refusal. He did not argue with Brahm over any misassessment of the Berlin situation. Instead, Schnitzler wrote in his diary that the absence of an erotic motif was mainly responsible for the rejection.

In the same letter in which he rejected Bernhardi, Brahm explained why he could not envisage his accepting the directorship of the famed Viennese theater. "I am not as tactful as Max Reinhardt," he wrote, "that I publicly announce my refusal; no, I remain the same irreligious, non-Jewish Jew you have always known."

The critic **Leo Berg** (1862–1909) was an equally vigorous advocate of modernism. He supported only those writers who went along with the new reality, but he was vehemently opposed to such trends as the cult of Wagner, nation worship, submissiveness to authority, and unwarranted optimism. He disliked the youthful Nietzsche in whom these traits were manifest, but he was appreciative of the older Nietzsche who had sensed the malaise of his time: *Deutschtümelei*, philistinism, and excessive Romanticism.

Berg recognized the issues over which the now fifty-year-old battle against Heine had been fought. Where Brahm worshipped the very German Heinrich von Kleist and shrugged off the democratically minded

Friedrich von Schiller, Berg leaned toward the latter—and even far more toward Heine. Earlier than most, Berg recognized in Heine a true modern who understood the complexity of life and the inability of any one system to satisfy all of it. Heine comprehended the inadequacy of all-embracing doctrines, rejecting them as false tenets spawning new prejudices and coercion. Berg's admiration for Heine was also evident when he sometimes referred to *Durch* (*Through*), the literary society he directed, as "Das jüngste Deutschland" ("The youngest Germany"), reminiscent of the young Germany movement to which Heine was sometimes said to belong.

Berg sought to enter the minds of conservative critics like Karl Goedeke, Max Hein, and Heinrich von Treitschke, all inveterate foes of Heine. "German literature," he imagined they might think, "is in a terrible state. What has happened to the good old poetry from Goethe to Uhland? Who ruined it? Of course, the Jew Heine. Oh, these Jews who apply their disreputable wit to everything, who know neither reverence nor morality, this homeless, pitiable people." In Heine's enemies, the Jewish critic saw the many faces of Jew hatred. Hauptmann and Ibsen were threatened by the same combinations of nationalism and conservatism—forces that arrogantly claimed the right to be guardians of public morality.

REALISTS AND NATURALISTS

Not a critic, but playwright and novelist, **Franz Held** (1862–1908) continued in the tradition of the problem play, giving it a distinctly pessimistic tinge. In his short life, which ended in insanity, Held made clear his utter terror in the face of the human condition. He was frightened by, among other things, an exploitative bourgeoisie that disinherited nonconformists, socialists, and Jews like himself. This ruling class did not even attempt to hide its greed and was willing to sacrifice both human health and safety for it. In a long dramatic poem, "Gorgonenhäupter," and a play, *Manometer auf 99* (*Pressure Gauge at 99*), his best-known works, Held portrayed the outer limits of human ugliness and despair.

His sympathy for the downtrodden was as patent as his anger at their oppressors. Held classified Jews with the downtrodden. In a minor poem he related the tale of the maiden Noemie, purchased from pirates by the Cimbrian King, who forces her to become his wife. Upon his death, as custom requires, she is burned on his funeral pyre. But on reaching Walhalla, she is not admitted to the Germanic heaven, and even her children reject her as a Jew when they join her.

Held was repeatedly attracted to the theme of Cain and Abel, brothers who stand for different principles and fight each other to the death. In *Manometer auf 99*, the Goldschmidt brothers are outwardly fraternal, but there is an underlying deep hostility. It derives from a number of reasons: the polarity of attitudes between businessman and poet, realist and dreamer, liberal and socialist. The brothers are also infatuated with the same woman and are considering the same candidacies for the Reichstag. One brother is killed, though not by the other, yet he becomes remorseful and goes mad. It should be noted that Held was just as distrustful of the "noble" idealist as the hard-headed realist. He hated machines and the way they could damage human lives. His sensitive characters were fearful of losing their sanity, a fate that befell Held in his early forties.

Today **Georg Hirschfeld** (1873–1942) is remembered chiefly as one of the heralds of the new drama, the trumpeter of Hauptmann's glory. In his early years he exhibited the promise of becoming a major dramatist in his own right. More than Hauptmann, he remained faithful to the original naturalism. Perhaps it was this failure to change that cost him any claim to greatness.

Hirschfeld's heroes are usually misunderstood artists—brooding, sensitive men who have been broken by misfortune or unresolved conflicts. The old polarity of "poet and merchant" is never far from the surface. Though some of the businessmen-fathers are admirable men, exploited by ambitious and greedy wives and indolent, manipulative sons, it is generally a younger son with an artistic bent who is destroyed. Forever on the brink of despair, Hirschfeld's artists are sometimes too unvaried not to grow wearisome with time.

Die Mütter (*The Mothers*) may be Hirschfeld's finest play. The maid recalls that the artist-hero used to go to the "Jewish Church" when still a young man. He left his parental home expecting to stand on his own two feet; then he ran off with a young working class woman who supported and protected him, until he was forced to admit that his psychic resources were exhausted. *Agnes Jordan* features a more clearly identifiable Jewish milieu and could well be—in the words of Arthur Eloesser—Hirschfeld's "contribution" of a Jewish family to naturalism.

Slowly, a Jewish type was emerging in plays with a realistic-naturalistic bent. Many characters were not identified as Jews but were readily recognized as such. Jews saw themselves in this portrait and so, gradually, did Christian writers like Fontane, who were beginning to comment without animosity on a *genus judaicus*. Generally, the Jewish hero—and perhaps his creator—was frail, neurotic, and a courageous though often inept fighter for his ideals. Even when these ideals were social in nature, they seemed to rest on a solid moral base. The modern Jewish hero was a product of the cities and would never consider living elsewhere. He was deeply disturbed by an ever-broadening industrialization and the steady conquests of the machine. His sympathy was with the workers; he resented what the machine did to people physically and psychologically.

Georg Engel (1866–1931) generally granted his characters more free will than did naturalist writers, often presenting them with a choice between city sophistication and country simplicity. Engel was one of the very few Jewish-born writers who occasionally dabbled in *Heimat* (homeland) literature. In *Zauberin Circe* (*Enchantress Circe*) (1894) Engel examined the impact of a sophisticated Berlin woman, a Jewish banker's wife, on a young physician from the provinces. The villain is neither the flirtatious enchantress nor the promiscuous girl the hero met on arrival in Berlin, but the city itself that destroys honesty, goodness, and simplicity—Engel's rustic values. But the countryside is not necessarily more moral. In *Der Ausflug ins Sittliche* (*Excursion into Morality*) (1901) a colonel who is ruthless in his dealings with workers, brutally selfish in his relations with his wife, and ultrareactionary and anti-Semitic in his politics, is chosen to be the head of a "Society for Moral Regeneration." His hypocrisy is exposed by his nephew, a former seminarian and now a Social Democrat. The nephew is rejected by the villagers, but a young woman from the nobility recognizes him as the moral person and his uncle as the epitome of hypocrisy and evil.

Engel again quarreled with false spirituality in *Über den Wassern* (*Above the Floods*) (1902). Pastor Holm—rigid, ambitious but dedicated — has come to the island to teach the inhabitants the value of labor. He exhorts them to construct a dam, which is built but breaks, causing the loss of many lives. Through further plot complications Engel makes his point: Christianity has lost its originally noble character and has adopted values divorced from both compassion and human service. A biblical play *Hadassa* lacked both moral insight and passion, as did most of his later works.

The early fiction of **Hans Land** (Hugo Landsberger) (1861–1938) leaves no doubt about his social involvement and protective attitude toward workers. It reveals as well his sense of the ironic and understanding of those twists of fate that can turn success into failure, wealth into poverty, beauty into ugliness. This trait is especially present in *Stiefkinder*

der Gesellschaft (*Stepchildren of Society*) (1888). One of his "stepchildren" was the daughter of a highly placed official. Her face is disfigured by pockmarks. Her sole yearning is for one night of happiness. She is given that night but pays dearly for it. In another sketch a pastor never ceases to warn his daughter against sensual passion, only to fall shamelessly in love with a maid. Another tale recounted the tragic yet noble end of the pianist whose fingers no longer accept his command. The author's heart reached out to those hurt by a cruel, inscrutable fate, but he also cared for those oppressed by society's rules.

Land's workers have not attained that stage of development at which they become conscious of their oppression. In *Vom neuen Gott* (*About the New God*) (1891), young idealistic intellectuals try to bring the wisdom of Marx and Lassalle to factory workers. Soon the idealists are rejected equally by the bourgeoisie they come from and the proletarians to whom they extend a helping hand. Land deeply sympathized with the young idealists who were not uncommon on the labor scene at the turn of the century.

Three other writers that fit the mold of the modern problem author are **Konrad Alberti** (Sittenfeld), **Ernst Rosmer** (Elsa Bernstein, née Porges) (1866–19?), and **Felix Holländer** (1867–1931).

An inveterate traveler, Alberti was often attacked for the sexual content of his work that brought him into frequent conflict with Kaiser Wilhelm's censor. One of his common themes was the struggle of the weak against the strong. He was critical of those who, in their drive for status, power, and wealth, would ruthlessly sacrifice the weak under their control. Stupidity usually won over intelligence in Alberti's generally pessimistic fiction; similarly, injustice triumphed over right and brute power over goodness and truth. *Wer ist der Stärkere?* (*Who is the Stronger?*) not only demonstrated his values, but also showed that he was more adept at logic and voicing indignation than he was at imagination and inventiveness.

Elsa Porges assumed a male name as did other gifted women writers of her century. As the wife of Munich playwright and lawyer Max Bernstein, she felt a particular need for separate identity. In her plays Rosmer-Porges created female characters who were strong, emancipated, and self-directing. Men, by contrast, tended to be weak and dependent on their women. Strength, however, did not diminish the gentleness of her female characters, who were also warm, thoughtful, and vulnerable.

Rosmer's themes and language often shocked her contemporaries.

Reference to body functions was judged vulgar and tasteless. Yet her words were not designed to shock but grew out of her need to reflect reality. In *Johannes Herkner* (1904), the sculptor-son of Pastor Herkner falls in love with the Jew Miriam Tachau, sister of the baptized editor Dr. Sigmund Tachau. Symbolic of the avant-garde rootless Jewish intellectual, Dr. Tachau approves of Herkner's erotic adventures until he discovers that Miriam has been his nude model. When the old pastor dies, disappointed that his son persisted in his hedonistic ways, the sculptor's guilt prompts him to forsake his art. Miriam and the artist's sister steer him back to it and to a new sense of responsibility, epitomized by his marriage to Miriam. In *Wir Drei* (*The Three of Us*) (1893), a weak, indecisive writer leaves his simple, decent wife for the favors of a liberated woman. It is the latter who engineers the reunion of the couple. Rosmer's Jewish characters are neurotic intellectuals between cultures, uprooted and tossed about in opposing currents. However, Rosmer wrote little of a specifically Jewish nature.

Felix Holländer's literary life was limited to the early and late years of his career. In the middle portion he acted as Max Reinhardt's close collaborator. His *Jesus und Judas* (1981) thematically resembles *Vom neuen Gott*) (*About the New God*), in which the scion of a middle class family befriends workers, hoping to become their savior. Circumstances, however, force him into the role of Judas. Holländer was aware that more is needed than goodwill for successful involvement in the social struggles of the time.

In 1892, Holländer published another proletarian novel, *Der Weg des Thomas Truck* (*Thomas Truck's Way*). Here another would-be Jesus becomes a Judas. Thomas Truck naively believes that he can circumvent both Marxist dogma and the bourgeois police. With time he realizes that he will always be rejected as an outsider by the socialists and as a socialist and traitor by the authorities. Truck is gradually driven to the ultimate act of despair: suicide. In *Ackermann*, Holländer mixed greed, infidelity, revenge, and obsessions to create a thoroughly pessimistic play. Though a conscious Jew, Holländer rarely used Jewishness for creative purposes. He saw himself, as many did, as a contributor to German culture who also happened to be a Jew.

● ● ● ● ●

Self-deprecators

T he hatred of Jews that flared up anew in the 1870s never really abated. It was aimed at the presence of Jews as foreigners in Christian Germany; it attacked their economic and political power and their social and political status; it labeled all Jews as alien and corruptive; and it called for control of their presence and influence. Hatred of Jews began to have racial overtones as well: Jewish blood must not become a threat to pure Teutonic blood. The anti-Jewish campaigns were waged in the *Reichstag* (German Senate), in daily newspapers, in journals of opinion and scholarship, in books, from pulpits and from the orator's and professor's lecterns. The political participants came mostly from the right, though from the left socialists began to propound their own negative thoughts on Jewish capital and exploitation. Intellects and creative artists (Wagner, Treitschke, and Freytag) lent an aura of respectability to the anti-Jewish arguments. What nearly all anti-Semites had in common was their view of Germans as victims and Jews as victimizers.

The Jewish writers of comedy and problem plays and novels, the adherents of social realism and naturalism, did not seem unduly troubled by the rising tide of anti-Semitic rhetoric. To be sure, they reacted forcefully against all prejudice—against that toward the Jew but also against prejudice directed toward women and the economically helpless. Reacting to anti-Semitism was sometimes the last vestige of their Jewishness.

However, there were other writers who could not as easily shake off what they heard about themselves as Jews. With little positive Jewishness to provide a defense, they internalized the vile attributes attached to the Jewish label. Their perception of self was split. While they knew, of course, that many of the arguments to defame Jews were simply vicious, they perceived in other defamatory assertions a grain of truth. The Jews, for whatever reasons—their different history, their behavior resulting from centuries of persecution, the slanders against them—had been publicly transformed by the dominant culture into badly flawed, if not ugly and hateful, beings.

The artists affected by the anti-Semitic wave felt impelled to depict characters who had become victims of their low self-esteem—in some instances a reflection of their creators' own inner turmoil. Why did they create characters who could not act naturally out of genuine desires of their own, who could only react to outside hostility? Why did they create only characters who were so ashamed of their own Jewishness that they went to absurd lengths to conceal it? Why did they feel compelled to fight duels over the slightest hurt and wince at the mere mention of a characteristic generally ascribed to Jews? Perhaps these authors needed to agree with the anti-Semites that some Jewish traits were indeed despicable, and that some Jews such as themselves were conscious of the traits and deplored them. For them the time had come, not to prove Jewish virtue, but publicly to dissociate themselves from Jews who lacked it. Obviously, the creators of these characters perceived serious patholog- ical problems in many Jews of their time—problems that needed to be removed if Jews were to become whole and healthy members of German society.

There were others, of course, who diagnosed almost identical flaws in the Jewish psyche but reached different conclusions. Theodor Herzl and Max Nordau also depicted weak, nervous, self-hating Jews, whose insecurity could be dissolved only by normalization of the Jewish condition through a nation of their own. Out of this overall concern for the health of the Jewish psyche in the concluding decade of the nineteenth century the Zionist idea, previously a fragile plant at best, burst into full bloom.

The most gifted of the self-analyzing writers was **Ludwig Jacobowski** (1869–1900), who died at an early age after a promising career as poet and novelist. Leo Wolff, the hero of *Werther der Jude* (*Werther the Jew*) (1892), is the most clearly delineated and convincing of the self-hating Jews. Leo Wolff is a composite of undesirable traits, less in the eyes of the Gentiles than in Jacobowski's own. A student in Berlin, Wolff has impregnated a sweet Gentile girl whom he loves but eventually ruins. Wolff consorts freely with fraternity brothers, some of whom are vicious Jew haters, and lives in constant fear that his banker-father will disgrace him through some dishonest business transaction. The father does, indeed, contribute to the financial ruin of the parents of Leo's best friend, and the son rushes home to make amends. His accumulated neuroses lead to a breakdown. Thus, he is unaware that in his absence from Berlin his pregnant girlfriend has killed herself. Overwhelmed by his own guilt Leo Wolff shoots himself.

Wolff judges Jews by a standard different from the one by which he measures Gentiles. He is obsessed by the fear that Jews will cheat in business, that *Börsenjuden* (stock exchange Jews) conduct themselves ludicrously in public, that Jews might behave improperly in love or speak German with a Yiddish word order or a *Mauschel* ("Jewish") inflection. He sees Jewish aberrations where there are none, apologizes for nonexistent moral and social inadequacies, and demands of Jews a code of conduct that would help him relieve his anxieties. Hatred and fear fuse into one when he reads of a Jew in an unsavory context. Wherever he finds a negative news story, he searches in secret terror for a Jewish-sounding name. He feels ill at ease on Christian holidays. He is attracted to Gentiles only, although Christian religious elements repel him as much as the Jewish teaching he has received.

It bothers Leo Wolff that the older generation, which he sees as forceful and businesslike, does not suffer from Jewish anxieties as he does—he who is young, modern, assimilated. Yet, in his view, it is precisely the older generation that is responsible for the increasing prejudice he and the young are experiencing. It does not occur to Leo that anti-Semitism might be the problem of the one who hates rather than the one who is hated.

Not unlike Jacobowski, Wolff expects the end of anti-Semitism to coincide with the moral regeneration of the Jew. Leo dismisses the remarks of reasonable Gentiles who emphasize the irrational nature of anti-Semitism which, they tell him, exists independent of any action by Jews, good or bad. Instead, he accepts the judgments of Jew haters as facts. But when the most poisonous Judeophobe of his fraternity denounces a young boy as a "Jew-boy," Leo challenges him. The reader quickly realizes that Leo Wolff is not fighting for his own honor or that of a Jew, but merely to avoid any suspicion of Jewish cowardice. This novel is structurally flawed, but it should be viewed as one of the most instructive about the psychological pressures on young Jews in the late nineteenth century. The Werther of the title is a residue of Jacobowski's original intention to write an epistolary novel in the style of Goethe's *Die Leiden des jungen Werthers* (*The Sorrows of Young Werther*).

Some observers have seen in this novel a fictionalized autobiography. Undoubtedly, Jacobowski personally experienced some of Leo Wolff's conflicts; even more surely he noticed them in other Jews. But it is in no way autobiographical as far as the externals of Jacobowski's life or specific incidents are concerned. The author spent many years of his short life in the employ of Jewish community agencies and successfully engaged the anti-Semitic demagogue Hermann Ahlwart in a lengthy polemic.

Similarly torn is the main character of *Schmelz der Jude* (*Schmelz the Jew*) by **Ferdinand Bronner** (1867–1948) who wrote as Franz Adamus. Born in Auschwitz, he spent the better part of his life as a schoolteacher and wrote but sparingly. Like Leo Wolff, Schmelz is a member of an anti-Semitic nationalist fraternity bearing the Germanic name of Nibelungs. Schmelz will go to any length to conceal his Jewishness. Not only does he regret the day when Jews exited from the ghetto, but he wishes them out of existence altogether. He even blushes at the sight of a Jew with an allegedly Jewish characteristic. Not only has he changed his name, but he lives in dread that something within him will betray his origin. He requires repeated assurances of his Aryan appearance. He has nearly convinced himself that his mother is a Silesian peasant, not Jewish at all, and that his father is not really his father. A Zionist at a public meeting arouses his ire, as does a Jewish peddler who offers his wares during a fraternity meeting. Finally, his father appears at the same meeting and suffers a stroke as he confronts his son. Even the anti-Semitic Nibelungs find Schmelz's conduct reprehensible. As he sits by the bedside of his paralyzed father, Schmelz is finally overtaken by remorse.

Jacobowski and Bronner were also patient explainers. But they no longer explained what Jews would be capable of doing if given a chance. These authors explained to Jews and Gentiles alike what irreparable harm the hatred of Jews had done to the psychology of the Jew. At least to a degree, Werther and Schmelz are accusatory figures who pointed a reproachful finger at Jew baiters, wherever they may be. In the process, they confessed freely to pernicious qualities that ravaged the Jewish psyche. The hope of Jacobowski and Bronner for a reformed anti-Semite was minimal; they seemed to be counting in part on a reform of the Jewish makeup. Very tentatively, they suggested a moral regeneration of the Jew. In the process they forgot that the moral regeneration of the Jew had little to do with anti-Semitism.

The turn of the century brought other examples of Jewish characters afflicted by a wholly destructive pathology. The hero of *Ketten* (*Chains*) (1908) by **Herman Reichenbach** (1869–1924?), Siegfried Lehmann, has chosen a military career, but officer status is available only at the cost of conversion. He conceals his baptism from his father and his Jewish origin from his fellow officers. He even pretends not to know his father's best friend who comes to visit him. Insulted by other officers, Lehmann dies in a duel. *Großstadtjuden* (*Big City Jews*) (1910) gives a graphic account of Viennese Jews in a state of psychic and moral decay. Self-deprecation, self-hate, and outright Jewish anti-Semitism placed Reichenbach's characters in absurd and paradoxical situations. Jews looked for Gentile marriage partners even with haters of Jews. In an attempt to cleanse themselves of their impure blood, some Jews went to ludicrous extremes.

Vienna apparently had no monopoly on pathological self-hate and social climbing. In *Millionär (Millionaire)* (ca. 1910) by **Arthur Landsberger** (1876–1933), a repugnant woman pushes her husband into a mad scramble for power and prestige. Twice she persuades him to cheat her own father out of a fortune, and when he dies, she will not attend his funeral largely out of dislike for the Jewish village of her birth. When she converts to Christianity, the act is as casual as slipping into a new dress.

In spite of the prominent role **Max Nordau** (1849–1923) played in the history of Zionism, historians have largely ignored his play, *Dr. Kohn* (1894), which also portrayed the progressive malaise of the modern Jew. Leo Kohn has failed to obtain a professorship because he chooses to remain a Jew. He falls in love with Christine Moser. Her father is a baptized Jew whose family barely remembers he had once been a Jew. Moser will accept Kohn as a son-in-law, provided he converts. This wish is understandable, for Moser's family consists of extremely anti-Semitic clergymen and generals. In the end, Moser's son, infected with the anti-Semitic virus, shoots Leo Kohn in a duel.

In a frank conversation between Dr. Kohn and Moser, the latter had stated his policy: to keep a low profile in the family, never to mention his origin, not even to his children. By the next generation, this origin will be forgotten. The more Kohn listens to Moser, the more he identifies as a Jew. The conversation also hints at why Nordau advocated "the muscle Jew," the Jew of physical strength and courage who will not cave in to intimidation.

In his early writings, Nordau had mistakenly presented anti-Semitism as a specifically German phenomenon. The Nordau who wrote *Dr. Kohn* knew better. There was but one remedy for the fearful, twisted Jew of the Diaspora: instead of veiling his Jewishness, he needed to be proud of it and nurture it. Only the normalization of the Jewish condition, impossible in the dispersion, could eliminate the extremes of Werther, Schmelz, and Moser.

The impetus for the political Zionism of **Theodor Herzl** (1860–1903) was also based on the realization that Jews were an ailing people, obsessed with money, insecure in spite of the power that money conferred. The Jew bowed outside, cringed inside, even if there was an occasional show of bravado. *Das neue Ghetto* (*The New Ghetto*) (1894) painted an unflattering portrait of the family of a stock exchange speculator. Herzl's hero, Dr. Samuel, expects to marry into this family. Not a strong play, it is interesting, as is Nordau's, for a conversation between Samuel and his Christian friend. The Christian has taken Samuel to task for being willing to join the speculator's family. A break occurs with the Christian friend. Samuel will remain with his *Börsenjuden* (stock market Jews), good or bad, contemptible or not. With Jews he belongs, and with them he will stay. Would his Christian friend forsake his group because, inevitably, it had undesirables in its midst? Samuel admits that he can tolerate some Jews only through sheer determination. Jews have to be led to a new and better path: the normalization of the Jewish condition through the acquisition of a land. In their own country they would carry their heads high and their souls would not be rent by conflicts of loyalty, inadequacy, and self-deprecation.

The culture critic **Samuel Lublinski** (1868–1911) rejected the notion of "prideless reform" of Jewish character and urged instead a sense of oneness, of belonging to one another, perhaps a form of Zionism. Jewish culture had become a nomad culture, in perpetual discord with the people among whom Jews were living. But for Lublinski "nomad" had positive connotations. It meant young, striving, becoming, as yet incomplete, and full of inner strife. Try as they might, the Jews could not fit in; their participation in the affairs of their adopted country was essentially unwanted. Jews must not expect recognition for their writers and artists. It was far wiser for them to consider ways of reestablishing pride in themselves and their heritage than to make a contribution the native culture would be happy to do without. Jews could afford no further spineless concessions to the outside world.

Revulsion over alleged Jewish qualities was in the air when Zionism appeared as the bright hope for correcting the deficiencies of Jewish personality. Whatever new problems Zionism might bring in its wake, they seemed minor in comparison to what was happening to the attitudes of Jews toward themselves. The other solution, Jewish moral reform from within, implied acceptance of the hateful characterizations of the anti-Semites, the very tendency that the self-deprecators deplored. It was neither a realistic nor an honorable solution. Rather than yield to the enemy, the Zionist alternative offered a rich measure of hope, even if that solution still appeared beyond reach in 1900.

● ● ● ● ●

Self-haters

T he authors just discussed presented an array of self-hating Jewish characters. Their purpose in creating these near caricatures was to motivate readers to consider the unhealthy trends in young Jews. Their message was didactic: young Jews needed to change their ways of thinking and acting, preferably by finding new sources of self-respect.

There were also writers with less benevolent intent behind their anti-Jewish outbursts. The anti-Semitism of this group was unmistakable, although the degree of virulence differed from one writer to the other. In a real sense, these authors resembled the characters created by the previous group. Since the source of self-hate lay in relationships to parents, the Jewish community, and individual Jewish types, biographical factors become more significant than heretofore.

For the philosopher of language, novelist and essayist **Fritz Mauthner** (1849–1923), the dilemma of dual identity as German and Jew did not exist. Few writers were more eager for the label of German and more callously frank in shedding the name "Jew." Mauthner's family in Bohemia had already detached itself from Judaism and perhaps passed on its negative attitude to the son. Mauthner's mother retained many of the Frankish resentments of the region; his father also mocked Jews but preferred a Jewish education for Fritz to a religious vacuum. The young Mauthner thoroughly disliked the Yiddish he heard and made fun of the inept religious instructor who was assigned to him. He and his classmates taunted this teacher with questions about Jesus and made it clear they did not regard him as a qualified member of the *Gymnasium* (prep school) staff. As suggested by his novel *Der neue Ahasver* (*The Latest Ahasver*) (1882), Mauthner sensed some profound religious longings in adolescence. An eclectic Judaism, he wrote, might have found him receptive. Instead, what he was taught turned him against Judaism, which he left early in life.

Culturally, Mauthner identified with the Germans, and politically, he supported Bismarck's policies. Later, he endorsed pan-German aspirations. In Berlin he was disgusted with the commercialized literature of the press which was largely in Jewish hands. What we know about Mauthner's Jewish attitude stems from his *Prager Jugendjahre* (*A Youth in Prague*); his *Erinnerungen* (*Memoirs*) (1918); his letters to Gustav Landauer; and correspondence with his niece, the writer Auguste Hauschner. His dislike of Christianity was as pronounced as his distaste for Judaism; in Christianity he abhorred, above all, the omnipresence of religious dogma.

Besides blaming Judaism for some of the evils in Christianity, Mauthner denounced many Jewish beliefs as "negative." The notion of "chosenness" was pure arrogance, he asserted. Heaven and hell as places for reward and punishment struck him as harmful concepts. The question has justly been raised about how much Mauthner knew of Judaism and whether his sources were legitimate.

Though he condemned anti-Semitism, having been victimized by it for his *Sprachkritik* (*Critique of Language*), he blamed Jews more than Germans. He proposed that anti-Semitism was not related to religion but to Jewish failure to shed every vestige of distinctiveness. The German nationality could tolerate no alien substance; not only should all Yiddishism be eradicated, but also Jewish character traits that Mauthner found unattractive.

After reading Salomon Maimon, Mauthner confessed to feeling singularly affected: he discovered in himself Jewish ways of thinking and feeling. The discovery must have been painful since Maimon was what Mauthner despised above all: the Polish Jew. Actually, Mauthner's most pathetic demonstration of self-hate centered on his contempt for Eastern Jewry. Although in a letter to Auguste Hauschner he disclaimed having demanded that the German border be closed to incoming Eastern Jews, he declared he would not apologize if he had made such a demand. And he also abhorred profit-oriented Berlin merchants. What about Martin Buber, his friend and Gustav Landauer's friend? Although he considered Buber a valuable human being, Mauthner referred to him as a "Polish Jew" and "atheistic Zionist."

Mauthner regarded the Jewish problems as trivial, and he was annoyed when a Jewish journal claimed him—as he sarcastically commented—for the chosen people. He also derided the Jewish editor who had asked him whether he had really converted. Mauthner responded sharply that he was above such nonsense and that he was proud to have dispatched to the editor the nastiest letter he had ever written.

In any genre he attempted, Mauthner was far stronger on abstract formulation than on either feeling or imagination. The absence of the latter may explain the impression of callousness he often created. He often voiced his craving for unity with the blond majority. His desire for assimilation was total, surpassing that of his young contemporary, Walter Rathenau, ardent patriot and later foreign minister of the republic. Though Mauthner thought of Jews as a people with a distinct personality, he never considered Zionism as an answer. Perhaps he simply did not think enough of the "Jewish problem." Perhaps, too, he wanted the extinction of Jews as a people—not, to be sure, physical extinction, but an end to their existence as a distinct group in the West. Whereas he applauded Bismarckian German nationalism, that of the Jews was unthinkable.

According to his copious writings, **Maximilian Harden** (Felix Ernst Witkowski) (1861–1927) was an aggressive German nationalist. To his many enemies of the right and left he was only Isidor Witkowski, the Jew. Not long after his onetime friend Rathenau was assassinated in Berlin in 1922, Harden was nearly beaten to death on a street in the same city. In his final decade Harden recognized the implausibility of his previous positions. Too much of his credibility had been used up for a new Harden to make an impact. He died a bitter and broken man.

The child of an unhappy marriage that ended in divorce, Witkowksi escaped from home to join a theatrical troupe. During his ten-year stint as an actor, he converted to Protestantism. When the strain of touring forced him out of acting, he turned to theater criticism. Here he espoused modernist trends, but preferred Strindberg and Wedekind to Hauptmann and Sudermann. Soon his passion for theater yielded to a pervasive passion for politics, which may have originated in an invitation from the recently dismissed Bismarck to visit him at his estate. The event made of Harden a lifelong worshipper of Bismarck and an implacable foe of William II. Harden's criticism implied that William merely struck an aggressive pose but was not at all aggressive, merely awkward. Harden was more expansionist than the kaiser. He voiced dismay that the heavy outlay in armaments failed to lead to the firing of even a single bullet. In his columns Harden played a distasteful role, virtually persecuting Prince Eulenberg and his entourage for their homosexuality. No moralist, Harden merely wanted to rid the emperor of advisers he judged dangerous to the national interest.

Harden's anti-Semitism manifested itself in his acrimonious attack on pro-Dreyfus forces in *Die Zukunft* (*The Future*), the journal he edited for over thirty years. The Dreyfus Affair, he contended, was a further expression of the struggle between tradesmen (Jews) and warriors (generals). It was advantageous, he stated for "rich Jews to make

sacrifices in clearing a son of Shem of the most shameful of crimes." The
Dreyfus case would have assumed smaller proportions "if the condemned
man had not been a Jew, if a race famous for its strength and cohesive-
ness did not fight for his innocence and its right to live." Overnight, Jews
had turned Zola into the "brightest light of Israel." An inveterate enemy
of the press, Harden denounced as Jews the Paris correspondents of
German newspapers in Paris.

Upon the outbreak of pogroms in Russia, Harden assailed Jews
more mercilessly than Plehwe, "the butcher of Kishinew." He came close
to presenting Plehwe as a victim of the "sons of Israel." German-Jewish
journalists, he demanded, should admit that their hatred for Russia
resulted from her denial of rights to Jews. While he claimed to understand Jewish hatred for the czarist nation, he insisted that "the German
flag must not be misused and Germany harmed." Until his conversion
to liberalism in 1918, Harden sided on every issue with German national
interests, often to the detriment of Jewish safety and rights. The most he
offered to Jews was to publish now and then a review of a religious-
cultural book, such as Buber's *Hasidic Tales.*

Harden evinced greater fairness toward Zionists than toward
Diaspora Jews. After publishing Walter Rathenau's *Höre, Israel (Listen,
Israel)* (1902), a book not without its own hatred of Jews, Harden offered
Theodor Herzl an opportunity to respond. Herzl, who was trying to
secure the kaiser's cooperation for Zionist settlement plans, knew he
would antagonize the kaiser if he wrote for the journal of his archenemy.
But a pro-Zionist article did appear in *Die Zukunft* at varying intervals.

When Harden hated, he hated without restraint. His tone was ugly,
envious, and spiteful when he wrote his editorial following Rathenau's
assassination. (Harden had wanted to be foreign minister, but Rathenau
had been offered the position.) Erich Gottgetreu saw in the unworthy,
tasteless editorial Harden's need to rant against himself. "Identification
with German-ness,"Gottgetreu wrote, "had ended in catastrophe for
both." Harden had come to realize too late that there was no escape
from the limitations of his origin. In 1923 Theodor Lessing commented
on the shift in Harden's speech from "we" to "you" when he referred to
Germans at the trial of the assailant who almost killed him. Paul
Coßmann believed that Harden's tragedy could be traced to his obsessive
need to prove that a man of Jewish origin could be an ardent patriot. In
effect, he did not convince those Germans who would not be convinced,
and he ended up becoming a spectacle of pathology.

The young writer whose name has become synonymous with Jewish
self-hate is **Otto Weininger** (1880–1903), whose *Geschlecht und Charakter*

(*Sex and Character*) (1904) aroused much public attention in its time. Weininger wrote of the "nothingness" of Judaism, the dangers implicit in the Jewish mentality, and the desirability of an Aryan victory over inferior non-Aryans. Although Nazis were later to quote him, Weininger, despite all his contempt for things Jewish, would have been aghast at any maltreatment of Jews. Women and Jews, whose perennial debilities he deplored, were still human beings, and he would have objected to ill-treatment of any persons, regardless of what he thought of them.

Relationships in Weininger's family were not close, and later Weininger found it difficult to establish deep human relationships. Otto Weininger's father repelled any attempts at friendship or intimacy with his son. Though the younger Weininger had friends, they were not the kind with whom he could share his inner turmoil. The facile explanation of homosexuality as the cause of his hostility to women has not been proven in any form.

Weininger used his original studies in biology in his attempt to prove that women were inferior. He then searched for a principle that distinguished men from women. "The female is purely sexual," he concluded; "the male is also sexual." Woman received her worth through man; only through his wishes and adapting to his ideals could she truly find identity. Woman's consciousness was dull and weak, her concepts vague. Pure man existed in the image of God, of the absolute (Something); woman, as also the woman in man, was the symbol of Nothingness. Moral tensions were absent in her; she had no conflict with nature.

Always concerned with guilt and morality—the word "criminal" occurs in his writings with disturbing frequency—Weininger repudiated those qualities in himself that he judged base: the woman in him and his Jewishness. Both were marked by the same insufficiencies and represented the same Nothing, that is, the absence of ethical commitment and the incapacity for a "higher life," a striving for God. His observations were based wholly on the rootless, nonbelieving Jews of Vienna, who were indeed oftentimes beyond religion and faith. These skeptics were prone to becoming victims of the "very low ideas" that Weininger detested. These lost souls whom Weininger had in mind had strayed far from the paths of the fathers into whose traditions Weininger fitted more than into those of the Viennese Jews of his time.

In pronouncing the Jew the nonbeliever *par excellence* who viewed nothing as holy and inviolate, Weininger merely proved his total ignorance of the Jewish past. He continued in the same vein when he called Jewish religious services "abstract idolatry" on the one hand and "lacking in all mystery" on the other. According to Weininger, Judaism was a slave religion, for Jews were not even permitted to utter the word

"God." Jewishness is only an idea, he said; it does not stand for either a people or a religion. Little more than a turn of mind and a psychological and mental direction, Judaism meant weakness of substance and character; to Weininger it was the negation of the absolute. Little wonder that Weininger embraced Christianity, but only in a variety of his own fancy.

Weininger killed himself only four months after publication of his brilliant but perverse book. He hanged himself in the house in which Beethoven, his idol, had died many decades earlier. Arrogance had mixed with despair, histrionics with terrifying moral earnestness, creating in Weininger a desire to be more than human.

Theodor Lessing said of **Arthur Trebitsch** (1880–1927) that he was a Jew who prayed to the Germanic god of war, Wotan. Indeed, Trebitsch, whose life was spent near or inside the borders of insanity, worshipped strength, power, and war. Unlike Weininger, who merely despised Jews for their inferiority, Trebitsch would have liquidated them all.

In Trebitsch's Viennese home, pro-German sentiments entailed deprecation of Jews. "See, I don't look Jewish; look how blond I am," reflected the mood of the household. Yet Arthur's older brother, Siegfried Trebitsch, writing after World War II, expressed the highest regard for his father who, more than other businessmen, was sympathetic to his son's literary ambitions. Siegfried, the future translator of Shaw into German, became as transnational as Arthur had become a racist-nationalist German. In his autobiography Siegfried remained silent on his brother's peculiar doings. Instead, he alluded to his own friendly contact with Theodor Herzl and his own suffering at Nazi hands.

Siegfried must have been embarrassed by the memory of Arthur, who had actually allied himself politically with Austro-German anti-Semites, including Nazis. For a matter of months, the latter even appointed him their local leader. Though the Nazis saw in him an effective anti-Semitic orator, they soon remembered his origins and dismissed him. Moreover, they discovered that Arthur had a superb talent for making enemies, even among his ideological comrades.

Arthur Trebitsch's main opus, *Geist und Judentum* (*Spirit and Judaism*) (1923), brought into view his mounting paranoia. He never ceased referring to the *Chavruse* (band of Jews) that would have him jailed or committed. He exhibited his intense dislike of the modern world, the omnipresent exploitation of the many by the few, but he also deplored such developments as industrialization and automation. Like Hitler, he detested the church and its clergy. Whatever and whomever

he hated he equated with Jewish spirit. All he abhorred in himself was
similarly labeled.

Theodor Lessing (1877–1933), who invented the term "Jewish self-
hate," was himself afflicted with it. The author of *Der jüdische Selbsthaß*
(*Jewish Self-Hate*) (1930), he spoke frankly of his own migration from
Jewish anti-Semitism to a personalized vision of Zionism. Even as he
told of his present beliefs, it became all too apparent that he had not
shed all vestiges of earlier credos. Lessing's youth was marred by his
parents' wretched marriage and by his tyrannical father, who punished
his son severely for his failures in school. Theodor discovered he was a
Jew when a fellow student commented on his origin. His mother
explained what a Jew was by referring to an acquaintance who wore a
caftan and *peyes* (side curls). Lessing called this an unhappy introduction
to the sense of difference.

First a physician, then a philosopher, the early self-hating Lessing
looked upon Jews as all intellect, removed from nature; he saw them as
decadent, inferior to the blond, blue-eyed people he met in his circles.
One such person was Ludwig Klages, a member of the Stefan-George-
Kreis, an anti-Semite, whom Lessing propelled further in this direction.
Lessing intemperately attacked Samuel Lublinski for his "Talmudic
cultural criticism," an assault that drew a strongly negative reaction from
the youthful Thomas Mann. Theodor Lessing's witticisms at Jewish
expense reached their apex when he returned from a trip to Galicia.

Klages broke with Lessing because Lessing was a Jew. At around the
same time Lessing learned about the Zionist option. Then Lessing made
a sudden turnabout. The new Zionist now belittled Teutonic attitudes
and also espoused socialist and pacifist causes. In 1925 Lessing publicly
questioned Hindenburg's suitability to be president of the Reich,
comparing the old general-idol to a St. Bernard. This led to his dismissal
as Professor of Pedagogy and Philosophy at Hannover. Moreover, the
article netted him the permanent animosity of militant nationalists, Nazis
included. When the Nazis came to power, two of them fired shots into
Lessing's private room at Marienbad, fatally wounding him.

The main targets of the young anti-Semitic Lessing had been
Geist—intellectuality, social ethos, meliorationism—all of which he
equated with modern Jewry. Against these qualities he opposed soul,
blood, the subconscious primordial nature, and cosmic metaphysics. A
streak of intellectualism even persisted after he had begun to view *Geist*
and gentleness as desirable values. Now he could bewail German hatred
of *Geist* in the same memoirs in which he criticized Walter Kerr and
Siegfried Jacobsohn in terms the Nazis would have approved. In his later

years his yearning for death as a theme, overexaltation of Judaism, and extreme dislike of things German become a trifle suspect. Though he viewed himself as a contemplative poet rather than the polemicist he was, the war within is still perceptible to the modern reader.

The Jewish mission struck the adult Lessing as twofold: Jews were ideal mediators between Europe and Asia, between Nietzsche and Buddha, but they were the symbol of the future hope of peoples, as the carriers of all that was universal and fundamentally human. He still regretted that the Jewish people, once close to nature, should have been divorced from it through endless persecution. Now they had become claustrophobic, a people without a country. It was equally tragic that in the nineteenth century Jews should have allowed so much to disappear that was worth saving. For quick and cheap recognition they had adopted unworthy characteristics. Fortunately, a counterforce had been generated in the form of Zionism, which rejected lopsided intellectuality and decadence and forced the integration of *Geist* into a healthier frame.

The Jews' history of suffering had both negative and positive effects. Among the former was the willingness to accept guilt for the misdeeds of one of their own. The result was often a sense of worthlessness and its extension, self-hate. But their own suffering made them sympathetic to that of others and converted them into leaders of the oppressed everywhere. However, Lessing persisted in the view that this same history led the Jews to overvalue spirit and logic at the expense of the aesthetic and the truly religious. Ironically, Lessing was struck down by others who also praised the spontaneous, the irrational, and the earthly, as well as will and energy.

It is evident that the self-haters reacted with particular vehemence to their inferiority status and the psychological aberrations compelled them to identify with their blond, blue-eyed, normal, and uninhibited neighbors. They envied and resented these neighbors whom they could not actually touch. They turned their emotional anger and frustration on their own group. In the process they evolved theories that were designed to be respectable, even though their own emotional base was not. Clearly, they were psychologically and morally the prime victims of their status—and especially their pathological reaction to it.

• • • • •

III

The War and Its Aftermath:

New Functions and Pressures

The period immediately before, during, and certainly after World War I witnessed a rich flowering of German-Jewish writers. They ran the gamut of enthusiastic nationalists to equally enthusiastic internationalists, from liberals to socialists, from assimilationists to Zionists. One fact went unchanged: They remained conscious of—or otherwise in conflict with—their German environment and sought to overcome their feelings of nonacceptance by supplying continued proof of their goodwill and citizenship in order to gain approval. They also flung the gauntlet of defiance at their enemies, thereby letting them know that Jews would be themselves, with no apologies for who they were, and heedless of what others might think of them.

Nationalists

Considering the challenge to prove their German-ness, it is astonishing that the number of superpatriots among the German-Jewish writers remained small. Patriotism, after all, would have been the simplest and most direct way of demonstrating that they belonged and deserved to belong. Perhaps they knew deep in their hearts and minds that displays of patriotism would have incurred the displeasure of Christian patriots who thought they enjoyed a monopoly on love for the fatherland. They would resent the efforts of upstart Jews to express patriotic sentiments they believed to be legitimately theirs and theirs alone.

Nevertheless, there were two or three writers who unabashedly sang paeans of love to their country. Perhaps never in literature has a single poem dogged its creator's life so thoroughly as did the poem by **Ernst Lissauer** (1882–1937) entitled "Haßgesang gegen England" ("Song of Hate against England") (1915). For a whole year during World War I the poem elicited enthusiasm. Then yesterday's hero became today's villain. Lissauer's foolish, immature patriotism was never forgiven, and many were gleeful when in the 1930s he was treated like any other Jew. Yet the "Haßgesang" had its precedent in Kleist's comparable poem

105

during the Wars of Liberation. That, however, was a century earlier, and the poet was a German Christian.

Lissauer composed long poems of love for the German language, German soil, and the German landscape. It is easy to imagine his intense disappointment when the nation he had cherished cast him out, rejecting any claim he had to being German. His poems after 1933 mirror his bitterness.

Being Jewish, which Lissauer never denied, meant belonging to a particular religious community. By accident he had been born a Jew; by accident he was born in Germany, making him accidentally a German Jew. His political and cultural communities were matters of choice. He chose enthusiastically to be a German and he developed this identity with all his resources. He never doubted that the German and the Jew could peacefully coexist within his breast. However, he probably never realized how much he subordinated his Jewish to his German self. Judaism was a religion, and he was not especially religious.

Lissauer was born in Berlin and died in Vienna. In 1907 he published "Der Acker" ("The Soil"), poems longing for land and nature, the city-dweller's pining for the purity away from the asphalt environs. In isolation, some lines could be construed as voicing the aching for the land he never had. His best volume was *Der Strom* (*The Stream*) (1912), which revealed greater aptitude for the epigrammatic than the lyrical. While Lissauer's language is masculine and vigorous, his poems lack the musicality and sensibility of a great poet.

Then came the fateful lines, and all else dissolved. None of his criticism or historical dramas—*York* (1921), *Das Weib des Jephta* (*Jephta's Wife*) (1929), or *Luther und Thomas Muenzer* (1929)—could obliterate his one error. Lissauer left for Austria in 1924, to remain there until his death. Before Hitler, he sided with German nationalists in Vienna. After the advent of Hitler, his lyrics revealed his return to the monotheistic divinity of the Jews.

Like many nationalists, Lissauer rejected all rampant individualism. He condemned those who would not submerge their individual selves in community, a people, a nation. In his eyes, the Jews were not a people or nation, and there was no Jewish land in which they could immerse themselves. There was only the German nation for German Jews. He had visited the ghettoes of Poland and had returned feeling no kinship with the "strangers" he had encountered. Zionism struck him as a horrendous idea, a threat to his German identity. Jews had one overriding task: adapting to the markedly different countries in which they lived.

A late poem such as "Ein Mensch ruft zu Gott" ("A Man Calls Out to God") (1933) manifests Lissauer's despair and his return to the God of Israel:

Du deutsche Sprache, meine große Mutter,	Thou German language, my great mother,
Ihr Judenväter, ihr deutsche Väter,	You Jewish fathers, you German fathers,
Jesais, Luther,	Isaiah, Luther,
Ich Ausgesähter,	I, uprooted [?],
Ich Windverwehter,	I, blown away by the wind,
Ich Ausgedroschener,	I, thoroughly thrashed,
Ich hebe mich noch ein Mal wie der Rauch,	I lift myself once again like smoke,
Der steil emporstieg aus dem Opfer jenes Abel	That rose straight up from that sacrifice of Abel
Und rufe auf zu Gott mit grauem Rauch.	And call up to God with gray smoke.

The war lyrics of **Walter Heymann** (1882–1915) rivaled Lissauer's in the intensity of patriotic sentiment. For Heymann, war was a means of finding dignity and meaning in history. Early in the war, he died for these beliefs on the Western front.

Though Heymann was economically independent and could devote himself fully to literature, he produced very little. He had published a volume of poems called *Nahrungslieder (Tableaux of Sustenance)* (1909). It was his *Kriegsgedichte und Feldpostbriefe (Poems and Letters from the Front)* and *Die Tanne (The Fir Tree)* that gained him his short-lived fame.

Heymann loved everything about Germany as well as his *Heimat,* or native region. In 1914 he volunteered for the war in spite of being ill-suited for combat. After repeated requests, he was assigned to a regiment and experienced the exhilarating proximity of battle. Unlike Lissauer's "Haßgesang," Heymann's lyrics contained no hatred for the enemy. He appears to have felt no conflict between his love for humanity and his enthusiasm for the war. He hardly ever alluded to his Jewishness. Perhaps involvement in the war was his last hope for oneness with the German people. Certainly, the sense of comradeship is strong in his poetry:

Wenn einer von euch fällt,	When one of you falls in battle,
der stirbt gewiß für mich,	He surely dies for me,
Und ich soll übrig bleiben?	And I am to be spared?
Warum denn ich?	But why me?

Surely, Lissauer and Heymann and other forgotten patriotic poets were aware of the never-ending anti-Semitic debates. Certainly, they had not been spared, any more than other Jewish youths, the epithets of "dirty Jew" in their younger years. Did they rise to supernatural moral heights to forgive the hurlers of insults, slurs, and retorts targeted at them as Jews? It would seem unlikely. It is more probable that they preferred to be on the other side, with the myth-making Germans rather than the myth-victimized Jews, thereby perhaps escaping the worst forms of victimization. It was more comforting to belong to the definers of quality than to those defined. What more honorable way than to identify with the stronger and strengthen notions of German beauty, German strength, and German heroism?

● ● ● ● ●

Expressionists

T he full-fledged nationalists chanted hymns of love for Germany and approved the war, one group glorifying armed conflict and the other expressing violent hatred for the enemy. The Expressionists, who came into vogue at the same time, were unabashedly critical of Germany. Increasingly they turned against the war, and in some instances they advocated pacifism. The nationalists can be seen as extensions of the defensive-apologists, with patriotism the criterion for acceptability rather than the outmoded "virtue" of the nineteenth century. The Expressionists, many dismissive of Judaism, can be construed as modern equivalents of the defensive-aggressors, with a thoroughly rebellious attitude toward the value-setters. What the few nationalists and the many Expressionists had in common was a moral earnestness and intensity of purpose. These qualities were enlisted in the service of Germany: the nationalists gave unreserved approval, and the Expressionists underscored flaws, failures, weaknesses, and shame—criticisms that were as yet beyond the conscious-ness of the public at large.

Expressionism took hold in the years immediately preceding World War I and declined in the early 1920s. Jews played a dominant role in every facet of Expressionism. In poetry, they invented daring new images and used the myths of every continent. In drama, their innovations presaged the theater of Brecht. The novel was not the favorite medium of the Expressionists, yet they contributed noteworthy and intriguing examples.

Perhaps Expressionism had best be left imprecisely defined. It had an early and a late phase, each with a distinct focus. The phases had in common a vigorous extension of the old Impressionism, in which the artists detached themselves from concrete pictures to delve into their own sensations and inner reactions. Expressionism dealt with a state of soul and mind; was wholly subjective; and often became abstract, allegorical, visionary, or ecstatic. But note: it was intellectual rather than emotional. An amalgam of private intellectual images, Expressionist poetry was a reflection of the soul seeking expression. The technique proceeded from the outside to the inside, though the reverse was possible. Communication was indirect and quickly "changed frames."

Novelty in themes matched newness in form and style. God, man, brother, and peace were the high-frequency words in the Expressionist vocabulary. As focal points, they were separate and yet interrelated. The kingdom of God was a commonly stated goal, but it was really a new kingdom of man in which brotherhood and peace would reign supreme. Some settled for an ecstatic kingdom in which the divine embrace was somewhat less fervent. If man was central to their thinking, it was less man in contradistinction to God, than man as opposed to the machine, mass production, the impersonal city, or the loss or absence of community. If brotherhood was the ultimate yearning, the self would merge with other selves into a common bond. Human divisions would be obliterated, whether they were those of nationality, race, or religion. Expressionism spoke of the new man; for some this was to be a "new man" in the Nietzschean sense, for others just as strongly anti-Nietzschean.

For the early Expressionists the communion of man with the divine represented the highest goal. (Expressionists with this orientation are referred to here as communionists.) Later Expressionists centered on human affairs with aspirations, including the abolition of war; liberalization of sexual relations; revision of the penal code; elimination of the death penalty; and the battle against clericalism, the church, parliaments, and, above all, the "hypocritical morality" of the corrupt but outwardly respectable bourgeoisie.

Expressionists viewed themselves as ethical idealists, distinctly different from equally idealistic but doctrinaire Marxists about them. Unlike the Marxists, they would not be bound by inexorable historical laws. Kurth Pinthus summed up their political activism as "political poetry of a high order" that was disinterested in such banalities as the victories and defeats of political parties. Theirs was the politics of humanity that would culminate in "a temple of art and statesmanship." Their outlook was patently transnational at a time when nationalist fervor was at its high point. Their cosmopolitanism and political internationalism set them sharply apart from those with wartime hysteria. Coupled with irreverent views of the social status quo, this heterodoxy called attention to the

Jewishness of many of the Expressionists.

In a well-known essay, Alfred Wolfenstein posed the question of why there was vigorous Jewish participation in the Expressionist movement. His answer was vague and inconclusive. Perhaps he was attempting to be too subtle. Could it not simply be—new concept or old—that Jewish writers had shed the ancestral faith and had found a new spiritual home in Expressionism or some in socialism—secular counterparts to the lost faith? A poetic movement of yearning for human love, Expressionism also promoted the social justice of old, the concern for the forgotten and indigent, the victims of traditional privileges. The movement had a more human face than socialism, although after the decline of Expressionism, some adherents found the nearest alternative in Marxism. Others, it should be noted, turned toward a mystical union with the nation, a yearning embodied in Nazism.

The often anthologized poetry of **Ludwig Rubiner** (1882–1920) pleaded for peace and social equity. The very titles of his volumes articulated Expressionist values: *Der Mensch in der Mitte* (*Man in the Center*) (1917) and *Die Menschheit schreit* (*Mankind Screaming*) (1918).

America and her cities often served as Rubiner's purgatory. In "Die Stimme" the poet heard "the voice" among African-Americans who humbly turned up the whites of their eyes in anguished pain; he heard it among starving Jews kneaded together in greasy ghettoes; and among exhausted, weakened workers, three million of whom die, the hapless victims of the new "factory system." The voice was audible, too, among women exploited by bordello masters who robbed them of their hard-earned money. In "Das Licht" ("Light") Rubiner again depicted American urban centers as dehumanized jungles of teeming masses of blacks, Jews, and other dominated ethnic minorities of whatever color and complexion. Europe also came in for criticism. In "Stimme über Barbaropa" ("Voice over Barbareurope"), Rubiner declared war on those who declared war. In typical Expressionist fashion, he condemned fathers and the older generation as symbols of hypocrisy, fraud, and meanness.

Rubiner's often naive idealism spilled over into literature itself. Here, as in society at large, he resented elitism and egoism and faulted Goethe's Olympian detachment and seeming unconcern with human welfare. When a magazine appeared with unsigned contributions, Rubiner applauded the authors' self-effacement in favor of a focus on better ideas and living.

In his final two years, Rubiner found increasing comfort in the progress of the Russian Revolution. He knew Russian well, and while he was not uncritical of unfolding events, he perceived in the new society and antibourgeois state the fulfillment of his dreams.

From the first, the difficult, abstruse work of **Carl Einstein** (1885–1940) was more rational and philosophical than ecstatic or communionist. His tale "Bebuquin" (1912), with its disjointed images and seemingly absurd dialogue, foreshadowed the surrealist movements to come.

The son of a Hebrew schoolteacher, Einstein was to die by his own hand when the Nazis invaded France, his home for many years. Throughout his adult life, he had argued against a life of comfort and tranquility. But even he was not prepared for the turmoil of the 1930s and the quick Nazi victory in 1940. Einstein had been radicalized by World War I, which led him to participate in the street fighting in Berlin in 1918–1919. He fought alongside the Spartacists without ever formally joining their ranks.

His thought defies categorization. In "Bebuquin" (1912), *Der unentwegte Platoniker* (*The Steadfast Platonist*) (1918), and the Jesus playlet "Die schlimmste Botschaft" ("The Fatal Message"), his ideas revealed a nihilist whose nihilism led neither to indifference nor to hopeless resignation. Einstein was skeptical about virtually all transmitted truths; their falseness, he asserted, would inevitably be exposed with time. He sympathized with modern man who lacked firm values to cling to, having abandoned old ones as invalid and spurious. However, Einstein felt that this difficulty confronting modern man did not excuse him from his supreme task—that of thinking. Everything, objects included, existed only in relation to human thought. Yet even this Platonism, when closely examined, was profoundly cynical. This unorthodox writer was also a fertile art critic.

The themes of **Albert Ehrenstein** (1886–1950) are typically Expressionist. They revolved about man's suffering—especially that of poets—the horrors of war, the crimes of the military and their political counterparts, and industrialization with its pollution of cities.

Two childhood factors conjoined to produce this poet's sense of alienation and helplessness—poverty and Jewishness. Raised in a poor section of Vienna, he learned early the effects of unemployment, unsanitary conditions, tubercular disease, and various forms of human depravity. From his earliest years insults from Christian children made him conscious of difference and inferiority. On a visit to his grandparents in Slovakia he witnessed a Catholic street procession that deepened this feeling but turned him resolutely toward Zion and Jewish identification. But this greater awareness did not prevent him from being sarcastic about Jewish ritual, the pretentious delivery of rabbis, the "ugliness" of Yiddish, and any allegedly Jewish characteristics. Though there were hints of self-deprecation, he identified himself publicly as a Jew and defended coreligionists from unwarranted attack.

Inner conflicts took their toll. His initially close relationship with Karl Kraus turned sour, but so did many of Kraus's friendships. His quarrel with Max Brod was a better indication of his deteriorating emotional health; his literary fortunes declined. His work came to be filled with forebodings of impending doom. The advent of the Nazis drove him first into Swiss exile, then to North America. After Hitler's defeat, the now wholly demoralized poet returned to Switzerland and then went back to the United States. There he died, forsaken and forgotten in a hospital ward.

The novelist Ernst Weiss wrote that Ehrenstein's narrative *Tubusch* (1912) inhaled and exhaled ghetto air. In Ehrenstein's grotesque hero, Weiss discerned "the eternal Jew clad in the iridescent, often-mended beggar's garment of destroyed illusions." Alternately playful and ironic, Ehrenstein's wit merged in *Tubusch* with a deep sense of humanity. The narrative is suffused with the hope of a better world inhabited by better people. Perceptibly, but less than in his lyrics, Ehrenstein revealed his impatience with the ever-silent God who does not react to the cries of human anguish and suffering. In *Briefe an Gott* (*Letters to God*) (1922), Ehrenstein despaired that he must empty his messages into a gigantic void. Here he became the angry, admonishing, prophetic Jew infuriated with the injustices of the world. But the *Letters* are less accusatory of man than of the supposedly omnipotent, omnipresent divinity that refuses to engage in any dialogue that would explain his action or inaction.

The poet's *Selbstmord eines Katers* (*Suicide of a Tomcat*) (1912) has been likened to Kafka's animal fables. However, though Ehrenstein sometimes visited Kafka in Prague, no link of influence has been plausibly established.

The literary fortunes of **Alfred Wolfenstein** (1888–1945) rose and fell with the Expressionist movement. During the decade in which it flowered, Wolfenstein's verse was marked by great vitality. Unfortunately, as the movement failed to adapt to changing conditions, so did Wolfenstein. His work may also have been damaged by the chasm between his outer enthusiasm and optimism and his inner despair and forebodings.

Wolfenstein often seemed out of step. In the brief months of the Soviet Republic (*Räterepublik*), in Munich Wolfenstein edited *Erhebung* (*Revolution*), but the time for *Erhebung* was already past. He still visualized the glories of a utopian world when Germany was struck down by defeat, hunger, and cold. While the darkness of his vision deepened in the postwar world, with few glimmers of hope penetrating the gloom of exile in France, the strain of surviving World War II was too much. In 1945 he killed himself in Paris.

His successful period, the Expressionist decade of 1912–1922, produced his first collection of verse, *Die gottlosen Jahre* (*The Godless Years*) (1914), denouncing city life with its lovelessness and estrangements. During the first World War, Wolfenstein was attracted to Kurt Hiller's pacifism, which was oriented more to "Geist" than to politics. The strong attraction of the ethical socialism of Landauer and Eisner is also manifest in the poems that advocated change in society, but without bloodshed. Wolfenstein's sense of political realism was as undeveloped as that of the men he admired. Ernst Toller, Landauer, and Eisner believed that revolutions should adapt themselves to the ways of the poet, not the reverse. Yet Wolfenstein could barely conceal the *Angst* behind his proclamations of the omnipotence of poets and artists, those magnificent geniuses with a unique gift for revealing truth to the unseeing masses.

His essays in *Erhebung* (1918–1920) still lauded, in rhapsodic terms, the creation of the "new man" in an age of chaos and despair. He was more brilliant than persuasive in his attempt to liken Jews, the perennial outsiders, to the Expressionist poets, who were forever on the periphery of society. Both were homeless, alienated, and tossed between the deafening city and a nature from which both were estranged. Poets and Jews experienced more deeply the ruthless assault of war, of the military, and of discord. Jews celebrate life but cannot forget that life is full of strife and is a never-ending battle. The Jewish spirit is just like that, he wrote: conscious of the conflicts of existence but determined to be victorious in the end. Poet and Jew think in terms of the eternal and are adamant about emerging victorious over faddism, fashion, and the materialistic attitudes of the mob.

Though **Alfred Lichtenstein** (1889–1914), **Jakob van Hoddis** (1887–1943), and **Ernst Blass** (1890–1939) wrote little, each was recognized chiefly for one poem, and their rare jewels enhanced the Expressionist accomplishment. All three men had brief literary careers and led lives that ended tragically. Lichtenstein fell in battle in the third week of war; van Hoddis suffered a total mental collapse; Blass went blind and died in Berlin on the eve of World War II. Though skimpy, their work showed them to be innovators of language, and the substance of their poems fitted snugly into the Expressionist emphasis on universality, brotherhood, and social reform.

Lichtenstein is remembered for his 1913 poem "Dämmerung" ("Dusk"), which has often been anthologized. He also wrote prose sketches that were much in vogue. They were a curious mixture of black humor, pathos, and longing for a better existence. His best-known figure was the poet Kuno Kohn, generally interpreted to be Lichtenstein's inner self. Lyrics by the fictitious Kuno Kohn bore the same characteristics as the narrative in which Kohn played the dominant role: insanity, nonsense, sexual fantasies, and death consciousness. Kohn suffered richly, loved abundantly, and was obsessed with the need to be a poet.

The pathetic life of Jakob van Hoddis (Hans Davidson) has not diminished the exquisite and very original eight-line poem "Weltende" ("End of the World") that sounded the opening gong in the Expressionist campaign. His total output consisted of twenty poems. Van Hoddis spent the last thirty years of his life in institutions or in the homes of families willing to care for him. Deported in 1942, he was presumably killed in Auschwitz.

Ernst Blass's *oeuvre* consists of four slender volumes, nearly all written during the "Expressionist decade." Then he and his muse parted ways, and he turned chiefly to criticism. Again one poem, "Die Straße komme ich entlang geweht" (I Come Strolling down the Street) (1912), serves as anchor for his reputation.

In **Ivan Goll** (1891–1950) Expressionism found its most cosmopolitan expression. Born in Alsace of an Alsatian father and a mother from Lorraine, he studied in Strasbourg and Paris and began writing in both French and German. Goll made his literary debut with *Lothringische Volkslieder* (*Lorraine Folk Poems*) (1912) and followed the same year with *Der Panamakanal* (*The Panama Canal*). Goll spent the war years in Switzerland, where he met Claire Studer, who, as Claire Goll, also became a poet of note. After a stormy "nonlegal marriage," disrupted by numerous affairs (she was the mistress of Kurt Wolff, Rilke, and Jean Painlevé), and two suicide attempts by Claire, the liaison culminated in marriage.

Goll looked upon himself as beyond national conflicts and war, and especially beyond tensions between the two nations whose cultures he loved and between which he wanted to serve as a bridge. *Requiem pour les morts de l'Europe* (*Requiem for the European Dead*) (1916), of which he provided a German rendition, *Requiem für die Gefallenen von Europa* (1917), was almost wholly devoted to the theme of building bridges. Goll settled in Paris after 1919, dabbling in a surrealism he never fully accepted. After 1921 he chose to write in French.

In Goll's writings, communionist longing—a craving for God and the infinite—and social conscience fused more completely than in most Expressionists. The poem on the Panama Canal speaks enthusiastically of the canal's potential for joining peoples together and for the enrichment of lives everywhere. But in the same vision the poet is appalled by the denial of passage to some people and by the enslaved human labor that is passing through the canal. As in so many of his works, he mingles eternal hope with shattering disillusionment.

In many of his lyrics Goll deplores the loss of humanity. His critique of contemporary Europe is harsh and biting. "What importance does the individual still enjoy in the city?" is the question posed in the prologue to a later work. "One could no longer hear one's voice," he complains, "drowned out as it was by horns, record players, turbines, iron, asphalt. I was yearning for a single plaintive voice, for a human cry." Modern man is torn, split into parts, with no part having a sense of the other, the whole man lacking in responsibility. No wonder he is rent by boredom and lack of direction and that he is "incapable of giving purpose to his existence."

Mélusine (1922), a play that foreshadows the techniques of Brecht and Ionesco, involves the marriage of a mermaid to a real estate broker. The basic theme revolves about the craving for a fresh and innocent nature. This Rousseauist vision can only be a hope, given the nature of human history and modern advances in technology. In an essay, linked to Mélusine, he wrote:

> God is no longer a topic of conversation; the notion of Fatherland is dead; father, wife, bride, family, none is able to provide significant conflicts. Revolutionary drama is dead. Toller is great in prison, journalistic-dull on the stage. There is truth in the idea that conflicts diminish when binding values such as religion, honor and love have fallen into bad times. With old values gone, the age of a new stage has dawned.

Many of Goll's Jewish poems are in a collection of five centering about "Noemi," which echoes with the plaintive strains of the women of Judea. Yet, as one critic put it, they are only variants of the eternal themes of hope and failure, happiness and want, faith and disappointment, yearning and hard reality. Noemi, the title heroine, repeatedly alludes to the destiny of the Jewish people, the God Years, the Temple Years, the Ghetto Years. Here, as elsewhere, Goll senses greatness alongside legitimate complaint. He achieves in these poems a biblical style consonant with the Hebraic themes. He succeeds with the Job poems that he attempted at different periods of his life, the final version in the posthumously published "Niela" (a reference to the final prayer in the daylong Yom Kippur service). The dying poet yearns for oneness with God, whom he has vainly sought to understand, against whom he has railed and revolted, and whom he now serenely accepts along with his own mortality.

Perhaps alone among the Expressionists, Goll was a conscious Jew who, according to Claire, regularly attended Yom Kippur services. His was not a Jewish life, but his experiences were those of a Jew of his time.

Walter Mehring (1896–1981) was, in succession, an Expressionist, Dadaist, political chansonnier, humorist, playwright, and novelist. Exile took its toll on Mehring, who never regained after 1933 the recognition accorded him after 1916. In that year, along with Georg Grosz and Wieland Herzfelde, Mehring founded a German Dadaist movement proclaiming its resolve to liquidate bourgeois institutions and support all revolutionary movements. He was even then composing polemic quips for *Die Zukunft* (*The Future*) and *Die Weltbühne* (*The World's Stage*) and reciting witty poems in Reinhardt's cabaret "Schall und Rauch" ("Noise and Smoke"). His early Expressionist works, *Die Frühe der Städte* (*Young Years of the Cities*) (1916) and *Ketzerbrevier* (*Notebooks of a Heretic*), are filled with pain, hurt, and passion—also typical components of his humorous works.

Mehring's father, the editor of *Ulk,* a humorous magazine, was often summoned to the censor's office for transcending the "bounds of acceptability." His son's polemics skirted the same limits. After 1921 he did not always find the German climate congenial. He began to spend long periods in Paris, his eventual home, though the advent of Hitler forced new peregrinations on him, including an unsuccessful stay in the United States. Mehring attacked the privileged classes, the secret private armies, corrupt officials, bourgeois hypocrisy. He lacked moderation in nearly all he tried; he hated and loved with equal abandon.

Echoes of Expressionist techniques resound in his 1928 drama *Der Kaufmann von Berlin* (*The Merchant of Berlin*), staged by Piscator. His use of Jewish and Nazi characters in odd combinations failed to amuse or instruct. *Müller, Chronik einer Sippe* (*Muller, Chronicle of a Clan*) (1935) was more successful. This witty response to Nazi racial teachings shows Germans living, loving, raping, and being loved and raped, first by Romans, then by Frenchmen, Russians, Swedes, and Jews. The current Müller is an anti-Semite, though his wife is Jewish (she had nursed him back to health after a serious wound in battle). He refuses to divorce her. Mehring mercilessly portrays Germans as stupid believers in obedience and authority, and in supposedly all-knowing *Landesväter* (sovereigns). He felt they possess a unique talent for acting against their own interests. With more balance this novel could have had a greater impact than it did.

Carl Sternheim (1878–1942) represents early Expressionist drama through the abstract, allegorical quality of his characters, his style, his refusal to imitate nature, and his willingness to let inner attitudes surface as he saw fit. But he is neither a communionist like the early Franz Werfel nor a social activist like Rubiner. He comes closer to Frank Wedekind, and perhaps the early Heinrich Mann to whom the Expressionist label has but limited applicability.

Sternheim is difficult to define or classify. Arnold Zweig attributed his many contradictions to the Jewishness with which Sternheim never came to terms. Sewald places Sternheim's dilemma as one of "unsuccessful assimilation." The author's poor mental health, which required repeated sojourns in rest homes, confirms the thesis of unresolved tensions, some of which were assuredly connected with his Jewishness.

Neither the biological nor the cultural legacy from his wealthy banker-father pleased him; he was more grateful for what is received from his Lutheran mother. He considered his father's heritage as vague and tainted by money, stock markets, philistinism, and urban, bourgeois values—all of which he despised but felt drawn to. His mother's background stood for religious and cultural stability, along with honorable traditions, and it was somehow related in his mind to that aristocratic element with which he sympathized. Sternheim suffered: he was from the city, not from the country; from the bourgeoisie, not the nobility (nor the proletariat, which he praised at times). He also belonged, like it or not, to a literary culture based on market value as much as on the intrinsic merit of the product.

Sternheim's most impressive plays form part of his *Szenen aus dem bürgerlichen Heldenleben* (*Scenes from Heroic Bourgeois Life*), of which the Maske trilogy is the most distinguished. The plays, held together by the collective title, offer a satiric portrait of the Wilhelminian middle class, all too ready to sacrifice love, understanding, compassion, or art in a vain pursuit of wealth, prestige, and power. Sternheim strips layer upon layer of hypocrisy from seemingly innocent language and harmless actions. His ability to unmask the truth behind pious platitudes is one of his prime assets as a writer of comedies of manner and character.

The older Maske of *Die Hose* (*Bloomers*) is willing to profit from his wife's mishap—dropping her bloomers accidentally during a royal parade. Initially he punishes her but quickly realizes that her "carelessness" will net him a higher income from rents paid by two men who had witnessed the affair and were entranced by her charms. This rent, he has figured out, will enable the Maskes to have the heir they have long wanted. Maske is quite willing to tolerate the advances of the men in whom Frau Maske has a keen interest. But the men are only talkers and dreamers. One, the poet Scarron, prefers jotting down his impressions of surrender rather than achieving it.

In contrast to the ineffectual dreamers, the philistine Maske is at least real—but dishonorable. Scarron is neither. The poet, who initially despises the barrenness of Maske's psyche, comes to admire his masculinity, genuineness, and strong will. In later Maske plays, Sternheim returns to the incident of the bloomers as a precipitating cause for further grabs at power and attempts at upward mobility.

Sternheim turns out to be a master of converting the trivial incident into significant events. In *Bürger Schippel* (*Citizen Schippel*), a major play, the action again focuses on the acquisition of earthly goods and prestige. Although Sternheim disapproves of the false respectability that veils despicable actions, he cannot fully conceal his admiration for the successful go-getters. He also exhibits a liking for an effete, yet powerful officer class at one end of the spectrum, and to the lowly, disenfranchised workers at the other. To the bourgeoisie, who nevertheless attract him, he attaches all guilt for war.

While Wolfenstein equates the Jew with the poet, Sternheim is inclined to identify Jews with money, capitalism, and corruption in literature. Only two Jews are not negatively drawn, one a *Kammerdiener* (valet), the other an artist. The poet-merchant dichotomy exists alongside that of father and son. Sternheim never forgave his sire for being a Jew, and he resented all that this Jewish identity had come to mean in his own mind. His knowledge of Jews seemed limited to his father's milieu and to the Jews he met in the publishing world. Sternheim did not get along with some of the publishers, for example, Kurt Wolff. What Sternheim knew of Jewish tradition he may have gleaned from anti-Semitic rather than Jewish sources. His compelling need to be with the dominant group did not engender any affection for Jews whom he perceived as obstacles to his acceptance. When he failed to obtain a literary honor, which he thought should be his, he blamed the snub on his Jewish birth. Like so many of his *confrères,* Sternheim spent much of his life abroad, mostly in Brussels. During the war he escaped deportation only through the intervention in that city of influential acquaintances.

Sternheim was not far removed from the self-haters. He found no redeeming value in Jews or their way of life. He saw only Rothschild and was blind to Landauer and Buber. Here was one writer whose vision was clouded by personal conflicts and prejudices.

Also half Jewish, **Walter Hasenclever** (1890–1940) wrote Expressionist plays that were more sensational than sound. In *Der Sohn* (*The Son*) (1914), a twenty-year-old refuses to be intimidated by his authoritarian father and joins a revolutionary club, but is forced by the authorities to return to his father. In despair, he pulls a gun on his father. He does not shoot, but the father, horror stricken, dies of apoplexy. With this play, *Vatermord* (*Murder of One's Father*) becomes synonymous in Expressionist theater with killing history, authority, bourgeois existence—all *bêtes noires* of young Expressionists.

Hasenclever was wounded in the first World War and hospitalized. In such poems as "Der Retter" ("The Savior"), and again in "Der politische Dichter" ("The Political Poet") (1919), he denounced the war and clamored for recognition of a common humanity. To the poet he assigned a special, even revolutionary responsibility. In *Antigone,* the tyrant Creon functions as a double for Wilhelm II, and Antigone turns into a radical pacifist. Hasenclever committed suicide in a French internment camp in 1940.

Much of Expressionism was thus characterized by a lofty idealism, a deepened sense of compassion for human suffering, and a demand for lowering barriers—both national and religious. Expressionists battled German nationalism and militarism as incarnations of all they viewed as evil. They were equally appalled by Jewish nationalism the few times they dealt with that notion. While the yearning for the divine was powerful in the communionists, it rarely expressed itself through Western religions, which they denounced as equally separatist.

During its decade of dominance, Expressionism crashed against the rock of nation worship and xenophobia. The idealism of the universalist poet was repudiated or ignored by the establishment forces it ceaselessly attacked. Even when these forces should have been repudiated by defeat in a war they helped engineer, they were quick to regroup and emerged between 1919 and 1923 stronger than ever. The partyless, unaffiliated idealism of the Expressionists was overcome by the reemergence of powers they could not hope to conquer. Expressionism was forced to self-destruct. Its idealism was not lost but allied itself with existing political movements. As previously noted, some Expressionists turned to communism, others to Nazism. Jews could hardly turn to the latter; increasingly they veered toward various brands of socialism.

• • • • •

Socialists

F rom the very beginning there were Jews in the socialist fold. The socialism of Moses Hess was briefly mentioned in relation to his Zionist ideas. The near anti-Semitism of Karl Marx has been discussed too often to bear reviewing here. Less well known are the ambivalent attitudes of **Ferdinand Lassalle.** A disciple of Marx, Lassalle outstripped him in political skill and succeeded where Marx failed—in creating a political instrument, a party to promote the socialist cause.

Jewish problems concerned Lassalle (1825–1864) only in his younger years. In his teens, this spoiled son of a Breslau businessman was greatly troubled by the pariah status of Jews and their passive, unheroic attitude toward the destiny others would determine. To a youngster with his romantic imagination and fiery temperament, Jews were people to be profoundly pitied for their unwillingness to resist their treatment as outcasts. "Even the Christians wonder at the sluggishness of our blood—wonder why we do not rise in revolt and rather die on the battlefield than in the torture chamber," Lassalle wrote. He imagined himself at the head of a defiant Jewish army, drawing his sword on behalf of his hapless people. At fifteen he wrote:

> Indeed, I believe that without observing the traditional Law, I am one of the very best Jews. Like the Jew in Bulwer's *Leila,* I would risk my life to lift the Jews from their oppressed state. I would not even fear the guillotine, if I could make them into a respected nation once again.

Near the halfway mark of his short life, Lassalle proclaimed his interest in Reform Judaism. But he soon turned to his second religion, Hegelianism, and thence to the championship of the oppressed. Though not a trained attorney, he defended the interests of individuals, such as the curious Countess Hatzfeld, and even Heine. With the Countess's case settled in her favor, his involvement with the interests of the laboring classes could finally occupy center stage. This new champion of the proletariat believed Jewish equality to be part of a larger question.

Eventually he moved closer to the anti-Jewish prejudices of Marx. An apologetic note crept into his love letter to Sophie Sontzeff:

> Will you be able to bear the [second] blow which I must now give you? Sophie, I am—a Jew! My parents are Jews, and even though I am in my innermost self no more a Jew than you are, I have never renounced the religion in which I was raised, for I have never seen my way clear to adopting another. It is true that for your sake I would be willing to become a Christian. Should this become an indispensable condition, I would probably agree. All the same, Sophie, I should find it hard. Not that I have any liking for the Jews, whom, generally speaking, I detest. For me they are no more than the extremely degenerate sons of a great and long vanished past. During long centuries of slavery they have acquired the characteristics of slaves and that is why I cannot endure them.

This is an echo of his complaint in his diary entry at age fifteen. But now the desire to help had disappeared. Shortly after he wrote this love letter, he confessed that he detested two groups, literary people and Jews, and it was his misfortune to be a part of both. Lassalle, in turn, was treated as an object of Marx's contempt. From London Marx denounced him for his speculations and bourgeois lifestyle, both aspects of the Jew incarnate, the man of money. Although Marx and Engels shamelessly accepted his loans and offers of support, they used such derogatory names for him as "Baron Itzig" ("Baron Trendy"), "Jüdel Braun" ("Little Jew Brown"), "Ephraim Gottscheit" ("Ephraim God-dog"), and "Jakob Wieselthier" ("Jacob Weasel"). Lassalle was especially suspect to them because his family had come from the Polish border, and "pomade and makeup" hid neither a lack of *Bildung* nor a greedy, selfish nature.

While the theoreticians amused themselves at his expense and issued directives from the safety of England, Lassalle risked repeated jailing, exile, and the abuse of a hostile German middle class. To some degree, Lassalle enjoyed the aura of martyrdom. Subsequently, Marx and Engels had to concede that Lassalle had become the most effective instrument that labor had in Germany. Unfortunately, Lassalle's romanticism, with its notions of heroism and its premonition of death, continued to haunt him. He died tragically in an absurd duel. This inexplicable action, one of many in his life, left little doubt that his fall was voluntary.

Although some Jews and ex-Jews were in the socialist camp from the beginning, World War I steered many more in a socialist direction. This was especially true for those whose views evolved from Expressionism. Many of the Expressionists found the Marxist brand repulsive with its harsh intransigence, its formulaic language, and its one-sided, determined interpretation of all phenomena. The Expressionists stood for egalitarian ideas and for a social justice that never forgot human nature or shed its ethical and humanitarian components. They were reluctant to concede too much power to the state. The anarchistic streak in their thinking easily rivaled that present in Marxist thought.

Ethical socialism often lacked a sense of realism, as evidenced by the failures in Bavaria of Kurt Eisner, Gustav Landauer, Ernst Toller, and others who participated in the Bavarian Revolution and the short-lived, ineffectual Soviet-style government they established. Perhaps they recognized in theory that revolutionary times required the use of harsh means. *Gesinnungsethik,* as Max Weber dubbed the morality of impractical socialists, was a luxury in an age of turmoil and revolt. Private citizens, but not those intent upon creating a "just society," could indulge in politico-moral narcissism. Thus, Alfred Wolfenstein was appalled by the need to deploy military and police power, and even Ernst Toller, though minister of war, found it hard to accept the violent means of revolution. Some, like Rubiner and Friedrich Wolf, soon to enter the communist camp, demanded the employment of drastic measures.

It has been suggested that Jewish socialists could never cut the umbilical cord that linked them to ethics and spirit. They could *think* utopian and social goals; they could be effective critics of existing shortcomings and call vigorously for total change. But they lacked the ruthlessness essential for effective action. Civil and physical courage were abundantly present, but Jewish socialists lacked the will to perform actions that would dirty their hands, spill blood, and subordinate human lives to the ruthless pursuit of needed goals.

Jewish socialist loyalties were thin; these socialists were far more concerned with the economic power of Jewish banking families than with Jews' second-class status. Prejudices, discrimination, even persecution would be removed with the advent of the socialist society. Like all religions, Judaism was atavistic, palliative, sedative—the last tool of a dying caste. What was admirable in Judaism had been incorporated into socialist thought. As for Jewish ethnic identity, it had ceased two thousand years ago, and the remnants were the result of outcast status that united Jews in misery. In effect, Zionism was an evil dream.

Besides a basic devotion to social justice, Judaism and socialism shared a this-world concept of the messianic expectation. Alfred Döblin was to call Marxism "secularized messianism." Similarly, Friedrich Heer was prompted to declare that so deeply had messianism penetrated socialism that both Marxism and bolshevism had become unthinkable without the messianic foundation. There was also antagonism and incompatibility. Socialism could never detach itself from Marx's view of Jews as hagglers, barterers, and exchangers of commodities. They were irremediable peddlers. Marx accepted too willingly the views published by his erstwhile friend, the radical atheist Bruno Bauer, who derogated Judaism as the cult of egoism. Moreover, Marx had internalized many of the contemporary economic and social prejudices by his acceptance of them as he sought to distance himself from his origins. His modest dose of self-hate that diminished somewhat with time became in its turn part of the socialist catechism. This did not prevent others, notably the Russian anarchist Mikhail Bakunin, from discerning the same dark characteristics in Marx himself.

While much of Hess's literary output and that of the early Lassalle fits into the aggressor typology, most socialist writers are hard to place in relation to the primary attitudes toward both Jewishness and Germanness. They minimized the significance of their own Jewishness and of the Jewish question in general. They were as aware as others of the hatred of Jews and sometimes fought it even as they shared in certain of its tenets. The socialist writers were not timid people. They were outspoken, and their defiance of the economic establishment frequently caused trouble with the censor or landed them in jail. They belonged to a new breed for whom the institutions of their times were outmoded, as were most current beliefs. They thought the Jewish condition shameful because it consisted of capitalist exploitation by Jews in some instances and the legacy of a slave tradition and psychology in others. Improvement in the Jewish condition came to be seen less in drives for emancipation than as part of a general meliorism following a broad overhaul of society.

For three action-filled months between November 1918 and January 1919, **Kurt Eisner** (1867–1919) was a daily headliner, known for his bloodless November revolution and his unconventional tenure as prime minister of Bavaria. He quickly became a discredited idol, and, finally and dramatically, a victim of assassination.

He belongs only marginally to literature. He was a political journalist, editor of the socialist *Vorwärts* (*Forward*), a biographer, historian, and an occasional poet. At a time when most literary men were becoming politicized, Eisner's politics was "literaturized." In fact, he was eventually dismissed from his *Vorwärts* post because his aesthetic leanings at times overshadowed his socioeconomic interests. The head of the Bavarian government filled his speeches with classical allusions. As prime minister, he presided over public political gatherings that began with poetic readings and symphonic music. In the eyes of many, the wisdom of such programming was suspect in a city that was starving and freezing in the aftermath of military defeat. When Eisner publicly demanded that Germany admit to her war guilt—a clumsy attempt to prove that a new Germany had been born—his fate was sealed. He was an outsider, an "other," a traitor. The hero of November had become the villain of January.

His theater criticism and journalistic essays were repetitive to the point of monotony. Among his pet peeves were the Prussian aristocracy and its officer class. His idols were the common people, helpless, exploited, and unaware of their condition. Eisner was more charitable as a political writer than as a drama critic. Perhaps he feared less harm in the early demise of a play than in a politically irresponsible statement.

Eisner became protective of Jews only when they were under attack. He rarely criticized them as a separate or distinct group. The few times he dealt with a Jewish subject, he did so sympathetically. Hermann Cohen, whose lectures Eisner attended with fascination, sought to direct him toward Judaism, but to no avail. However, when asked why he would not convert to Christianity, he responded that he would never leave a despised and persecuted community. Toward other religions he showed the same detached respect as toward Judaism. Eisner was the idealistic, universalist Jew who looked beyond Jews, Bavarians, and Germans to an international community of brothers and sisters.

Gustav Landauer (1870–1919), a minister in Eisner's short-lived cabinet, wrote novels, novellas, and literary and theater criticism. His literary reputation was eventually overshadowed by the distinctness of his socialist thought. Anarchist and ethical rather than Marxist, this socialism served as an inspiration to many. Yet right-wing commentators denounced this gentle and quintessentially honest man as a political monster.

Landauer's socialism was grounded in his compassion for the deprived and his distrust of both the state and politics. Although he was often doctrinaire, he exercised independent judgment and remained open to new and different ideas. He wanted to serve the human community, but not through class struggle or bloody revolution. His distrust of the state was rooted in his conviction that centralization inevitably meant distance from the people the state was to serve.

Robert Weltsch spoke of the "deeper layers of Landauer's mind," which were "of a semi-religious nature." For Landauer the roots of evil lay not in the social structure alone, but "in the human heart unable to create a true sense of community based on love [or] brotherhood."

Landauer's correspondence comprised exchanges with Martin Buber, whom Landauer influenced considerably; with Fritz Mauthner, the self-rejecting Jew; and with Constantin Brunner (Leo Wertheimer), a convert who regarded Jesus as a representative of pure Judaism. In letters to one or the other, Landauer denounced those Jews who had discarded their Jewishness to participate in humanitarian, universalist movements. Jews, maintained Landauer, were a people with a distinctive culture that found expression in the wisdom of the Psalms or the thought of Spinoza. When Mauthner diminished his own Jewishness and derided Landauer for attaching importance to his, Landauer stated his own hierarchy of priorities. "First I am a human being," he wrote, "then I am a Jew, next a German, then a South German, and finally an I." His recognition of Jewish peoplehood did not blind him to faults that history had spawned in Jews. He despised *Börsenjuden* (stock market Jews) but added that they were not money-crazed just because they were Jews. Anyway, these Jewish stock market speculators were few and far between. Most likely it was the Jew in him—a Jew in the prophetic tradition—that made him revile stock market Jews.

If there was to be a betterment in the human condition, it would come about, he argued, as a result of the improvement in human attitudes rather than through sweeping political change. The latter was veneer; the former was substance. Landauer's great hope rested with small communes, which, in the long run and with altered human relationships, could cause the state to crumble. His definition of socialism shows his distance from Marxism. Socialism was "the attempt to steer one's life toward a bond of common spirit of freedom, that is, religion." Every individual had an obligation to participate in this effort to bring about the desired social communal state and recognize in it—especially if he or she was a Jew—the coming prophetic, messianic era.

Landauer made sacrifices for his ideals. Twice he was jailed, first for inciting to riot in his publication *Sozialist,* then for a press attack on an official. When his journals were suppressed or ceased publication, he published German renditions of British literary works. In this attempt to acquaint Germans with literary England, he was assisted by his second wife, Hedwig Lachmann, a poet and translator of note.

After Eisner's revolution, Landauer hoped briefly that a new spirit had been born and the power of the state could be broken. Soon, however, Eisner's compromises disillusioned him, though he remained loyal to his chief. Moreover, he could not tolerate the communists—not yet called that—who increasingly dominated the government after Eisner's assassination. He retired. In spite of this retirement, when

radical right-wing forces toppled the government, the White Guards
seized him and brutally killed him in a prison yard. He never suspected
their intention.

Revolutionaries who would not spill blood, Eisner and Landauer
became the first major victims of pre-Nazism. Only a few weeks
separated the two men in death. But in the four years that followed their
murders, a streak of assassinations struck down nearly four hundred
"traitors," men who had been opposed to the lost war and supportive of
peace and the new republic. The victims also included Jews like
Rathenau, who had impassionately defended Germany, opposed an
armistice, and crucially served the nation in war. Though on opposite
sides of the political fence and aligned differently on economic questions,
Landauer and Rathenau were united in their faith in the supremacy of
the spirit. Perhaps it was this *Geist* which the rising men of blood, soil,
and iron could not tolerate.

Some have labeled **Erich Mühsam** (1878–1934) a harmless *café-
Literat* (café satirist); others called him a true revolutionary. He was
both. Always struggling to make ends meet, he entertained in cabarets
and sometimes did serious work in journals. Mühsam was an inveterate
rebel who played a leading role in the Munich Revolution of 1918–1919.
He suffered for his involvement in the Soviet-style government with
many years in prison.

Recent studies have shown that the eccentric and unruly Mühsam
was less hostile to Jews than critics once believed. When Jews were
publicly assailed, he just as publicly came to their defense. He then
insisted that the Jewish prophetic vision represented a major step
forward in world thought. Under Landauer's influence, he had come to
see Jews as a people. He denounced anti-Semitism as a foul attempt of
the privileged to divert attention from their unsavory manoeuvers. He
wrote during the Beilis case involving a charge of ritual murder: "At this
moment I am conscious of my solidarity with every Galician horse trader,
just as Spinoza and Heinrich Heine would be." For him, Eastern Jews
were not unwanted outsiders, a threat to the impression of *Bildung* and
Kultur which German Jews were still trying to convey. It was incumbent
on Western Jews to assist their Eastern brethren in distress. But try as
he might, Mühsam could not bring himself to favor or even envision a
Jewish state.

Mühsam did not enjoy a happy childhood; the relationship to his
father was strained. His father came from an orthodox home but seemed
to live in fear that some external factor would set him apart from the
Christians of Lübeck. At his father's insistence, Erich tried to become a

pharmacist, but the boy had neither the patience nor the temperament. On his twenty-second birthday he inserted a "declaration of no love to my father" into his diary. Yet, his father had good reason to be concerned about his undisciplined son, who had been expelled from school. Finally, Erich Mühsam left Lübeck for a long period of vagabondage, eventually settling in Munich's Schwabing area, where he began writing in the prewar years.

Rebellion permeates his fiction. His story "Carmen" (1912) features a struggling Jewish poet at odds with a society he loves to shock. There is significance in the choice of *Kain* as the name for his first journal. In the drama *Judas* (1921), which dealt with the anti-war strikes of 1918, he exculpates a modern Judas for his betrayal. For Mühsam, Jesus was a Jew who left Nazareth to make the poor happy.

But not all of Mühsam's Jews are sympathetic rebels. In *Die Hochstapler (The Impostors)* (1906), he paints the greed of a Jewish real estate broker. The Jew speaks jargon when dealing with money matters. His Jews are either money worshipers or rebels.

Far more important as a writer was the equally tragic figure of **Ernst Toller** (1893–1939). Where his onetime colleagues Eisner, Landauer, and Mühsam were killed by "premature" or actual Nazis, Toller could no longer bear what life had served up to him and died by his own hand.

Toller imbibed Expressionism more deeply than did other socialist writers who began in this vein. While he sat isolated in his fortress jail for five years, the world was changing, and he was not given an opportunity to change with it. After his release from prison for his share in Kurt Eisner's *coup d'état,* his literary production declined in quantity and quality. Upon his release, he never lost the sense that the world had passed him by.

"A Jewish mother bore me," Toller wrote in 1933, "Germany nurtured me, Europe shaped me, my home is the earth and the world my Fatherland." None of these sources treated him kindly. He suffered as a Jew without recognizing any redeeming worth in this identity. Germany proved fickle, first dealing shabbily with him and then casting him adrift. European culture had proven deceptive, and Germany had punished him for seeing the earth as a home and fatherland. Toller's autobiography may have been his most accomplished literary work. It disclosed a young man committed to ideals that demanded greatness. An ardent German patriot before the outbreak of war, he volunteered enthusiastically for frontline service. When he recognized both the government's deceit and his own folly, the ensuing revolt quickly turned him into a socialist. Though not averse to Marxism, he was more truly the exponent of a humanitarian socialism with justice for those who had none. He immersed himself deeply in the Bavarian Revolution and became minister of war in the government of the Soviets. For participating in these events Toller received a lengthy prison sentence. By the late 1920s, his utopian vision seemed more remote than ever; his prison years—indeed, his life—impressed him as a dreadful waste. After 1933, the forced exile in France and England, his briefer stay in the United States, and his whole Ahasver-like fate plunged him into an ever-deepening depression. One day in New York, his suitcases already packed for a return to England, he hanged himself—probably on impulse and in despair, in a New York hotel room.

Toller possessed civic and physical courage in abundance, but he lacked the ruthlessness, the kill-to-win instinct for his activist and revolutionary efforts to succeed. He had proven himself exceptionally brave in war and equally courageous in the courtroom in which he heard himself denounced as a killer. When an offer of freedom was extended while he was in prison, he rejected it as dishonorable. He continued to languish in his cell, but his thoughts returned to the events that had brought him there. In this frame of mind he wrote his finest plays.

Biographical elements course through his plays. *Die Wandlung* (*The Change*) (1919) focuses on a young man who had sought service to the Fatherland because this tie would bind him to other Germans. Instead, the war convinced him of the desirability of human brotherhood. Though crammed with rhapsodic monologues and alternating scenes of dream and reality, *Die Wandlung* may be the least Expressionistic of Toller's early plays. Much more so is the memorable *Masse Mensch* (*Man and the Masses*) (1920), now a classic, in which a female socialist revolutionary speaks for him. This heroine is alienated from her bourgeois husband, but she is also repelled by *Namenlose* ("Nameless"), the impersonal Marxist activist who orders ruthless killings in the name of the masses. The heroine has been arrested for her revolutionary activity and is about to be executed when her husband comes to her rescue in the name of "all right-thinking people." She is still appalled by his values and also turns down the offer of *Namenlose,* whose proposed rescue involved killing a guard. The woman shares the real-life Toller's dilemma. She can no longer be a part of the bourgeois world, her past. Nor can she accept the blood-soaked revolution, the supposed future.

The theme of the perils of social actions and nonaction recurs in *Die Maschinenstürmer* (*Machine Wreckers*) (1922), which Toller also wrote while at Niederschönefeld Prison. The setting is nineteenth-century England. Workers feel threatened by machines that endanger their livelihood. Only one man recognizes that the machines should not be destroyed but made useful to the workers. The masses reject his moderate arguments, suspect him of treachery, and kill him. In spite of his continued support for workers, Toller does not indiscriminately side with them.

In *Hinkemann* (1923), Toller returned to a contemporary German setting. The hero has lost his sexual organ in war, a loss that has devastated him as a human being. It has ruined his marriage to Grete, whose lover delights in humiliating Hinkemann. To punish himself, Hinkemann has taken the debasing job of biting through the necks of rodents at public fairs, perhaps also to prove in this manner his remnants of masculinity. But underneath this seemingly ruined man there remains a decent, sensitive, and compassionate human being who empathizes with the poor, the sick, and the disgraced. It is evident that the Expressionist Toller's faith in the "new man" is on the wane and that a terrifying reality has taken hold of him.

The deep sensibility of this writer, who wanted barriers removed between all living things, manifests itself in his fascination with several swallows who had nested near his window in his prison cell. The nest was destroyed by order of the warden. Two more times the swallows rebuilt their nest, and again it was destroyed. Finally, the swallows gave up, and the female died. Toller reported these observations in several letters from prison; they also formed the basis of his *Schwalbenbuch* (*Book of Swallows*) (1924), a little jewel of poetry.

Toller was still to write other plays, none the equal of *Masse Mensch* or *Hinkemann*. They reflect their author's increasing fear of impending barbarism, premonitions of war, and a return to medievalism. His novel *Justizerlebnisse* (*Experiences with Criminal Justice*) (1927) delineates the politicization of justice in Germany and the psychological and political terror plays of the classes in power. His final plays, for many years available only in English translation, demonstrate his lowered expectations, the death of hope, as in *Hoppla, wir leben* (*Aha! We're Alive*) (1927).

Except for his early years, Toller's Jewishness was not a problem for him. As a child he had learned that as a Jew he did not belong to a favored species, that Jews lived apart from others, that rumors about them were ugly and ridiculous. But then a Polish worker's son asked Toller whether the stories about him, a young Pole and worker, were all that different. Peculiarly, Toller felt they were not, apparently unmindful of a Jewish history of minority status *everywhere* with accompanying vilification and persecution. Toller accepted anti-Semitism as a disagreeable fact of life, to be fought but to be regarded as part of a restructuring of society.

Early in life he lost belief in God and also abandoned the Jewish ritual practices which had been observed, though casually, in his home. He was interested in Jews as second-class citizens, not as a people with a history or a worthwhile way of life. He remained a Jew because he was born one, and no other faith appealed to him sufficiently to warrant a change. He was a friend of people and peoples, not of just one group, be it German, Jewish, French, or Chinese.

He valued the international character of Jews. That is why he was doubly incensed at those Jews who strove to be more German than the Germans. In his deepest self Toller expected more from Jews, whom he wanted, nevertheless, to be integrated without distinguishing marks into a universalist society.

•　•　•　•　•

The George Circle

I n the middle of the nineteenth century, Jews had flocked to comedy. Toward its end they had championed the social realism of Ibsen and Hauptmann. In the early decades of the twentieth century, many were attracted to Expressionism. Some were lured by different brands of socialism.

Still others were rotating about the complex and enigmatic **Stefan George** (1868–1933). Why would such diverse personalities as Karl Wolfskehl, Friedrich Gundolf, Edith Landmann, and Berthold Vallentin fee drawn to the bizarre Rhinelander? Was it George's teaching that everything should be viewed *sub specie aeternitatis* (in its essential form) that seduced impressionable, floundering young Jews? Was it the rigid discipline he exacted of his disciples? Wolfskehl likened him to a god. Perhaps "Georgean Law," as some suggested, constituted a Torah of the arts. Some critics related Buber's Hasidic legends to certain emphases in George's teachings.

The Jewish question occupied a place of some importance in the George Circle. The group around the Master, as many called him, included virulent anti-Semites such as Alfred Schüler and Ludwig Klages, whose fanatical hatred of Jews sometimes foreshadowed the Nazis' in intensity. Some George followers eventually joined the Nazis, and George himself was accused of being sympathetic to them. However, not only did George maintain his distance, but he voluntarily exiled himself in 1933. That same year he chose a Jewish disciple to turn down, on his behalf and in his name, the prize offered him by the Nazi Ministry of Culture.

Anti-Semitism cannot be placed at George's doorstep. There were, however, isolated statements recorded by the disciples that could be construed as irresponsibly critical, but these could be counterbalanced by others protective of Jews. Toward Judaism as such George was indifferent.

George evolved from classicist to romantic to symbolist and back to classicist. Evolution also characterized his sociopolitical views—to the extent such questions interested him. But it is clear that George enjoyed the company of Jews—women even more than men, despite his homoeroticism and undercurrent of misogyny. George, who never owned a home of his own, spent weeks at a time at the Wolfskehls' in Munich or the Vallentins' in Berlin, to mention but two of his hosts.

The life-styles his autocratic behavior imposed on his followers were often the cause for ruptures in their relationships. He interfered unabashedly in marriages and careers. Hugo von Hofmannsthal's father insisted that his son break with George before a deeper relationship could be forged. The friendship with Rudolf Borchardt never flourished as George had hoped. Wolfskehl, whom George tolerated, was the most independent of the disciples. Gundolf was less fortunate, and a total rupture was inevitable. The anti-Semites Klages and Schüler broke with George, and the former even sued him. George agonized over the terminations but remained determined to steer the faithful toward a *Wiederaufbau* (reconciliation).

Distinctive, often original, George's thought was aristocratic, elitist, anti-democratic, and universalist. He never succeeded in reconciling the Platonism and Nietzscheanism that rivaled each other for his attention. He remained outside the dominant trends of his time and disliked transient currents and faddist idealism. In his emphasis on personal worth and nobility, the special prerogatives of the exceptional person, and exclusivist esthetics, he ran counter to the spreading European egalitarianism. In a period which treasured nationalism as the ultimate good, he repudiated it. When literature was becoming politicized, he became increasingly apolitical. He was anti-materialistic when many confessed frankly that materialism, for them, was the only value. Regressive and progressive elements coexisted in his expression of hope for European unity of the spirit. He was uncompromising in his stress on quality and independence of thought.

There were also dangerous facets to his views that he could not foresee. His concept of the new *Reich* (empire) was comprised of elements that were partly antique and partly medieval, and his notions of leadership and service were ideas that encouraged the Nazis in some of their dubious pursuits.

Karl Wolfskehl (1869–1948), earliest and longest lasting of George's followers, still referred to him as the Master and to himself as the "Ever Faithful." At that time Wolfskehl, a blind old writer said to be dependent on stipends from Zalman Schocken, was living in exile in New Zealand. The disciple in Wolfskehl manifested itself in many ways. Most students of Ibsen's drama searched for the social reformer, but Wolfskehl concentrated on the man of soul and intellect, on his uniqueness, and reacted negatively to any suggestion of a social tableau or the notion of mob and mass.

Wolfskehl's rejection of French novelist, biographer, playwright, and musicologist Romain Rolland's pacifistic appeal of 1914 to German intellectuals must be explained against the Georgean complex of values. On the surface, Wolfskehl's response would seem to be that of a zealous patriot. A closer reading, however, reveals little interest in German policies. Wolfskehl's response focused on the ideal inherent in national effort and on the defense of a unique German culture. Wolfskehl and Gundolf were considerably more patriotic than George, who thought a German naval defeat might make Germany more modest and less stridently nationalistic. But the Christian George was not called upon to prove he was a German.

In prose and poetry Wolfskehl alluded to the thousand-year history of his family in the Rhineland and to the Tuscan-German-Jewish elements that molded him. Wolfskehl lost his mother early in life, but through the generosity of his banker-father, he managed to live in comfort. Before he lost his wealth in the inflationary years, he and his first wife Hannah frequently entertained George along with other followers.

Wolfskehl's Jewishness did not *follow* his German-ness—it was not exclusively the result of insecurity or rejection. As early as the first decade of the century, he had felt drawn to Zionism and had attended the Uganda Zionist Congress at Basel. He retained a friendly interest in the Zionist concept. But when Hitler forced him into exile, he opted for New Zealand rather than Palestine. Enough of George's influence remained to make him shy from political movements. He preferred the solitude of a distant, culturally undeveloped land.

His strength as a poet lay in his innovative, delicately chiseled language. His themes were modern despite the recurring echoes of ancient myths. Filled with longing for the divine, his lyrics mirrored his awareness of flux, metamorphosis, sensuousness, and balance. He yearned for greatness in himself and others. After 1933, other themes appeared: exile and return, destruction and renewal, longing and fulfillment, death and rebirth. His later poems pondered his altered personal circumstances and those of fellow exiles. What has survived from pre-Hitler years was loyalty to the word and appreciation of its significance. He retained the sense of mystery and awe he had discovered long ago. Wolfskehl's involvement with the Holy Man, which Gundolf gently mocks as his "oriental quest," emerges in early poems in the *Jüdischer Almanach* such as "Das Zeichen" ("The Sign") and "Vom Nebo" ("About Nebo"). Composed in the infant years of Zionism, "Das Zeichen" foreshadows the future:

Ja, die Botenscharen winken.	Yes, the swarms of messengers beckon,
Gürtet euch, ihr Fahrtgenossen!	Gird yourselves, traveling companions!
Tausend trübe Jahre sinken,	A thousand gloomy years fall,
Freudenfluten sind ergossen,	Glad tides are poured out,
Wo die alten Wasser flossen,	Where the old waters flowed,
Helle Morgenblitze sinken.	Bright flashes of morning sink.

In "Vom Nebo":

Leises Geräusch dringt bis zu mir hinauf.	A faint noise penetrates up to me.
Ein Lufthauch bringt die Dufte der Verhei-ßung	A breath of air brings the scents of promise
Von unserem Land, dahin ich euch geleitet,	From our land, to which I led you,
Dahin ich selber nie gelangen soll.—	Which I myself am never to attain.
Wie weit mein Blick: Er segnet eure Tracht,	How far my look: It blesses your native costume,
Fruchtschwere Niederungen, grüne Weiden.	Low-lying areas heavy with fruit, green meadows.
Ich hatte gerne meiner Brüder Herd . . .	I would have liked to see my brothers' hearth . . .
Auflodern sehen auf der Heimatscholle . . .	Flare up on native soil . . .
Ihr Tagwerk noch geweiht—doch ich erkenne	Their day's work still consecrated—but I recognize
Die dunklen Wege, die du mich geführt	The dark ways you led me
Bis hierher auf die letzte Bergeshöhe.	Up to here on the last mountain height.

Wolfskehl's longing for Zion is nostalgic rather than, as Franz Rosenzweig once put it, the symbolic quest for a better life. George accepted Wolfskehl's "Aus den alten Wässern" ("From Ancient Waters") for his *Blätter* (*Leaves*), perhaps as an expression of "Jewish spirit."

Just as the biblical subject of Saul is among the poet's first poetic-dramatic efforts, so another, *Hiob* (*Job*), helped close out his career. Through Saul's dark destiny Wolfskehl had conveyed his own sense of alienation in a foreign land. Through Job, he poses the eternal questions concerning his own sufferings: blindness, exile, oblivion.

Dionysian intoxication coexists in Wolfskehl's lyrics alongside dark

Germanic brooding, Jewish suffering alongside Jewish hope. They often make for an imponderable mix. More than most, he knew how much he owed to German and Jewish *Geist*.

Like Wolfskehl, **Friedrich Gundolf** (Gundelfinger) (1880–1931) was born in Darmstadt, the son of a professor of mathematics with social and religious interests. A warm friendship linked Wolfskehl to Gundolf until the latter's early death. Gundolf was an enthusiastic patriot in World War I, eliciting from Romain Rolland the acid comment, "Gundolf est un imbécile." He served first at the front, then in the military press corps.

As one of the most influential professors of literary history at Heidelberg in the 1920s, Gundolf propagated the Master's teachings, even after friction developed over George's objections to Gundolf's marriage. This quarrel led to total severance of relations, much to Gundolf's chagrin. A renowned literary historian and critic, Gundolf had come close to dominating German literary studies before his premature death.

Whereas Wolfskehl's Jewishness pulsated in his whole being, Gundolf's was bloodless. A master of wit, he often deployed it at the expense of Jews, their customs, and their religion—but above all, their aspirations to nationhood. His sensitivity to anti-Semitism was such, however, that he rarely indulged in these remarks in public. Like many apologists Gundolf was unhappy about journalistic attention to Jewish matters. In letters to Wolfskehl, however, he could mercilessly mock Wolfskehl's interest in Zionism. The charge of self-hate has but limited validity; Gundolf was simply an uneasy Jew. Yet he remained a Jew and even belonged to the Heidelberg congregation. His self-characterization as an "old pagan" confirms the ambivalence of his position, as did the observations that he wished to serve Shakespeare, not Jehovah.

In the church of Stefan George, Gundolf was dubbed John, Wolfskehl was called Peter, and Friedrich Wolters (often anti-Jewish in his utterances) was Paul. Among the scholars surrounding George, Gundolf was undeniably the most promising. He had a genuine Heinean talent for satire, to which he did not dare to give free rein. His often unreasonable attacks on Heine suggest a form of self-chastisement or at least a conscious effort at distance between his natural proclivities for lightness and charm and the rigid, often ponderous tone of the Georgean cult.

Like other followers, Gundolf remained a hero worshiper. Besides his reverent book on George himself, Gundolf singled out Caesar, Goethe, and Shakespeare as idols. He himself called his Caesar worship a fetish. The Roman represented for this German Jew an exemplary fusion of spirit and action, of will and transcendence. Unlike Napoleon, another man of action, Caesar did not sacrifice harmony or allow himself to be governed by his own demons. He remained human, as ruler, Roman, and classicist. Gundolf recognized in Shakespeare and Goethe the ultimate that literature has produced. In discussing their lives, he attempted less a biography than a recounting of examples of their uniqueness. Gundolf used these great writers as a means of transmitting a view of the world as *Bildungserlebnis* (educational experience).

In line with George's wishes that the disciples accept "regular positions" in academic fields, they made distinctive contributions. **Berthold Vallentin** (1877–1933), a lawyer, wrote a *Napoleon* which, like Gundolf's *Caesar*, smacked of hero worship. Napoleon was a more likely hero for a Jew because the Napoleon cult among German Jews was by no means confined to the young Heine. Vallentin brought the Corsican to life and gave him heroic dimensions. **Edith Landmann** (1877–1951) recorded the Master's pronouncement on a variety of topics. More than others, she addressed many questions to him about Judaism and its practitioners. Her *Transzendenz des Erkennens* (*Transcendence of Knowing*) provided a philosophical extension of George's thought. Conscious thought, she stated, was originally not intended for practical use at all, and pure thought could only be captured in pure poetry, divorced from utilitarian concerns. **Edgar Salin** (1892–?), a political scientist, and **Ernst Morwitz** (1887–?), a literary scholar, provided personal recollections and interpretations of George's verse, respectively.

The most eminent historian of the group, **Ernst Kantorowicz** (1859–1963) is best known for his worshipful study of the Hohenstaufen Emperor Frederic II. Kantorowicz—who, like Morwitz, concluded his academic career in America—had fought with the right-wing Freikorps in Bavaria against the Soviet-style government.

Other scholars and writers who were exposed to the Master's influence were **Erich von Kahler** (1885–1970), **Arthur Salz** (1881–19?), and **Margarete Susman** (1874–19?). They belonged to the circle only briefly or peripherally.

Vera Lewin has provided this explanation for the presence of Jews in the George entourage. For Jews, she maintained, he represented "measure, center, and reality." Those in his group expressed the urge to be "redeemed from individual loneliness" and corroborated their belonging to the intellectual elite of Germany. Above all, they sensed in George's absolute code the "rigor of the Jewish Law."

Clearly, George and his Jews lived together and inspired each other's works. Whereas socialists and Expressionists used German culture as a vehicle for achieving human kinship, especially in socioeconomic and cultural terms, George's Jews benefited from the Master's teachings in an older, yet different way to achieve community with Germany and her culture by plumbing the divine recesses of art.

• • • • •

Editors and Critics

J ewish editors and critics who moved to the forefront between 1900 and 1925 were often harsh and intemperate in their judgments. But they also advanced the careers of men and women who were sounding a new note in German letters. However, in their attempts to become creative artists in their own rights, they were only moderately successful.

Moritz Heimann (1868–1925), the power in the publishing house of S. Fischer, was fictionalized by Jakob Wassermann as Melchior Ghisels in *Der Fall Maurizius* (*The Case of Maurizius*) and lauded by Hauptmann as the conscience of German literature. It was Heimann's unenviable fate to be thought of more as a friend and counselor to the great than as an accomplished writer in his own right.

As editor and critic, Heimann furthered the careers of Hauptmann, Wasserman, Loerke, Stehr, and others. In general, his criterion for literary quality was "proximity to life," which Shakespeare and Goethe possessed among the classical writers, and Tolstoy, Dostoyevski, Ibsen, and Hauptmann exhibited among the contemporaries. He found *Lebensnähe* (closeness to life) in Hauptmann, but little in Paul Heyse, Theodor Fontane, neo-romantics, and borderline realists. He sought fairness for writers, and the polemic spirit so prevalent in Kraus, Harden, and Kerr was missing in this more judicious critic.

He was the son of poor, strictly observant Jews, the only ones in a village of peasants in Brandenburg. A lonely child, he was much given to dreaming. He came to know the peasants and painted them with affection, yet unsentimentally. Julius Bab was to remark that there was nothing of the *Großstadtjude* (big-city Jew) in Heimann and that urbanity and sophistication had passed him by. Heimann began writing as a student in Berlin, and before long he was a reader for Fischer, a position that evolved into that of editor-in-chief and decision maker for the house. He remained in that post until a terminal illness confined him to his home in the early 1920s.

Heimann should be classified with the liberal tradition. Truth for him lay in neither extreme, nor necessarily in the center. There were many intermediate positions between the middle and the extremes of the left or right. He had a keen sense of the possible, which generally guided him on sociopolitical questions. Though an admirer of Bismarck, he was an advocate of citizen participation in the political process. He demanded a strong political commitment on the part of the artist. But politics was more than what was commonly perceived. He called it "the only, or at least the first and most immediate form of *Geist.*"

His fiction lacked imagination but possessed nearly all other virtues. His characters were victims of their limitations, especially in what they expected of themselves and others. He had a clear preference for the active person who errs rather than for the passive individual who never lives. Moreover, what he calls a *Novelle* is often little more than a psychological study.

Jew and Prussian co-existed peaceably in this man. After all the turmoil to which nineteenth-century Jewry had been exposed, Heimann looked upon modern Jews as amorphous and almost undefinable. He deplored the fact that Jews did not even seek to define themselves but allowed others—including anti-Semites—to do the defining for them. Yet he himself assumed the traditional defensive stance when he urged that the Jewish issue be removed from the "combat zone." Jewishness, he believed, should be neither an object of attack by anti-Semites, nor an expression of inordinate pride by overly conscious Jews. In an essay on conversions, Heimann pitied those who escaped from Judaism without having anything better to escape to, especially not to a Christianity in which they believed even less than in Judaism. Should Jews turn to Zionism, the great new hope? While he was not unsympathetic to its aspiration, he believed its greatest value to be the hope it afforded the oppressed Jews of Eastern Europe. He also had personal reservations about Herzl as leader of the movement. Also, would Jews have the talent for maintaining a state, an ability perhaps lost over the centuries, even if a gift of land were made to them? As for himself, he was both hopeful and skeptical. He would have to follow the dual track of German and Jew, a course he deemed wholly compatible, even if he did not underestimate the difficulties involved.

Thus Heimann's Jewishness was a Jewishness without emphasis of any kind. Jewish tradition filled him with a healthy respect, as evidenced by his review of Buber's *Geschichten des Rabbi Nachmann* (*Tales of Rabbi Nachmann*). Contemporary Judaism, with its rampant assimilationism and the emptiness of its rabbis' sermons, left him indifferent at best.

The influence of **Alfred Kerr** (1867–1948) as theater critic was less uniformly benevolent than Heimann's. Kerr could be gentle and charming, but he might also be harsh and sardonic. Kerr had a distinctive talent for the quick, incisive phrase. His style often seemed jerky and nervous, as though he needed to rush on to the next idea. Though Karl Kraus, Kerr's bitter foe, satirized Kerr's writing, Kerr was equally unimpressed with Kraus's, in spite of the latter's reputation as a master of the German language. Their witticisms at each other's expense lacked taste and hardly offered exalting entertainment.

Kerr often praised the work of men he personally disliked and castigated that of authors he admired. Still, he could be cruelly unjust and ugly, as demonstrated by his cheap revelation of the affair of a police commissioner with the actress Tilla Durieux. Mainly a theater critic, Kerr deprecated this art as secondary and justified it only when it was integrated into a broader view of life. He quickly stripped a play of its false trappings, sought a meaningful core of *Lebensnähe,* and then proceeded to delineate the individuality of actors and actresses. Elizabeth Bergner and Albert Bassermann were the prime recipients of his interest.

An inveterate traveler, Kerr was away from his desk for three to four months a year. He had full command of several languages—later he was to write in both French and English—which helped him to write travel books, for which his style and outlook seemed especially well suited. He was an effective interpreter of other cultures. Max Brod greatly preferred Kerr the travel reporter to Kerr the theater critic.

Though of the moderate left, Kerr volunteered for the Kaiser's army. He even wrote patriotic war poems. In subsequent years, Kerr claimed that he supported Germany in the war but was opposed to the war itself. After the war he was greatly dismayed by the failure of the new republic to assert itself. Again and again he chided it, though not destructively *à la* Tucholsky, chiefly for its failure to deal incisively with Hitler and others intent on its demise.

Kerr gives an animated account of his trip to Palestine in 1903 in *Die Welt im Licht* (*The World under Scrutiny*). He entitled the segment "Jerusholaim" and announced that he would approach his account from the vantage of the insider. Tears welled up in him, he writes, as he espied the Palestinian coast: "There, there before me, rises the land of the Jews." He is struck by a strong, vigorous Jew who assists him, a blond man in his forties. Was he seeing in the ancient land a more noble human type than the Diaspora Jew in Berlin? The land itself is infinitely rich, and every plant and flower evokes biblical memories. "Samson and Bar Kochbar, bold and strong" receive him at the gate of the ancestral land and remind him of the wondrous, unbowed people, "burned, martyred, oppressed, slain—but above extinction." This ancient people, he says, is really the most liberal and open, though it is also the newest and youngest after two thousand years of history.

Kerr believed that the Jewish contribution had been dimmed, nearly lied out of existence by enemies over the centuries. But it survived just the same. How foolish and narrow are those who painted portraits of Aryan glory and Jewish infamy! Where are their uniqueness, their strength, and their moral vision! When Kerr touches the Wailing Wall, a powerful longing overcomes him.

Max Brod was interested in Kerr, in part because of their common enmity toward Kraus. Brod had doubts about Kerr's brand of German-ness and Jewishness. He was especially suspicious of Kerr's stress on the Jewish contribution to civilization. According to Brod, Kerr wrote as though it were his task to instruct the Germans how quickly or slowly they should go forward. He was not a *"praeceptor Germaniae,"* for this was not a proper task for a Jew. If Kerr did, indeed, assume this role, he was the antithesis of his friend Rathenau, who believed Jews had nothing to teach and everything to learn from the superior Germans.

Also a theater critic and an historian of drama—as well as a director of the Lessing Theater—**Arthur Eloesser** (1870–1914) studied under the anti-Semitic historian Heinrich von Treitschke. He was disappointed not only in Treitschke's view but also in his lack of method. Abandoning history, Eloesser turned to drama. When his *Das deutsche bürgerliche Drama im 18. und 19. Jahrhundert* (*German Middle Class Drama of the Eighteenth and Nineteenth Centuries*) was well received, Eloesser considered an academic career. But it still required baptism, a step he rejected outright. The academic approach never disappeared entirely from his criticism, a drawback for reviews that appeared in the daily press, mostly the *Vossische Zeitung* (*Voss Newspaper*). After 1933 and before his emigration he contributed frequently to the *Jüdische Rundschau* (*Jewish Review*).

Ephraim Frisch (1880–1957), a creative artist in his own right, was a discoverer of new talent. He promoted the reputation of Leo Perutz, Felix Braun, Kasimir Edschmidt, and even Brecht.

Frisch had his early education in the chederim and yeshivas of Galicia and completed his formal studies at the University of Kiel. His work is characterized by an unusual diversity of knowledge. As an editor, he was open to the new and the old, the conservative and the radical. He considered himself—and was, in fact—a moderate who supported the German position in World War I. It has been suggested that he needed to dispel any suspicion that one reared in a non-German environment might show insufficient loyalty to the Kaiser and *Vaterland.* Eventually, he was to denounce the war as inhuman and divisive.

A wide-ranging essayist, he could not shake off the influence of that genre from his attempts at fiction, represented in the main by *Zenobi* (1927), a surrealist Kafkaesque work. (A work of great promise, "Gog and Magog," was frequently interrupted by illness and left incomplete at his death.) The main character of *Zenobi* was "an actor, but no artist, a confidence-man, but no criminal, a knight but no hero." "Die Legende von Kuty" ("Legend of Kuty"), set in a *shtetl* (one of the former Jewish village communities in Eastern Europe), was originally intended as a prologue to "Gog and Magog" but can surely stand on its own merit. Those who read "Gog and Magog" (see Rev. 20:8; biblical personification of the nations that, under Satan, are to wage war against the kingdom of God) in manuscript thought it had the potential of becoming *the* Jewish novel of our time and Wolf Brandes, the protagonist, a Jewish Hans Castorp, the representative, "healthy" bourgeois protagonist in Thomas Mann's *Der Zauberberg* (*The Magic Mountain*).

His Galician childhood inculcated into him a sense of Jewish life known to only a handful of writers. His "Legend of Kuty" is steeped in Jewish suffering and messianic hope. Rabbi Mosche exclaims, "Woe, oh woe, this generation is too weak to receive the Messiah." Whereas most German-Jewish writers knew of Jewish external relations, Frisch also knew the internal workings.

When all is said and done, the fact remains that Frisch viewed most questions from the standpoint of the universalist. It was only after Hitler's assumption of power that Jewish questions absorbed his attention more than others. Frisch was another writer whom the Nazis reconverted into a Jew.

As a British subject **Monty (Montague) Jacobs** found himself in some difficulty at the outbreak of World War I. He became naturalized and entered the service of a kaiser he disliked. After the war he served the *Vossische Zeitung* (*Voss Newspaper*) in various capacities. In 1939 he emigrated to England, his father's home country.

His book-length studies—*Maeterlinck* (1901), the first in German on the Belgian symbolist; an edition of the works of Achim von Arnim (1908); and an edition of Johann Peter Eckermann's *Gespräche mit Goethe* (*Conversations with Goethe*) (1913)—exhibit little literary focus. Jacobs was a moderate and tolerant critic, formal to the point of reticence, open to persuasion. He was a German version of the British gentleman. A major achievement was his advice to Ullstein, in the 1920s, to publish Erich

Maria Remarque's *Im Westen nichts Neues* (*All Quiet on the Western Front*) (1929). Unlike Heimann and Kerr, he favored subjective literature and the presence of a strong individuality and a distinctly personal language.

Restraint also marked his Jewish attitudes. He never denied his Jewish origin, but he did not make much of it. He disapproved when Arnold Zweig's *Die Sendung Semaels* (*Semael's Mission*) was called a "Jewish tragedy." Tragedies were indivisible; they could not be Jewish or Christian, German or English. While conceding to Jews a common racial basis, he placed the natural and cultural awareness of being German above the blood ties of Jewishness.

Although most influential critics were centrist in their views and supported the German war effort, this was not true of **Herwarth Walden** (1878–194?) (Georg Levin). As editor of the Expressionist vehicle *Der Sturm* (*The Storm*), he provided a forum for innovators in any art medium. A *Verein* (fraternity) Walden established had participants of the stature of the Mann Brothers, Döblin, Lasker-Schüler (whom he married), and Wedekind. To protect the "artistic integrity" of his authors, Walden often fought battles on their behalf with publishers, over both content and finances.

While his interests included all the arts, Walden's own greatest competence was in music. Then, rather suddenly, Walden abandoned music and the other arts for the sake of socioeconomic causes. In the 1920s he became as committed a communist as he had previously been a champion of the muses.

In 1932 he emigrated to the Soviet Union, which, even as Mother Russia, had caught his fancy. But just as cosmopolitan Berlin had disillusioned him with its gradual Nazification, so before long Moscow became a source of disenchantment. Stalin's ideas on art differed radically from his own. Although he withdrew dutifully from argument, only occasionally contributing an article to *Das Wort* (*The Word*), it was not enough for the Soviet potentates. Even as director of a language school he fell into disfavor. In 1941 the Stalinist police arrested him, and he was never heard from again.

The only religions Walden cultivated were those of art and radical socialism. He detested nationalism and ethnic identities—whether Jewish, German, or Russian. Only the world could claim his full allegiance.

Also a universalist critic, **Siegfried Jacobsohn** (1881–1927) was more radical in his positions than were Heimann, Kerr, Jacobs, and others. He was fearless, an aggressor-apologist who ruffled the feathers of generals, industrialists, and professional patriots. He transformed the highly regarded *Schaubühne* (local theater), once wholly devoted to theater, into the *Weltbühne* (world theater), with vastly expanded concerns. By daring to publish exposés of illegal rearmaments and the resurgence of the military, he managed to attract both controversy and enmity. Under the later brief editorship of Kurt Tucholsky and that of the tragic Carl von Ossietsky, the *Weltbühne* was to take on an even more radical complexion.

At age twenty, Jacobsohn was invited to review plays for *Welt am Montag (World on Monday)*. Although his youthful critiques were very stinging, Jacobsohn nevertheless won the respect of older critics like Paul Schlenther and Arthur Eloesser. However, the people Jacobsohn had hurt were waiting for his first mistake. The moment came when he was accused of plagiarizing a few lines, a fact he attributed to his exceptional memory. At twenty-three, he seemed a has-been.

As a critic, Jacobsohn leaned toward the experimental and looked upon the likes of Brahm as heroes of a bygone day. Brahm was hopelessly *démodé* in this postwar period. A good theater needed new authors, new themes and viewpoints; the young critic found them in the works of Wedekind and Strindberg and in the staging of Reinhardt. He was disrespectful toward the Expressionists, with some exceptions.

When the war altered the face of Europe, Jacobsohn demanded a new substance and image for Germany. From the first, he endorsed the new republic, but like many of his contributors he was critical of many facets. Unlike Tucholsky, he never lost sight of the fact that, in spite of numerous shortcomings, the new regime constituted a positive advancement.

It was less as a Jew than as world citizen that Jacobsohn demanded an end to attacks on them. The fact that the enemies of the Jews were also his enemies as a writer made his defense of Jews appear more authentic and convincing.

• • • • •

Women Writers

The salon hostesses of the early nineteenth century had a significant impact on the nexus between German and Jew. They achieved it by stressing their *Deutschtum,* which at that time inevitably meant a diminution of their *Judentum.* Nearly all converted, and one or two skirted the boundary of self-hate.

Among the women who were born in the nineteenth century, but lived well into the twentieth, two—**Else Lasker-Schüler** and **Gertrud Kolmar**—were not only poets of the first order, but richly utilized Judaic traditions in their artistic expression. Lasker-Schüler died in Jerusalem during World War II; Kolmar, hindered by an ailing father in her plan to leave Berlin, never managed to leave the city. She was deported to the East and died in an extermination camp.

The women writers were aware that they were doubly oppressed, both as Jews and as women. In their ethnic battle the Jew in them often yielded to the German. In their sexual struggle, they were destined to remain female. As women they knew there were millions and millions of other women similarly dominated by men. But there were fewer Jews with whom to share their burden of ethnic oppression.

Throughout the nineteenth century, male Jewish writers and female Christian authors knew that they were bound together by the bond of oppressed status. George Eliot wrote about the problems of Jews in *Daniel Deronda.* Though George Sand wrote only rarely about Jews, she wrote frequently about other oppressed groups—to wit, workers and peasants. Like Jews, women writers—whatever their origin—could not always write naturally or spontaneously any more than Jews could. While Jews worried about being too Jewish and not German enough, women were fearful of appearing aggressive, unfeminine, and male. Women writers realized that dominated status involved a degree of role playing and assumed hypocrisies.

The heroines of **Anselma Heine** (1855–1930) have typically feminine occupations but occasionally question the superiority of those who employ them. She was aware that writing made her, in a sense, special; after all, she was close to Arthur Eloesser and met Ibsen and Nietzsche.

In her writings, Heine's younger women often try vainly to instruct their mothers in new modes of conduct. Much of her fiction has foreign settings.

Doris Wittner's (1880–1937) most revealing novel deals with Heinrich Heine's relationship to his "mouche," *Die Geschichte der kleinen Fliege* (*The Story of the Little Fly*) (1915). She depicts the great poet as pleasant, loving, and more sinned against than sinning. Wittner emphasises Heinrich Heine's awareness of the greatness of Jewish tradition. She is effective in reconstructing his visit to Frankfurt's *Judenstadt* ("Jew Town"). For her, Heine is a true artist, too free and critical to stay with any single cause. Wittner attributes Heine's feud with Börne to Heine's many-faceted nature in conflict with the fanatical single-mindedness of Börne.

Wittner's book appeared during the war. Of course, a book on Heinrich Heine in wartime, published against a backdrop of well-fanned flames of nationalism, called for extreme caution. Therefore, in her introduction she makes the poet more German than he was. "Hot German blood was coursing through his veins. . . ." Then she gives a hint of felt constraint: "May the German people, under the sign of the *Burgfrieden* (truce), finally see this poet in the light of true understanding, without idealization. If the German people could see him in this fashion, their sense of justice would be honoring not Heine, but the German people [themselves]." The *mouche*, for her part, appears as a self-confident, emancipated woman who offers the great poet warmth and solace in his mattress grave.

The humorous and once popular **Alice Berendt** (Alice Hertz) (1875–1938) achieved her effects by offering caricatures of bourgeois types, particularly their predilection for social climbing. Especially in her later life, she also dealt compassionately with serious issues like poverty and unemployment. While *Die Bräutigame der Babette Bomberling* (*The Fiancés of Babette Bomberling*) (1914) is representative of her first period, *Rücksicht auf Marta* (*Taking Care of Marta*) is typical of her later writing.

Berendt demonstrated her own independence by becoming a foreign correspondent and by living in Italy for many years. After 1935, she made Italy her permanent home.

Even more sprightly are the novels of Lorraine-born **Adrienne Thomas** (1897–1980), whose women are between cultures and animosities and are also caught up in the games of sex. Her heroines see through the Franco-German tensions that disturbed their youth. Their thinking is independent enough to peel off layer after layer of lies and hypocrisy in the beliefs and actions of adults.

These writers are clearly second-raters, significant only because they represent fiction by women trying to gain a foothold on a literary scene dominated by men. They must take a back seat to **Else Lasker-Schüler** (1869–1945), who has been justly regarded as the foremost German-Jewish poet since Heine. Karl Kraus and Gottfried Benn, among others, have praised her highly as a lyrical "phenomenon." Her imagery was boldly innovative and her idiom provocatively different. But her work also breached that thin line that separates neurosis from psychosis. It often brings to mind the willful child who never quite reached maturity but then surprises with the power of knowledge and insight.

If a childhood of love holds the key to a healthy adult life, then Lasker-Schüler should have led a life of emotional well-being. Her father possessed the wit to make her laugh, and her mother displayed qualities the daughter was to praise in numerous lyrics. Was her childhood, in fact, so happy that upon reaching adulthood she still longed for its shelter and security? Neither her first marriage to the physician Lasker, nor her second to Herwarth Walden, nor her many affairs offered the satisfaction and beauties she remembered from her childhood home. Perhaps the single exception was her liaison with the vagabond poet Peter Hille, a brief idyll which ended with his premature death. She enshrined his memory in her *Peter Hille Buch* (*Peter Hille Book*). Lasker-Schüler had a son, born out of wedlock; she bestowed on the sickly youngster all the maternal affection that she herself had received.

Upon the collapse of her marriage to Walden, she embarked on a nomadic hotel life and café hopping. Beset by increasing poverty, she lived outlandishly, dressed bizarrely, and invented names for her literary friends. Karl Kraus became the "Dalai Lama" or "The Cardinal," though one letter, full of praise and affection, ended abruptly with "I hate you." Exile after 1933 hardly changed her ways. She first emigrated to Switzerland, then increasingly "heard the call of the Jordan" and traveled several times to Palestine. Eventually she took up permanent residence in Jerusalem. There are descriptions of her stalking the ancient city, dressed quaintly, her hair disheveled. On occasion, she collected herself sufficiently to give poetry readings. She kept writing up to her final days.

From her first to her last volumes, her themes were loneliness, escape, faith, and hope. The poems were enveloped in a world of wonders, of Mediterranean and Oriental colors and scents, or imaginary adventures reminiscent of the *Arabian Nights*. This variegated, private world mixed Jewish mythical elements with others of Germanic, Egyptian, and Christian origin. In this universe of a distraught adult who was bereft of attachments but not of memories, the poet yearned for new human contacts and outlets for her love-filled self. Increasingly she took refuge in a world of dreams. The voices she heard created visions of the apocalypse to come. When her *Arthur Aronymus* was initially performed in Zurich, Ernst Ginsberg wrote that few in the audience suspected that the poet's dream-anxieties were about to become reality.

Lasker-Schüler's religiosity, including her Judaism, was intensely personalized. From her *Hebräische Balladen* (*Hebrew Ballads*) (1920) to her final works, her poems about Abraham and Isaac, Jacob and Esau, Moses and Joshua (she often dealt in biblical twosomes) bear only a superficial resemblance to biblical accounts. Similarly, her fantasy rabbis of "Der Wunder Rabbi von Barcelona" ("The Marvelous Rabbi of Barcelona") and of *Arthur Aronymus* are creatures of her playful and often humorous imagination. Historical truth yields in her work to the dictates of personal needs. Lasker-Schüler is fascinated with Hasidism and kabbala, but again one apprehends the poet rather than movement or text. Her religious needs are felt, as is her appreciation of their artistic usefulness to her. Jewish tradition is more the poet's tool than her source or objective.

Priority words in her vocabulary are time, heart, conciliation, and Jerusalem. Time represents the transient, the ephemeral, the insignificant, and the material. Being qualified with time suggests rotting and victimization. To time she opposes the eternal, the quest for the one and only God. She evinces a special fondness for the *shmah* because this call and prayer symbolize the everlasting. The heart elicits positive responses, connoting the reaching out for the eternal. Distraught and nervous during her last years, the poet wailed increasingly about the divisions within her, the noisy battles between *ich* and *ich*. Finally, the idea of conciliation in her poems evokes such images as rabbi and bishop sitting down at a table and breaking bread together.

Although she frequently alludes to pogroms, which she calls timeless and placeless, she clings to the hope that meetings of Christian and Jew, German and Jew, will someday materialize. Even as the cataclysm approached, she did not forsake this hope. For her, Jerusalem epitomized the gate to Heaven, the antechamber to God, the saintliest place on earth. Jerusalem was godliness and timelessness and the keeping of the promise of heart and conciliation.

Lasker-Schüler was that rare phenomenon of her time, the apolitical writer. Even when she wrote her early social drama *Die Wupper* (from the name of a river), she had neither reformist nor socialist intent. She merely painted the dehumanizing and hence ungodly ways to which the machine had subjected the workers. She trotted out three characters, abandoned by God and man alike, to whom, in this non-dramatic drama, she extends her hand in sympathy and compassion.

Palestine never meant to her a potential conflict between Jew and Arab. Nor had it much to do with colonialism or Zionism. She could only think of the *Hebräerland* (land of the Hebrews) and of the *Bibelland* (land of the Bible). The Hebrews and the Bible were timeless, their nation was the land beyond lands. Far from a political issue, Palestine is a revelation that burns men's souls. The pioneers settling here were seeking not gold but God. They are eager to be near the Wailing Wall where, if one listens intently, one can hear whispers of wisdom.

At times, Lasker-Schüler indulges herself by assuming oriental rather than biblical identities. Her canvases become a veritable potpourri of colors. Other poems take her back to Berlin, where she plays out her love-hate relationship to the city. When she came increasingly under financial strain, she published everything in newer collections, including—indiscriminately—poems and essays, autobiographical vignettes, and biographical sketches.

Lasker-Schüler belongs to the *poètes maudits,* those poets who suffered grievously for the uniqueness of their vision. Like George Sand before her, Lasker-Schüler loved scandalously. About the erotic, she wrote that "the physical act out of which the human being is born is sometimes so impossible that it is justified only when two people, out of sheer love, cannot help but engage in it." It is remarkable that this Bohemian child-woman, with her wild humor, boundless imagination, and grotesque life-style, should have written some of the finest verse about a religious tradition that is rocklike in its consistency.

Whereas adversity nearly brought Lasker-Schüler to the brink of insanity, it generated new strength in the quietly attractive figure of **Gertrud Kolmar** (1894–1943). To judge by the biographical facts available and her letters to her sister, Kolmar possessed enormous inner resources. She was a remarkably forthright person, sensitive and receptive to new ideas. She knew what needed to be done and was prepared to do it. While all about her was crumbling in the fateful years from 1940 to 1943, she sensed that events were pushing her inexorably toward the abyss.

First she had to abandon the house in which she had grown up, secure and loved. The Nazis transferred her and her ailing father to "Jew houses," the beginnings of a new ghetto. A very private person, Kolmar had to live in crowded apartments, to eat and sleep with many. She relates her anguish as old people vanish into nowhere and are replaced by new ones who will soon share the same uncertain fate. She tells of having to work in a factory with its stultifying routine. She looks upon everything as educational rather than painful, and she feels new strength welling up within her. She distinguishes between outer and inner acceptance. Though her nerves are tensed to the breaking point, she refuses to yield to despair.

She sees herself as a person apart in the factory and she knows that others perceive her similarly. She also notices that the emotionally tarnished are drawn to her, perhaps because she intuitively knows their needs. She is both shocked and elated by her encounters at forty-eight with a young man of only twenty-two. She is angry only once, and then by the shoddy taste of a woman who puts crosses on walls all about her.

Kolmar, whose real name was Chodziesner, spent most of her life in Berlin. She was a cousin of Walter Benjamin and spent many hours at his home. Her father, a distinguished lawyer, had played a leading role in the famed Eulenburg Case. As a child she was more interested in animals than in toys; she studied English and French—which she later taught—then Russian, and, toward the end of her life, Hebrew. The memory of her one great love—the lover is never identified—nourished her for the remainder of her life. The abandoned and childless woman looms large in her work, as do children generally.

Kolmar dealt more frankly than most women writers with eroticism and female sexuality. Nearly one hundred poems focus on women at different stages of their lives—as girls, lovers, mature persons, and old adults. The women are mostly independent persons, giving and humane. Even where they seem outwardly dependent, they remain inwardly free. Kolmar's love poems extend beyond male-female relationships to love of nature, the earth, and the hapless creatures inhabiting it, especially children and animals. From there it is but one step to an equally gentle love for the people from whom she issued and who are suffering once more.

She trembles for Jews, their anguish in history. She rejoices in their survival after endless threats to eradicate them. Just as in her dreams she could identify with the abandoned women of history—e.g., Napoleon's Walewska—she can also transform herself into a Jewish woman of bygone days. In "A Jewish Woman" (*Eine Mutter,* 1965; re-titled *Eine jüdische Mutter,* 1978) she writes, "I was there before great Rome and Carthage were, because in me the altar fires ignite/of Deborah and her tribe." She likens persecuted Jews to towers that God has let fall into ruin, yet which stand for ages. In "Wir Juden" ("We Jews") she whispers as to a lover, "Ich liebe dich, ich liebe dich, mein Volk,/ Und will dich ganz mit Armen umschlingen heiß und fest." ("I love you, I love you, my people/And want to embrace you firmly and fervently.") And while other nations were able to develop freely, actively, and normally, Israel suffered a martyr's torment and death. Sensing the worst is yet to come, she speaks to Israel, vowing to arise and "stand like a triumphal arch above your cavalcade of anguish":

> I will not kiss the arm that wields the weighty scepter,
> Nor the brazen knee, the earthen feet of demigods in
>   desperate hours;
> If only I could raise my voice to be a blazing torch
> Amid the darkened desert of the word, and thunder
>   JUSTICE!   JUSTICE!   JUSTICE!

Yet the end is near, and she knows it. She feels "the fist that drags my weeping head toward the hill of ashes."

Death also ends Kolmar's novellas. In *Eine Mutter* (*A Mother*), a Berlin Jew, Martha Judassohn, is terribly withdrawn. She weds a Christian engineer whose father had warned him that Martha looks like an Old Testament Jewess. Only sexual attraction unites them. When he leaves her upon the birth of a daughter, she is forced to leave the child with a neighbor. One day the child is missing; eventually, she is found, the victim of a rape. Martha's schemes at revenge fail, and her life collapses. This is a cruel story, repeating the motifs of the abandoned child, the sexually savage woman, the fierce mother.

In the quiet, poetic *Susanna,* Kolmar broadens her range. Here a tutor, much like Kolmar herself, helps a mentally disturbed child who loves animals. Susanna believes her pet harbors the soul of King David or King Saul. The youngster is glad she is Jewish. "You, too?" she asks the tutor, who confesses that she has almost forgotten her origin. Susanna instructs her tutor. "Every book, I was told, had to be read from the first page on. The Bible is the only exception. It you can open anywhere because it is the word of God." A young Jew, as misshapen in body as she is in mind, falls in love with her, but she prefers a mysterious Herr Rubin. In an attempt to follow him, Susanna dies.

Kolmar's intense love of history led her to the controversial figure of Robespierre. Her study unveils a keen understanding of the dynamics of revolutionary action and a deep sympathy for the oppressed, who can achieve change only through drastic means. Her involvement with Russia is not necessarily related to the Soviet Revolution, though also not wholly divorceable from it.

In spite of the relative paucity of her production, Gertrud Kolmar merits a place commensurate with that of greater poets. She created a universe of her own in which kindness, justice, boldness, and honesty played a most admirable role.

•   •   •   •   •

Uneasy Assimilators

F rom the 1840s to the Jew debates of the 1870s, the road to assimilation seemed relatively unobstructed. Occasional rebuffs or implied pressures to prove their German-ness notwithstanding, those Jews who wanted to enter the mainstream of German culture could do so. However, after 1880, new waves of anti-Semitism caused some of the more radical reactions already discussed, from self-deprecation and self-hatred on the one hand to total defiance, disinterest, or Zionism on the other.

Other writers were emerging, mostly born in the 1870s or 1880s, who opted for a clearly assimilatory course, but then had occasion—at different times—to wonder about the wisdom of this choice. Casting their lot with Germany and trying to help to make her a better nation did not seem appreciated. Whatever they did, they were still seen as aliens and interlopers.

Georg Hermann (Georg Hermann Borchardt) (1871–1943) wrote novels that commanded attention in their time and still merit respect in ours. Among them are his "Jewish novels": *Jettchen Gebert* (1906)—indisputably his masterpiece—and its less impressive sequel, *Henriette Jacoby* (1908). Other works of distinction were *Die Nacht des Dr. Herzfeld* (*The Strange Night of Dr. Herzfeld*) (1912), a novel of alienation, and *Kubinke* (1910), the story of a Berlin coiffeur. *Der Rosenemil* (*Rosy Emil*) (1935) was written when Hermann was already in exile. Numerous other works failed to attain the standards of his better earlier fiction.

Hermann was an undistinguished student until courses in the *beaux arts* opened a new world for him. He had to earn a livelihood, however, and art offered little hope in that regard. Still, he kept studying it with a focus on the Berlin of the *Biedermeier* era. Not only did he produce *Das Biedermeier im Spiegel seiner Zeit* (*Biedermeier as a Mirror of Its*

Times), but the period also served as backdrop for *Jettchen Gebert,* one of the very few worthwhile family novels in the history of German-Jewish letters.

The novel was probably begun in 1896 but not published until 1906. It was set in a period about seventy years earlier. The Geberts (an actual name in the author's ancestry) are a tightly-knit clan, stable and rooted, knowing the difference between right and wrong, their obligations to one another and the outside world. But not all are lovable. They have their foibles, especially on the female side. The males are successful business-men, wholly honorable, compassionate, and supportive of each other. The youngest brother is Jason, secretly in love with his niece Jettchen. He is the family intellectual, approved and accepted despite this "flaw." His friend, the Gentile writer, Dr. Koseler, loves Jettchen, too, and she loves him. Nevertheless, she has been promised to young Jacoby, a businessman from the Eastern provinces. He is uncultured, unrefined, hardly the man Jettchen should marry. Yet she does marry him. The union is not consummated; Jettchen flees into the night.

The Geberts of Berlin have a considerable distaste for the Jacobys in the Polish border area. They are without *Bildung*; their business practices are sharper, less honorable, their language is laced with jargon, their manners uncouth. The Jacobys have never heard of Heine, a contemporary of theirs. The oldest Gebert indulges in Yiddishisms, too. His first twenty years coincided, after all, with the dismantling of the ghetto—they cover the last twenty years in the life of Moses Mendels-sohn.

This story of a Jewish family barely out of the ghetto contains virtually no references to Jewish practices, not even to the High Holy Days. But Jettchen and Uncle Jason jointly attend a Christmas celebra-tion. (The same absence of Jewish practice—but perhaps not of feeling—holds true in the sequel, *Henriette Jacoby,* which recounts Jettchen's affair with Dr. Koseler, the effects of which lead to her suicide.)

The Geberts have quickly adapted to German life. Though the word Jew is hardly mentioned in the two books, theirs is a distinctly Jewish family. But this is communicated by means of inner intangibles rather than by external signs. Anti-Semitism is mostly absent from both novels, as is concern with intermarriage.

The protagonist of *Die Nacht des Dr. Herzfeld* is as deracinated as the Geberts are rooted. Hans Kohn has characterized the actions of the hero as "the last disguise in which Ahasuerus, in his endless metamor-phoses, appears to us." Herzfeld's outsider status must be attributed in part to the distance between his current self and his presumed origins.

Hermann, however, was not attempting to demonstrate a thesis. Herzfeld's urban companion, a Christian, is suffering only slightly less from the pangs of urban uprootedness. Herzfeld's Jewish heroes, especially after 1923, become more consciously Jewish.

In an essay Hermann admitted that Jewish problems had not existed for him before the war, emerging only in the early 1920s. Though his Jewish characters move closer to center stage, Arthur Sakheim's view that he could easily visualize Hermann in the company of Leopold Zunz, Samuel Holdheim, Edward Gans, or Ludwig Philippson seems terribly exaggerated. Only the growing awareness of hatred of Jews, of non-acceptance, forced Jewish life on him, even in artistic terms.

Culturally, Hermann envisaged little conflict between being a German and being a Jew. Religiously, he confessed, "in precisely the spot where the religious organ is supposed to be, there exists in me a huge gap. . . . All concepts on which a religion is built are incomprehensible to me." While Judaism did not interest him, he denounced Christianity as the "destroyer of classical antiquity" and as "one of the great misfortunes that could befall the world." The young Hermann also opposed the emerging Zionism. Yet by 1919 this antipathy had weakened. If Zionism was a haven for persecuted Eastern Jews and offered a spiritual-cultural center for Jews all over the world, it had to occupy a place he could respect.

He had always held onto his Judaism, he wrote. Though he had previously worn it "as a vest under his jacket," he now wore it *over* his jacket. Hostility toward Jews had steered him toward a more consciously Jewish attitude. When Martin Buber published a special issue of *Der Jude* in 1925, in which prominent Jews and non-Jews discussed "die Judenfrage" ("the Jewish question"), Hermann was horrified by what he read. If the Jewish situation looked that way to Aryans whose humanity was above suspicion, what would it be like in the minds of others?

He now felt impelled to refute false impressions. German Jews *were* an integral part of the German people, entitled to live in Germany as much as any other group. Jews were *not* the materialists they were made out to be, but a people who had given Europe her basic laws, religion, theater, journalism, and many literary traditions. They were *Erlöser* (redeemers) and revolutionaries and had provided outstanding examples of self-sacrifice for ideas. Hermann rejected the notion that Judaism was a burden to Jews; instead Jews honored and respected the Jewishness in them as it lent support and security to their *Lebensgefühl* (sense of life).

This defense was in response to attack. Nevertheless, no matter how defensive he sounded, Hermann could not become an ethnocentric Jew any more than he could ever be a German nationalist. Intense group loyalty was foreign to him, and he was content to be German and Jew in one frame. That was his choice, if he had one. But he was becoming more and more aware that he would not be given this option. The German humanistic tradition, he concluded, that of Goethe-Schiller-Herder, was less firmly entrenched than he had thought. Germans were proving to be poor keepers of the seal of humanity. When he wrote these skeptical words, he did not anticipate the barbarism that would engulf Germany a decade later and of which he was to become a victim.

There was much controversy about the literary worth of **Jakob Wassermann** (1873–1934). Some placed him alongside Thomas Mann. Lion Feuchtwanger dubbed him a German Dostoyevski. Still others viewed him as a mere entertainer who craved cheap popularity by translating news stories into fiction. Oskar Loerke curtly dismissed *Christian Wahnschaffe* (*The World's Illusion*) (1918) as pure *Kitsch*.

Some of Wassermann's troubles lay in the fact that he aspired to more than he could deliver. Also there ran through his novels a romantic streak that seemed at variance with their somber nature, thereby creating an inner dissonance. None of this detracted from the fact that Wassermann was an interesting and exciting—though by no means easy—storyteller.

While critics could never quite decide whether he was a metaphysical writer, a social critic, a romantic, or even a radical moralist, Jewish readers were often equally puzzled. Some thought that his Jewishness constituted the primordial source from which all else derived. Others have just as vigorously minimized any Jewish influences on his work. The fact remains, however, that Wassermann broached the dilemma of German and Jew more directly than most writers.

Until his mid-twenties, Wassermann was a wretchedly unhappy young man. An unsuccessful father and a none-too-loving stepmother created an uncongenial home atmosphere. After many quarrels Jakob was shipped off to an uncle in Vienna who briefly showed him some understanding and also gave him a job. The experiment in business was short-lived. Wassermann now wandered through Germany, unsure of his next meal or lodging. Hurling himself into the fray of Schwabing's Bohemia failed to end his depression. Some stability reentered his life when he became amanuensis to Ernst von Wolzogen. From there he graduated to a minor editorial post with *Simplizissimus,* where Thomas Mann was his co-worker.

His first novel, *Die Juden von Zirndorf* (*The Jews of Zirndorf*) (1897), presaged his literary characteristics: a heavy and ponderous style, a proclivity for mystery, uncommon names for his characters, and a sense of timing for unraveling his mystery. Both then and later his heroes were young and solitary men, deeply tormented and functioning outside the mainstream of society. They gain strength as the story unfolds, though they move tortuously toward a climax. Wassermann's greatest weakness is the intrusion into the narrative of essays and ideas that interrupt its smooth flow.

The early novels, among them also *Caspar Hauser* (1908) and *Das Gänsemännchen* (*The Little Goose Man*) (1915) already encapsule future themes: evil, suffering, indifference to the lot of others, justice or the lack of it, illusion and reality—and above all, the incapacity to feel. *Caspar Hauser* is Wassermann's fictionalized account of the real-life tragedy of the animal-like seventeen-year-old who appeared out of nowhere in Nürnberg in 1828. How this youngster, believed to have been the illegitimate offspring of a royal house, was maltreated by different people for different reasons—and eventually murdered—makes suspenseful and thoughtful reading. In *Das Gänsemännchen,* Wassermann offers a middle-class family portrait at the turn of the century. His artist-hero struggles to survive in the face of a hostile society and its contradictory demands. The hero has been dreaming of transcending the egomania that is flourishing all about him. Trying to surmount it, he is nearly destroyed by it.

Christian Wahnschaffe, a mammoth two-volume novel, was widely translated, but it diluted Wassermann's reputation at home. Written during the war, it has a fairy-tale effect, as the rich young man of the title divests himself of his wealth to live with the poor and neglected. The novel reflects the influence of Buddha and Tolstoy, but Christian is also the Expressionists' New Man, who fights the generational battle and destroys all his father, an industrialist, has stood for, as well as his own youth and upbringing. In his search for meaning and values, Christian and others often seem posturing, histrionic—in short, unconvincing.

Wassermann created many Jewish characters, but only *Die Juden von Zirndorf* can be called a Jewish novel. In the myth-laden prologue with its rich colors, Jews respond to the exciting news that a Messiah has arisen in faraway Smyrna. They are jubilant that this Messiah, Sabbatai Zvi by name, has come to end centuries of torments and that now, at last, the return to Jerusalem will be possible. The caravan sets out for the East. En route, the Jews encounter a returning group, who conveys the dreadful message that the Messiah has once again proven to be false. For a fleeting moment the near realization of the ancient dream had transported them into unknown regions of joy, in the process loosening old and confining bonds. They turn around, go back to their native region, and settle in what they ironically call *Zionsdorf* (Zion village), a term soon to evolve into Zirndorf.

Two hundred years later, the descendants of the original pilgrims find Zirndorf in a state of disintegration. The hero of the novel, Agathon Geyer, a man of kindness and heart, has severed all ties with the ghetto. The old religion strikes him as ossified and unrelated to life. Agathon will not deny his blood ties to Jews, but he pines for absorption into the German community.

Geyer thinks about his fellow Jews. They lack self-assurance, tremble at the thought of the future, and think they are hopelessly exposed to danger. Agathon's father, Elkan Geyer, is an anxiety-ridden man. Opposing this mentality is the patriarchal Gedalja, a man of pride and unconquerable spirit, unbending, but also unbent by the blows administered by God and Christians. On the Gentile side, Wassermann gives us the writer Gudstikker, who approves of individual Jews but deplores their collective power. He rejects their acceptance as a group as well as their demands for equality.

Wassermann examines his Jews physically, psychologically, and morally. The red-haired messenger of the "Prologue" has "Jewish eyes"; they are full of restlessness, haste, inner discord, vague supplication, and suppressed warmth. These eyes are "now glowing with passion, now losing it in melancholy." What happened after the Jews settled in Zirndorf? "The Jew became a *Kulturmensch,* and some claim it was pretense," says Wassermann. They claim he became a corrupter and seducer. For many he was "an actor that was a real human being, capable of beauty yet ugly; lustful and ascetic; charlatan and dice player, fanatic or cowardly slave—the Jew is all of these. Did time transform him into this, or did history, or pain, or success? God alone knows."

What were the sources of Wassermann's information about Jews? He tells us that he first associated with them in Vienna. While he had noted ample differences among them—as he did among Gentiles—he found certain traits more prevalent among Jews. They were more active and mobile than Gentiles; they sought quick friendship and intimacy; their opinions were apodictic; they were given to idle reflection, pondering uselessly over the simplest things. They indulged in hair-splitting arguments over truths that one could verify merely by looking; they were docile and submissive when pride was indicated but often appeared assertively boastful when modesty was in order. They were unconcerned about either dignity or restraint. They had neither talent nor taste for metaphysics, and their rampant rationalism impeded deep and wholehearted relationships. In ordinary Jews, the aversion to the "metaphysical" resulted in worship of success and wealth, in a frenzied competitiveness. In more special Jews, it led to an unfitness for intuition or ideas. "Science was the idol; intellect the undisputed master; whatever eludes quantification was inferior."

Perhaps it was for this reason that Wassermann was skeptical about Jewish claims to creativity. Two years after making these assessments in *Mein Weg als Deutscher und Jude* (*My Life as German and Jew*) (1921), he modified them when he distinguished between Oriental and European Jews, less in an ethnic than a mythical sense. "The Jew as a European can only be a *Literat* (man of letters), as Oriental he can be a creator." The difference was between withering and blossoming, individualism and belonging, anarchy and tradition. As a European the Jew is a man who relies on himself and strives to cut himself off from the past—partly because environment, education, and a sense of duty tie him everywhere to it. Wassermann's Oriental Jew is sure of himself, aware of his blood ties; a noble consciousness links him to the past, and a deep moral sense and personal responsibility obligate him to the future. This Oriental is no sectarian, fanatic or pretender; he is merely a human being cognizant of his origins.

On the surface, Wassermann's vision of the Oriental Jew seems to correspond to the image of the proud, upright, and idealistic Zionist. In fact, it did not. Zionists were nationalist Jews; and Wassermann, who had called the nineteenth century one of nationalist insanity, disapproved of all nationalism. If Zionism were to become a reality on Palestinian soil, Jews would become a laughingstock. During 1800 years of exile they had lost the ability for political leadership. Also, settling on a soil of their own as a political unit, they would cease being Jews. Wassermann never deviated from this view. At the same time, he remained uncomfortable with his negative stance on Zionism. Increasingly he recognized the need of Eastern Jews to find a refuge. But would not a nation willed into being be artificial? And would Herzl, the writer and man he knew, be able to function as a political leader?

A far deeper reason for Wassermann's cynicism about the Zionist option lay in his total lack of solidarity with other Jews. Though he wanted Eastern Jews to be secure, he had no sense of fraternity with them. In their being and language they were strangers and, at times, repugnant to him. Wassermann felt shame over this attitude and frankly hoped others would not share it. Deep inside, he sensed that the Eastern Jew was entirely a Jew and he, a German Jew, but a poor facsimile. In any case, Eastern Jews were different people with whom he had little in common.

Wassermann was the archetypal defensive-apologist Jew, intent upon proving something to Germans, who, he sensed vaguely, were uninterested in his proof. Like other apologists, he thoroughly disliked Heine. He was patently afraid of seeing the immoral, clever, sometimes *rough* and sometimes over-refined Heine as a specimen of German Jewishness. Similarly, his Diaspora mentality produced fears and discomfort in him while he was in Vienna, a city with highly visible Jews in the arts and professions. The questions he asked his German friend in *Mein Weg als Deutscher und Jude* (*My Life as German and Jew*) (1921) were permeated with defensiveness: Were these books, even though written by a Jew, not those of a *German* writer steeped in the German language and in German culture? His German friend answered evasively, exactly the response Wassermann had dreaded. Wassermann never lost sight of the fact that Jews understood his work far better than Gentiles, although Jews were reluctant to believe in the creative genius of one of their own.

The desire and need to be accepted as German has seldom been stated more forcefully than by this excerpt from a conversation between a Jew and a German:

> Jews, Germans, this separation of concepts was beyond my understanding; I could not, would not, accept it. . . . Wherein lay the source of the separation? I asked myself. In religious belief? I don't have Jewish religious beliefs. In blood? Who is to arrogate to himself the right to differentiate between different types of blood? Are there pureblooded Germans? Haven't Germans mixed with French emigrés? With Slavs, Northerners, Spaniards, Italians, most likely, too, with Huns and Mongols when their hordes flooded German lands? . . . And is it conceivable that the two-thousand-year existence of Jews in the West should not have affected their blood . . . through air, soil, history, destiny, action, involvement, even if we excluded actual physical intimacy? Are they of a different moral makeup, of different human character?

Toward the end of his life, Wassermann had given up asking rational questions of German friends. German arrogance toward Jews sickened him. It seemed to increase German coarseness and alienated Germans further from the humanistic spirit. Wassermann died only months after Hitler's takeover and was acutely aware that the tragedies of the past were to be replayed. Toward the end of his autobiography he raised a few bitter, denunciatory points to which he supplied his own reactions of hopelessness and despair. Nothing, but nothing, could gain acceptance for the Jew.

Wassermann echoed Auerbach's desperate "I have lived in vain . . ."; he concluded that it was

> [V]ain to adjure the nation of poets and thinkers in the name of its poets and thinkers. Every prejudice one thinks has been disposed of

breeds a thousand others, as carrions breed maggots.

Futile to present the right cheek after the left has been struck. It does not direct them to the slightest thoughtfulness; it neither touches nor disarms them; they strike the right cheek, too.

Vain to interject words of reason into their crazy shrieking. They say: He dares to open his mouth. Close it for him!

Futile to act in exemplary fashion. They say: We know nothing. We have seen nothing. We have heard nothing.

Vain to seek obscurity. They say: The coward! He is trying to hide, driven by his evil conscience.

Futile to go among them and offer them one's hand. They say: Why does he take such liberties with his Jewish intrusiveness?

Later Wassermann pointed both sadly and indignantly to the example of Walter Rathenau, patriot *extraordinaire*, German savior in World War I, noble soul, man of spirit. He, too, was viewed as the eternal alien, intrusive in his wish to contribute, destructive of true German value, and destroyed for wanting to help.

Wassermann was working on a novel of "Jewish destiny" when death aborted this effort. Its proposed title was *Ahasver*. He did not live to see that even the option to migrate would not long be open and that all would vanish as did his dream of coexistence and fusion.

In some minor writers the path to assimilation is obstructed not only by the Germans, but also by Jewish historic memory. To the universalist **Ernst Heilborn** (1867–1941), merging into broad humanity is less promising for Jews than it first appeared. In *Die gute Stube* (*The Good Room*) (1922), he characterized Henriette Herz's early nineteenth-century salon as one of admirable tolerance and Rahel Varnhagen's as suffused with an equally desirable *Geist*. Blending into the existing social landscape is more difficult in the novella *Erwachen* (*Awakening*) or in *Die kupferne Stadt* (*The Copper City*) (1918), in which an assimilated banker, whose moral values have become suspect, rediscovers his roots and the road back to integrity through the intervention of a mysterious Jew from the East.

J. E. Poritzky (1876–1935) came to Karlsruhe from his native Poland when still young. Generally preferring the drama, Poritzky wanted to serve as a bridge between Eastern and Western Jewries as well as between Jews and Gentiles. In a story called "Joel Klugau," part of a collection *Die da müde sind* (*They Who Are Tired*) (n.d.), a gifted young Polish Jew comes to Berlin to prepare himself for the rabbinate. As a result of his partly secular studies, his traditional beliefs are weakened. Joel Klugau first questions his suitability for the rabbinate, then the rabbinate itself, and finally all religion. He also falls in love with a delightful Christian woman. Unexpectedly he is summoned back to Poland; the old rabbi has died and he is to assume his responsibilities. He commits suicide rather than live a life of sham.

The story is rich in irony, a quality that made Heinrich Heine very attractive to Poritzky. "How Shall We Understand Heinrich Heine?" is the title of an essay by Poritzky, in which Heine stands out because no single system contained for him the whole and only truth.

Though in his later years **Franz Hessel** (1680–1746) wrote mostly *Konversationsromane* (conversational novels), *Der Kramladen des Glücks* (*The Junkshop of Happiness*) (1913) had a more serious message. He cautioned Jews against "premature universalism" and parents against letting youngsters grow up in a social and religious vacuum. Gustav, the Jewish youngster, has one demoralizing experience after another among Christian youngsters. He finds some human relationships in a Zionist organization, but earlier experiences come back to haunt him. He belongs nowhere. Parents, Hessel cautioned, cannot raise their children as though the age of human kinship had arrived.

• • • • •

Voices from Vienna

At the turn of the century, Wilhelmine Germany zealously promoted economic and military growth. Literature sometimes moved with, but more often against, this current. Novels, dramas, and poetry became increasingly politicized.

Not so in Vienna and Prague, bastions of the Hapsburg Empire. Under the aging Franz Joseph, the multinational Empire showed signs of tottering. But in the last decade of the century, its literature was beginning to flourish as never before. Neither Vienna nor Prague was linked to rapid industrialization. Their literature resisted politicizing, and social questions remained on the periphery. Perhaps foreshadowing the decay of the millennial empire, the literature of both cities reflected the weariness, exhaustion, trauma, and mystery of old age and death.

Fin-de-siècle Vienna has been portrayed as a city given to joy, *Gemütlichkeit,* and the celebration of life—all against the stench of decadence. Self-indulgence was a way of staving off the inevitable; it was one last fling, characterized by that *douceur de vivre* that has so often preceded revolutionary change. The aristocracy danced itself into a frenzy of sensory delight, and the bourgeoisie, as always, emulated it. Workers grumbled without much expectation of ameliorating their condition. But workers do not make literature. Those who did see themselves as writers met in their preferred coffeehouses, discussed their problems and projects, and were amused or frightened by the "characters" among them. In Vienna, as in Berlin, hatred of Jews was receiving a new impetus. Karl Lueger, soon to be Mayor of Vienna, was advancing his own version of anti-Semitism, and other demagogues succeeded in competing with him.

J. J. David (1859–1906) does not fit into the portrait of decadent *fin-de-siècle* Vienna. The terms *Leid* (pain, sorrow) and *leiden* (to suffer) occur with exceptional frequency in his *oeuvre.* They reflect not only the poverty and illness which afflicted him most of his life, but that which he also imposed on his fictional characters. However, when David refers to suffering, he has in mind that caused by God and fate rather than the

160

evil perpetrated by men.

Lifelong indigence and disabilities in hearing and seeing darkened the outlook of this naturalist. David rather stoically accepted his fate and expected others, similarly deprived, to do likewise. Yet he could not always contain his self-pity. If he blamed anyone or anything, it was the impersonal city, in which evils were lurking everywhere and no one was greatly concerned about the fate of his neighbor.

In spite of the tragic mood permeating his work and the intense pain felt by his characters, they try desperately to conquer what fate has in store for them. Only some succeed; others die "by the wayside"—the title of a successful work. Moreover, there is irony in the defeat ultimately suffered by David's characters. One dies immediately after he has passed his exams with flying colors and becomes eligible for the position he has always craved. Another is equally close to the goal of a lifetime when he is struck down. Yet not all is gloom. There are heartfelt human relationships and, in a different vein, a profound appreciation for landscape. The Austrian and Swiss-Italian Alpine regions are drawn in detail, and the mood they convey often influences the inner state of the characters.

David often used Jewish characters whose Jewishness is incidental. He wrote about them because he knew them best. He wrote about Moravians for the same reason. He was also familiar with the lives of peasants, impoverished students, and the indigent in both cities and villages.

The ingredients of his fiction are already announced in his first work. A disheveled Jewish mother (the epitome of disintegration) and her inept, Talmud-studying husband have neglected their little daughter, Fanny. The father has lost his business, spent time in prison, and escaped from his former home to hide in this village, where they are the only Jews. The mayor, a Christian peasant, is aware of the deplorable conditions in the Jewish home and summons the derelict parents. He decrees that Fanny must attend school, even a Christian school if necessary. The mayor's two sons are to keep a friendly eye on the neglected child. As they grow older, Fanny—a near–prostitute—comes between the two brothers, and the younger one is killed. The father's goodness has brought misery to all.

From a Jewish standpoint this story is unique. Few Jewish writers had ever used an immoral Jewish woman to destroy, even unintentionally, a Christian male. Poverty in Jewish fiction is common: slovenliness, indecency, or degeneracy are not. David delves into young Fanny's heart:

> As she listens to the Lord's prayer, she was not thinking of the one and only good God . . . she thought of a God who was hostile to her, of

whose goodness she could not partake. When at the end of the school day all intoned "Ein' feste Burg" she was silent; but in her deepest being she felt the abyss that separated her from all others; she also sensed her loneliness and isolation. She did not even feel pain which can lead toward good; no, she only experienced envy, envy for all those who belonged to a community from which she was excluded without knowing why.

Jews are usually outsiders in David's work, more excluded than self-excluding. When the Jewish medical student Siebenschein asks a Christian why it is so important that his parents flaunt their *Deutschtum,* the non-Jew regards him with pity and disdain. Siebenschein is portrayed as tense, nervous, and ambitious—all much more than Christian students. He also shared "some of the arrogance of his race for whom book wisdom and learnedness were always of the highest importance, right next to earning a livelihood."

In his late works David was increasingly drawn to the religious wars in his native Moravia. In such novellas as *Ruth, Gold,* and *Der neue Glaube (The New Faith)*, he examines first the birth of religious passions, then the quarrels, and finally the fanaticism that lead to death and destruction. While he is sympathetic to religion as meeting man's inner need, he cannot comprehend how one religion would deem itself superior to another. He is puzzled that people should go to war over the unknowable.

David's feelings for Judaism or Jews become manifest in his "Jewish poems." Jewish life has been characterized by homelessness, alienation, the sense of difference, and, in a child, the failure to comprehend why he should be treated differently. "Ich bin aus Judas finsterm Stamme/Du bist ein blond Germanenkind" ("I come from Judah's dark tribe, you are a blond Germanic child") is the refrain of "Von Zweien" ("About Us Two"), a verse dialogue between a Jewish boy and a Christian girl. In "Ein Judenkind" ("A Jewish Child"), a Jewish girl, "homeless and captive," saw before her mind's eye the "broken members of the tribe whom divine wrath smashed to pieces." German lances and British swords have done irreparable harm to her hapless people. A powerful yearning awakens in her for the cedars of Lebanon and the rose valleys of Ein Gadi. While present, this longing for the lost land is not strongly developed.

Religious protest pervades David's poetry. In "El Shaddai" the poet wonders why God does not act upon his knowledge that warmth, love, and compassion are needed in this cold universe. David's poem on Job is weak, whereas "Rachel's Tears," about the suffering of her people, is an inspired work.

In his essays, too, David occasionally touched on a Jewish subject. His eulogy of Herzl stresses the dead leader's determination to end Jewish suffering when he had barely experienced it in his own person. He marvels at Herzl's courage and skill in dealing with a kaiser, a sultan, a pope. How could this Viennese dandy he had known so well stir the masses of Eastern European Jewry, when he had so little in common with them? Yes, Herzl was right. These masses must be resettled—Palestine was possibly a premature choice—in order to live unfettered and like human beings. That David's motives are not entirely altruistic is evidenced by his assertion that these less cultured, *ungebildete* Eastern Jews must not threaten the hard-won gains of Western Jewries.

David's gloomy view of the Jewish condition must be fitted into his general pessimism. His fictional Jews have no desire to be anything but Jews, but this Jewishness is pale and diluted, as is David's own.

Unlike David, **Peter Altenberg** (Richard Engländer) (1859–1919) belongs to a small group of *fin-de-siècle* Viennese writers who epitomize "decadence." Literary historians who have used this term freely have defined it as all that weakens, makes impotent, causes lethargy, and exudes morbidity. Decadence has also come to mean nervousness, excessive refinement and culture, and preciousness. It implies aestheticism, pessimism, skepticism, melancholia, immersion in sensuousness and eroticism—all to enable one to forget or escape.

Altenberg's numerous books consist mostly of aphorisms, short poems, and impressionistic observations. They cover the gamut of human activity in a mood that shifts from anger to self-pity, from aggressiveness to quiet charm. In a sense, they are diaries without time entries. Anything Altenberg saw, heard, or thought could generate an interesting and sometimes poetic comment. He was unselective in what he wrote. As a consequence, much of his work is uneven, repetitive, and indifferent to literary traditions and reputation. His oft-quoted saying that all he wanted was for the world to be a bit better because he briefly inhabited it, was more of an afterthought than a purpose.

Altenberg (or "Der Peter," as he sometimes called himself) confidently dispensed advice on all sorts of subjects. Then, only a few lines down, he displayed insecurities so severe as to disqualify him entirely as a counselor. He was the master of the short sentence; occasionally, his endurance permitted a two- or three-page commentary. Yet even critics who scoffed at Altenberg called him an "Original," a unique figure. For nearly thirty years, Arthur Schnitzler—writer, physician, and psychologist—grappled with a play featuring an Altenberg-type character. Eventually, Schnitzler gave up, conceding that he could never capture all of the character. He had his problems with Altenberg's "poses and contradictions"; Schnitzler could not even resolve his own ambivalences about the man. Information received from Altenberg's brother, who was seriously worried about Peter's alcoholism and repeated stays in sanatoriums, did not help, nor did anything else he tried.

Kurt Bergels was also puzzled. He placed Altenberg somewhere between "a poet and a *Literat,*" with a special gift for the miniature impression. But Altenberg was also a neurasthenic, a man of childlike purity, an idealist and reformer, a Viennese precursor of the "Beatnik" to come.

Others noticed chiefly the unsavory aspects. Not only was Altenberg hopelessly attracted to "all women," but he loved them from the time "they no longer soiled themselves" to the day they died. He loved them tenderly and fiercely, worshipped the "female personality," and experienced fits of jealousy if one of his "girls" showed interest in another man or proposed the erotic games he himself enjoyed. He especially liked chambermaids, cleaning women, waitresses, and servant girls. This did not mean that he could not appreciate *les grandes dames,* but they played a less conspicuous role in his life.

Altenberg did not advocate the advancement of women's rights, nor did he care about helping women of the lower classes. His social conscience remained undeveloped. "Der Peter" simply believed that adorable women deserved the best. Women represented a tragicomic chapter in the life of this intelligent but ill-behaved child. "Der Peter" himself suspected that the child in him lived on. "All went well with me," he wrote, "until I was to be independent and responsible for myself." His respectable bourgeois family allowed him broad freedom, and he abused it. He gave up his university studies and, for a short time, became a bookseller. Soon he was in the grips of a wholly Bohemian existence, moving from hotel to hotel, café to café. Alcohol joined an unbridled eroticism to preclude ever again even a semblance of stability.

This virtual alcoholic delighted in writing books on hygiene. His panaceas were maximum exposure to fresh air, minimal clothing, simple dietary laws—the "new Kashruth" in the language of scoffers. His advice was peremptory in tone, and he repeated his recipes for good health in books that allegedly dealt with different subjects.

In 1915 Altenberg added the war to his subjects. He denounced it as wrong, but for strictly human—not political—reasons. He sympathized with the underdog, whatever the color of his uniform, for the underdog was the common soldier who risked his life. For him Altenberg was willing to do battle for three years.

Although Albert Ehrenstein spoke of Altenberg's "Jewish humor" and described his wrath as that of an Old Testament prophet, he failed to make a convincing case. While Altenberg was born a Jew and associated with Jews, in most ways he was peculiarly un-Jewish. Both the man and his life were singularly undisciplined and shapeless, hardly the attributes of the Old Testament prophets or their descendants. Instead, he belonged to that army of rootless modern Jews and others, the ailing and the suffering, those whose lives were cruelly torn asunder and could not be put together again. He loved aimlessly and undiscriminatingly; he suffered, and he both enjoyed and resented his suffering. He was not an untalented writer, not without occasional originality and depth of insight, but he lacked the sense of order that would give form to his perceptions. From the standpoint of Jewishness especially, Altenberg was an anomaly.

Though "decadence" cannot be applied to the life of **Arthur Schnitzler** (1862–1931), his early dramas dealt with characters afflicted with it. Schnitzler observed neurasthenics with a clinical eye. While he examined them sympathetically, his aim was not to pass judgment but to extract, so to speak, psychological truth. While Freud was making the study of the subconscious the basis for future studies of man and his inner turmoil, Schnitzler—in the same city and at the same time—had come to startlingly similar insights. But where Freud was credited with being one of the pathfinders of modern man, Schnitzler had to content himself with being the foremost dramatist of the dual monarchy.

Even this status was threatened for a time. After World War I, it was fashionable to write off Schnitzler as passé, as the chronicler of a world now dead. His frivolous lovers were gone, together with the "*süße Mädel*" ("sweet girls"). Small and poor postwar Austria could no longer indulge in games and duels over love and honor. But while the world of the Hapsburgs had vanished, along with Schnitzler's settings, his finely honed psychology had not. More than ever, this psychology seemed to be the psychology of the future, and his dramas and narratives invited comparison with the works of Proust and Chekhov. With them, too, the core of hard truth transcended the antiquated societal structure.

Schnitzler's dramas did more than probe into the subconscious, detecting and explaining changing moods and needs, uncovering real motivations. He is profoundly touched by the anguish and pain of his fellow man. Although he shies away from metaphysical speculation, and God and religion play a minuscule role in his work, his basic questions are serious and eternal: illness, death and the fear of it, broken relationships, necessary but mutually exclusive solutions, psychological

and physical handicaps. In spite of his early involvement with melan-
cholics, eroticists, and devotees of illusory pleasures, Schnitzler had high
expectations of life. He valued it, notwithstanding his awareness of
ugliness, destruction, and the omnipresence of death.

Schnitzler was spared the conflict of so many young Jewish writers
between a businessman-father and an artistically inclined son. The
dramatist's father was a physician, a throat specialist whose work brought
him into professional contact with actors and singers. This world of
theater enchanted the son, and his adult world was initially split between
medicine and drama. The two proved mutually supportive until, in his
middle years, Schnitzler increasingly turned to drama and eventually gave
up his practice.

Such early short plays as *Anatol* (1893) and the full-length *Liebelei*
(*Light O'Love*) (1896), a curious blend of love and death, quickly caught
the attention of the theater-going public. Later plays reveal far greater
maturity. *Der junge Medardus* (*Young Medardus*) (1910), *Der einsame Weg*
(*The Lonely Road*) (1911), and *Professor Bernhardi* (1912) fit less readily
into a mold and add social and moral issues to psychological perceptions.
Narratives that have survived are the novellas *Sterben* (*Dying*) and the
longer *Leutnant Gustl* (1901).

Schnitzler did not surround himself, as did his contemporary,
Gerhart Hauptmann, with admirers and disciples. When he met
Hofmannsthal, Beer-Hofmann, Werfel, and Altenberg, members of the
Young Vienna group, at a café, he was seeking a community of spirit,
not literary adoration. He approached his friends as he did his characters, with quiet comprehension, a measure of sadness and resignation
that never let him forget the torments of the human condition. At the
same time there was subdued joy in knowing them.

Though Eros intruded himself into many Schnitzler dramas, he
played the absolutely dominant role only in *Reigen* (*The Merry-Go-
Round*) (1897), a series of ten dialogues of people in pursuit of lust.
Banned in most cities and performed only in 1920, this daring play of
musical chairs in sex was appreciated by thoughtful critics, while others
were outraged by the titillation it might provide and "its cheap attention-
getting appeal."

In response to his work, Austrian anti-Semitism, never far beneath
the surface, rose to have a field day. In *Reichswehr* and other right-wing
organs, Schnitzler was denounced for moral depravity that could only
issue from corrupt (read "Jewish") minds. Jewish brashness and
violations of Austria's Catholic traditions were faulted by the military
and clergy alike. The upper classes were equally displeased, especially
when they remembered how Schnitzler had demystified the social and

cultural poses of their caste. Both German nationalists, whose hatred of Jews had a racial tinge, and conservatives, whose brand was more religious and cultural, had found a new and inviting target.

Schnitzler was only moderately sensitive to anti-Semitism and appeared almost resigned to it. After 1902, he concluded, however, that whereas he might leave anti-Semitism alone, it would not leave him in peace. As with Herzl a decade earlier, it began to trouble him; it followed him into his clinic and writing studio. In 1908, he wrote *Der Weg ins Freie* (*The Road to the Open*), his long novel on the Jewish question.

Der Weg ins Freie is a sprawling and awkward novel. The characters are mere abstractions of ideas; the dialogue is wooden. The former engage in long, introspective analyses that may be interesting but are poorly inserted into what action there is. Every strand of Jewish opinion of the time is present in the story, which revolves around the love of the Baron von Wergenthin. Each view is analyzed, argued, attacked, defended. Why every Jewish character should need to wash dirty linen before this Christian nobleman is hard to fathom. Leo Golowsky is the spokesman for the rapidly growing Zionist position; Heinrich Behrmann stands for the assimilationists. Middle-ground attitudes are also presented to the baron, who is naturally baffled by the swarm of contradictory arguments. Wergenthin sympathizes now with one, now with the other.

Basically, Schnitzler perceived the Jewish dilemma as the outgrowth of two thousand years of unique history, with minority status a constant. This status and what it connoted doomed Jews to contempt, suspicion, and fear. The isolation of their lives that disturbed so many was not generally of their choosing; in at least equal measure it was imposed from without.

No solution was the answer for all. Every Jew had to find an inner road for himself. Zionism, for example, was not an answer for every Jew and certainly not for Schnitzler. But it constituted an advance for those to whom mere tolerance by a majority was no longer satisfactory. Also, there were Jews who were persecuted and did not want to knock beseechingly at an alien door. But why should Palestine be the chosen country of refuge? The link to so distant a past was tenuous. What could this faraway Oriental land mean to him, an Austrian writer, expressing himself in German, a man whose friends were in Vienna, who grew up there, who had always worked in this city? Schnitzler's own view is voiced by the older Ehrenberg, who is devoted to Zionism until he returns from Palestine determined to fight his battles in Vienna in spite of all difficulties and the security and freedom of the distant land.

Thus, unlike many who rejected Zionism, Schnitzler had few illusions about the limitations of his life in Vienna. He and other Jews would simply have to adjust. It was dangerous for Jews to feel secure in a host nation, even if for a while during their sojourn, they were not actually harmed.

Schnitzler was, therefore, equally skeptical of assimilation, though in some form it was inevitable. Jews had to make sure they could accept themselves, be at peace with their heritage, and develop fully what they felt was within their being. He was at a loss to comprehend the thinking of Karl Kraus or Otto Weininger, fellow Viennese who wanted to escape from their origin and who regarded it as odious or disgraceful.

In 1912 Schnitzler wrote *Professor Bernhardi,* a powerful play on the miscarriage of justice perpetrated against a Jewish physician. By then he was convinced of the utter unavoidability of the anti-Semitic phenomenon. This realization made him look into his past. At every level of education he had been harassed by officials, by envious and ambitious colleagues eager to displace Jews. It was present in his father's clinic, which served as the setting for the Bernhardi drama.

Schnitzler bared a stronger resentment of anti-Semitism in *Professor Bernhardi* than in *Der Weg ins Freie.* The physician, head of his clinic, is at first maligned, then imprisoned, until finally he becomes the focus of an unwanted *cause célèbre.* Schnitzler parades several Jew-hatred myths, which were then mouthed not only by the masses, but also by physicians, politicians, and so-called protectors of the arts. Schnitzler exposes their motives, which are selfish. In his calm, elegiac manner, he unveils the hypocrisies behind their pious attitudes and clichés. As for Bernhardi, Schnitzler has him accept his destiny as just another unhappy fact of life.

The drama unfolds when Bernhardi bars a priest from entering the sickroom of a dying patient. This patient is convinced of her recovery, and Bernhardi felt duty-bound to make her final hours as comfortable and anxiety-free as possible. The priest sees matters differently and, supported by a nurse, allows the case to become a major incident. Screaming headlines read that a Jew has prevented a priest from exercising his duty in Catholic Austria. The repercussions are great. Bernhardi's deputy at the clinic joins forces with a former colleague, now a government minister, and feeds hate-filled lies to the anti-Semitic press. Bernhardi is suspended. A parliamentary interpellation splits the deputies along conservative and liberal lines.

Like *Der Weg ins Freie, Professor Bernhardi* underscores the disarray within contemporary Viennese Jewry. Not all the Jewish physicians at the clinic support their chief. There are timid Jews on the staff as well as Jews turned Christian. Schnitzler leaves no doubt as to the fear, shallowness, and treachery that prompt their actions. Even the once-Jewish lawyer whom Bernhardi retains does not adequately defend his client, for fear of casting suspicion on his recent conversion. The Zionist supports Bernhardi vigorously, but the latter finds his aggressive manner as unpleasant as any other. Moreover, he, too, has a goal in mind other than justice for Bernhardi. Like his hero, Schnitzler prefers moderates, be they Christians or Jews. One of the physicians confesses that he had been an anti-Semite in his youth, and he is still an anti-Semite—only now he is equally anti-Aryan.

Schnitzler brings a quiet, objective approach to most of his subjects, including the Jewish situation in Vienna. He depicts the shenanigans of a majority group—Christians—that dominates a dislocated, psychologically defensive, and reactive minority in its midst. Being a Jew was not a cause for undue pride and certainly not a reason for shame. A Jew was what he was—a human being, a European, an Austrian, a physician, a writer—yes, and a Jew—not necessarily in that order. Of these identities, the Jewish one might be the most difficult to nurture, but it was worth nurturing nonetheless.

While Heine was the greatest Jewish-born poet writing in German and Kafka the most original novelist, Schnitzler was unmistakably the most eminent dramatist. He was an innovator in psychology—Freud's literary "double," as the founder of psychoanalysis once called him. He created new and different characters, dealt with new and different problems, and while some of these have now vanished into history, the underlying view of man has not.

A liberal, he can yet be fitted into the "aggressor" tradition in that he was remarkably unconcerned about public reaction. Not combative, not a lover of feuds and polemics, Schnitzler was adamant about defending his private self, and he rejected intrusions of all kinds. If he was not more of a Jew, it was not that he did not care, but because his own Jewishness was only one aspect of many identities he cherished.

"Decadent" fits to a near perfection the *oeuvre* of **Felix Dörmann** (Felix Biedermann) (1870–1928). A volume of poetry significantly entitled *Neurotica* (1891) was followed in 1900 by *Die Zimmerherren* (*The Lodgers*), a drama regarded by some as having paved the way for Schnitzler's *Reigen*. (Neither play could be staged before 1920, years after each was written.) The hero has slept with the maid as well as two of her mistresses. His *ennui,* even with sex, leads to impotence. In *Die Liebesmüden* (*Tired of Love*), a frustrated wife seeks to procure an innocent young girl for her impotent husband, hoping he will regain his vigor. Though the plan fails, the husband is reunited with so devoted a wife. In *Frühlingsopfer* (*Sacrifice* *of Spring*) (1919), Schnitzler again deals with sexual sacrifice and impotence.

Dörmann used a line in *Die Liebesmüden* that he might have written for himself. "It is remarkable," he wrote, "how many people are oldest when they are youngest." The youthful Dörmann, influenced on one side by Baudelaire's *Flowers of Evil* and on the other by his own alternately agitated and fatigued state, is filled with a longing for death. He seems to have seen and experienced it all; there is little to look forward to in the way of new joys. As Dörmann aged and his love pangs diminished along with his *Weltekel* (revulsion to the world), his poetic powers also declined. Although this Austrian Impressionist gave little evidence of Jewish interests, he was often attacked as one of the corrupt sons of Israel.

The only truly Jewish writer in Young Vienna was **Richard Beer-Hofmann** (1866–1945). His two biblical dramas, *Jacobs Traum (Jacob's Dream)* (1914) and *Der junge David (Young David)* (1933), are characterized by a keen poetic sensibility and broad universality of outlook. The seven tableaux that comprise *Der junge David* have great breadth but are ultimately exasperating for the reader, who can barely keep up with the vast cast of characters.

The paucity of this poet's literary output has kept his reputation from flourishing. Sometimes he would publish nothing for a whole decade. Beer-Hofmann was a trained lawyer who entered literature late with a volume of two novellas. One of these, *Das Kind (The Child)*, involves the representative Viennese characters of the time—people suffering from psychic exhaustion and moral lethargy. A disappointment, crisis, or death merely strengthens the craving for pleasure, but it is pleasure without enjoyment. Yet in this novella the hero returns to sanity upon the death of his child. The tragedy leads him to assess not only his life, but the purpose of existence. In Sol Liptzin's words, Beer-Hofmann's novellas initially point out man's "insignificance in the universal order, the assertion of the guilt of the creator toward even the most insignificant of his created subjects." But this poses the corollary question "of the necessity of man in this world, the responsibility of individuals toward this fate, the relations of parents to children and of children to parents."

This is also the theme of the often-anthologized poem written two weeks after the birth of his daughter Miriam. "Schlaflied für Miriam" ("Lullaby for Miriam") has been acclaimed by many, from Kerr to Rilke, as a jewel of thought and feeling. Here again, the poet finds relief from cosmic loneliness by listening to an inner voice, establishing some kind of mystical union with his forebears, and thereby celebrating the mystery and unity of life. In fewer than five stanzas the poet reflects on life's uncertain beginnings and the even greater uncertainties that surround its end. He speaks of man's solitary wanderings during his earthly life and laments the human errors repeated in each generation. Nevertheless, behind all the negatives the poet senses a divine design, a mysterious continuity that belies futility and chaos.

The same polarities of transience and eternity, life and death, emptiness and meaning pervade Beer-Hofmann's only novel, *Der Tod Georgs* (*George's Death*) (1900). The melancholy aesthete, in the style of Schnitzler and Oscar Wilde, is identified as a Jew only in the latter parts of this short novel. Having faced human destiny through the proximity of death and having finally assumed responsibility for his existence, the hero wants to discharge his obligations as an individual and as a part of the Jewish people. The obligations of the latter are to teach divine justice to all the nations. The hero is aware that in the lives of those whose blood courses through his veins "justice was present like the sun whose rays never warmed them, whose light never shone for them, yet before whose brilliant splendor they reverently protected their pain-covered forehead with trembling hands." These were ancestors forced to migrate from land to land, disgraced, ragged, scorned by all for the very condition to which these others had subjected them. The forebears maintained their dignity and self-respect, kept worshipping their God, proudly so, and "not as a beggar honors an almsgiver, but calling out in their suffering to the Lord of Mercy, to the God of Justice."

Jacobs Traum followed an impressive drama, *Der Graf von Charolais* (*The Count of Charolais*) (1904). The dream was originally conceived as a prologue to the David trilogy. As it turned out, it surpasses *Der junge David* as biblical drama. The frame is supplied by Jacob's theft of his blessing and his encounter with the angel. The two brothers Jacob and Edom complement each other: the former is the dreamer, the artist, the man of developed sensibility, able to perceive a deeper reality. Edom is the practical man, the man of matter and action, the hunter in need of earthly goods even as he observes the divine law.

The action follows the biblical tale rather closely. The most dramatic and yet poetic scene is the meeting of the brothers on a mountaintop, enveloped in the mist of early morning. Beer-Hofmann has filled Jacob with mysterious questions which echo the fears, doubts, and promises of his ancestors. He has just set free his slave "after equal dialogue." Suddenly, against this spiritual backdrop Edom appears with murderous intent. Skillfully and courageously, Jacob first neutralizes his brother's hate, then transforms it into friendship. He assures Edom that he is not inferior to him: "God needs me as I am, and He needs you in other ways. Only because you are Edom, may I be Jacob." All individuals, like all peoples, have an appointed task; all are God's children and equally important to him.

As soon as Edom has disappeared, a man at peace, the angels appear, and Jacob besieges them with his questions. What is the meaning of existence? Why does God allow suffering, even cause it? The angels respond evasively. They reiterate God's promise that Abraham's seed will receive "the fat of the land." Jacob rejects God's promise. He wishes neither dominion nor special status for himself: "Could I be blessed when all suffer, when all approach me by day and by night, when man and beast and herb and stone moan to me with mute eyes, imploring an answer of me?" Jacob is assured that, after the demise of then-existing civilizations, his progeny will continue to exist as a living testimony to God's eternal world. "But Israel's seed will die a thousand deaths and a thousand times will rearise from the dead."

Through Samael-Lucifer, Beer-Hofmann discusses the Jewish future. Others may, indeed, bow to the testimony on the mountaintop, but the Jewish mouth pronouncing it will be bloodied. Yes, and Israel will know no rest, have no home, become a victim of the whims and sins of others. Samael-Lucifer continues: "Every people to which you attach yourself will burn you out like a cancer. You, the beloved of God, shall be hated more than a poisonous plant or an evil beast." Nevertheless, Jacob accepts the role as God's chosen emissary and the mission it connotes with all its perils.

Beer-Hofmann's language is sparse. His imagery conveys the primitive herdsman's society which can yet touch on the divine. The poet-dramatist knows when not to broach what cannot be stated in language. He shuns cheap devices when he deals with the sense of the divine. He is explicit, however, when detailing the high cost of chosenness to Jews.

Der junge David was envisioned as the first installment in the life of the King, but it can stand on its own merits. The youthful David, like Jacob, has deep insight into the human heart. He knows that King Saul, who once loved him, now senses "the icy shadows of evening descending upon him" and that he—as a young man—serves as a constant reminder of this falling curtain. This David is neither a heroic fighter nor a psalmist. He has experienced more than many older men. He has known the proximity of death, the dilemma of conflicting loyalties, the unpleasantness of being called a traitor. Unwittingly he has been involved in murder. More and more he has felt the need to fathom the cruelty of the divinity he worships.

Beer-Hofmann's preoccupation with choice permeates his entire work. Many of David's choices have had a stigma attached to them. He has sworn loyalty to a group hostile to his people, and he will cling to this impossible position. Though diplomats in his entourage scoff at honor and dependability, they constitute for him an indispensable foundation for relations among people and of people with their God. Though Saul has persecuted him, David's joy upon being crowned is marred by the memory of a once-satisfying friendship. When David wonders what his future holds and what will become of him, a woman answers with the author's wisdom: "What ultimately becomes of all of us, dung of the earth! Perhaps a song—this, too, is soon wafted away." He must let God's stars guide him to complete his earthly mission. The young king accepts his Covenant with God as Jacob did. He announces royal policy: he will not extend his power, employ force or aim at the enslavement of neighbors. He wants an end to pain and oppression. He yearns for the seeding of a new spirit.

Some of the words Beer-Hofmann puts into David's mouth reflect the author's alarm at what was happening in Germany. The warnings against ultra-nationalism and territorial expansion are clear. King Saul at his most evil could not conceive of the tortures that were being reported from across the border. Extreme ethnocentrism had always been repugnant to Beer-Hofmann as a human being and as a Jew. Jews, too, must guard against it, he says. Therefore, he sees Jews as a community of men and women with common memories and experiences. The memories were partly positive in that they consisted of moral messages propounded by the prophets of Israel. But the community was also held together by recollections of sorrows and suffering, the refusal of others to accept Jews for what they were.

Beer-Hofmann belongs to the few who sought to articulate Jewish mission and destiny. Though he dealt largely with the moral message, he did not teach or preach. His dramas offered guideposts for living, for finding purpose and direction in human existence. For Beer-Hofmann, Israel's moral code transcends time and place.

Karl Kraus (1874–1936) was only slightly removed from Beer-Hofmann in his moral vision, but a huge gap separated both writers in their assessment of the Jewish role in achieving it.

Satiric genius and self-appointed protector of the German language, Karl Kraus was a fierce warrior against all he judged false and corrupt. For this reason he became an implacable foe of the modern press and its *feuilletons,* the psychology of the subconscious, and the growing materialism of his time. Since, according to Kraus, the press was Jewinfested, the psychology in question a Jewish "invention," and the institutions of materials in Jewish hands, Jews bore a heavy burden of blame for the evils he discerned. There were other *bêtes noires* in Kraus's view of the world, and somehow he was able to connect Jews to most of them.

Kraus had no qualms at all about lambasting "the children of Israel" for contributing to the ills of the world. His attacks on them could reach such intensity that the impression of self-hate had to gain currency. His hateful, vicious, often tasteless criticisms, his cheap imitations of Jewish speech and discourse, and his desire to distance himself from Jews were often repugnant. His callous use of ancient prejudices, which he merely dressed up in modern garb, resembled the most harmful of medieval Christian slanders.

Nor should Kraus's assaults be likened to those of Heine and Börne, distantly related ancestors. They, too, sported an occasional anti-Jewish quip and could be highly critical of Jewish philistinism, but theirs were the reactions of insiders deploring the status quo and hoping for improvements in the Jewish condition. Moreover, when Jews were under attack by Christians, Heine and Börne would leap to the defense of their former brethren. Not so with Kraus who, all too often depicting the Jew as an arch-villain, transcended any reasonable self-critical stance. There is nothing at all protective about Kraus's assaults. Also, when other writers imitated Jewish speech inflections, or "mauscheled," their intent was not necessarily aggressive. Kraus's "Jew speech" perpetuated stereotypes of Jewish greed, profiteering, exploitation, and hunger for power. As Harry Zohn, a thoughtful Kraus student put it, some pages could have come straight from the *Stürmer* (i.e., as propaganda from members of Hermann Göring's storm troopers). The satirist's often sardonic strictures against the Jews—Berthold Viertel euphemistically called them the castigations of an Old Testament prophet—did not diminish greatly until *Die dritte Walpurgisnacht* (*The Third Walpurgis Night*), his final book, published sixteen years after his death. Here at last a softer tone prevailed, and a more generous set of comments replaced the denunciations of old.

Kraus was born in a small town north of Prague. His father, a businessman, placed no obstacles on his son's road to literary success. Among the apostates, Kraus enjoyed as happy a childhood as any. In 1877 the family moved to Vienna, his home for life. At the university Kraus rarely attended the law lectures for which he had registered but pursued literary interests instead. He began with theater reviews for Viennese newspapers. Like other Jewish writers, he frequented coffee houses but was not fond of them. A brief flirtation with acting redoubled his determination to devote himself to letters. He sent short pieces to the *Neue Freie Presse,* a paper he pilloried throughout his life.

Die demolirte Literatur (Literature Demolished) (1897) was Kraus's first major collection of satire. The occasion was the destruction of the Café Griensteidl, the favorite haunt of Jewish writers, whom Kraus mercilessly lampooned. Kraus urges the members of "Young Vienna" to pack up their belongings, which consist of lack of talent, cheap showmanship, girls, and incorrect language. His main victims were Beer-Hofmann, Dörmann, von Andrian-Werberg (a half-Jew), and Salten (who was sufficiently incensed to attack Kraus physically). Peter Altenberg, a lifelong Kraus protégé, escaped unscathed, and Schnitzler emerged partly intact. About Schnitzler, Kraus said he had "plunged deepest into this shallowness and is most deeply immersed in this emptiness."

Although *Eine Krone für Zion (A Crown for Zion)* (1898) was published near the time Kraus converted to Catholicism, it bore much more the characteristic of a newly acquired socialism. Zohn has called this a superficial essay which remains "a significant document in Kraus's forty-year war against part of his own self, his roots, and certain aspects of his own intellectuality." The title is a pun, *Krone* signifying both a royal crown and the old Austrian monetary unit. Like other Jews, Kraus had been asked to contribute a shekel for the Zionist cause, which Kraus called "anti-Semitic." If Kraus ever had a Jewish position, it was wholeheartedly assimilationist. He could not generate an ounce of sympathy for Herzl's political Zionism, which, like other nationalisms, struck him as divisive. More than others it was artificial. He could understand the desire to rescue Eastern Jews, but he believed that socialism—not a superimposed sense of nationhood—would achieve this result. The satirist could not envision the elegant Jews of the West engaging in the proposed agricultural schemes. How could King Herzl create Jewish heroes? No, it would be simpler if the program were reversed: "The most refractory Zionist could easily be civilized and turned into a European in only a few years." The vulgar anti-Semitism of the masses might have disappeared but for Zionism, which lent it new impetus.

These and other books were often collections of articles that first appeared in *Die Fackel (The Torch),* the periodical he began publishing in 1899 and which, after the initial years, he wrote almost in its entirety. Publication ceased only with Kraus's death in 1936. Greatly admired by the younger generations for its aggressive, fearless mocking; its pleas for sexual freedom and for intellectual and spiritual integrity; and its comic assaults on the liberal press, economic corruption, and cultural disintegration, *Die Fackel* was dreaded by the bourgeois establishment, which felt its secret vices had been mercilessly exposed. In the 1930s the fortunes of the journal declined markedly. In its heyday, the meager cultural readership in Austria was divided into pro- and anti-Fackel circles with sharply drawn battle lines.

One of the first collections with a common theme was *Sittlichkeit und Kriminalität* (*Morality and Criminality*) (1908). Although hardly a defender of women's rights, Kraus was willing to grant women greater freedom in the sexual realm. He ridiculed the duplicity of men, especially lawyers, who condemned by day what they practiced by night. He was loath to judge what seemed to him consonant with human nature. He lashed out at the press for the contemptible manner in which it reported crimes. In *Die chinesische Mauer* (*The Chinese Wall*) (1910), Kraus broadens his war against the *Neue Freie Presse*, apparently siding with a deputy who alleged that "culture is what one Jew copies from another." He looked upon this deputy as a more honest promoter of cultural progress than the Jewish editor of the newspaper he hated. He tells of the tricks he has played on this newspaper— tricks which did, indeed, succeed in making the prestigious *NFP* appear ludicrous. His humorous attacks are marred by his cantankerousness, his sacrifices of truth to the gods of cleverness and wit, and sometimes his wanton destructiveness. His underlying seriousness is not helped by these sundry excesses. His attempted slaughter of the *NFP*, justly regarded as a great European paper, was often demeaning. Yet it was not entirely without reason that he deplored journalistic power in the modern state, in which an invisible government ruled instead of the apparent one.

Kraus fueled the fires of anti-Semitism further by his attacks on Heine, a perennial object of controversy. Unlike Auerbach or Riesser, who fulminated against Heine because he endangered the image of Jewish virtue, Kraus agitated against the earlier poet-satirist as the originator of the *feuilleton*, that diseased French import: "Heine so loosened the corset of the German language that today every little merchant can fondle her breasts." The *feuilleton*, Kraus maintained, has debased thought with its superficial Gallic brilliance that covers a large core of nothing. Kraus was pained by the fact that the public will always prefer the showy, charming Heinean French import over the deeper thought conveyed in exquisite German. But dislike of Heine extended beyond the *feuilleton*. He despised Heine's vaunted cynicism, calling it a stale pie of woe and wit; Heine's verses, he said, are but operetta lyrics, often merely "scanned and rhymed journalism." Only the serious poems of the *Romanzero* gained Kraus's approval. The question is too obvious: Was Kraus deeply envious of Heine's light, effortless style, when his own was heavy, labored, and opaque? Could Heine have been the artist against whom Kraus privately measured himself?

World War I affected the direction of Kraus's work. His keen insight into language convinced him early on of the chasm between pious assertions and impious actions. During the war he became more aware than ever that innocent language covered distorted uses of patriotism, vicious profiteering from the misfortunes of others, including those who had died in combat or were about to do so. His vision of the war and the world to come was apocalyptic, as suggested by new titles such as *Nachts* (*At Night*) (1918) or *Weltgericht* (*Day of Judgment*) (1919).

Kraus's most significant work may well be the 800-page unstageable play, *Die letzten Tage der Menschheit* (*The Last Days of Mankind*) (1922). All of the satirist's themes and causes converge here. Protectiveness toward language, distaste for many bourgeois values, dislike of the fact-and-fancy press, carping at materialism—all are being linked to wartime events. The action of the play is minimal, but clever and witty talk with Krausianisms abounds. The play is noteworthy also because Kraus here bids farewell to a monarchy he had cherished.

This most continuous and comprehensive of his books features over five hundred characters, none developed, but jointly offering a panorama of the allegedly depraved Vienna of the war years. He continues to levy dangerous charges against Jews, going so far as to claim that Jews had spread the poison that is money and in the process had enslaved innocent princes and innocent peoples. The old accusations are revived and continue as one of the author's staples into the early 1930s.

Then came Hitler—not to Austria in Kraus's lifetime—but to neighboring Germany. He began to make his presence felt everywhere. To Hitler, Kraus was only another non-Aryan. And Kraus? "Mir fällt zu Hitler nichts ein" ("On the subject of Hitler no ideas come to me"), he commented lamely. This was not entirely accurate. In *Die dritte Walpurgisnacht,* originally intended for *Die Fackel,* he engaged Nazis in a disputation, in which he accused Hitlerism of all he had ever fought. Its propaganda, language, literature, and culture were a shock such as he had never anticipated. Here his comments on Jews were the mildest of his career. Apparently, he did not wish to be an anti-Semitic bedfellow to the barbarian in Germany.

The renewed interest Kraus's work received after 1960 should be attributed to his verbal dexterity more than to his ideas. To be sure, his thought could boast a certain consistency, but it was a tiresome, repetitive over-consistency. Nevertheless, this monarchist, socialist Dollfuss supporter who existed between worlds, and never entirely within one, had a basic and undeniable integrity. If there was the moral earnestness of the Old Testament prophet in him, as claimed by

Berthold Viertel, there was also the weakness of ordinary men.

A notch or two in ability below those discussed was **Felix Salten** (1869–1945), remembered today for *Bambi* and other animal tales. He belonged to the circle that comprised Altenberg, Beer-Hofmann, Schnitzler, and, at one time, Karl Kraus, with whom Salten had a severe falling out. The fact that Salten was a successful *feuilletonist* at the *Neue Freie Presse* could hardly endear him to Kraus.

In several of his short plays and narratives, Salten pitted characters of supposed rectitude and little humanity against others less rigidly virtuous but all the more compassionate. Marked by humor and a mild eroticism, his dramas lack direction. The same holds true for his *Simson* (*Samson*) (1928), a novel. While following the Biblical tale too closely, Salten remade Delila into a good person, herself brutally victimized. There are several themes, each insufficiently developed.

Salten was a friend of Theodore Herzl's and was generally sympathetic to Zionism. In 1925 he undertook a trip to Palestine, which resulted in the glowing *Neue Menschen auf alter Erde* (*New Men on Old Soil*). His leftist political orientation often expressed itself in witty cabaret appearances.

Roda Roda (Alexander Rosenfeld) (1872–1945) enjoyed exceptional popularity in the city's cabarets. His ethnic puns, sketches, narratives, and plays created mirth wherever he appeared. Many were collected and added to an already prolific production.

The son of an officer and himself commissioned, Roda Roda frequently drew on military life for his cabaret performances and writing arsenal. Though he lost his commission for supposedly degrading the military, Roda Roda was less a satirist than a good-humored verbal prankster who had no desire to destroy the object of his spoofs.

He was conversant with many of the languages of the empire and relied heavily on this talent for his ethnic humor. He treated all groups alike, with gentle barbs, sketching broad characteristics of Jews, Poles, Slovaks, and Germans. Not all were flattered by his attention, and the Nazis were among the most grievously offended. The Weimar years, which he spent mostly in Munich and Berlin, where his home served as a center for literacy discourse, were the time of his greatest popularity. In 1933, he returned to Vienna; in 1940, he came to the United States, where he died.

Roda Roda moved in territory bounded by literature, journalism, and the cabaret. Fifty books, each not terribly distinguishable from the other, attested to a loyal public. Some of his pieces were of dubious morality and were said to be emblematic of the morbidity of Austrian-Jewish literature. Yet his Jewishness, wholly assimilationist, was weak at best.

Hugo Bettauer (1872–1925) was only a marginal figure in terms of serious literature. He is more interesting as a person, both for his unorthodox views and his uncommon courage, for which he paid with his life. He was assassinated in 1925 by a crazed right-wing fanatic.

Bettauer used the novel as just another platform for his ideas. He had few literary pretensions and was satisfied if his one-dimensional characters moved through the novel to demonstrate his convictions. They are invariably entangled in actions that reflect social injustice. Bettauer recognized human stupidities and was sufficiently outraged to expose them mercilessly. For many he was an *Unbequemer,* a troublemaker, eager to stir up his readers.

Although he was born in Berlin and worked there as a journalist as well as in the United States, he wrote most of his novels in post–World War I Vienna. His novels had American or Viennese settings. They were popular, partly because of the great clarity and also because they foreshadowed the technique of the cinema. They were much less popular in religious-conservative circles, for they had already singled him out as an enemy for publishing a sexually oriented magazine.

Bettauer is always on the side of the underdog. In *Das blaue Mal (The Blue Stain)* (c. 1926), the underdog is a mulatto, rejected alike by American blacks and whites. Bettauer's view of America is jaundiced, in part because of racial discrimination and in part because of the emphasis on "the almighty dollar." In *Das entfesselte Wien (Vienna Unchained)*, Bettauer continued his battle against greed and advocated his ideas on women's liberation. He rejected the false sex standards of the past and suggested the feasibility of trial marriages—if there are to be marriages at all. Many of his ideas on sex and women's rights were expounded in *Er und Sie (He and She)*, a journal later known as *Bettauers Wochenschrift (Bettauer's Weekly)*. His most imaginative work is *Stadt ohne Juden (City Without Jews)* (1922). What would Vienna be like without Jews? A Catholic chancellor, with strong right-wing views, expels Jews and is hailed for his bold action. He expels them, not because he hates them, but because he recognizes their superiority, which enables them to control the inferior but decent Austrian rural population. This rustic element, the chancellor thinks, must be preserved at all costs. Soon after the Jews have left, the economy weakens, the arts dry up, and the universities become mere shadows of their former selves. The entire society is diminished and breaks down. Even those who had most enthusiastically greeted the Jews' expulsion—and had initially benefited—now demand and even beg for their return.

Bettauer loudly asserts the Jews' presence and demands recognition of their uniqueness, even where that uniqueness is less than admirable. Nowhere does he praise Jewish "virtues." In fact, he is peculiarly aware of the vices that derive from the Jews' affluence and business acumen. What is totally lacking in Bettauer is any genuine interest in Jewish life, beyond noting the contributions Jews have made to the world. Even more lacking than a respect for Jewish tradition is a sense of people-hood. The Jews in the novel accept as perfectly natural and acceptable any further limits placed on immigration from the East, for Jews from Poland and Russia are a culturally retarded group. By contrast, Bettauer demanded full rights for all Jews, Eastern or not, already in residence.

In spite of making the Viennese conscious of the value of a Jewish presence, Bettauer was a Jew without Jewishness, a man who defended Jews not because they were Jews, but because they were oppressed human beings. For his limited Jewishness and unpopular views, Bettauer had to pay with his life.

The multi-ethnic character of the Hapsburg Empire put less pressure on Jewish writers to prove their *Deutschtum.* Most of the Jewish writers within the confines of the dual monarchy wrote in German, thus recognizing the German language as the medium. Writers of other nationalities were fighting for the acceptability of their respective languages as suitable vehicles for literary expression. But while Viennese Jewish writers were spared the national struggle, they were beset by the demon of religious animosity from an all-powerful, monolithic Catholicism. From this most ancient branch of religious anti-Semitism sprang other varieties that were economic, social, and cultural in nature.

In spite of an anti-Semitism that was—certainly in rhetoric—more virulent and constant than any propounded in Germany, there is less evidence of reactive pressures on the part of Austro-Jewish writers. They seemed to take matters in stride. Only Schnitzler confronted hatred of Jews specifically, and he could do so with detachment and objectivity. The reactions of Bettauer were a case apart. Only one of the writers, Richard Beer-Hofmann, dealt with Jewish tradition and destiny. The variety of literary interests in general was as great as that of Jews in Germany. It ranged from decadence to depth psychology, from the evils of poverty, to those of wealth, from the moral quest in a conventional frame to that operating outside such a structure.

•   •   •   •   •

Prague Writers

Prague and the rest of the country soon to become Czechoslovakia suffered less acutely from the sense of impending doom. The city's links to the Hapsburgs had become weak, and the dominant Czech population would actually welcome the dissolution of the Empire. The German-speaking minorities of Prague, including Jews, had more binding ties to the Hapsburgs, especially Franz Joseph, whom they viewed as their protector. Jews often had good cause to feel trapped between Czechs and Germans, both of whom made their lives difficult. Though "city of the three ghettoes" may be an exaggeration, the three groups hardly lived in loving togetherness.

In Prague, as in Vienna, the Jewish writers met in cafés, but also even more often in private homes. They knew one another, for they had sometimes attended the same *Gymnasium* (academy), and their relationships dated back to early adolescence. They possessed enough common bonds for cultural historians to link them by the label of *Der Prager Kreis* (The Prague Circle).

The myth-laden city itself played a large role in shaping the character of its literature, but so did the ethnic tensions and the sense of impending change. The legends of Prague convey more mystery than do those of most cities. Fantasy and past horrors are resurrected by edifices, monuments, memorials, and cemeteries. The tale of the High Rabbi Löw, buried in the famed Jewish cemetery, and the Golem he brought to life clearly suggest the distinctly folkloristic quality of the city.

Appropriately, it was Prague that gave birth to the God-seekers Brod, Kafka, and Werfel, though each writer pursued his own distinct road to the divinity. That road, however, is rarely recognizable; it is enveloped in mysticism, the occult, and concealment rather than in revelation. The realistic narrative seemed a rarity.

One of the few realists of that time, almost forgotten today, is **Auguste Hauschner** (1850–1924). Born and raised in Prague, she became a lifelong resident of Berlin. She was one of the few Jewish writers in Germany to attempt a family novel, *Die Familie Lowositz* (*The Lowositz*

Family). The Lowositzes lived in Prague at the end of the past century. The father knows but one duty: to provide the *parnose* (all family needs). But the Jewish ritual observed is empty and routinized. Young Rudolf Lowositz is the idealistic, searching protagonist who is repelled by the family's materialism. He is also alienated by his Jewish teachers, whom he finds dull and hypocritical, more prone to torment than to inspire. He is also tortured by a cruel Gentile mathematics teacher who assigns problems to him about Jews in quest of dishonest profits. Rudolf is strong, stubborn, and defiant. In many ways he typifies the ethnic dilemma of Prague Jews. He feels thoroughly German, and he has a low regard for Czech culture but is sympathetic to its desire for recognition. As a Jew, he belongs to neither group but is wooed and ultimately rejected by both.

Young Rudolf has been seen as a re-creation of Fritz Mauthner, Hauschner's childhood friend and relative. While Hauschner maintained her contacts with him, she also entertained cordial relations with Gustav Landauer and Max Brod, both of whom served as counterweights to the often self-hating Mauthner. Both pro- and anti-Jewish attitudes are mirrored in this novel, Hauschner's most serious work. Much of her fiction fits the label *Unterhaltungsroman* (popular novel).

Hugo Salus (1866–1929) was described by Max Brod as an unqualified assimilationist. While this may be an exaggeration, Salus did hope, all else failing, for full Jewish absorption into the host society. But Salus often made use of Jewish folkways and observances in his poetry, plays, and occasional fiction.

Salus was a highly regarded gynecologist but also, at the turn of the century, the most respected Bohemian poet writing in German. This man, who physically resembled Heine, appealed greatly to the ladies, whose beauty he chanted in verses that sometimes strove to be Heinean. Salus, however, lacked Heine's frivolity and naughtiness and without them could not recreate the easy charm of the earlier poet.

He drew much of his material from the ethnic groups among whom he lived and worked. In one poem he remembers the origin of the famed crucifix on the Charles Bridge, framed by Hebrew letters; the poet relates how this statue was financed by penalties inflicted upon a Jew. Salus speculates on the unknown fate of this Jew, whose cries to heaven and complaints on earth keep ringing in the poet's ears.

The volume *Glockenklang (The Sound of Bells)* (1911) contains many poems of Jewish interest. In "Das Lied des Bluts" ("The Song of Blood"), and less directly in "Die ewige Mutter" ("The Eternal Mother") and "Der Heimatlose" ("Homeless Man"), Salus centers on a favorite theme: continuity and generational linkage, blood ties and memories of suffering in common. "Das Ahnenlied" ("Song of Our Forefathers") is also reminiscent of Beer-Hofmann's "Schlaflied für Miriam." Salus's verse lacks the conciseness of Beer-Hofmann's but compensates through spontaneity and sincerity. Other poems bemoan the tragedy of those without a land of their own, and who, in the search for asylum, are compelled to beg at the doors of strangers and are coldly rejected by them. Salus concludes with "Doch bald erwachst auch du zum Traume/Und sollst dir deine Heimat gründen." Zionism was in the air, and even assimilationists sometimes inhaled it. Other poems disclose his interest in the Bible, and in his twin lyrics, "Der Todesengel" ("The Angel of Death") and "Die Seele" ("The Soul")—which he called Talmudesque legends—he displays at least some knowledge of the oral tradition. Perhaps it was inevitable that as a lifelong resident of Prague, he should fall back upon the legend of "der hohe Rabbi Löw."

Of his two verse dramas, "Susanna im Bad" ("Susanna Bathing") is the more interesting. Salus fills the apocryphal biblical tale with psychological and ethical interest. Because of its inherent eroticism, the one-act play was not performed, though it was written in excellent taste.

His collections of novellas display far more skill with imagery than with narration. "Simson" is betrayed more by an inscrutable fate than by Delila. Salus's ghetto tale *Die Beschau* (*The Inspection*) takes great pains to explain the practice of visiting and inspecting a marital prospect, but the writer leaves no doubt that it had to be abandoned. The Talmudic student Daniel, unaware of nature or of his body, is made conscious of both by Eva, a girl with natural instincts. In making David aware of nature and sex, Salus invokes the *Song of Songs,* from which David quotes copiously as he makes love to Eva. *Die Beschau* is a ghetto tale *à la* Kompert, with reminders of Greek on the one hand and a foreshadowing of Freud on the other.

Salus had Jewish perspicacity, respect for religious texts, and compassion for past trauma. He prayed that homelessness could finally end. If no other home could be found, then the Jews had to make the best of the situation and mingle with the nations around them.

Also belonging to the Prague Circle, though somewhat on its periphery, were the poet and translator **Friedrich Adler** (1857–1918), the anthologist-poet-translator **Camill Hoffmann** (1878–1944), and the neo-romantic, Expressionist poet **Paul Adler** (1878–1946). Paul Adler wrote a legendary tale, *Elohim* (1914), almost impenetrable in its mixture of Talmudic, kabbalist, Christian, and pagan elements. Its title notwithstanding, it is at best a work of marginal Jewish interest.

Far more important were the tragedies of **Paul Kornfeld** (1889–

1943), who made a place for himself in communionist Expressionism. His essay, "Der beseelte und psychologische Mensch" ("Spiritual and Psychological Man") is essential background to a comprehension of his dramas. "Souled man" was the inner man—substantive, spiritualized, capable of experiencing life from the inside—while psychological man could be studied from the outside. Kornfeld regards the body as the prison of the soul. Only through the latter can man aspire to godliness and immortality. The body is but a clump of earth, food for worms, incapable of medieval Christianity. But other facets, especially of soul, call for the sanctification of daily acts and suggest many of the *mitzvoth* (commandments, precepts) demanded of the Jew.

The downgrading of psychology manifests itself in Kornfeld's tragedies, notably *Die Versuchung* (*Temptation*) (1917) and *Himmel und Hölle* (*Heaven and Hell*) (1919). These eerie bloodless plays are singularly lacking in emotion. They convey man's own struggle with himself, his God, his fellow men. The plays, which lend themselves to wildly different interpretations, revolve about existence and soul, good and evil, and redemption through understanding and involvement with others. Kornfeld is often as close to Catholic notions of grace as he is to Jewish ideas of a freer ethical choice.

In its barest outline, *Die Versuchung* discusses melancholy Bitterlich's murder of a bourgeois philistine, a man without a soul. This is actionless drama with frequent monologues which, along with the dialogues, border on the absurd. In *Himmel und Hölle,* Count Ungeheuer ("Count Monster"—Kornfeld's characters have allegorical names) suffers from total inability to relate to others. Unable to express the love he feels for his wife Beate, he invites to his house the ugly prostitute Maria, who calls herself a human castoff, a worn-out beast. It is she who redeems Ungeheuer by sacrificing herself for others. She even takes upon herself the guilt of Beate, who has slain her child. Maria is executed for Beate's crime.

Here, too, the action is negligible and thinly motivated. Kornfeld repeats certain phrases in the manner of Maurice Maeterlinck. The repetitive phrases are in contrast to the effervescent exclamations of love or self-disgust.

All of Kornfeld's work is non-political. He is distrustful of meliorist schemes and the deceptive actions of statesmen. In an age of revolutions he remained deeply skeptical of their value. Life was unkind to this ungainly, quiet little man who labored hard for achievement and recognition. More often he had to settle for undesirable attention. He spent his first and last years in Prague and his middle years in Berlin, where he was Reinhardt's dramaturgist. During a brief stint as head of the Darmstadt Theater, he invited the Habima, precursor to today's Israeli National Theater. Its ethnic style failed to charm the provincial critics and spectators. After some controversy, Kornfeld resigned. He also seemed to resign from life. Although in 1941 he was given the opportunity to avoid deportation, he refused to be saved. He lacked the strength to renew the eternal battle.

Although **Ludwig Winder** (1899–1946) had the makings of a gifted writer, he could not fuse the parts into a memorable whole. It was Winder who, after Kafka's death, gradually assumed his place at informal meetings of the Prague Circle.

His novels often depict the results of unresolved conflicts in childhood. Theodor Glaser of *Die rasende Rotationsmaschine* (*The Furious Rotation Machine*) (1917) is determined to turn his position of newspaper editor into a source of trans-European power and influence. This pathological desire for recognition, Winder has the reader believe, originates in Glaser's ethnic need for *Geltungsgefühl.* His fierce ambitions and savage hatred border on mania. In an attempt to do away with himself (for universalized hate includes self-hate) Glaser kills a sparrow, an act that ends his career. Left to his own ruminations, Glaser, who never accepted himself as a youngster, sees the life before him as wasted time.

Thematically different is *Die jüdische Orgel* (*The Jewish Organ*) (1922), Winder's most important novel. The *Weltfremdheit* (alienation) of the hero's Talmudically trained father is suggested in the novel's opening sentence: "Wolf Wolf, a servant of God, found out about his wife's pregnancy only in the seventh month." Albert Wolf, his son, grows up a victim of his father's religious obsessions and falls prey to another obsession, sex. After a long, unwholesome affair with a Hungarian girl, he returns home to find his father dying. Out of guilt he takes on his father's persona and marries the unattractive niece of the head of the congregation. One day, after finishing his prayers at the shul, he "saw that God did not live in this temple . . . God lived where men were living, hating, loving, sinning and repenting, not in this temple of paid *schnorrers.*" Albert Wolf starts a new life as a doorman in a house of iniquity, demonstrates kindness toward a dying girl, is fired, and becomes "a peddler in purity" who knows "the characteristics of men and the secrets of God." Jewish practices come in for pitiless criticism as he condemns the divorce between Jewish educational goals and natural human development.

Max Brod commented that somehow he never discussed Judaism with Winder, who had different ideas from his own. While Jewish negativism—or apathy—bothered Brod in others, it did not in Winder, whose sincerity and seriousness he judged above approach.

There has been some speculation about Winder's last years. Some claim he turned to Communism, while others thought he had embarked on a serious religious search, perhaps in the hope of finding a God other than the strict Jehovah. He shared with other Prague writers a basic pessimism about the human condition which the elusive divinity seemed disinclined to alleviate. Winder never abandoned the Jewish fold, however critical he was of what he found there.

Oskar Baum (1883–1941) was blind by the age of 12, and his friends had good cause to marvel at his strength and affirmation. His early novels center on blindness. As he explores the inner lives of the sightless, he reproaches those who would substitute pity for the more strenuous effort to help them lead useful lives.

Baum's Expressionist play *Das Wunder* (*The Miracle*) (1920) is thematically a cousin of Georg Kaiser's *Gas.* His sympathies lie with the endangered and exploited, though Baum refused to translate his leftist leanings into political partisanship, for politics was repugnant to him. The play also makes clear his skepticism about grand solutions. For these, he substitutes a strong faith in the exceptional person. In the play, Paul, the protagonist, seems doomed from the beginning to be misunderstood and eventually crucified. While average people resent in him the artist-inventor, the more gifted want what he cannot give. *Das Wunder* is more pessimistic than Baum's fiction about blindness. In *Das Wunder,* mere survival seems a miracle, and being understood more than one has a right to expect.

Baum wrote some novels of Jewish interest. *Die böse Unschuld* (*Evil Innocence*) (1913) depicts Jewish life in Bohemia against a backdrop of Czech-German nationality conflicts. In *Das Volk des harten Schlafs* (*People of the Deep Sleep*) (1937), Baum turns to the kingdom of the Khazars for his time and place. In this historical setting the reader recognizes the situation of contemporary Jewry under the Nazi yoke. His Jews are courageous and highly skilled in the art of war; moreover, they demonstrate uncommon endurance in the face of ruthless oppression. However, the novel is marred by awkward narration, stilted dialogue, and lack of political subtleties.

This blind writer, who grew up in a milieu of pronounced Jewish awareness, never abandoned his commitment to Jewishness. He was critical, however, of Jewish elders for whom Judaism signified improved status and social recognition. What it should mean, he asserted, is the yearning for God, be it through art, beauty, service to one's fellowman.

There should be nothing parochial in Jewishness, which can only be enriched through proximity to the non-Jewish world. The latter, in turn, can benefit greatly from contact with Jews. Until the end Baum kept hoping for a successful fusion of the particular and the universal.

A friend of Kafka's, **Ernst Weiss** (1884–1940) was burdened in his adult life by precarious emotional health. Weiss studied medicine in Vienna and counted Freud among his teachers. Nothing came of his wish to become a surgeon, for his nervous disposition precluded this practice. Instead, he sailed the oceans as a ship's physician. He visited India, China, and Japan, and his animal fables about the tigress "Naha" were made possible by his familiarity with exotic locales. His medical background also served him well, for he frequently used doctors as his protagonists.

Weiss never married, and his animosity toward women was a probable factor in his friend Kafka's breakup with Felice Bauer. After he gave up medicine, Weiss moved from city to city. He was in Munich when Hitler's rise prompted his return to Prague. When Hitler followed him to renewed exile in Paris, Weiss, emotionally exhausted, drowned himself in a bathtub in a sleazy Parisian hotel.

The confidence and capacity to live preoccupied him in many novels, though occasionally he addressed other issues. In *Boetius von Orlamünde* (1928) he delved into social snobbery that is suddenly undermined by poverty. Another novel, *Georg Letham, Arzt und Mörder* (*George Letham, Physician and Murderer*) (1931), combined scientific know-how with the temptation to kill. The protagonist of *Ich, der Augenzeuge* (*I, the Eyewitness*), published posthumously in 1963, is the physician who treated Hitler during his hysterical blindness in 1918. This physician detected a criminal element in his patient's makeup and carefully followed his career. He was ultimately punished for his intimate knowledge of the *Führer*'s questionable past.

Whereas Weiss warred with the institutions of his time, he was far more concerned with his own battle for life and an easier coexistence with fellow humans. In the absence of such rapport, he began a long and private dialogue with God. In such early poetry as "Der Versöhnungs-tag" ("The Day of Atonement") (1920), he carried on his disputation with God as well as with the "counter-God." The poet engages in an angry revolt against the vaunted charity of a divinity that is hardly charitable. God's omnipotence seems tragically misused.

Given his own psychological ambivalences, it is natural that Weiss should have been intrigued with the biblical figure of Daniel. In his novella of that name (1920), Weiss depicts a man who recognizes the truth, but cannot act on it, who is emotionally stunted and thus but half a man. A victim of God and circumstances, Daniel is abandoned by a father more eager for Nebuchadnezzar's favors than for sharing the privations of his wife and newborn son. He is also abandoned by his mother and angry at the father who had saddled her with a child, only to pursue his own pleasures. The youngster grows up, detached from the suffering of others, emotionally undeveloped. He can distinguish between good and evil, but he dissociates himself from any struggle over them.

After Kafka's death, Weiss's fiction assumed more and more of the features of Kafka's work: enigmatic contradictions, fog-shrouded situations, unusual father-son relationships, preoccupation with guilt. Weiss's work became ever more threatening, but then it also represented a world that seemed headed for disaster. The physically abused and financially embarrassed Weiss, sensing the Nazis' breath down his neck once more in 1940, announced to Soma Morgenstern that he had become an orthodox Jew. While Weiss had never fought his Jewishness, he had not shown any particular interest or devotion. If the "conversion to orthodoxy" did occur, it was almost surely the expression of ultimate despair.

Though Heinrich Heine and **Franz Kafka** (1883–1924) are the towering figures of German-Jewish writing, the mention of them in the same breath seems preposterous. Heine was controversial in his lifetime and beyond; Kafka was barely known in his brief occupancy on earth and was only recognized two decades after his death. Heine drank to the fullest from the cup of life's pleasures. In contrast, Kafka was ambivalent about life, and the very notion of pleasure mystified him. While the nineteenth-century poet laughed at life and the powerful, the twentieth-century novelist's hallucinatory visions caused him to shrink more and more into himself. Heine was deeply, though not always seriously, involved in the sociopolitical struggles of his day; for Kafka they had little existential value. Heinrich Heine mocked the distant, morose God, only to embrace Him, however tentatively, in his final years; Franz Kafka never ceased to question God's mysterious designs. After 1826, Heine often attacked Jews, calling himself a Jew one day, a Christian the next, whichever suited him at the moment. Kafka mentioned Jews in aphorisms and diaries, but according to some, Judaism was the very essence of his writing. Kafka as poet was caught in continuous contradictions, his sincerity and seriousness open to question. Kafka's contradictions were probably intentional—even systematic—and they were enveloped in mystery.

On the surface, it would be difficult to conceive of two writers more distant from each other than Heine—the Rhenish lover of beauty, the singer of sweet songs of love and nature, the scoffer at systems and ideologies and assorted sacred cows—and Kafka, the Bohemian fantasist-moralist, the very symbol of anxiety and alienation, of human powerlessness and of metaphysical protest, the master of "parable and paradox." Beneath the surface, however, both are united by the common bond of Jewish historical memory. Though they react differently to the fear of hostile authority, Heine and Kafka experience a vague yearning for the divine, even if they display varying temperaments in their quest.

The presence of Jewishness in Kafka's *oeuvre* is no longer subject to doubt. Whether that presence was truly significant (as Max Brod believes) or more moderate (as Eric Heller, Heinz Politzer, and recent biographers lead us to think) admits only a subjective judgment. This judgment, in turn, rests on one's own reading of Kafka or, more precisely, on one's own experience read into his work.

This Jewishness is most obvious when Kafka is viewed in conjunction with biographical information and weakest when considered through the fictional works alone. Thus, it is helpful to know that at a particular time, Kafka was warring with his father, the symbol of power, practicality, and business acumen; or that, during the preparation of a novel, he was attracted to a visiting Yiddish theatrical troupe; or that, at another time, he was studying Hebrew and contemplating a trip to Palestine. But even if the reader knows none of these facts, the brand and degree of his insecurity and sense of alienation would suggest that his narratives were written, if not by a Jew, then by someone with a Jew-like background or set of experiences.

Jewishness touched on Kafka's existence in many ways. His father was barely one step out of the ghetto and only two notches away from the "jargon." Few fathers, of course, have played a more pervasive role in the life of a writer-son than Hermann Kafka. When Franz wrote his *Brief an den Vater* (*Letter to My Father*), he reproached the latter, among many other complaints, for not instilling in him a more meaningful attitude toward their common Judaism. Hermann Kafka rose to be a giant in his son's mind, to become as one with all other authority figures: God, the Emperor, the courts, the police, bureaucrats. In the nightmare-ridden cubicles of his mind, all father-authority figures used the right—as his own father did—to judge the hapless son and dispose of him in life and death.

Hermann Kafka never suspected the devastating effect he had on his son, whom he loved dutifully and understood little. And so the son kept measuring himself against the cold, constantly busy, uncomprehending father and found himself frail and weak, unsuited for the role his father was playing. The thought of a fatherhood of his own was forbidding, and even the role of husband seemed beyond his strength. The letter to the emasculating father spread light not only on Kafka's disturbed inner life, but also, as mentioned before, on his craving for a Jewish involvement in his younger years. The son's indictment of his father's failure is revealing:

> [I]t would have been possible for us to have found each other in Judaism or at least to have found in it a point from which we could have traveled the same road. But what kind of Judaism did I get from you! In the course of the years I have had three different attitudes toward it.

> When I was a child I agreed with you, and reproached myself for not going often enough to the synagogue, not keeping the fasts, etc. . . . I thought I was doing you an injustice, not myself, and the feeling of guilt, always ready to hand, overwhelmed me.

> Later, when I was a young man, I couldn't understand how you, with the insignificant fragment of Jewishness you possessed, could reproach me out of godliness, as you put it, with not making an effort to put the same insignificant fragment into practice. It was really, as far as I could see, nothing, a joke—not even a joke. On four days a year you went to the synagogue, where you were at least nearer in spirit to the indifferent than to those who took it all seriously, went through the prayers patiently as a formality, sometimes astonished me by being able to show me in the prayerbook the place which was just being chanted—besides—and that was the main thing—whenever I was in the synagogue, I could twist and turn about as much as I liked.

In the elementary school he attended, all the pupils were Jewish, though the classes were taught in alternate years by a German, a Czech, and a Jew. In the *Gymnasium* Kafka encountered nationality disputes; he was not alone, however, since there were many Jewish youngsters. Among themselves they debated the Jewish problems current at the time. In 1897, the Basel program of the new Zionism beckoned for approval on their part. Kafka was opposed to it, favoring instead a humanitarian socialism. It is unclear to what extent he regarded this socialism a solution to the problem of anti-Semitism and rootlessness. In 1902, Kafka and Brod (who attended a rival *Gymnasium*) became good friends, and Kafka later admitted that he came increasingly "under Max's influence." As Brod more and more ardently embraced Zionism, Kafka absorbed at least some of his ideas. Certainly, there is evidence of a moderate rapprochement with Zionism after 1904. When, in 1911,

Prague Zionists established a meeting-place in the ancient *Rathaus* (city hall) which was to help educate the Jewish proletariat on the English model, Kafka actively participated in the project. In spite of his shyness, Kafka read to his group from Kleist's novella *Michael Kohlhaas*.

He was brought still closer to Jewish culture by the now oft-discussed visit to Prague of a theatrical group from Lemberg that performed Yiddish plays in Yiddish. He initially attended at the urging of Max Brod. His diaries make clear his fascination with Eastern European Jewish practices, the "jargon," the plays' roots in Jewish folk experience, and the very alien format of the presentation itself. For a while, he could be seen at almost every performance. He seems to have been smitten with one of the actresses, and he established a friendship of some duration with Isak Löwy, the lead actor, from whom he received further "lessons" in Jewish lore and drama. He felt impelled to study the Jewish past and immersed himself in Graetz's *History*. Some months after meeting Löwy, Kafka organized a lecture by the actor at the *Rathaus* and introduced it with a few remarks of his own in Yiddish. But the case some critics made for the immense impact of the visiting theater on early writing such as *Das Urteil* (*The Judgment*) (1912) is only mildly convincing.

Some of Kafka's early tales appeared in Jewish periodicals. "Der Hausvater" ("The Housefather") was published in *Selbstwehr* (*Self-defense*), whereas some of his animal parables were selected by Buber for *Der Jude* from a complement of twelve stories which Kafka had sent in characteristic indecision.

In the decade left to him, Kafka battled with illusion, insecurity, and his marriage dilemma. The social changes wrought by war and the altered status of Prague—the establishment of the new Czech state—all left him untouched. Yet he had always been sympathetic to the cultural aspirations of Czech writers.

While Kafka's biographical links to Judaism are clear, especially so in his final year or two when he lived with Dora Dymant, the tie-in to his fiction must remain speculative. The Jewish aspect of his work is every bit as enigmatic as the problem of reading Kafka in general. The attempt to interpret a Kafka fabulation dogmatically, and from one standpoint to the exclusion of others, is doomed to frustration. Kafka's admission that he did not "understand" his stories and could not always grasp what had flowed from his brain to his pen cannot be wholly dismissed. "Do you find a meaning in 'The Judgment'?" he asks Felice Bauer in a letter. "I don't and can't explain anything in it." Even if we don't take these words literally, it would be presumptuous to adhere only to *one* interpretation, be it theology, Marxism, or Judaism.

Thus, Kafka's novel, *Das Schloß* (*The Castle*) (1929), has been seen as man's accession to grace, but also as the Diaspora Jew's ubiquity. The village will not fully accept the Jewish surveyor, and the castle excludes him outright in spite of vague promises of a job or contract. Does it mean that no degree of assimilation is acceptable to those who determine acceptability, that the attempt to please or oblige is an exercise in futility? Or does it allude to the arbitrariness of a willful divinity presiding over a kingdom of heaven whose ways will always mystify man? Or does it mean one of several other possibilities? As though anticipating the reader's craving for clarity and somehow wishing to obvert it, Kafka sneaks in here and there a line that eliminates both certainty and logic. Thus, about the castle as a symbol of grace, as the heaven on earth, we are told that things in the castle are no better than down in the village.

Similarly, *Der Prozeß* (*The Trial*) (1925) may be read as a parable of metaphysical guilt, the passing of moral judgment, and the inscribing of it—the passage, in fact, as one critic put it, from Rosh Hashana to Yom Kippur. Or one may think of the Jew condemned everywhere by the accident of birth and the fact of his mere existence—like the protagonist Kafka who does not know why he has been arrested and is unable to find out. But are not the heroes of both *The Castle* and *The Trial* symbols of exclusion and alienation, terrified and puzzled by life's enigmas, and doomed to a state of chronic anxiety? Is this in the main a Jewish oppression, or is it the oppression of twentieth-century man, threatened by forces too powerful for him to control and too complex for him to identify the component parts? The world of *The Trial* is full of ambivalent relationships, weird chains of command, secretive judges, elusive prosecutors, and exasperatingly self-important bureaucrats. Nightmarish settings serve as courtrooms in which vague, unexplained charges are presented, many of them seemingly baseless, and yet they end in a judgment of death by execution. All authority seems to fuse into one, and it derives from an undefinable source. One could almost say that *Der Prozeß* is the modern version of Kleist's *Michael Kohlhaas*.

In the three tales sometimes published as *Die Söhne* (*The Sons*), authority again proves oppressive. Whether it is the absent God who imposes enigmatic sentences—changing one son into an insect, another to suffer death by drowning—or whether it is fathers who maim or kill, or bosses who are terrifying in their contradictory commands and evaluations, the sons find themselves in perennial uncertainty, a state of chronic anxiety and self-doubt. Authority on any hierarchical level crushes the helpless sons, that is, the pitiful creatures inhabiting this earth. Of course, if one is so inclined, one can again equate the sons with Jews, hopelessly at the mercy of arbitrary rulers. Like the sons, the Jews have overestimated their security in every generation, to be struck down again and again.

But why assume that Kafka was so parochial in his thinking as to see only Jews as objects of non-ending persecution? Why not the Czechs, the Bohemians, the Hussites and the Ruthenians? Had not all people in a sense become Jews? Had not Jewish suffering and peril become universal suffering and peril? If the fate of his characters had only a limited sectarian or ethnic interest, the world would no longer be intrigued with the Kafka puzzle so many years after his death. Instead, the debate goes on, almost everywhere and recently even in Prague. Kafka would not remain buried in the Jewish cemetery, as his unique vision of human destiny demanded his resurrection.

The debate continued unabated. Whom do critics see now? asks a French student of Kafka. Is it the surrealist, the Expressionist, the apologist for Kierkegaard, the Freudian? Is Kafka, studied and restudied, an atheist or a tireless God-seeker? Is he a mystic or a Zionist? Is there more to him than the frightened seer of emptiness and alienation, the prophet of the executioner's universe? In a different vein, was he so disgruntled with assimilated Judaism that he contemplated the road to conversion? Were most critics wrong and Max Brod, the friend, right in perceiving strong affirmationist and optimistic elements in Kafka's works?

But Brod, too, concedes that Kafka used his narratives to vent doubts and tell "how man confused and missed his way." In his *Aphorismen (Aphorisms)*, Brod maintains, Kafka sought to redirect man, ever so subtly, to a new path. The road signs may be poorly marked, but the road is there. But is Kafka's positive voice universal, or does it speak only for the writer, for whom writing was "a form of prayer?" Brod claims a broad universality for Kafka:

> His efforts were directed toward inner perfection, a stainless life. . . . For he was wholly occupied with the striving for the highest ethical pinnacle a man can attain—a pinnacle which in truth scarcely can be attained. He was filled with a drive, intensified to the point of pain and semi-madness not to brook any vice in himself, any lie, any self-deception, nor any offense against his fellow-men—this passion for perfection often took the form of self-humiliation, since Kafka saw his own weaknesses as though under a microscope, magnified to many times their size. How he despaired of himself on account of these weaknesses, longing as he did for intimate fusion with the Pure, the Divine, which in his Aphorisms he described as the 'I destructible'.

The often-reproduced photograph of the mature Kafka shows a gaunt, haunted face, brooding, sensitive, bearing the marks of hurt, pain, *Angst,* on essentially soulful, sympathetic features. The face bears a disquieting, almost supernatural resemblance to photographs of survivors of concentration camps, as they emerged from captivity twenty years after his death, still stunned, from a penal colony that made his own nightmarish visions seem benign.

Thieberger was struck by the possibilities for protean explanation of Kafka's aphorism: "A cage went in search of a bird." The cage is both prison and protective wall, symbol and reality, paradox and gallows humor. To him, the richness of Kafka as well as the difficulties and elasticity are cohabiting in this one paradoxical statement. It is one of the characteristics of Kafka's *oeuvre* that the more it is explored, the more it deepens speculation.

Though new literary heroes abound on the horizon, Kafka remains one of the most widely read authors of our time. Literature has not been the same since this man, devoted to writing as a sacred enterprise, catapulted into the limelight after 1945. In Kafka, the melding of German and Jewish culture, enriched by the moods of Prague, wrought a revolution in the novel and in the view of the post-Auschwitz-Hiroshima world—which, however, he never knew. Equally important, he conveyed the anxieties of twentieth-century man.

Hermann Ungar (1893–1929) was no Kafka, but his novels had a distinctly Kafkaesque streak. In *Die Verstümmelten (The Mutilated)* (1927) and *Die Klasse (The Class)* (1927), Ungar created characters pitifully unadaptable to life. The protagonist of *Die Verstümmelten* was traumatized by a hated father's incestuous relationship with his sister (the hero's aunt). His obsessive memory propels him into a sexual relationship with a widow with frightening characteristics of her own. He seeks out other grotesque creatures: a once generous friend whom illness has transformed into a sadist; a former butcher who has become a nurse and murderous religious fanatic. A similarly frightening cast peoples *Die Klasse,* in which the teacher, Joseph Blau, unable to relate to his wife, students, and colleagues, becomes responsible for the death of one student and nearly that of another. He eventually redeems himself by saving the life of yet another of his charges. Ungar's Jewish characters share with their non-Jewish confreres the numerous psychomoral handicaps that make his landscape so bleak and barren.

Sandwiched between Slavs and Germans, Czech Jews developed literary moods and strategies that feature enigma, paradox, mystification, arcanum. Whether their terror and despondency were a response to their precarious position or to the overall history and mood of the region must remain conjecture. At least one member of the Prague group, Franz Kafka, managed to give his private anxieties and dread a universal significance that has helped shape attitudes toward the modern world.

• • • • •

IV

Gathering Clouds:

Jews Exit from German Life

The Beginning of the End

Not even during the years 1919–1923, which Golo Mann has characterized as the most serious of popular German anti-Semitism, did a Cassandra foretell the end of German-Jewish life. Jewish writers were not endowed with greater vision than other Jews. In 1918, no one would have predicted that German-Jewish togetherness would disintegrate in less than 20 years.

However, there are occasional flashes of intuition. In a story, "Gespräche mit dem ewigen Juden" ("Chats with the Wandering Jew") (1921), Lion Feuchtwanger related this nightmarish vision:

> And then the room grew much larger and became a huge square filled with smoke and blood. Towers of Hebrew books were burning and funeral pyres were built, high up into the clouds, and men were being charred, countless men, and the voices of priests were chanting "Gloria in Excelsis Deo." Long lines of men, women and children were dragging themselves across the square, coming from all sides; they were naked or in rags, and they had nothing with them but bodies, charred, dismembered, broken, hanged, nothing but bodies and the scraps from book scrolls torn, violated, soiled with excrement.

Yet, like all others, this same Lion Feuchtwanger underestimated the Nazi danger. In *Erfolg (Success)* (1930), perhaps the first anti-Nazi novel on record, he painted a contemptuous portrait of the chauffeur Kutzner, a double for Hitler.

No one seemed to recognize the vitality of the Nazi movement, its proclivity for brutality, its willingness to shove the past overboard and to create its own morality. The Jewish artists did not divorce themselves any more than the average person from what had preceded Nazism in history. When they thought of persecutions, it was in terms of the past—economic restrictions, some graffiti on houses, slurs in the streets, perhaps even a beating, though most likely in some other town. The recurrence of such past unpleasantness was unlikely, they felt, in the enlightened Germany of today. Jewish intellectuals had not always recognized that the Germany of Goethe and Kant had given way to a worship of Germanic tribes and other primitivism. The writers' alleged intuitive powers and intellectual insights failed totally to conceive of the horrors to come.

Once Hitler was in power, recognition of a new reality came more swiftly. Before the last cinders of the Reichstag fire had been cleared away, many of the writers were in exile. Some who counted on the good sense and perspicacity of the German people waited. They did not always leave in time.

Once abroad, they enlisted their talents in battling the Nazi foe. The power of the pen was not, however, as great as it was alleged to be, especially not when a ruthless enemy played without rules. For the Jewish writers, too, came the devastating realization that the number of their readers had shrunk pitifully and that their works, often in German and untranslated, were enlightened only to those who, like themselves, no longer needed enlightening. They were frustrated that citizens in their host countries ignored their warnings—that, in fact, Frenchmen, Englishmen, and Americans suffered from the same limited vision that had afflicted them earlier. In some countries, they were regarded as uncomfortable, irritating foreigners.

Life was not easy for the Jewish writers in their various new homes. The few publishers-in-exile had to be circumspect in their investments and could publish little of what was submitted, even by previously established writers. As a result, many authors depended on refugee relief organizations for their daily bread or took on the lowliest of jobs. A few were strengthened by the challenges; others proved inept in meeting them. There were suicides throughout the Nazi years, especially, however, from 1939 to 1942, when it appeared that Hitler might be invincible and continued struggle seemed in vain—or they found the very notion of a Hitlerized world insufferable.

Nearly all had to change residence repeatedly. Those who initially opted for Vienna or Prague had gained only three to five years of grace. The refugees in Paris or in the Riviera town of Sanary-sur-mer fled to England or the United States. For Jewish writers who came to the United States for their first or last stop, America proved to be a friendly but difficult country. Severed from their own language and culture, largely unknown, incapable of grasping a new brand of cultural egalitarianism, Jewish writers were often unhappy and associated with others in the same depressed state. In spite of physical security and countless acts of generosity by their hosts, life for many of the exiles had lost its meaning and charm.

Since they had not adjusted to their new life, they clung to the hope of returning to an idealized former life. Of those who actually returned to Germany after the war, few remained for long. The old relationships were good, but new ones were difficult to forge in the light of the past. An invisible wall had been erected which would darken German-Jewish togetherness for generations to come.

•   •   •   •   •

Apostates

For a brief period before 1933, **Alfred Döblin** (1879–1954), Expressionist novelist and stylistic innovator, immersed himself in the dilemma of living as a German and a Jew. He emerged from the experience with a serious indictment of Western Jewry in general. His conversion to Catholicism in the disastrous days following Hitler's victory in France in the summer of 1940 was the result of profound anxiety and deep inner crisis. Yet it cannot be divorced from the void he perceived in Occidental Judaism.

Döblin was born in Stettin, the son of a tailor and his middle-class wife. The father coldly pursued his pleasures, neglected the family, and eventually took off with a young woman. In 1888 the impoverished mother moved her children to Berlin. "I belonged to the poor," Döblin wrote later. "This determined my whole nature. To this people, this nation I belonged: to the poor."

Döblin observed no Jewish practices in this emotionally barren home except for the observance of the High Holidays. He had heard, he stated, that his parents were Jewish and that he belonged to a Jewish family. The anti-Semitism he encountered in the streets and in school did not greatly disturb him. His Jewish instruction consisted of some Hebrew, a little literature, and early Jewish history. They did not intrigue him. He had studied enough language in school, and between the Odyssey and the Nibelungs he had had his fill of legend: "As for the teaching of the actual religious element—I read it and listened to it. No real feeling was aroused and no permanent attachment developed." He apprehended the divinity not through Jewish teaching, but through Hölderlin and Dostoyevski. Even the declaration "Thou shalt have no other God, for I am the Lord, your God" impressed him as vacuous and uninspired. He wanted and needed a less distant God. Later, after he read Kierkegaard, his need for a nearer divinity deepened even more.

He was well established as a physician and writer when the 1920s produced pogromlike outbursts in Berlin. Zionist leaders urged him to help assess the situation. They also invited him to visit Palestine, an idea alien to him. But he did become sufficiently concerned to want to learn more about Jews. "I could not consider my friends who called themselves Jews as real Jews. They were not, either in their faith or language; they were the remains of a vanished people who had been assimilated into their environment. I, therefore, asked myself and I asked others: Where are there Jews? I was told 'in Poland,' whereupon I traveled to Poland."

In *Flucht und Sammlung des Judenvolkes* (*Flight and Settlement of the Jewish People*) (1935), written a decade after his return, the future convert chides Jews for having no Jewish values. Jews in the West have only disdain for their religion mixed with some hatred, he notes. German Jews had been cheated in their emancipation pact with the German state, which abrogated the agreement after luring Jews away from their secure existence. Willingly, humbly, they suffered repeated rebuffs in the vain hope of a more genuine acceptance. They were simply unwilling to recognize that they were not welcome. Their mistaken rush toward *Deutschtum* had inevitably meant their flight from Judentum. As a result, Judaism fell into disrepair. What was left was a falsification of its nature, a Christianity without Christ. When they dissolved as a people with distinct practices and values, they also lost their God—the real center of their religion. Jewishness had become only a burden, an obstacle to career and to social and professional equality.

Döblin's indictment continues. What Jews secretly hope for in the West is the fulfillment of a wish: "Beginning today, you are not Jews, you have never been Jews, all your birth records have been blotted out . . . you are German, Swiss, Austrian. You may now leave." With the realization of this wish, real prayers of thanks would be heard in the magnificent reform temples that have been erected.

While he speaks sardonically of German Jews—and discusses them virtually as an outsider—he points respectfully to the authentic Jews he met on his Polish journey. Their identity as a people had been kept intact, and it was still possible to be a Jew. But even there, especially among leftists, he had detected the first signs of disintegration. He feared that only one generation separated the young Polish Jews from the errors already perpetrated by their Western brethren.

Eastern and Western Jews had in common the external enemy. Their common misfortune stemmed from a defeat suffered two thousand years ago and from which they had never recovered. It had imposed on them, in the Diaspora, a recurring pattern so obvious that it had gone unnoticed. There is flight from the old and then search for the new home. When the enemy reappears, there is first the attempt to appease him. When this is impossible, the Jews leave once more, and the process is repeated.

Döblin's assessment of Jewish helplessness is reminiscent, almost in wording, of Wassermann's description. If the Jews are poor, they are offensive to the eye. If they are rich, they have robbed their Gentile neighbors. If they are religious, theirs is the wrong religion. But if they are irreligious, they become corruptors, subversives, *Kulturfeinde* (enemies of culture). Whatever they do or are, their prospects are equally poor.

This destiny was not divinely decreed. When Jews had a country of their own, God had chosen them to be proud and strong. Suffering, which had led others to revolt, had made Jews passive. They *read* Torah: they did not *live* it. Döblin asks Jews to return to Judaism's proud spirit and cease practicing an inactive, ghetto-inspired worship of it. Jews should follow Abraham's example, claim free land and occupy it.

In western Europe, the coupling of the acquisition of land with the national idea might be reactionary. For Jews, it would be liberal—a vital, new, and vigorous idea. A Jewish people united on its own soil will "allow the Jewish shadow to fall normally, and a Jewish plant to grow straight."

Though Döblin advocated a Zionist solution, Palestine was hardly a personal dream. His own assimilationist "disease" had progressed too far to permit a cure. When Hitler threatened him a second time in defeated France, he visited a church, and the image of the nearer and gentle Jesus offered more hope and solace than the remote and abstract Jehovah. He converted to Catholicism soon after his arrival in Californian exile after much illness and sorrow, and after experiencing renewed poverty and neglect in the countries that had received him.

Berlin Alexanderplatz (1929) had been translated into English, but its author remained unknown in the United States. This is a work of immense vitality and vision and often suggests James Joyce. A novel of proletarian existence, it combined some techniques of Expressionism with a thorough grounding in psychiatry and sociology. The novel may be less grandiose than Thomas Mann's masterpieces, but it is more modern, anticipating in many ways the fiction of Günter Grass. Eastern Jews living in Berlin frequently cross the path of the hero, Franz Biberkopf. They are generally presented in a favorable way, endowed with mystery and wisdom.

Döblin's other major novels had not been translated. Their metaphysical content and spiritual quest—clothed in Expressionist garb and innovative language—were alien to the American spirit. Döblin owed his brief employment in a Hollywood studio less to admiration for his work than to the spirit of charity toward displaced artists. Neither the captains of the American film industry nor American publishers cared to invest in a writer whose work dealt with Eastern and Western mysticism, the desire to bring Eastern spirituality to a consumerized Western world, or the notion—before the atom bomb—that science without goodness and godliness might drive man to the very abyss.

Döblin's brilliant trilogy of the German Revolution of 1918—published long after the events depicted—mixed fictional with historical figures. Entitled *1918,* this mostly political fiction, which made for ambitious reading, ranks somewhat below his religious-spiritual work. The novels mark him as a man of the left, with a far greater respect for the half-demented revolutionary Rosa Luxemburg than for the moderate pseudo-socialist Friedrich Ebert, the villain of the first segment. *1918* is deeply pessimistic, which, however, does not hold true for *Hamlet oder die lange Nacht nimmt ein Ende* (*Hamlet, or the Long Night Draws to a Close*) (1956). Here he voices a mild hope for a new Europe.

Neglected and frustrated in America, Döblin was among the first to return to Germany, where he briefly edited a journal. He soon found the post-Nazi climate uncongenial and returned to Paris, site of his first exile. He continued writing in the French capital until his death.

Like Döblin, **Hermann Broch** (1886–1951) was a seeker of the absolute. His religious conversion, not without some conviction, should not be construed as a valuation of Catholicism over Judaism.

If Broch failed to attain the summit of literary recognition—his reputation has increased with time—it was not for want of extraordinary gifts. His late literary beginnings are in part responsible, along with exile, which gave him but few years to write on native soil. Until the years after World War I, when his father's textile business declined, Broch was active in the family's factory. A many-faceted genius, Broch invented a machine and later headed the company. His father surmised correctly that his son—already in his mid-thirties—never had his heart in the textile industry. Broch himself later described his association with family and business as sheer hell. Though sparing in self-revelations, Broch left no doubt that his life was dominated by his business-centered father.

Nevertheless, he managed to give some shape to this life. At the very time he began dabbling in literature, he devoted long hours to mathematics and the sciences, which he was studying at the university. He would at times frequent Vienna's cafés in the company of Altenberg and others of the Young Vienna group.

Broch developed two character flaws that were to plague him throughout his life. One was an insatiable appetite for women; the other his inability to hold on to money when he had it and to earn it again after he had lost it. After 1928 when the business, now under his direction, took a marked turn for the worse, he never again enjoyed the comforts that were once his own.

Like Döblin, he found little in Judaism to attract love, reverence, or loyalty. Upon marriage, he converted. But in an age of racial anti-Semitism, his Christianity did not prevent imprisonment after the *Anschluß*. Released, he quickly left Austria for an exile frequently marred by privations.

Broch felt some attraction to the integral Jewishness of Eastern Jewry, especially the Hasidic brand. In the *Schlafwandler* trilogy (*The Sleepwalkers*) (1930–1932), many Eastern Jews appear, and the attitude toward them became a gauge by which to measure the decay of values and the loss of the Absolute. Even before his conversion Broch became an adamant fighter against anti-Semitism, perhaps for the very reason that it served as a cultural barometer of the worth of people.

Die Schlafwandler addresses the disintegration of German values as a prelude to Nazism. Broch is inventive and develops character and movement to reflect the increasing relativism which he finds wanting and dangerous. His style is consonant with the mood, ideas, and characters in each segment of the tripartite work.

The initial volume starts with 1887. Stability rules the tradition-bound land, but it is a painful, stultified tradition, epitomized by the cold and sterile von Pasenow family. Here Broch's style is formal, restrained, and conservative, as though to mirror the archaism that suffuses the tale. Then, as dehumanization and war draw near, Broch's language loosens perceptibly, reflecting the growing anarchy. In the revolutionary postwar years, as society is torn from its moorings, Broch resorts to loose associations of words and concepts, at times a deliberate dissociation. His language reflects times that gallop toward disaster. Though he varies locales, the constant is a Germany militarizing or suffering the consequences of militarization.

The characters develop in line with Broch's notion of the flow of history. The class awareness of von Pasenow dooms him to boredom, discontent, and the inability to enjoy the one real love offered him. His opposite, another nobleman, Bertrand, has gone into business and embodies movement and life but is regarded as a traitor and seducer by his class.

In *Der Anarchist* (ca. 1903) August Esch, a bookkeeper, dreams of a better world, but against a backdrop of sex, greed, and crime. His dream had been vaguely humanitarian and socialist at first, but after some reverses and disenchantment, he retreats more and more into a dangerous world of wishfulness.

Completed shortly before 1933, the final volume, *Der Realist*, concentrates on the tumultuous postwar years. The protagonist Huguenau foreshadows the Nazis to come. Huguenau, the realist, i.e., opportunist and criminal, benefits from the brutalization that followed the defeat. He can kill with ease; his conscience has been silenced. Evil has become banal, and the time is ripe for crime. Men such as von Pasenow, the romantic, and Esch, the dreamer, have left the door ajar for Huguenau to enter.

The culture critic in Broch found, however, some stabilizing forces that had not caved in. In them neither the notion of humanity nor the quest for the Absolute was dormant. Neither a woman from the Salvation Army nor the Hasidic Jew Nuchem is touched by the decay. Having existed all along on the periphery of society, they have escaped the infusion of its poisons. Though theirs are traditional religious values, their lives enclose none of the anachronisms or modernist excesses of the main characters. Nuchem's family is the epitome of warmth and feeling in human relationships. What is lost in the trilogy is, in the final analysis, God himself, even if Broch speaks only of the loss of *Erkenntnis* (recognition, perception, knowledge).

The loss of *Erkenntnis*—a virtually untranslatable term—reappears as a prime theme in *Der Tod des Vergil* (*Virgil's Death*) (1945), which "interprets the visions of Vergil and depicts the age from whose bloodshed and convulsions Christianity was to be born." In a dialogue between Vergil and Augustus, the poet reveals that knowledge and truth are perennial goals. When the Emperor inquired if Vergil had attained this *Erkenntnis,* the poet responds that no one can. The loss of the divinity is the prelude to the rawest craving for power, with devastation and destruction ominously following one another.

Broch's political values are unmistakably conservative, leading some enemies to label him a crypto-fascist. The truth is that in all domains Broch strove for progress, but only within continuity and with due respect for what had preceded. In the *Anarchist* portion of the *Sleepwalkers,* the labor organizer may alone have Broch's full approval. In monetary and mercantile societies and governments and their equally materialistic parties and constituencies, Broch perceives the demolition of values most clearly.

Far from being the reactionary depicted by some, Broch is closer to that specifically Austrian brand of Marxism which targets a reconciliation of socialism with capitalist features. Also, in his final years, Broch seriously proposed an international university that would study political psychology and mass hysteria. It was to plan, with scientific precision, varying models of democracy, peace, and humanitarianism.

Broch's attitudes toward his Jewishness cannot be divorced from his disillusioning family experiences, his unfulfilled longing for wholeness and the divine. In a sense, he reacted, as did Döblin, against his family values, including the anemic Jewishness they represented and their debasing need for acceptance. In their joy over a favorable balance sheet, they tended to forget not only human values, but the God who had once been central to their being.

Seekers of the divine—Broch, Döblin, Werfel—found Judaism wanting. Perhaps they never understood its essence, having experienced only what they looked upon as empty ritual and routinized synagogue attendance, if that. They equated it with the spiritual void in the home. If God was not among the Jews they knew, He must be elsewhere. It is significant that only the impoverished but spiritually rich Jews of the East enjoyed their respect. Here, too, it was the case of a religion in a place where they were not. It was easier to turn a Western Jew, a Jew of *Bildung,* into a Western Christian than into an Eastern Jew.

Obsessed with God after a godless youth, Prague-born **Franz Werfel** (1890–1945) found himself powerfully drawn to Catholicism in his final decades. His actual conversion, claimed by some, is doubtful; his spiritual conversion is not. In 1945 Franz Werfel was buried in a Catholic cemetery with a priest in attendance.

Werfel was probably more attracted to Catholicism than alienated by Judaism. While he never felt much enthusiasm for his native religion, he never withheld his respect. Jews as such remained a special people for him, chosen to deliver the divine message to others. He esteemed the dignity with which Jews had borne their suffering. As a celebrant of life, he revered the Jews' determination to live and triumph over their enemies. Out of respect for Jewish history and his own sense of integrity, he refrained from abandoning a harassed community in its most tragic hour.

Werfel's Jewish family history was less than felicitous. Though his father cherished the muses, he wanted his son to continue his business. Any ambition beyond met with disapproval. Werfel's mediocre school-work merely strengthened the father's resolve to see Franz established in a business of proven quality. Even after Franz had amassed considerable fame for *Der Weltfreund (Friend of Humanity)* (1911), the father sent Franz to Hamburg to gain business experience. But Werfel wrote poems when he should have been examining ledgers, and one day he flushed his business papers down the toilet. The act led to a virtual rupture with his parents; it was not a formal break, nor were there violent scenes, but a gradual distancing and infrequent visits.

In the early years of the war Werfel served in an artillery regiment; then in 1917, he was reassigned to the press corps in Vienna, a city he called his home until the *Anschluß*. After the war he flirted briefly with radicalism, then made an about-face and adopted generally conservative positions. After Hitler, he sought exile in southern France, and, following an adventurous escape across the Pyrenees in 1940, he enjoyed major successes in America. Hence he was spared the economic hardships that afflicted Heinrich Mann, Döblin, and even Brecht.

Weltfreund and similar poetry had constituted a declaration of love to humanity. It was a feeling, warm-hearted, soul-stirring work that sought to eradicate lines that separate one group from another. Voicing discontent with the present and yearning for the future, Werfel set a tone that many Expressionists were to follow. The war demolished both their illusions and Werfel's. *Der Gerichtstag (Day of Judgment)*, written in 1916–1917 in the trench but not published until 1919, expresses the searing pain of the lover of a world that has gone mad. The poet's heart is still aglow as he prays for a bond among all people. The prospects are less good; the world is torn by lovelessness. Any why this lovelessness? People have lost consciousness of their divine origin. The author argues with a God whose redemptive plan now strikes him as questionable. The poet's soul is divided and longs to become one again. He feels unclean and pleads repeatedly, "Reinige mich, reinige mich!" ("Cleanse me!")

The spiritual nature of man is also the theme of *Der Spiegelmensch (Mirror Image)* (1920). Troubled by the evil he has done, Tamal seeks admission to a monastery. Inadvertently, he releases his other self, "der Spiegelmensch," from the mirror which has contained him. That self represents Tamal's very earthy drive for wealth, power, sex. Under his tutelage, Tamal commits actual and probable crimes, from seducing his best friend's wife to killing his father, from promising Utopia to society to brutally betraying it. Werfel solves his dualist dilemma: he kills Tamal and thus chokes off the *Spiegelmensch* within. Unity remains an elusive target.

Before 1927, the word "Jew" occurs sparsely in Werfel's vocabulary. His universalist longings transcend any group interests. However, the Jewish presence surges in *Paulus unter den Juden (Paul Among the Jews)* (1926). Writing this play, Werfel confessed later, was painful as he depicted the great and tragic hour of Judaism when the nascent Christianity severed the umbilical cord from the mother faith. The wise Jewish scholar Gamaliel has learned that his former student Paul has returned to Jerusalem a completely changed man. Gone is the nationalist zealot who had induced the High Priest's son into a frenzied revolt against Rome. Stunned also are James, Jesus's brother, and Peter, the disciple.

Gamaliel pleads with Paul to return to the ancestral faith. Yes, he concedes, Jesus was a holy man of God, and a wrong judgment may have been passed against him. But Jesus was not the son of God: "Out of human beings like ourselves, renewal cannot come." Gamaliel is adamant that Jesus was only a man. The Messiah has not come; the Messiah belongs permanently to the future. Unable to persuade the new Paul, as committed to his new cause as he had been to his old, Gamaliel fears impending disaster. On the eve of Yom Kippur, as was the custom, the High Priest had chased a he-goat into the desert, laden with the sins of the people. This time the goat ran back into the Temple. An ill omen! Gamaliel dies and his body is carried off. The Roman governor Marullus, a treacherous politician, resorts to a pretext to introduce into the temple the image of mad Caligula. One of Paul's disciples, disenchanted with his master, kills himself. Jewish misfortunes mount. Peter, witness to the chaos, announces that the hour of Christianity has struck.

Though Werfel aimed to strike a balance, he could not conceal his Christian sympathies. He respected the Jewish positions he depicted, but he would go beyond them. The Judaism of Jesus's time was stagnant and ripe for change or renewal. The change called not for an abrogation of Torah, but an extension of it—through new revelation.

Werfel sometimes deploys Jewish characters to deal with Christian concepts of sin, grace, and redemption. In "Der Abituriententag" ("Graduation Day"), a novella, a brilliant but unattractive and clumsy Jewish boy is psychologically abused by an envious and often cruel Christian youngster. Years later, the Christian has become a prosecuting attorney, and before him appears an alleged sex murderer whose physique and mannerisms remind him of his own crimes toward the Jewish youngster. In a moment of moral panic, he hurls himself at the murder suspect, embracing him in a gesture of penitence, only to realize immediately that this was not the youngster he had injured.

Again, in *Barbara oder die Frömmigkeit* (*Barbara, or The Pure in Heart* (1929), Werfel pits the selfless piety of the maid Barbara against the intellectualized Christianity of the Jew Engländer. Engländer, who bears some resemblance to Werfel, visits a Hasidic community and urges its members to accept Jesus as the Messiah. If Engländer rejects baptism, it is only because he does not wish to be seen as an opportunist. Engländer's brand of Christianity and resulting conflicts lead him to a tragic end. Claiming to be the bishop of all the Jews who believe in Christ, he attempts to gain access to the Archbishop's palace. But instead of being admitted to His Eminence's presence, he is shipped off to a sanatorium.

In 1929, Werfel undertook his second trip to Palestine. He found the country more developed. In Jerusalem, he met some Armenians, victims of Turkish persecutions a decade earlier. The experience was to culminate three years later in *Die vierzig Tage des Musa Dagh* (*The Forty Days of Musa Dagh*), a grueling epic of genocide. The novel could serve as a warning to humanity that the fate of the Armenians might be in store for others. The Armenians know they are not being slaughtered for anything they have done, but for who they are.

This novel, as memorable achievement, is one of the few in which father-son relationships are strong. In *Die Geschwister von Neapel* (*The Siblings of Naples*) (1931), paternal authoritarianism leads again to family disasters. Father-son relationships may symbolize here also the relationship between Judaism and Christianity: "Whosoever sees his father sees God. For this father is the last link in the unbroken chain of ancestors which join Man to Adam and through him to the origin of creation." But "whoever also sees his son, sees God. For this son is the nearest link which joins ties to the Last Judgment and Redemption."

Der Weg der Verheißung (*The Eternal Road*) (1935) was written at Max Reinhardt's bidding, not long after Hitler's rise to power. Here a group of Jews is awaiting a judgment of life or death. A Mephistophelian visionary keeps belittling Jewish history and "unmasking" Jewish strengths as cowardice and God's support of Israel as a curse. As always, Werfel the half-convert voices his respect for the Jewish past and its moral grandeur.

When, after serious illness and several dangerous months in occupied France, Werfel's escape route took him to Lourdes, he vowed—so various accounts have it—to tell the story of St. Bernadette if ever he should inhale free air again. The result was *Das Lied von Bernadette* (*The Song of Bernadette*) (1941), which became an enormous success in the United States, assuring him a life of comfort in his new country. The novel confirms the seductive power that natural and selfless piety always had on him. It also confirmed how far his Catholic sympathies had progressed.

To the very end, Werfel was eager to balance his Catholicism with his Jewishness. In *Jacobowsky und der Oberst* (*Jacobowsky and the Colonel*) (1945), a play set against the Nazi victory in France, a Polish Jew—witty, wise, and mentally superior—is engineering an escape in the company of a bigoted, love-struck Polish colonel. The colonel's impressive claims of achievement are not matched by the facts. Jacobowsky's responses to the colonel leave little doubt as to where Werfel's sympathies lie. Nevertheless, the main point of the play focuses on the respect that two very dissimilar people can develop for each other. Jacobowsky is an artist in survival, in spite of little physical heroism; the colonel is poorly equipped to survive, in spite of ample bravery.

A work he did not live to complete, "Stern der Ungeborenen," ("Star of the Unborn"), shows that Werfel could not carry the Jewish-Christian dialogue beyond its earlier confines. Unlike Döblin, who found Judaism wanting, Werfel merely wanted it enlarged. He saw in Christianity an addition, not a repudiation. What is more difficult to understand in Werfel is his pronounced later conservatism, which made him intolerant of most progressive and all socialist thought. He remained opposed to militarism and social oppression, but his Catholic-inspired politics moved him ever closer to the positions held by Rome.

Although the spirit of his grandfather, Samson Raphael Hirsch, the great theorist of neo-Orthodoxy, permeated his childhood home, **Karl Jakob Hirsch** (1892–1952) ended his life as a Christian. This painter and stage designer, author of the impressive *Kaiserwetter* (*Emperor Weather*) (1932), had strong spiritual needs which Judaism apparently was unable to fill. Increasingly, he saw himself as a "solitary wanderer in the chaos of a universe that once had direction." Jewish ritual had long ago ceased to have meaning; the "punishing Jehovah" was more intimidating than trust-inspiring, and in the difficult years of his American exile less available than the Jesus of love. Hirsch made it clear, however, that his baptism in no way altered the ethical traditions in which he had been raised. The account of his conversion is alternately touching and naive. The impact on him of the film version of Werfel's *The Song of Bernadette* is described as significant. As for Zionism, he detested it with the same intensity with which he rejected German nationalism.

Kaiserwetter is reminiscent of Thomas Mann's *Buddenbrooks* in its emphasis on disease and death. It echoes Heinrich Mann's *Der Untertan* (*Little Superman*) in its insistence on the rotten underpinnings of German bourgeois life. Through the repeated intersecting of the careers of an opportunistic, ruthless climber, and a lawyer who embodies individualism, Hirsch depicts the seemingly well-regulated lives of Germans under the Empire—stable, orderly, predictable, but concealing behind the facades shallowness, dishonesty, and perversions. Here, as in less significant writings, Hirsch searches vainly for the lost faith of his youth.

It is doubtful that the apostates ever gave Judaism a serious chance to meet their spiritual needs. For the most part, they equated it with the formalistic and loveless ritualistic practices of their homes. Little happened in later life to remove the ideas formed in their early years. When the religious need grew more urgent and intense in the critical period of Nazi expansion, the nearer figure of Jesus offered, moreover, greater solace than the distant, invisible God. The teachings of the Father seemed worn and confused compared with the simpler, more direct offerings of the Son.

•　•　•　•　•

New Masters in Historical Fiction

As Nazism became more and more ominous, a number of Jewish writers resorted to history to clarify the present. This process accelerated after Hitler's domestic and military successes rendered the Thousand-Year Reich a distinct possibility. Some have charged that recourse to historical fiction constituted a retreat from reality; others claimed it was a conscious effort to analyze the present more dispassionately and with greater distance. Also, since the world had not collapsed as a result of the historical disasters depicted, the novels offered some hope that the Nazi regime, too, would pass into oblivion and civilization would survive.

The most adept and successful of these political-social, historical novelists was **Lion Feuchtwanger** (1884–1958), whose copious *oeuvre* comprised novels of Jewish experience, works that were part of the anti-Nazi struggle, and others that addressed problems of revolutionary methodology. He returned to Jewish themes throughout his career, turning to the anti-Nazi struggle mainly in the 1930s and 1940s and to the revolutionary dilemma in the years following World War II. Frequently, these themes were intertwined.

Feuchtwanger's excursions into Jewish history had convinced him of certain constants. Throughout the centuries, in antiquity (the Josephus trilogy), the medieval period (*Raquel*), the eighteenth century (*Jud Suess*), or contemporary history (*The Oppermanns*), Jewish psychology had become reactive and defensive. Feuchtwanger associated Jewish values with a fearless and exalted sense of justice and a love and respect for Torah that lent Jews uniqueness in history.

Born in Munich of Orthodox parents, Feuchtwanger remained in that city until the Nazis' rise made him and others seek refuge in Berlin. Because of the hateful climate in his native city, his memorable *Jud Suess* (*Jew Suess*), written years earlier, was not published until 1925. In this fictionalized account of the unscrupulous eighteenth-century court Jew, Suess is depicted as both victim and victimizer. In the end, there is something heroic about his desire to die a Jew, when other options for survival were available. Though the doings of the all-powerful Suess threaten their safety, the Jews of Württemberg combine in an effort to save their fallen coreligionist. What holds Feuchtwanger's Jews together in this novel, as in the similarly conceived *Raquel, the Jewess of Toledo* (1954), is the meaning, knowledge, and lesson of the Book: "They bound it with phylacteries round heart and head, they fastened it to their doors; they opened and closed the day with it; as sucklings, they learned the Word, and they died with the Word on their lips. From the Word they drew the strength to endure the piled-up afflictions of their way."

These novels of court Jews, powerful advisers to ruling princes, spell out the futility and transience of earthly power. The court Jews' almost "mystical knowledge" often produced in them an enigmatic and even supercilious smile which provoked their enemies. Yet, on the whole, Feuchtwanger was hardly a parochial writer, and some of his Jews are less than admirable characters. Some are intolerant and even fanatics, others exploiters and financial manipulators. But even these usually have some redeeming qualities.

With the exception of his novels of revolution, Feuchtwanger includes Jewish characters in his novels. All feel insecure in the host nation and are conscious of the dangers from enemies known and unknown. Whatever services they render to the host society, they are at the whim and mercy of others. Josephus is patronizingly addressed as "my Jew" by Vespasian, and his sons are sacrificed by other Emperors. In modern times, the Oppermann brothers have enjoyed wealth and prestige but stand helpless with the advent of Hitler. Feuchtwanger's Jews, whether Roman, Egyptian, or Spanish, are thinly-disguised, assimilated German Jews who overestimate their acceptance by the host society. To some degree, Feuchtwanger's Jewish novels are histories of anti-Semitism. Still, there is no paranoia in his fiction, no lachrymose account of the Jewish past. On the contrary: the novels are suffused with optimism, as though the Jews would emerge victorious over their tormentors in the end.

While shying from any notion of Jewish chauvinism, Feuchtwanger was attracted from the first to Zionism, without ever being able to embrace it fully. A state of their own would offer persecuted Jews a refuge and a cultural center to world Jewry. It would normalize the Jewish condition. In *Josephus* (1932), he had depicted Jews in a country of their own, committed to agriculture, the trades, statecraft, and even the military. (He inserted battle scenes into *Josephus* to illustrate how a poorly equipped Jewish army distinguished itself against the Roman legions.)

His skeptical humanism, growing Marxism, and anti-nationalism kept him from becoming more than a Zionist sympathizer. He was excited by the idea which Yohanan ben Zakkai expounded in *Josephus*—that the Jewish nation would be unique in its cohesion without the material base of a state. Through the Academy Yohanan was to establish, through their learning, and their Book, Jews would attain a *consensus omnium* on vital questions that would permanently bind them together. After 1940 and his own harrowing flight from France, Feuchtwanger finally agreed that "no nation, no large group of men, can exist in airless space, where only ideas are housed. A nation must have a ground on which to stand, a State."

Although *Jud Suess* (sometimes called *Power* in English translation) first introduced Feuchtwanger—he had written copiously before, mostly plays—his *Josephus* trilogy may be his finest effort in interpreting the Jew in the modern world. The polarities nationalism-internationalism, religion-secularism, spirit-matter, father-son, and Rome-Jerusalem are skillfully integrated into the plot to provide a distinctive vision of Jewish destiny. Set in ancient Judea, Egypt, and Rome, the *Josephus* novels were written when the author's life was seriously imperiled by Hitler, who by the 1940s was master of Europe.

Feuchtwanger's initial interest was the theater. His plays were concerned with such questions as Asia vs. Europe, Buddha vs. Nietzsche, power vs. renunciation; he was convinced that a wave of Asian beliefs would soon engulf Europe. Then the war and its aftermath greatly politicized him, and he added social and economic problems to his repertoire. Increasingly, too, he became preoccupied with the role of the artist, especially social involvement and responsibility. While he wavered for a long time, he sided ultimately with activism. He used his pen to counteract Nazi propaganda, to ridicule the Nazi leadership, and to find parallels for their misdeeds in history. Still later, he examined the dynamics of the French and American Revolutions and the impact of the one on the other.

Even after he had settled in the socialist camp, he never allowed himself to become doctrinaire. The story remained paramount, and he never sacrificed it to an idea, however cherished. To every socialist argument advanced by a character, he had a liberal position argued by a different person. His socialism can easily be passed over in his fiction, but not in his correspondence, in which he made it amply clear.

Feuchtwanger was relaxed about his Jewishness. He called himself a German, a Jew, a world citizen. No identity could claim him entirely. But he did not have the sense of being uncomfortably sandwiched among the three. His writing and language were German; his thinking was cosmopolitan; the beat of his heart was Jewish.

Feuchtwanger's self-definition is too catchy to be entirely believable, but it contained a degree of truth. In the postwar years, he refused to indict the German people and insisted on a distinction between German and Nazi. Unlike Döblin, however, he could not bring himself to return to the land of his birth, in spite of repeated invitations and proclaimed intentions to visit. And he never visited the Jewish state, although he believed its establishment was one of the proudest moments of Jewish history. Finally, socialist that he was, he could not follow his friend Arnold Zweig to the former German Democratic Republic (East Germany). No allegiance could claim him entirely, no more than it could Heinrich Heine, on whose *Der Rabbi von Bacharach* Feuchtwanger had written his doctoral dissertation. A German, a Jew, and a world citizen, he chose to remain in the United States, a country he frequently criticized and to which he had come in 1940. Although he had suffered some rebuffs at American hands, he felt comfortable in the United States and probably viewed America as the least of all evils and the best that life had to offer.

Max Brod (1884–1968) was a novelist, historian, biographer, and music and literary critic. He was a keen psychological observer, a religious thinker, and a writer of charm and persuasiveness.

Brod's intellectual evolution was complex. As a young man, he espoused "indifferentism," a belief based on the conviction that man did not have free will and hence nothing mattered. In *Schloß Nornypegge* (*Nornypegge Castle*) (1908), the "indifferent" hero is led to his inevitable destruction. Arnold Beer, the protagonist of *Arnold Beer, das Schicksal eines Juden* (*Arnold Beer, The Fate of a Jew*) (1912), is spared a similar fate through the patient guidance of an old grandmother whose speech is laced with Yiddishisms. *Jüdinnen* (*Jewish Women*) (1922) is a misleading title in that it does not touch on the lives of Jewish women as Jewish women; instead, the novel reflects Brod's growing estrangement from indifferentism and its replacement by a Jewish commitment. He also veered from the eroticism of earlier works toward more specifically ethical concerns.

Brod's Zionism, which dates back to 1913, was reenforced by anti-Semitic outbursts in his native Prague in the years 1918–1919, when he stood in the forefront of those who were defending Jews. In 1928, he undertook his first journey to Palestine, and ten years later he settled there permanently. He functioned as an adviser to Habima, engaged in various publicist ventures, and kept up his prolific production of novels and memoirs.

For a number of years Brod had some problems with Zionism. He was opposed to all kinds of nationalism, except the liberal Mazzini variety which aimed at the creation of a national entity by people of like background. But was Zionism just another brand of nationalism? Brod concluded that it was not. Unlike Arthur Koestler and Arnold Zweig, Brod never viewed it as separate from the Judaic tradition, but instead as an extension of religious emphases. What he advocated was an ethical nationalism which required that Jews become the first people to begin self-purification and thus cleanse the national idea of the filth that had blemished it for decades. By removing social inequities and establishing a just order, each nation—with the Jewish nation pointing the way—can achieve at once a national and universal mission. This is also Brod's concept of the "chosen people," with each people becoming a chosen one, and none forcing its answers on others.

The Arab problem preoccupied him as early as 1918 when he welcomed the idea of Arabs' cohabiting the land with Jews. The Arab presence would challenge Jews to demonstrate the inclusive nature of their national ideal. In the early 1920s, he was distressed by the ominous clouds darkening the Palestinian horizon and the incipient hatred between Jews and Arabs. Until the Nazi bloodbath he kept hoping that peaceful coexistence would be feasible. Then, in *Unambo,* a 1949 novel, he denounced Arab terrorism and British treachery. The events of the previous decade had hardened him. He was now convinced that no one would help the Jews if they did not help themselves. His uneasy suspicion of 1918 that his ethical nationalism might be utopian now seemed justified by events.

Brod believed that a Jewish state was not only essential as a place of refuge for persecuted Jews, but also as a site for Jewish psychological normalization. In his historical novel, *Reubeni* (1925), he had a false Messiah advocate a free Jewish Palestine. But Brod wanted a Zionist state for cultural as well as political and religious reasons. In the Diaspora, Jewish creativity had dried up because it had to feed itself parasitically off foreign materials. In an independent Jewish community, Jewish artists could generate and develop their own ideas and maintain full control.

The religious thought of Max Brod must be traced through several books. In another historical novel, *Tycho Brahes Weg zu Gott* (*The Redemption of Tycho Brahe*) (1915), a venerable rabbi instructs Brahe on the cause of his moral and psychological breakdown. Brahe learns that in single-mindedly pursuing his scientific investigations, he has forgotten his fellow man, lost sight of the unity in the universe, and failed in his duty and service to God.

In *Heidentum, Christentum, Judentum* (*Paganism, Christianity, Judaism*) (1921) and later in his briefer *Das Diesseitswunder* (*Natural Miracle*) (1939), Brod distinguishes between *edles Unglück* (noble misfortune) and *unedles Unglück* (ignoble misfortune). The former reflects the inability of humanity to transcend its natural limitations, to be more than it is. Noble misfortune is inescapable, unavoidable. Ignoble misfortune, on the other hand, is man-made and thus avoidable. It includes war, social injustice, and national feeling that goes beyond natural boundaries. However ingrained, this type of misfortune may be eradicated at some future time. Both misfortunes demonstrate the difficulty of a finite being placed in an infinite situation.

The uniqueness of Judaism, according to Brod, is that it has worked on the assumption that both misfortunes exist, and religion must address itself to both. Where paganism was solely concerned with the ignoble and Christianity mainly with the noble, Judaism alone recognized humanity's need for ministry in both. Judaism recognized the connection of the earthly with the divine, the worldly with the non-worldly. Brod calls the Mogen David the very symbol of this connection: two triangles, one from below, the other from above; and so intertwined as to have both parts as an indissoluble figure. God is one!

Because of its oneness, Judaism strikes Brod as the most concrete of religious systems. The many facets of daily living discussed in the Talmud are more than pagan commentaries on life. In Judaism, the rules of daily living are sanctified, eternalized. The true significance of Judaism has not been explored—to wit, the magnificent and miraculous interplay of Haggadah with Halakha of poetry and action, of myth and practice. Judaism seeks to provide a synthesis and strives for balance, harmony, and guides to meaningful living.

Brod deplores the fact that the Jews of his time are unaware that they are the carriers of a unique tradition. It is essential that they come to know it. Understanding the greatness of Judaism will improve the Jews' self-image and generate a more salutary attitude toward non-Jews. Why do so many young Jews find Judaism unattractive? Brod blames in part the overgrown Jewish "dogmatic garden," which is, moreover, inaccessible. Religious teachers are also guilty. They voice shock when spiritually starved youngsters turn to Christianity and blame the apostasy on the lure of a better job rather than on their own failures as transmitters of the Jewish message.

What should be the attitude of Jewish writers toward their host nation? Brod is one of the few to have publicly considered this question. He counsels a "detached love" for the culture whose language is used. He recognizes a contradiction in his terminology. What he suggests is the need to eschew both love and detachment. This task is difficult and delicate. Brod tips the balance himself when he states categorically that the Jewish writer must first find a firm anchor in Judaism: "Detachment can only be maintained by standing firmly on one's own ground. Detached love demands a balance of forces, but such a balance can be achieved only by opposing to the blandishments of a foreign culture one's own secure Jewish self."

In his late years in Tel Aviv, Brod often repeated himself in memoirs of a bygone era. But his study of the Jewish tradition led him toward a richer and more modern Judaism than other writers were able to discern. Brod could never accept Mahler's disinterest in his Jewish origin. Had Mahler known Judaism, Brod concluded, he would not have become a Jewish Christian. He would have known that the Christianity he admired was a veiled Judaism.

The preoccupation of **Bruno Frank** (1887–1945) with royalty and aristocracy set him apart not only from Feuchtwanger and Brod, but from nearly all Jewish writers of his time. The qualities he admired he found mostly in the nobility. For human improvement he relied on personal decency rather than social panaceas. He abhorred socialist-communist ideas on the one hand and the accumulation of wealth on the other. He found little value in organized religion. He loved and respected men of breeding and culture, all those who represented the true, the good, and the beautiful. Bruno Frank fits into the tradition of the nineteenth-century liberals for whom Jewish birth is incidental and who would not recognize any conflict in identity if there were one.

His literary output was minuscule, considering the length of his career: a few novels on historical figures, a few novellas, even fewer plays. While he wrote little of a specifically Jewish nature, Jewish characters appear from time to time. Almost without exception they embody the qualities Frank revered. Often, they are the trusted friends and companions of his aristocratic heroes.

Such historical fiction as *Trenck, Roman eines Günstlings* (*Trenck, Love Story of a Royal Favorite*) (1918), *Tage des Königs* (*Days of the King*) (1924), and even *Cervantes* (1934), his best work, lack political sophistication. He does better with a novella, *Der Goldene* (*The Golden Bug*), a contemporary tale of a man who rapes a woman, is incarcerated, and is maltreated by guards who have killed the "golden bug" which had offered him solace. How a human being overcomes a questionable action and regains his self-respect is told with a heavy dose of irony in *Sechzehntausend Francs* (*16,000 Francs*). Irony also marks the *Politische Novelle* (*Political Novella*), two-thirds of which consists of a dialogue between thinly disguised doubles for Briand and Stresemann, men of goodwill. While they devise a strategy for improving political relations between Germany and France, their Jewish aides discuss cultural improvements. After that lofty conversation, the German statesman ventures into the street and is murdered, for non-political reasons, while on a solitary walk. Good intentions are more fragile than evil.

Frank again deals respectfully with Jews in *Der Magier* (*The Magician*) (1918), in which a Reinhardt-type genius of the theater disappears after a spiritual crisis, turning up incognito in America where he directs Negro actors in plays of social significance. The Reinhardt figure is sensitive, wise, and restrained in judgment, searching for meaning in his existence. Like Frank's princes, he is motivated by his rich heritage of decency, justice, and charity. In *Der Reisepaß* (*Passport*) (1937), Frank describes the emigré environments of the 1930s and the high emotional toll of exile. Princes, scholars, and Jews suffer side by side. Through the romance of a prince and a Jewish woman, Frank may have wished to soften the terrors of exile with a fairy-tale flavor.

The historical fiction of **Alfred Neumann** (1895–1952) invites comparison with Lion Feuchtwanger's in that Neumann, too, wished to illumine the nature of power and those who seek it. With their varied locations, Newmann's novels were popular and lent themselves to screen adaptation.

Few of his protagonists are engaging figures—not in *Der Teufel* (*The Devil*) (1926), which relates the machinations of Louis XI of France and an adviser, nor in *Rebellen* (*Rebels*) (1927), which deals with the Carbonari Revolution, nor in *Guerra* (1928), a sequel to the latter. Neumann is profoundly skeptical of greatness and human nature and doubts these qualities exist in men of power. The early novels about the French Commune were written in Italian exile, later ones in France and southern California.

A liberal democrat, Neumann was nevertheless sympathetic to socialism and the plight of workers. He simply lacked faith in the political instrumentalities that would make grand designs a reality. Questions about the conditions of Jews intrigued him little, and he rarely addressed them in his fiction.

Jewish characters are also infrequent. In *Es waren ihrer sechs* (*There Were Six of Them*) (1945), based on the resistance of the Scholl siblings to Hitler, Jews serve to measure the humanity of pro- and anti-Nazi characters. In his novella *König Haber* (*King Haber*) (1926), Neumann created an all-powerful court Jew. In any comparison with Feuchtwanger's *Jud Suess*—perhaps because it is only of novella length—Neumann's effort falls short. Here a Jew of power wishes to put his illegitimate son (his child and that of the duchess) on the ducal throne and perishes as a result of his ambition. Haber's Jewishness is not defined, and his background is dismissed as "obscure." He wields his power discreetly, yet insiders know—and they bring him down. In doing so, they recognize in him a grandeur they had not previously suspected. If the reader knows that Haber is a Jew, it is because the nobelmen's objections to him carry the ring of old anti-Semitic prejudices. If Newmann's work has not stood the test of time, it may well be that he was a one-theme author.

Until age 35, **Ferdinand Bruckner** (1891–1958) used his real name of Theodor Tagger. As Tagger, he fitted into the prevailing Expressionist mode. In his rebirth as Bruckner, he turned to *Neue Sachlichkeit* (New Objectivity, a literary movement of the time) and a realism that earned him a niche in the history of drama.

Father-son conflicts abound in his work. He was born in Bulgaria of a Viennese Jew and a French mother. His parents separated when he was young. Raised as a Jew, Bruckner reserved his affection for his artistically minded mother. His father, a businessman, was austere and authoritarian. Bruckner's male characters are all obsessed with money, while his women bring cheer. Money is the enemy of the human values Bruckner portrays. The fathers represent a materialism that denies "the truly human." Bruckner never ceased to place the importance of the individual above the claimed needs of society.

Bruckner had a clearly international outlook, reflected in part in his use of French and British history in his dramas, but also in his love of translation. His novels *Elisabeth, Napoleon,* and the unfinished *Lafayette* were followed by subjects from the North- and South-American past. Nationalism was abhorrent to him, except for the late summer in 1914, when he was briefly infected by war fever. On the whole, he counted on the good sense and reason of individuals to overcome foolishness in society and to ensure that the rights of others would be respected.

When Hitler wrought havoc with Bruckner's humanism, the author wrote a classic anti-Fascist, anti-racist play. *Die Rassen* (*The Races*) (1934) tells the story of a young Aryan student in love with a young Jewish woman. The Aryan is initially apolitical and opposed to Hitler's

Brown Wave. Then he attends one of their meetings and falls under their spell. Now he participates in raids against Jews and repeats party gibberish. Meanwhile, the young Jewish woman (whom he has warned of her impending arrest) has developed into a fanatical jew, her defense against German self-glorification. Soon the Aryan recognizes his folly and regrets that he cannot return to what he had once been.

Bruckner's few Jewish characters are experts in survival. Even in the mid-1930s, he never questioned the likelihood that Jews would still exist long after Hitler had become a mere blot on history. But at no time can Bruckner identify with Jewish nationalism. The heroine of *Die Rassen* becomes less likeable as she becomes integrally Jewish. By contrast, he maintains a lasting respect for the Jewish past, which to him means loyalty to spirit and human dignity.

One does not have to read much of Bruckner to realize he has met one *Geldjude* ("money Jew") too many. The Jewish father in *Die Rassen* negotiates with the Nazis who, for a consideration, do not initially molest him. To keep his factory going, he sacrifices his safety, self-respect, and dignity. Bruckner belongs to that long list of sons of businessmen who rebelled against paternal values and used their pen in their war against the philistinism of the elders.

From the time of *Wer weint um Juckenack?* (*Who Weeps for Juckenack?*) (1924), **Hans José Rehfisch** (1890–1960), a trained lawyer, contrasted cold law with a humane conception of justice, advocated involvement in the effort for human betterment, and showed his awareness of the relativity of all perceptions.

Throughout his years in Berlin, Vienna, London, the United States, and again Germany, Rehfisch was a prolific writer, modern and sophisticated in outlook and skillful in dramatic movement. His dramatization in 1929 of the Dreyfus Case demonstrated his ability to reach the heart of a case quickly. Justice for the individual was being subordinated to national considerations, military advantage, and the preservation of "sacred institutions." Rehfisch made it plain that the deliberate sacrifice of one human being infected the moral health of a nation. Anti-Semitism is not the primary issue in the play, which Rehfisch wrote with the upsurge of right-wing radicalism in mind. His most sharply etched character is the culprit Esterhazy, the epitome of cynicism.

Rehfisch dealt with the major issues of his time. In *Der Frauenarzt* (*The Gynecologist*) he addressed the problem of abortion, in *Razzia,* a variety of questions. Less successful is *Nickel und die 36 Gerechten* (*Nickel and the Thirty-Six Just Men*), in which the Talmudic legend of the

Lamed Vovnikim receives uninspired treatment.

In both his historical and contemporary work, Rehfisch was a liberal writer, whose country was the world and for whom Jewishness or any other group identity was not of paramount importance.

•　•　•　•　•

Socialists Revisited

There were numerous socialist writers in the final decades of German-Jewish coexistence. The most important among them—and the one experiencing the most conflicts—was **Arnold Zweig** (1887–1968).

The decisive influence in Zweig's life was World War I. His memorable fiction centers on it, even if some novels were written years later. His wartime fiction shows Zweig's alter ego, the young officer Bertin, an enthusiastic supporter of the war at first and an ardent German patriot. Bertin evolves, however, into a supra-nationalist who develops a social conscience and moves more and more to the left. In fiction with a World War I setting, but written in East Germany after 1950, Zweig invests Bertin with fully developed social insights.

In his youth Zweig experienced both poverty and anti-Semitism. His parents sent him to a *Gymnasium,* but at sacrifice to themselves. He began writing at twenty, publishing in 1909 his *Aufzeichnungen über eine Familie Klopfer (Notes about a Family Named Klopfer).* According to one critic, this early effort foreshadowed his future absorption in things Jewish and European. Peter Klopfer is an ardent Zionist whose national convictions propel him to the shores of Palestine. But the book extends beyond Jewish themes, including those of aesthete and bourgeois, inhibitions, and letting go. The same themes recur in *Novellen um Claudia (Novellas about Claudia)* (1912), in which Claudia, just married, slowly sheds her inhibitions and yields to primeval instincts. Although the precious, overrefined Claudia struck the critic Moritz Goldstein as a "Jewish type," Zweig has both Claudia and her husband reappear in a later novel as Nazis. In several plays before the war, Zweig pondered Jewish questions, but he was not a skilled dramatist. *Das ostjüdische Antlitz (Face of Eastern Jewry)* (1920), based on Zweig's wartime experience on the Eastern front, showed the Jewries of Poland in a favorable light.

Had Zweig's work ended here, it would not be remembered. It took *Der Streit um den Sergeanten Grischa* (*The Case of Sergeant Grischa*) (1927) to inscribe his name firmly in world literature. The novel followed a helpless human being ground to death by an impersonal, overpowering war machine which, once set in motion, cannot be stopped. The novel was unequivocal in its anti-war, anti-militarist, international viewpoint and marked Zweig in the 1920s as a favorite target of right-wing Germans. Many of the characters of Grischa were to reappear in the other novels of the "Grischa cycle": *Junge Frau von 1914* (*Young Woman of 1914*) (1931), *Erziehung vor Verdun* (*Education at Verdun*) (1935), and *Einsetzung eines Königs* (*Crowning of a King*) (1937). Social and political issues gradually replaced psychosexual or aesthetic interests. Only his friend, Lion Feuchtwanger, could match Zweig's sophistication in depicting political planning and decision making, most of it behind the scenes. Premature Nazis (under other labels) show their brand of ruthlessness in novels set in 1915, suggesting his recognition of a type or form of prescience.

His outspokenness on the Nazi mentality compelled him to emigrate at the earliest possible moment. Where most writers chose France, Switzerland, or the Anglo-Saxon world, Zweig preferred Palestine. Though he was quick to express disappointment, his Zionism remained intact. More than others, he sensed the severance from European culture and knew that in a small, developing country there was only a tiny market for his works. Little by little, he recognized in Jewish nationalism qualities he had always denounced in the nationalism of others. He wrote *De Vriendt kehrt heim* (*De Vriendt Goes Home*) (1933), a weak and inconclusive novel on the emerging Arab-Jewish struggle. Zealotry on the Jewish side leads to a murder of a moderate Zionist, eager for understanding with the neighboring Arabs. Based on an actual case, the murder arouses doubt about the Zionism to which he has clung tenaciously up to this point.

Eventually, Zweig looked elsewhere, specifically in socialism, for a solution to the Jewish question. When Zweig returned to Berlin in the late 1940s, the Eastern intellectual elite welcomed him with open arms. He became convinced of the peaceful intent of the communist world and enlisted as a participant in the "workers' struggle for peace." He suspected that in the capitalist world some of the same greedy forces were operating which had been responsible for the disasters in Germany and Europe.

Der Streit um den Sergeanten Grischa may well be the foremost war novel of his time. Though there are no battlefields strewn with dead bodies, the novel illustrates the utter dispensability of human life in war. War operates in a realm of its own. Not even the chieftains themselves can control the destiny of the millions entrusted to them. Once the monster has been unleashed, it grinds its way forward in its own soulless, mechanized way. Victimizers and victims are both driven in unexpected directions; the only difference is that the victimizers often survive, while the victims rarely do.

Zweig's Jewish characters are varied: some are in uniform, others in civilian garb; they are officers and privates, businessmen and craftsmen, religious figures and irreligious ones. They sometimes seem idealized, as though the author needed to protect them from his anti-Semitic characters. Only figures like the elder Wahls, Bertin's in-laws, with their bourgeois attitudes and vacuous assimilationism, come in for criticism.

Most of Zweig's theoretical views on Jewish issues are found in *Caliban* (1927) and *Bilanz der deutschen Judenheit* (*Balance [sheet] of German Jewry*) (1934), both written in the shadow of Nazism. Zweig links Jews to the values he himself espouses. While disclaiming special virtues for them and denying particular credit for producing an Einstein, Freud, or Bergson—men who are individual phenomena—he commends Jews for having almost uniquely subordinated material to intellectual goods. Jews have always listened to scholars more than to people of wealth. The result has been an intellectual drive that has thoroughly influenced their *Weltbild* (image of the world). Along with the Arabs they have displayed a great capacity for mathematics. They have militated against war as the means of settling disputes, have demonstrated respect for the worth of the individual, and have argued for preservation of the heritage of all peoples. Since they entered the Western worlds, they have aligned themselves against the forces of barbarism and retrogression. By 1933, the year of Hitler's appointment as chancellor, Jews had given every indication of becoming the foremost representatives of Western European culture on the German scene.

Why then, Zweig asks, should such a people have been singled out for rape? Zweig, the disciple of Freud, holds to psychoanalytical and psychosocial concepts of prejudice. A keen example of the defensive-aggressor type, he blames German nationalism, ethnocentrism in general, and perennial Jewish minority status. The Jewish contribution itself is partly responsible. The powerful tradition of justice and *zedakah* (charity), of forward-looking social economic democracy, offended the ruling classes dismayed and threatened by lofty Jewish standards. As for the German, Zweig wrote in 1934, he "is as he behaves toward the Jews . . . a warning to everyone . . . [O]ur [Jewish] weakness is the measuring stick of the real maturity and strength of the powerful others."

He was pessimistic about the Jewish future. He deplored the Jews' reliance on human rights and education, constitutions, and other guarantees that have proven to be illusory bulwarks of security. It had been surprisingly easy for Hitler to abrogate the emancipation agreement with Jews and restore pre-Enlightenment conditions. Old views were reasserting themselves with frightening vigor.

Therefore, as Zweig had believed for twenty years, a Jewish home and state was a pressing need. Hitlerism merely confirmed an earlier conviction. Zionism was unlike the other nationalisms Zweig had always condemned. It merely aspired to statehood and reflected the desire of people with common background to determine their own destiny and assure their security. Jewish nationalism would be non-aggressive, would not be exclusive, tribal, or racist. Nor would it be encumbered by romantic-mystic trappings. In Palestine, Jews could develop freely, promoting their cultural and physical strengths. Jewish energy would be revitalized. A state of their own would end the pathological self-consciousness of Jews, the self-deprecation that bordered on self-hate, the lack of naturalness and spontaneity. The Jewish emotional apparatus would be repaired, inner divisiveness ended, and Jews aligned with other peoples that had a soil and nation of their own.

Jewish intellectuals would be among the prime beneficiaries. They would no longer have to whisper for fear their German status would be questioned. The fearful, neurotic Jew, a victim of Teutonic self-aggrandizement, had Zweig's contempt and pity. Zweig respected far more the Polish and Russian Jews, whose humanity, spirit of sacrifice, and capacity for work made a mockery of the German Jew's claim to *Bildung* and superiority. A Jewish homeland might become salvation to that shameful German Jew who prized a *Deutschtum* from which he was excluded and regarded his Jewishness as a cross to bear.

Whereas Zweig never changed his assessment of the Teutonic follies of some German Jews, he was forced to alter his appraisal of the Zionism evolving in his new homeland. The murder of Dr. Charles Arlosoroff disillusioned him about the desire of Jews to live side by side with the Arabs. The democratic-socialist basis he had envisioned for Jewish-Arab coexistence was not being created. Instead, the Jabotinsky wing of the movement created tensions that bode ill for the future.

Zweig's Jewish history is tragic. Never attracted to Judaism as a religion, he had identified with peoplehood and ethical-cultural Jewish values. A socialist Zionism had been his great hope for normalizing Jewish life. Then, to use his words, the road to Zion proved to be an illusion. The policies of the Yishuv, and subsequently the new state, repelled him, as his hopes for peaceful Jewish-Arab coexistence dimmed. In Marxism he found a new and total commitment. Now he saw Jewish problems only in the context of a socialistic reordering of society. Freud, Herzl, and Achad Ha'am yielded before the new god.

Of all the socialist writers, none was more completely socialist, more completely communist, than **Friedrich Wolf** (1888–1953). There is hardly a trace of Jewishness in his life or work. He grew out of the Expressionist movement and, like so many other writers, was radicalized by World War I. Chauvinistic excesses alienated this frontline physician, who soon refused further military service. In order not to attract public attention to this refusal, the authorities quietly transferred him to medical work unrelated to the war. In 1933 he fled to France, and then to the USSR, where he spent the war years. After 1945 he settled in East Germany, where, in addition to writing, he was given important assignments, including the ambassadorship to Poland.

His dramas were essentially dramas for social agitation. Whether he dealt with a peasants' uprising in the seventeenth century, the callous treatment meted out to pregnant proletarian women, or insurrection against the military, the social message was unmistakable and in line with party emphases.

Even his play against anti-Semitism becomes predominantly a Marxist play. *Professor Mamlock* (1935) bears some superficial resemblance to Schnitzler's *Professor Bernhardi*. Both hospital chiefs are beleaguered by anti-Semitism and treacherous, ambitious staff members. But where Schnitzler's play was barely political—perhaps anti-political—Wolf uses a sledgehammer to drive home the ugliness of Nazism. His message: fight the enemy with his own means. Surprisingly, Wolf's drama almost succeeds in spite of its heavy, didactic line. All his characters are flawed in their creator's view—with the exception of idealized workers and Mamlock's son, who alone stands up to the Nazis. Wolf conveniently forgets that the party and the workers surrendered to the Nazis with little more fight than anyone else.

Mamlock's Jewishness means nothing to him. His wife is a Christian, his daughter a near Nazi. She changes only as indignities are heaped upon her as the daughter of the Jew Mamlock. He is intent upon practicing surgery at any price. It is inconceivable to him that, as a former frontline fighter, repeatedly wounded, he should not be regarded as German. He lacks political awareness and urges his son to stay away from the "commies."

Wolf offers two rays of hope. The Nazi woman physician finds the dichotomy between the Nazi dream and the Nazi reality unbearable. She had been disenchanted with Weimar and the "Jewish influence," but what she sees now is infinitely worse. Besides this possibility of a change of heart, there is the hope of the "activist worker," who will continue the battle against the fascist oppressor. Mamlock himself ends his life after he finally understands that his colleagues have willingly signed a statement condemning him.

The author would have us believe that racism and anti-Jewishness are just symptoms of a diseased social order. At times, he speaks reverently of rights guaranteed to the individual, and one has to wonder what he thought of Stalin's policies in this regard. Wolf tries repeatedly to take the demonology out of communism. His concept of the movement seems as close to political reality as Mamlock's grasp of the goings-on about him.

Netty Reiling of Mainz, better known as **Anna Seghers** (1900–1983) studied art and sinotology and wrote a doctoral dissertation on *Jews and Judaism in the Work of Rembrandt*. Soon after, she joined the communist party and rarely touched on a Jewish subject.

She was in her mid-twenties when she discovered the huge gap between the haves and have-nots. In 1927, she wrote her first novel, *Der Aufstand der Fischer von St. Barbara (The Revolt of the Fishermen of St. Barbara)*, and about that time became a communist party member. Unlike Friedrich Wolf and Johannes R. Becher, fellow members, Seghers did not graduate from Expressionism. Her works are also less stark and harsh than theirs, but she is no less committed. Her break with her bourgeois past seemed abrupt and complete.

The time following the Nazis' seizure of power led her to adventures in France and Mexico. Some of these are recounted fictionally in *Transit* (1944), one of her better works. After the war she made her home in East Germany.

Her ample fiction is filled with sympathy for workers, peasants, victims of fascism, and even communists caught between governmental bureaucracies. She can envision change only along radical, Marxist lines. Her language ranges from the terse to the reticent. It appears cold, and cold, too, is her approach to her subjects. But she cannot conceal a warm heart that beats for the less fortunate and the oppressed.

Whether she depicts, as in her first novel, the hopeless condition in a village kept in tow by a monopoly and nearly destroyed by a revolt; or whether, as in *Der Kopflohn (Ransom)* (1932), she deals with the bestialization of a village in time of economic crisis; or whether she delves into the political failures of democratic parties in a German mining village, as in *Die Rettung (The Rescue)* (1934), she poses fundamental questions about the dynamics of political, social, and economic life. In each instance, she comes up with preconceived answers in the Marxist mold.

Described as "the story of exiles seeking permission to travel out of one country through another to reach haven in a third," *Transit* (1941) resembles most closely Seghers's own experiences as a political refugee. However, this novel does not compare in power with *Das siebte Kreuz* (*The Seventh Cross*) (1942). Here the commander of a Nazi camp has erected seven crosses on which to nail seven escapees from his camp. Six are found, returned, and meet their fate. The seventh is saved through the connivance of various Germans who, though afraid, dare for different reasons to help the escapee. The seventh cross remains as a symbol of hope for the inmates and others. The novel has been justly praised as *tour de force* by an author who had been away from Germany for nine years but was able to imagine a totally changed Hitlerite country.

Seghers's fiction displays the same indifference to things Jewish as that of her fellow communists. A few Jews appear more or less anonymously in *Transit*. There are references to anti-Jewish slogans, to Jewish children waiting in line for the parents' visa, little more. Even when a character has been designated as a Jew, as the physician who helps the escapee in *Das siebte Kreuz,* he is only helping as part of a humanity that causes and bears suffering. In her brilliant story, "Der Tanz der toten Mädchen" ("The Dance of the Dead Girls"), friendships with Jewish girls serve as a barometer measuring the moral and political hollowness of former classmates.

Rudolf Leonhard (1893–1953) had been at peace with his German-bourgeois environment until one New Year's Eve, when Martin Buber, Walter Hasenclever, and others presented to him "a different view of the war." It was the beginning of his political education, which took him more and more to the left. Disillusionment with the war was followed by postwar developments. He was sufficiently disenchanted with developments in Germany to choose Paris as his permanent residence. After World War II, he settled in the former German Democratic Republic.

Leonhard dealt with Jewish questions only in his early works. He wrote in praise of Polish Jews, the only ones he believed authentic. Later, he rarely identified any characters as Jews. Unlike other communists, he did single out Jews as receiving particularly inhuman treatment at the hands of the Nazis. In a touching story, "Das jüdische Kind" ("The Jewish Child"), a Nazi teacher forces a Jewish child to sing "When Jewish Blood Spurts from the Knife," a psychological atrocity that ruins the child's health. Leonhard's studied understatement augments the human horror of the tale.

More orthodox than Leonhard in their Marxism were the three Prague-born writers **Rudolf Fuchs** (1890–1943), **Louis Fürnberg** (1909–1957), and **F. C. Weiskopf** (1900–1955). The three held in common not only an unswerving allegiance to the party line, but also a deep respect for Czech culture.

Weiskopf especially had difficulty keeping his fiction from degenerating into mere party propaganda, and he was rewarded, along with Fürnberg, with major literary and political honors. Weiskopf was named Czech ambassador to Sweden and Peking. Though Fürnberg, like Zweig, had spent several years of his exile in Palestine, he turned increasingly anti-Zionist, convinced that the socialist rather than the national solution would put an end to anti-Semitism. Although **Arthur Holitscher** gave himself wholeheartedly to the "Moscow idea" after World War I, he never did so uncritically and refused to turn into the formula socialist that the Prague trio had become.

Holitscher fits no category. Where most Jewish writers were in conflict with their father, Holitscher never ceased lambasting the "cold, heartless, domineering bourgeoise" who was his mother. Revolt against his loveless home led him at first into bohemianism, and from there to endless travels and ceaseless changes in residence.

He began with such forgettable novels as *Weiße Liebe* (*White Love*) (1896) and *Der Golem* (*The Robot*) (1909); he next tried his hand at drama and poetry, and finally found himself with travel reportage. He had a rare gift for the quick, incisive impression, which then led him to an in-depth cultural analysis. His books on America paid tribute to the country's technical genius but severely castigated the exploitation of workers and the dehumanization of the assembly line. Holitscher opposed the first World War and wrote *Bruder Wurm* (*Brother Worm*) (1918), an impassioned plea for an international outlook and assistance to the lower classes. Though he turned to Moscow, he was disturbed that Russia should be the country for the socialist experiment.

In *Lebensgeschichte eines Rebellen* (*Biography of a Rebel*) (1924), he explained his attitude toward his Jewishness. He had always willingly embraced it, especially its religious and cultural values. Zionism, however, while a valid expression of religious longing for the lost land, could not count on him with its political nationalism. On the whole, he was astounded by the Jewish contributions to world civilization. But if Holitscher could appreciate Judaism, he could never forgive the Jewish woman who gave him life or the *Geldjuden* who made life miserable for their fellow beings.

There was little moderation in the social criticism of **Kurt Tucholsky** (1890–1935), a satirist in the aggressive tradition of Heine and Börne. The early nineteenth-century satirists had as their target the authoritarian, oppressive Metternich establishment. By contrast, Tucholsky regarded the ideals of the Weimar Republic favorably. There was simply too wide a gap between the stated aspirations of the Republican governments and their practices, which still smacked of the Wilhelmine era. By criticizing the Republic indiscriminately, Tucholsky was insensitive to the results of his satire and the damage it might do to the survival of the Republic. But there was ample truth in Tucholsky's contentions that the old power structure was still dominant and that the system of justice and the dynamics of governing had not adjusted to new conditions. As a socialist, he faulted social-democratic governments as not being socialist enough. Through his ceaseless attacks, Tucholsky helped weaken the foundations of the Republic.

Tucholsky did not think of himself as a politician with responsibility for actions taken. He regarded himself as a writer-journalist who could treat political topics from the perspective of the absolute. His responsibility lay in commenting discerningly on what he perceived in the actions of parliaments, courts, and cultural institutions. His view that his responsibility ceased when he turned over copy to the editor was unwise in the age of a rising Hitler.

His immoderate thrusts exposed him to the charge of bad taste as well as bad judgment. He overstepped many bounds, as have satirists before and after him. Some of Tucholsky's indignation at Republican failures died down only after 1933, when he turned silent in his Swedish exile. There in 1935, he committed suicide.

Today only the extremist Tucholsky is remembered. But there was a gentle side to him, even a romantic-bucolic side, seen in his first work, *Rheinsberg (A Picture Book for Lovers)* (1912), and his last book, *Schloß Gripsholm (Gripsholm Castle)* (1931). Far too often the satirist's power overshadowed the idealist's dream.

Even in school, Tucholsky developed a strong aversion to German self-aggrandizement, the near deification of the emperor, the rabid contempt for foreigners and their culture, and, above all, the glorification of the military. His first published piece in *Ulk* caricatured the Kaiser's alleged expertise in art. Upon the outbreak of war, Tucholsky was drafted, but the experience of war merely sharpened his antipathy for all nationalistic and militaristic fervor.

The soaring postwar inflation forced him to take a position with a large bank in Berlin, a city he disliked. He left the bank and city as soon as he could and became the Paris correspondent for the *Weltbühne* and the *Vossische Zeitung.* Like Heine, he loved France: her freedom, her people's willingness to challenge authority and be themselves. Upon Jacobsohn's early death in 1926, Tucholsky briefly assumed the reins at the *Weltbühne.* But he was now too restless to stay long. Soon he was back in France but later went to Sweden for his final years of depression and death.

Few of Tucholsky's books were written as books. Most were collections of parodies, fairy tales, fables, monologues, and assorted other short pieces that had appeared under five pseudonyms. Which pseudonyms he used depended on the target of the moment. Besides the general topics already mentioned, he gradually added the politicization of justice, the evils of the death penalty, parliamentary babbling, traditional diplomacy, the machinations of captains of industry and finance, and human foibles in general.

Tucholsky brought up his heaviest artillery for the controversial picture book *Deutschland, Deutschland über alles (Germany, Germany, Over Everything)* (1929), for which John Heartfield suggested appropriate photographs. Here his sympathy for the underfed, the poorly clothed, and the ill-housed proletarian masses finds its more forceful expression. Conversely, text and pictures condemn the strategies and pretentious behavior of the overfed—dressed in their tuxedos and top hats and eating at tables with white tablecloths and champagne glasses. Germany, Tucholsky attempts to show, is still not synonymous with "people," despite the pious rhetoric of babbling parliamentarians. The institutions of the Reich continue to protect the high, control the low, and disguise questionable practices with noble language. Tucholsky also runs roughshod over the aesthetic and cultural landscape—the ugliness of mailboxes, subways, comfort stations, and fads in architecture. The satirist had little tolerance for the predilection for sport, continued sexual censorship, or prevailing forms of entertainment. As though anticipating the complaint that he was writing a book hostile to Germany, he appended a paean of glory to the Germany whose landscape and language he would always cherish.

Among Tucholsky's subtler pieces are the Wendriner monologues, which also unveil many of his criticisms of Jews. Wendriner is a mentally and emotionally shallow businessman, a moral lightweight, interested only in improving his business. In the process he turns anti-intellectual, embraces German patriotism, is ever mindful of his comforts and convenience, and opens himself up to every whim and fad. The latter includes Nazism.

What is surprising is the fact that Tucholsky gives Wendriner a Jewish origin. Wendriner is wholly assimilated and has no greater wish than to be recognized as a German. At times, a German-Jewish expression reminds the reader of his descent. A telling example of his values is provided by Rathenau's assassination. The government has asked for a ten-minute period of silence, but this interferes with Wendriner's need to place a business call. Initially, he has hailed Rathenau as a great patriot and captain of industry, a statesman—in fact, the greatest. Then, as he becomes increasingly incensed over the telephone inconvenience, he starts disparaging Rathenau. A Jew should not call attention to himself as Rathenau had, thereby contributing to anti-Semitism, he says; and damned be the Republic with its revolutions, demonstrations, disorder. No wonder that in the episode "Under the Dictatorship" Wendriner is smitten with cleanliness, order, and romantic showmanship, losing sight of the essence and purposes of the movement.

The Wendriner pieces led to the charge that Tucholsky was just another self-hating Jew, but this allegation seems ill-founded. The Wendriner pieces were directed against a rootless, assimilated Jew who would be more German than the Germans, a man who stood for nothing and was nothing. After all, the rabbis in their pulpits were fulminating against the same type of Jew. That Tucholsky and rabbis might for once be of the same bent of mind was ironic, given that rabbis fare poorly in his remarks about them. His criticism: Jewish religious teachers fail to imbue Jews with courage and, in fact, fail themselves to give evidence of this quality.

On the whole, however, Tucholsky agonized little about Jewish questions. In 1929 he wrote that he kept silent on Jewish issues because they never intrigued him and, frankly, he didn't know "whether Zionists were on the right track or not."

Although he wanted no part of the Jewish dilemma, he did not succeed in keeping it at a distance. "People who want to hurt the Jew in me are usually wide of the mark," he wrote on one occasion, but later he appeared to change his mind. Although he had formally left Judaism in 1911, he knew now, toward the end of his life, that "leaving Judaism wasn't possible." Like Heine and Börne, he learned that neither his enemies nor Jews would let him forget that he was born a Jew.

In the words of Kurt Hiller, Tucholsky possessed those qualities for which Jewish intellectuals have been faulted since the days of Heine: disrespect for the past, excessive rationality, aggressive wit, and assertiveness. Eighty years earlier apologists had dreaded the effect of Heine on the German psyche; in the 1920s there were still some who feared the impact of new aggressors like Tucholsky.

In his final years Tucholsky was as disillusioned with communism as he had once been with the ill-fated Republic. In his despair, he turned—tentatively, to be sure—toward Roman Catholicism. This last step cast a new light on Tucholsky the man and made him as interesting to the psychoanalyst as to the intellectual historian.

The Prague-born journalist **Egon Erwin Kisch** (1885–1948) was known for causeries and reportages that were often reminiscent of Heine's. Early in his career, Kisch wrote for a chauvinist daily; there, he stated later, he learned to detect the lies and falsehoods behind pious phrases and "legitimate positions." He was driven into the Marxist camp by such diverse factors as the enthusiasm for war in 1914, the wound he received as a front-line solder, and his observations in his travels through many countries.

As a devout party member, Kisch continued to discover hypocrisies in the bourgeois world. But he failed to recognize any in the Stalinist world he championed.

The modern socialist writers were universalists who favored an "unlined society," i.e., a society without class, ethnic, or religious divisions. They questioned bourgeois acquisitiveness, competition, and exploitation. They proposed a new life for workers, colonized peoples, colored races, servants, and underlings wherever they were. They proscribed the nationalist concept, military expenditures, and clericalism. For Jews as an oppressed ethnic minority they had genuine sympathy. Toward Jews who had succeeded in the world of business and finance they attributed the less savory qualities of the capitalist exploiter. The Jewish-born communists thought of themselves as victims of fascism rather than as Jewish victims of Nazism. Their Jewish birth, even when they suffered because of it, remained incidental, the reminder of a meaningless and dead past. As for the new state of Israel, it became the Eastern outpost of Western imperialism. Just as Jewish communist writers at the time of the Stalin-Hitler Non-Aggression Pact had often sheepishly accepted it, so now their heirs repeated the same folly.

• • • • •

Assorted Writers

LITERARY AND CULTURAL CRITICS

Martin Buber was awed by the high artistic level of **Rudolf Borchardt** (1877–1945) but also frightened by the abysses in his personality. Sol Liptzin placed this cultural historian, poet, and translator among the "Jewish Aryans." Theodor Lessing counted him with the self-haters. While there is ample evidence for pathology in Borchardt's makeup, not all his dubious positions should be imputed to them. He carved a distinct cultural, national, and religious identity for himself.

Thus, he willed his Jewish origin out of, and an undivided German-Protestant identity into, existence. A poem on Dante and a study of Lassalle disclose his sensitivity to outsider status. His need for a German-Protestant self demonstrated how he had been victimized by the same tensions out of which many Jewish writers sculpted their work.

Borchardt's uncanny mastery of the German language enabled him to cast a translation into the mold of Luther's German or Dante's Renaissance Italian. His poetry has been likened to that of Stefan George; he was close to George without belonging to his inner circle. If Borchardt failed to become a great poet, it was owing to a lack of feeling and spontaneity. Couched in a style of endless interclausal constructions, Borchardt's culture criticism is marred by an ostentatious display of linguistic virtuosity that sometimes conceals the absence of original thought.

In his memoirs of childhood, Borchardt barely mentions his mother. He describes his father as mostly absent; on his rare visits, Borchardt viewed him as a stranger. French as well as German was spoken in their Königsberg home. At one point, Borchardt was shipped off to a tutor some distance away, perhaps to sever more completely the ties that still linked him to his imperfectly German home.

In later years, Borchardt painted an admiring portrait of his grandmother, whom he describes as descended from those cultured Königsberg families—not identified as Jewish—who were enchanted with poetry and the arts. This grandmother filled the youngster's head with patriotic episodes from the Wars of Liberation and a Francophobia that was to follow him through life. At one time Borchardt proposed radical extinction of decadent France, which he felt had outlived her greatness. In 1914, this burning patriot endorsed a ruthless annexationist policy.

A traditionalist in culture and politics, Borchardt disapproved of most trends in the Weimar years. He liked the poetry of George and worshipped as perfection the works of Hofmannsthal, who was embarrassed by his letters of adulation. It is anomalous that, like other Jewish writers before him, the arch-Germanophile Borchardt established permanent residence in Italy, where he remained until his death, his final months in hiding, in January 1945.

Residence in Italy can be explained in part by his intense love of antiquity. However, given his overall life span, Borchardt spent suspiciously little time in the Fatherland. He also engaged in precisely that activity for which Jews had acquired a reputation: translation, adaptations of foreign works, and interpretations of the non-German to the German. Perhaps Willy Haas best summed up the Borchardt phenomenon when he described him as a man "with a deep and unhappy sense of *Heimat* for the nation he chose to immigrate to."

In searching for Jewish sources in Borchardt's *oeuvre*, Werner Kraft asked these questions: Why did Borchardt, who knew of the Jewish historical contributions to morality and the idea of God, use the term "Oriental" in relation to Jews? Why did he hardly ever use the term "Jew" itself? Why, in the "Halbgerettete Seele" ("The Half-Saved Soul") or "Der Durant" or "Joram," must characters pass through "animalistic-Oriental" phases before they can reach purity and salvation? And why did Borchardt choose to cast the biblical Yoram (Jorum) into the German of Luther's Bible? Was his predilection for the archaic related to echoes he heard of ancient Hebrew? If there were faint reminders of Jewishness with which he felt uncomfortable, then the struggle of some characters to reach the ideal country assumes some significance.

But for the determination of Hannah Arendt and Theodor Adorno to collect and publish the key essays of **Walter Benjamin** (1892–1940), this critic's work might have been consigned to oblivion. His illuminating studies of Baudelaire, Kafka, Proust, and Brecht would not have become available to the English-speaking world. Benjamin's trenchant observations on language and his uncommon ability to characterize swiftly the individuality of cities he had known would also have remained hidden. Nevertheless, this very innovative critic is still only available to an elite. Benjamin remains difficult to read and is open to sharply divergent interpretations.

The son of a well-to-do Berlin art dealer, Benjamin was for some time under the influence of the progressive educator Gustav Wyneken but broke with him over his enthusiastic endorsement of World War I. When the great inflation of that period ruined his father, young Benjamin had to abandon his leisurely life of bibliophile, occasional critic, and man of epicurean tastes. His closest friend in Berlin was Gershom Scholem, who sought to steer Benjamin toward Judaism and Zionism. There was, however, the competing attraction of socialism, to which Benjamin yielded after reading Marx and Lukasz. Fortunately, he was able to develop independently of party lines. His account of his trip to the Soviet Union reads like another travel report and, in spite of an occasional nod of approval, is markedly cool in contrast to the reports of many Western visitors. After 1933, Benjamin wrote briefly under pseudonyms, then sought refuge in the Balearic islands and Paris. In 1940, while in flight, he stopped briefly at the Spanish border, panicked at reports of what would happen to him if he were caught, and took his own life.

Benjamin's criticism is less analytical than intuitive. In discussions of authors he may begin with an idiosyncrasy and from there broaden out to define individuality, essence, and significance. Streaks of romanticism, anarchism, and communism do not always co-exist successfully. Add to this the hope of Messianic salvation, and even a touch of violence and the resulting cultural cocktail can turn heady, indeed.

Scholem commented that his taciturn, often melancholy friend aspired to both Marxism and Judaism. In flirting with both, he could embrace neither. From Palestine Scholem kept urging Benjamin to come visit. He agreed, even learned Hebrew, and gave thought to settling there, but nothing ever came of his "resolve." Just as Benjamin doubted that his roots in the German language made Germany his real home, so he had similar reservations that his Judaism would enable him to reside permanently in Palestine. Much later, Scholem concluded that his friend might not have been happy in the land of the Jews. It was Benjamin's fate to remain the perennial alien who knew this was a constant in his makeup.

In Benjamin's essays, especially those on Kafka and Jewish memory, he spoke glowingly enough about the Jewish tradition to draw a warning from his friend Bertolt Brecht to not support Jewish nationalism. His masterful essay on Kafka came close to claiming justice as a Jewish concept. "The gate of justice," Benjamin wrote to a friend, "is study. And yet Kafka did not dare to tie to this study those promises which tradition has linked to the study of Torah. His helpers are communal servants who have lost the house of prayer, and his students are students who have lost Torah." If Brecht feared a political nationalism in

Benjamin, he was way off the mark. Benjamin's links were to the Jewish religious and cultural tradition.

JEWISH NOTES IN A MINOR KEY

The life of **Margarete Susman** (1872–1966), painter, poet, critic, and philosopher, was one of inner and outer turmoil. Some of it was caused by her mother's insanity and her own repeated bouts with emotional illness, and ultimately with blindness. She was on the verge of converting to Christianity when, literally on the eve of the announced step, she reconsidered and became wholeheartedly a Jew. She had the same experience of near conversion and "rebirth" as Franz Rosenzweig, whose interpreter she became. Her correspondence with Landauer shows her as a person of thought, gentleness, and wit, receptive to his ideas of ethnic socialism.

Unlike Rosenzweig, Susman failed to recognize the severity of German anti-Semitism. She liked to think well of people, was fundamentally apolitical, and spent most of her adult life in Switzerland. Yet, when World War I erupted, she hastened back to Germany, presumably to do her share.

After her reconversion to Judaism, she immersed herself with characteristic intensity in her Judaic studies. She began to depict Judaism as a strong and living religion that had given the world the hallowed idea of the one God. No, the mission of Judaism was not yet fulfilled; it had the power for further development, and its future was assured as an extension of a unique past. Her most important interpretation was *Das Buch Hiob und das Schicksal des jüdischen Volkes* (*The Book of Job and the Destiny of the Jewish People*) (1945), in which the fate of the Jewish people is evoked by that of Job. During the war years in Switzerland she had found solace and inspiration in ancient texts. Her stature as a poetic interpreter of Jewish history has not been fully recognized.

Martin Buber (1878–1965) will be remembered chiefly for contributions other than literary. He deserves mention, however, as a critic of substance and taste, as the translator of the Bible into German, and as the skilled narrator of Hasidic tales. This long-time editor of *Der Jude* was an inveterate traveler and lecturer who interacted with both Jewish and Christian intellectuals. His name looms large in cooperative endeavors with Gustav Landauer and Franz Rosenzweig. To judge by published conversations with the literary critic Werner Kraft, Buber seems to have read everything and thought about everything. Original insights are presented in precise, even clipped language and revolve about such diverse personalities as Paul Claudel, Schnitzler, Hölderlin, Kleist, Kafka, and Kraus.

In retelling Hasidic tales in superbly crafted German, he introduced the strengths and beauties of a constant and reverent way of life to an unstable, insecure, often confused world of German Jewry. Without idealizing the Hasidic tradition of wholly deprecating Western ways, Buber adamantly repudiated still-prevailing negative German assessments of Eastern Jews. It was over Wassermann's continued negative appraisals of Eastern Jewries that Buber discontinued the relationship. As much as any figure writing in German, Buber sought to build a bridge between Polish and Russian Jewries on one side and Western Jewries on the other.

Yet even Buber, an active and committed Zionist, felt the pull of German political and cultural pressure. In 1914, he was not above the war enthusiasm of German-Jewish circles. Landauer was sufficiently disturbed to write: "What a pity for Jewish blood; yes, what a pity for all mankind; what a pity they have erred into this war. . . . You will only discover too late the consequences that are still concealed today."

After war, revolution, Landauer's murder, and the violent reactions of a defeated nation, Buber realized that all rabid nationalism was evil. He proclaimed the worth of Hebrew humanism over the nationalist follies of the European nations. Later, he was to worry about the possible deterioration of Zionism into unhealthy attitudes that would be in conflict with Jewish tradition as he understood it.

His conciliatory position on Jewish relations with others extended to the Germans. After World War II, as he surveyed the totality of German-Jewish togetherness, he arrived at conclusions hardly shared by most emigrés: "The symbiosis of German and Jewish *Wesen* (being), as I remember it in the four decades I spent in Germany, was, since the Spanish period, the first and only one which received the highest confirmation of fruitful results that history is able to confer."

This same Martin Buber described the poetry of his friend **Alfred Mombert** (1872–1942) as "visual dreams involving aspects of creation." Others hailed it as "cosmic music" and placed Mombert alongside Heine, Wolfskehl, Lasker-Schüler, and Kafka, among the towering figures in German-Jewish *belles-lettres*. Though applauded by some in his lifetime, Mombert achieved genuine acclaim only posthumously. Before 1900, his verse was conventional, psychological in inspiration, and seeking musical effect. Then it became ecstatic in the ever more prevailing Expressionist fashion. It ended up as mystical visions, abstruse, often impenetrable, and with verbal images that were as original as they were mystifying.

The tribulations of Job and the haunting messages of the prophets were among the main biblical sources that inspired him. But to emphasize this Jewish element, as Julius Bab did, may be to pervert its significance. Mombert's *Nachlaß* (literary contribution), far more than works appearing in his lifetime, represents a clear measure of his Jewish consciousness. Once, however, when asked about his Jewishness, he referred to himself as an "Asian." He may have had in mind the Egyptian, Indian, or general Eastern mythologies he used alongside the Jewish.

In his trilogy *Aeon* (1907–1911), with its experimental style and music, the poet explored the relations between the world and the human soul. In Part II of the poetic drama he seems to examine the role of the self in the ongoing battle between cosmos and chaos. Part III deals with the "materialization of the human soul in the history of nations." His most ambitious and least penetrable work is *Atair.* In it he dares delve into the most challenging and forbidding of metaphysical problems.

Mombert cherished the German landscape. A passionate hiker, he explored with enthusiasm the regions about Mannheim and Heidelberg, the area in which he lived. Was it reluctance to abandon this landscape and forsake his hikes, or was it fear of severance from his linguistic roots that made him tarry in Germany longer than was safe? His bad timing landed him eventually in the French internment camp at Gours. But for the loyal efforts of his friend Hans Carossa, Mombert would surely have shared the fate of others transported from Gours to extermination camps. He remained in Gours just long enough for his health to be ruined. He died in Switzerland the year following his release.

Unlike Mombert, who sought to create myth and searched for the eternal, **Samuel Gronemann** (1875–1952) was content to poke fun at the tortuous doings of German Jews. In a fierce satire entitled *Tohu Wabohu* (*Chaos*) (1920), Gronemann displayed his virtuosity at caricature.

He also engaged in excessive preaching and teaching, and his comic ideas are often original. A Jewish character employs the worst of Talmudic casuistry to make a dishonest schnorrer-like letter appear honest. A former Jew is discomfited by being maliciously reminded of his origins. The board of a Jewish foundation passes on the application for a stipend of a well-known anti-Semite. A yeshiva student studies *Faust* via a Talmudic method.

Gronemann had once contemplated the rabbinate as a career but had settled for law. In World War I he met many Polish Jews and began to treasure their values, e.g., in his *Hawdoloh und Zapfenstreich* (*Hawdoloh and Tattoo* [military call to quarters]) (1924). Their Jewishness was whole, while that of the assimilationists at home was empty gestures and intolerable compromises. Gronemann chafed under the absence of Jewish pride and dignity. The German Jew will do anything to please the German Christian, he said. Instead of worshipping at the Teutonic shrine, German Jews should leave Germany to the Germans and claim Palestine for the Jews. In 1936 he emigrated to Palestine where he wrote, among other books, *Jakob und Christian,* a satire on Nazi racial doctrines.

The son of a tool manufacturer in Vilnius, **Arno Nadel** (1878–1943) was steeped in Judaism. Nadel spent most of his adult life as choir director of a Berlin synagogue. He first established his reputation in music when he collected Yiddish and Hebrew festival and love songs and translated them into German. Then he added painting and literature to his interests.

Nadel drew on the Bible for many of his subjects. His biblical figures often resembled Nadel's friends when in one or the other he perceived the essential trait of a biblical hero. Obsession with God, monotheism, and Hasidic tales and celebrations form his main themes. In his search for the eternal and for a cosmic vision, Nadel's efforts are reminiscent of Mombert's. The poems in the monumental *Der Ton* (*The Tone*) (1921) were ignored, largely because of their obscurities and abstruseness. Far more accessible but less original are his Nietzschean aphorisms in *Aus vorletzten und letzten Gründen* (*Of Penultimate and Ultimate Causes*) (1909), or the drama *Adam* (1917) or *Der Sündenfall* (*Original Sin*) (1920), a series of biblical scenes.

Nadel's work ranges from the naive to the complex. In "Chanukka" he implores the divinity to let Jews conquer, without arms, all of God's doubters and release the world from suffering. He pleads for peace, nonviolence, and the rejection of coarseness. "Purim" lauds the Jewish people for their thirst for the divine and their repudiation of temporal idols and powers. "Simchat Torah" beseeches Jews never to regard the Torah as complete, but perennially to try to realize it fully.

Evidently, Nadel looked upon writing as a means of conveying God's message. He did not regard himself as a revealer or prophet, but as a teacher who, more through the tone than the word, transmitted the monotheistic wisdom of centuries through verse sayings and images.

If Nadel has remained unknown in spite of the great personal cosmology of *Der Ton,* it is due only in part to the complexity of the work. In addition, there was the snobbery of the Jewish intellectual establishment, which did not accord equal consideration to a cantor's verses. This is unfortunate, given the fact that Nadel belongs to the few whose inspiration was predominantly Jewish and religious.

There were, however, other writers with a positive approach to their Jewishness. Among these was **Martin Beradt** (1881–1949), a lawyer who represented some of Germany's largest firms. The author of novels such as *Eheleute* (*Married People*) (1910) and *Der Neurastheniker* (*The Neurasthenic*), Beradt often dwelled on the chasm between people of action and people of contemplation. Apparently the pensive, sensitive, and often stimulating character cannot retain the combative qualities required in the businessman or lawyer. The former often turns out to be weak and maladroit, a variant of the schlemiel. Beradt's war novel, *Schipper an der Front* (*Schipper at the Front*) (1929) garnered him the enmity of the military. While there are some Jewish characters in these novels, Jews abound in *Die Straße der kleinen Ewigkeit* (*The Street of Brief Eternity*), published posthumously. It depicted sympathetically the lives and values of Eastern Jews who lived in the Berlin ghetto of the Grenadierstrasse. While Beradt shed the orthodoxy of his youth, he retained a lifelong regard for those who adhered to it.

Not orthodoxy, but reform, sustained **Emil Bernhard (Cohn)** (1881–1948), whose plays and novels bore the defect of most novels by rabbis: excessive preaching and interruption of a suspenseful narrative by short and long digressions. Bernhard defied the anti-Zionist stance of reform and early in his career endorsed Zionist aspirations. He was distressed by fellow rabbis who, in their zeal to modernize, surrendered much that was precious and unifying in Judaism. He disclaimed any desire to return to the past, insisting, however, that the spiritual unity that once existed between Eastern and Western Jewries be restored.

In his drama *Die Jagd Gottes* (*God's Pursuit*), a group of Jews is hiding in a synagogue, fearful of the Cossacks outside. In the evolving dramatic dialogues, the author touches on Messianism, the history of persecutions, the spirit and form of religion, and love and discipline in father-son relationships. Bernhard does not fully succeed in integrating his ideas into his drama. He does better in *Das Pantherfell* (*The Hide of the Panther*) (1951). Again he assembles a group, this time shipwrecked on an island. Biblical tales serve as background for stories within stories. Bernhard's talent was more narrative than dramatic.

Mildness, tolerance, and respect for a humane religious tradition permeates the poetry and fiction of **Ludwig Straus** (1892–1953). Having proven his business ineptitude, he was allowed, with the help of his

mother, to continue his academic education. He began to write during
World War I, which he attacked. His reputation as a poet was growing
when the Nazis ended his career. He chose Palestine for his new home.
There he perfected his Hebrew to the point of writing poetry in that
language.

The German and Jew in him lived without tension until 1920. The
virulent anti-Semitism which flowered at this time greatly strengthened
his Zionist sympathies. Poems on Palestine expressed his yearning for the
Urheimat (*ancestral homeland*) and his love of "holy earth."

The influence of Martin Buber, his father-in-law, appears strongest
in the narrative "Der Reiter" ("The Horseman") (1929). This tale places
genuine communication and empathy for the other at the zenith of
human values. Straus puts feelings above learning and ritual in this work,
which pits the scholarly Rabbi Naphtalie (called the Horseman), against
an Hasidic rabbi, intellectually his inferior, but possessing the gift to
heal, persuade, and attract Jews everywhere. Naphtalie remains skeptical
of his Hasidic colleague, even after the latter has saved his son. In crisis
upon crisis, the Hasid comes to the rescue of his learned but emotionally
arid colleague. Napthalie's dependence on him grows as he follows the
Hasid and finally dies in his arms.

Straus set his story in Eastern Europe. For him, the national Jew
and Jewry were one and indivisible, and Eastern Jewry could invigorate
with its strong feeling the cold rationalism of the Jews of Germany. It is
to Straus's credit as a literary craftsman that this gentle, inspirational
story does not turn maudlin and sentimental. His German renditions of
Ostjüdische Liebeslieder (*Eastern Jewish Love Songs*) reenforce the
impression of deep affection for the less-polished brethren of Poland and
Russia.

A century before **Jacob Picard** (1883–1967), Berthold Auerbach had
chronicled German village life, mostly that of Christians but peripherally
that of Jews as well. Picard has left the most remarkable portraits of
Jewish rural existence in the German language. His Jews are petty
merchants, and cattle and horse dealers. They are guided by "die alte
Lehre," the teachings handed down from generation to generation.
Village Jews have clung to this teaching tenaciously, sanctifying each
daily act, saying their daily prayers, and treating others as they themselves would wish to be treated. They have their problems and try to
solve them by honored and respected means. By day they trade amicably
with their Christian neighbors, each conscious of differences between
them, but convinced that these are surmountable with a measure of good
will. Christians were as used to seeing Jewish neighbors go to the

synagogue, as Jews were accustomed to witnessing the others attend church. If either failed to attend, it was a matter of curiosity, if not concern.

Picard presents uncomplicated Jews who know modern life but are minimally attracted to it. Like other humans, they are tempted by wealth or sex, but in the end moderation and human values triumph. Picard's Jews are warm, upright German equivalents to Sholem Aleichem's *shtetl* Jews. They are also related to heroes of earlier ghetto tales, but they are more up-to-date and more differentiated.

Representative narratives are "Der Gezeichnete" ("The Marked One") (1936) and "Die alte Lehre" ("The Old Teachings") (1934?). A novel, *Das Opfer (The Sacrifice)* (1934) showed him less skilled at handling longer materials. In his sparse work, some of it written in American exile, Picard presents men and women filled with Jewish belief and feeling.

Ludwig Meidner (1884–1966) was mainly a painter and wrote only when unable to paint. Friends often found him in his studio wearing his skullcap and sometimes interrupting a conversation because he had to "*davven minchah* or *maariv*" (say the afternoon or evening liturgy). A God-driven genius, Meidner was haunted by visions and apparitions which bordered on serious pathology. Some visions came after intense prayer, and he appeared especially susceptible upon the onset of the Sabbath.

Judaism was central in the work of this artist, who was destined to live in poverty, fear, and psychosis. *Im Nacken das Sternenmeer (In the Back a Sea of Stars)* (1916) abounds with prophets, visionaries, and biblical characters. Meidner expanded on this first volume of lyrics in *Septemberschrei (The Call of September)* (1918), replete with horror images of war and promises of eternal service to God. The war made a socialist of him. In his later works, he cast aside both his ecstatic Expressionism and socialism and found his sole support in religion. The advent of the Nazi horror demanded all the support he could muster.

A unique figure among German-Jewish writers was **Salomon Friedländer** (1871–1946), perhaps better known as Mynona. As Friedländer he wrote by day and was an organized, responsible, essentially conservative writer—and an outstanding interpreter of Kantian thought. At night he became Mynona, a Bohemian, an actor given to extravagant behavior and outrageous observations. Perhaps the two styles were to confound the world to protect his inner self against unwanted intrusions.

He came from the Posen area, in which "Protestants, Prussians, Catholic Poles and Old Testament Jews despised and hated each other in 'deepest peace'." Friedländer put his father, a physician, on a pedestal, and every comparison resulted in the author's self-deprecation. He first studied medicine but ended up with philosophy, toward which his brother-in-law, a rabbi, had steered him. In philosophy he began as a partisan of Schopenhauer, then converted to Nietzsche, and ultimately became a worshipper of Kant. Without Kant, he wrote, "mankind remains stupid, ugly, evil." He even wrote a "Kant for Children."

His many autobiographical sketches are clever self-deprecations that invited attention, however, to one "tired of his hard-earned obscurity." His wit, often at his own expense, was rarely malicious. Einstein seemed an unlikely target, but Mynona sensed in the proponent of relativity an opponent of Kantian thought. His tendency to look at great men *in specie aeternitate* led him into occasional polemics with key figures of literature and the arts.

As Mynona he is chiefly remembered for his "grotesques," which even he could not define. Perhaps they were to hold up to his readers exaggerated traits that they might recognize in their own existence and use to release tensions and provoke laughter. The "grotesques" were humorous pieces, even jokes, nearly all exposing human foibles and inadequacies. "Der lachende Hiob" ("The Laughing Job"), written after 1933, is said to have helped many an emigré laugh in the face of danger and death. However, Mynona had but a passing interest in social questions. Nothing temporary could engage this Kantian in search of the inner nature of things. Until the Nazi onslaught, Mynona was detached from Jewish concerns and seemed impervious to anti-Jewish slights. After 1933, he was drawn increasingly into the Jewish orbit. Perhaps governments were as transient as the problems that brought them to power. It was a transient government that drove the Kantian into exile and afforded him a narrow escape from death.

Richard Huldschiner (1872–1931) developed an early interest in Zionism. In *Die stille Nacht* (*The Silent Night*) (1904?), he kept repeating the point that Jews are living on hostile soil where pogroms have erupted in the past and will again erupt in the future. There is but one way of assuring Jewish physical survival and reestablishing Jewish pride, and this is not in God and prayer, but in Jewish *Volkstum* and the return to Zion. With a country of their own, Jews could enjoy like others a free life worthy of human status. His hero is Arbanel who, to the jeers of some and the applause of others, sets out for the Holy Land to translate his convictions into action.

Not only does Huldschiner provide authentic Jewish settings, but his holiday scenes are as real and festive as any found in German-Jewish fiction. Unfortunately, like some other writers with a Jewish orientation, he fails to integrate his thought effectively into his narrative. His characters are ideas that speak and act. But an enthusiastic Zionist novel in the year of Herzl's death was an act of commitment and courage.

• • • • •

Plaintive Sounds from Vienna

One of the great idols of **Hermann Kesten** (b. 1900–) was Heinrich Heine, whose skepticism, irreverence, and non-doctrinaire attitudes were also Kesten's own. "Heine was an ardent patriot," Kesten wrote, "whose fatherland was the whole earth."

Kesten's universalism allows no chosen people, German or Jewish, and also no chosen religion. In his exile, again like Heine, Kesten was intensely critical of Germany, while becoming most sympathetic to his fellow Jews. In a preface to a new edition of Heine's *Germany: A Winter's Tale,* in which he denounced the arrogance of Germans—in believing they could do away with Jews, capitalists, and socialists all at once—he pointed out the serious shortcomings of the Germans. They lacked the talent to become prophets like the Jews of old or to evoke pity as victims, as Jews had throughout the centuries. Germans were absurd pedants, radical in wrong domains of thought, clumsy in love, and backward in justice. Above all, the Teutons were pitifully deficient in the "spirit of fun." Like Feuchtwanger who had satirized Hitler in the person of a chauffeur, Kesten poked fun at a Hitler-type politician in *Scharlatan (Charlatan)* (1932).

Kesten was attracted not only to fellow-scoffers in the Heine mold, but also to God-seekers, even Christ-seekers, such as Joseph Roth and Alfred Döblin. He could also admire Max Brod for his literacy talent as well as his Zionist commitment. But Kesten himself was above nations, religions, ideologies, or movements. His role was to build bridges of understanding between them, demanding that each fulfill its own implied contracts with others and that they serve the human species.

His reputation would be more securely anchored if he had not spread himself so thin. He wrote short stories, novels, dramas, poetry; he was a critic, memorialist, translator, anthologist. He was not a profound critic, but rather a quick, intuitive sketcher of personalities and individualities. This same skill manifests itself in sardonic characterizations of his fictional heroes and anti-heroes. In fiction, he often squandered his gift on ill-chosen subjects, and a work such as *Glückliche Menschen* (*Happy People*) (1931) begins in one style and jarringly terminates in another. His novels have at their base a moral earnestness that no amount of erotic excess or self-deprecating wit can fully veil. The most immoral of situations—and they are numerous—have as their goal the illuminating of moral choice. In his fictionalized biographies of Ferdinand and Isabella (1936) and Philip the Second (1938), he delights in exposing vanities, hypocrisies, and absurdities—especially among those judged to be great and immortal.

Whatever his subject, Kesten refrains from religious or political partisanship. His post-holocaust novel *Die fremden Götter* (*Alien Gods*) (1950) reveals an equal distaste for fanatical believers and others who, chameleon-like, are attracted to any idea. In this novel he created an intolerant but well-intentioned nominal Jew who turned fanatically Jewish in the death camps. He now wants to save his daughter, who, in his absence, had been forcibly converted by nuns. The novel is directed equally against soul controllers and soul snatchers. In typical Kesten fashion, he has the daughter marry an atheist with the understanding that everyone be allowed to seek salvation in his or her own way. An intelligent writer, full of wit and irony, a man of many genres, between worlds and ideas, Kesten never offered more than the promise of greatness.

Robert Neumann (1897–1975), a native of Austria who lived variously in Germany, England, and Switzerland, is best known as a parodist, possibly the most versatile in German. Two years after he published *Mit fremden Federn* (*With the Pens of Others*) (1927), he also established himself as a novelist with *Die Sintflut* (*The Great Flood*), set in the time of the great inflation. His extensive business experience is also manifest in his other works. Like Kesten, this prolific writer spread himself too thin, condemning himself to the second rank of writers.

In 1939 he published a novel that focused on Jewish experience. *An den Wassern von Babylon* (*By the Waters of Babylon*) is set in prewar Palestine. Twelve Jews from different countries and backgrounds try to strike roots in a land of their own. The bus that is to carry them illegally into British-controlled Palestine meets with a terrible accident as it winds its way through uncharted terrain. Eleven passengers die instantly; only one manages to crawl away from the debris, a book in his hand. Then that book falls from his hand, opened to the page in which, in the Bible, God promises the land to Israel. Common desire and a common fate link the stories of the passengers, who come from the Carpathians, London, New York, Alsace, and Moravia. They all have a story to tell of Jewish fate and persecution.

In *Treibgut* (*The Inquest*) (1945), a British dramatist falls in love with a woman in his theater. After an intense but brief liaison, she commits suicide. The dramatist investigates her history and discovers that her psyche had been irreversibly shaped by the suffering Jewish people.

Stefan Zweig (1881–1942) was among the best-known writers of his time. He wrote one novel, several novellas, some plays, and several biographies that were more literary than scholarly. An accomplished translator, he was a catalyst for internationalizing national cultures. He made Belgian, French, Austro-German, and later Russian and British writers known to the world. Affluent throughout his life, he played a Maecenas role to several writers, especially Joseph Roth and Ernst Weiss, whom he partially supported in exile.

Not only was Zweig a cultural intermediary, but he also became a prime advocate of supranational ideas. Together with Romain Rolland, whom he translated, Zweig was justly seen as one of the chief pacifists of World War I. A man of peace at a time of frenzied nationalism, humanitarianism in an age of barbarism, Zweig was sensitive to the abuse he suffered. He was in many ways hyper-refined, almost *précieux*. Of course, he suffered even more grossly twenty years later with the degrading events of the Nazi era. Everywhere, the dictator's dark shadow loomed large. Though host nations treated Zweig well in exile and accorded him honors, the disillusioned world citizen could not tolerate either his own changed condition or the abysmal state of his beloved Europe. Given to depressions, he sought out the help of his friend, Sigmund Freud. There was now ample cause for depression, and in 1942, in Brazil, Stefan Zweig ended it all.

The scion of a wealthy Viennese family, Zweig fought many inner battles against the silver spoon, the life of comfort, refinement, and culture that he enjoyed. He was closer to his mother's family of distinguished lawyers, financiers, and professors than to his father's of merchants and manufacturers. Long before he received his doctorate, he had begun publishing in the *Neue Freie Presse*. He soon realized that a dearth of experience was hampering his growth as a writer. In 1902 he met the Belgian poet Emile Verhaeren and came under his influence. He also visited Paris to meet assorted cultural heroes in the French capital. Travels through Europe, the Orient, and North America soon followed. A meeting with Romain Rolland led to their pacifist manifesto. After World War I he settled in his villa on the Kapuzinerberg in Salzburg from which he could see, on the mountaintop of Berchtesgaden, the villa of the man who symbolized "the most dreadful defeat of reason and the wildest triumph of brutality" and who made him feel that "never had a generation suffered a more devastating moral retrogression from previous heights" than Zweig's own.

His selection of biographical subjects was determined by the human interest of their lives and the fact that they represented different facets of his own being and beliefs. Zweig was attracted to the new, the ever-receptive, and the daring, but even more to the tolerant and the non-fanatic. A biography of Erasmus (1934) and a shorter study of Montaigne represent aspects of his own detached self. Verhaeren and Rolland intrigued him as Europeans, though the former's vehement anti-German stance in World War I briefly alienated him. Among his *Baumeister der Welt* (*Master Builders*) (1935), he included Balzac, but also authors like Dickens, Stendhal, Dostoyevski, Hölderlin, and Kleist. His biographies, mostly of foreign figures, were to enrich the German spirit through the infusion of different ideas. But Zweig was also drawn to personages with noble aspirations which seemed about to be realized when chance, an unpredictable factor, intervened to cross their grand design.

This same attraction to those who succumb to the whims of fate is equally evident in several novellas. It holds true when Zweig deals with the young, as in *Erstes Erlebnis* (*First Experience*) (1911); with the mature, as in *Verwirrung der Gefühle* (*Entangled Feelings*) (1927), or with older people as in *Amok*. The novellas are marked by a lively imagination, narrative poise, and psychological insight. They are also marred by occasional stylistic carelessness and sometimes by preciosity. Zweig's characters are often in the grips of a passion and have complex and enigmatic relationships with one another.

Zweig's Jewish attitudes must be gleaned in the main from his autobiography and from those narratives that have some Jewish characters. In such stories as "Buchmendel," or "Der begrabene Leuchter" ("The Buried Candelabra") (1937), he shows his respect for the Jewish love of books and the Jews' desire to survive, respectively. Jewish history impresses him as that of a people uniquely dedicated to spirit over matter and peace over conquest. As night descended over Europe in the 1930s, he thought more and more often of the Jewish contribution to civilization: "Neither persecution, exile, inquisitions, nor pogrom could stamp out that invincible determination to create, which has demonstrated again and again Jewish intellectual fruitfulness, when and wherever the Jewish people were permitted to take part in the community."

Yet his respect for the Jewish past and values did not extend to such domains as religion or notions of peoplehood. No religion could claim his interest, and his reservations concerning Zionism manifest themselves most tellingly in his resistance to Herzl's imprecations, although Zweig liked Herzl and was indebted to him as a literary sponsor. Jewish nationalism, or what might pass for it, was as foreign to him as any other nationalism. In the Hitler years he appreciated the idea of a Jewish homeland, but homeland and nationhood were not synonymous. Zweig had little understanding of a vision such as Max Brod's, that Jews had to be a people again before they could work with others to build a universal community as envisaged by the prophets. Zweig had no patience with intermediate stages. He aspired directly to an "unlined" humanity. The collapse of this hope, with history flowing speedily in the opposite direction, wore down this gentle, refined idealist, who would not and could not live in a world without reason and hope.

Born into an all-Jewish environment near the easternmost outposts of the Hapsburg Empire, **Joseph Roth** (1894–1939) died, a profound Catholic sympathizer, close to the outbreak of World War II. As if his earthly journey were not troubled enough, Roth's death was due to acute alcoholism, and he became known as chief advocate of the Hapsburgs' return as the only salvation for imperiled Europe. Yet, earlier, Roth had been awed and enthusiastic about the Russian Revolution and had briefly flirted with Marxism, only to turn into an avowed foe. In the mid-1920s, he had also turned into an enemy of modernism in culture. "Idolatry," he commented, "begins with the worship of emptiness (*Leere*), the removal of distinctions, limits, contours, forms. . . ." Thus he condemned Joyce, Gide, Döblin, and himself as "splinter writers," in contrast to Scholem Asch, Kafka, and Rilke, who were writers of wholeness and distinction. But this increasingly conservative cultural critic never ceased to empathize with dominated, colored peoples, clamoring for their equality. (He also demanded equality for impoverished and maltreated whites.) A virtual beggar in his final years, Roth used his pen to make the fortunate more aware of the suffering of their fellow-beings.

Roth never knew his father and was left to the care of relatives. He was a first-rate student at the *Gymnasium* as well as in letters at the University of Vienna. As tutor in a wealthy home, he first witnessed the elegant manners of the aristocracy and copied them. For the first two years of World War I he served as a front-line soldier and then returned to Vienna to start a career in journalism. His *feuilletons,* most of them in the *Frankfurter Zeitung,* showed, according to Kesten, that he was a man of reason and peace, opposed to violence, the misuses of power, the abuse of language, the neglect of good books, and indifference to what happens to other human beings. Kesten placed this early Roth on the side of the good and the eternal.

Spent mostly in travel, his initial years with the *Frankfurter Zeitung* may have been the best of his life. Then came his wife's mental illness, his feelings of guilt, and the attendant financial worries over her permanent hospitalization. His slide into chronic self-pity was a mere overture to drunkenness. His situation deteriorated in the mid-1930s, when exile cut off his sources of income. He lived in hotels in Vienna, Nice, Amsterdam, Ostende, but mostly in Paris. He had become a "café czar," holding court, being pleasantly entertaining when he was not complaining or asking for help. He quarreled shamelessly with his benefactor, Stefan Zweig, over what he regarded as disappointing contributions to his sagging treasury.

Considering his sorry state, Roth managed a prolific literary production. In his first novels he was something of a skeptic, a rebel who depicted the sorry and disintegrating forces in man and society. Later novels reflected the believer, the classicist, and conservative. His undisputed masterpieces were the *Radetzkymarsch* (*Radetzky March*) (1932) and *Kapuzinergruft* (*Tomb of the Capuchins*) (1939). Other notable achievements were his *Hiob* (*Job*) (1930) and his magnificent novella *Die Legende vom heiligen Trinker* (*The Legend of the Holy Drinker*) (1939).

These and his "hotel novels" were deceptively tranquil and uneventful. Underneath the quietude he developed a heightening nervous tension. Stability and wholeness were illusory as disintegration was spreading, however imperceptibly. As the sense of doom enveloped Europe, Roth's work received a posthumous critical acclaim it had not always enjoyed in his lifetime. His voice and vision were increasingly perceived as prophetic.

Roth's novels had as their backdrop the collapse of the Hapsburg Empire, which he viewed as integral, supranational, and united by one church and one throne. Its fall was tantamount to the victory of such decomposing factors as growing materialism, nationalism, and racism, and the concomitant loss of balance, judgment, and taste.

Through the Trotta family, whose destiny he began to chronicle in the *Radetzkymarsch* and continued in *Kapuzinergruft,* Roth recorded this descent into disharmony and decay. While the founder of the Trotta "dynasty" was mainly concerned with establishing the truth of his role in saving the life of Franz Joseph, a truth unpardonably embellished in history books, his son had less lofty ambitions. He was content with his role of provincial administrator and his lusterless life of duty and routine. This son's son, the last Baron Trotta, no longer had any ideals at all. Given to gambling, drinking, and women, he barely managed to survive. He was a self-destructive loser, melancholy, craving for a better life, but incapable of marshalling the resources to attain this goal. This was also the flaw, Roth implied, the fatal flaw of the dying monarchy and of moribund Europe as well.

Roth was not, however, a man of profound sociopolitical insight. He was fascinated much more with the spiritual and cultural forces that were fighting the losing battle for survival with decency. If anything, Roth was lacking in political realism and sophistication. How else can one explain his frantic appeals, as late as 1938–1939, for a return of the Hapsburgs to the throne—at the very time that the Nazis were preparing their march on Europe?

Jewish characters were only on the periphery of most of Roth's fiction, but they were in the forefront of *Hiob,* written before Hitler's advent to power but following the onset of Roth's wife's illness. The setting of the first half of the novel was the Eastern European *shtetl,* but then it shifted to a New York Jewish neighborhood. Only the *shtetl* part succeeded. In the New York portions the novel nearly crumbled, as Roth lost his way in a maze of coincidences and miracles. While the *shtetl* sections rested on Roth's childhood experiences, the New York episodes had to rely on the observations that brief visits afford and the imaginative forces they set in motion. Ironically, it is in this most Jewish of his novels that the future near-Catholic appears in outline form, especially in his emphasis on the miraculous. The *Radetzkymarsch* and *Hiob,* however different, are linked together by the appreciation of past greatness and unity, the continuity that binds the generations together, and the dismay Roth felt over the breaking of this bond.

Hiob is the story of Mendel Singer, whom Roth describes as "just an ordinary Jew." One disaster upon another befalls Mendel: the birth of a retarded mute child, Menuchim; the conscription of his oldest son, truly a Jewish Cossack, into the Czar's army; the emigration to far off America of a second son, and the death of that son in war; his wife's death from grief; and his daughter's loss of sanity.

And what happens to the retarded child left behind in Russia, contrary to the advice of a "wonder-rabbi?" He appears miraculously at a Seder one night to which Mendel, a handyman in Brooklyn, has been invited as the mitzvah guest. Menuchim is now a famous orchestra conductor touring the United States. Months earlier, the lonely, abandoned Mendel had been powerfully touched by a recording entitled

"Menuchim's Song." The reader's credulity is strained by the disharmony of the fantasy of the last quarter of the book with the realism of the major portion.

Just as in his long essay *Juden auf der Wanderschaft* (*Jews in Flight*) (1927), Roth's treatment of Eastern Jewry in *Hiob* was warm and sympathetic. By contrast, he was critical of the assimilative tendencies in American life which destroy wholeness. For the human psyche and inner peace, Czarist Russia seemed almost better to him than democratic, multi-faceted America. Mendel's Americanized son Menuchim had become no less a stranger to Mendel than his lost son, the Jewish Cossack. If Roth is negative toward America as a prison of the spirit, he is also becoming negative toward women.

Of course, Roth realized that unlike the real Job, his Mendel has lost his faith, never again to regain it. But Mendel is made whole again and is partly reconciled with his God through the appearance of Menuchim, truly a feat of divine power and benevolence.

How is one to understand Roth's evolution from *shtetl* Jew to a Hapsburg partisan and near-Catholic? His biographer, David Bronsen, mentions a confession made by Roth toward the end of his life. In his youth, said Roth, he had been dazzled by German culture and eager to escape from the ghetto existence of Brody, his hometown. But he had realized that cutting himself off from his Jewish ties meant losing himself—i.e., no longer feeling comfortable in his own skin. He characterized his fascination with Catholicism as his "Jewish loyalty to the Hapsburgs." He had called the Hapsburgs the protectors of the Jews who were surrounded by hostile Slavs and Germans. But perhaps there was another reason. While the God of the Jews represented unity and wholeness, He may have been too remote for the despair and torment of Joseph Roth, for whom the world had suddenly become cold and forbidding.

Alfred Polgar (1873–1955), one of the few *feuilletonists* whom Kraus forgave for indulging in the genre, was a master of small prose and aphoristic wit. Non-doctrinaire, independent, receptive to the different, he admired the work of his friend Peter Altenberg, whose *Nachlaß* (works left behind) he edited. What Polgar's pieces lacked was clear direction and consistent viewpoint. His often harsh theater criticism, while incisive, failed to convey genuine love for the stage. Apparently neither books nor theater intrigued him, but life itself did. What Polgar detested was philistinism and double standards, both in everyday affairs and the cultural world.

In Vienna Polgar befriended the habitués of the Café Central, including Altenberg, Egon Friedell, Berthold Viertel, and Albert Ehrenstein. He collaborated with Friedell on several comic plays. In all he essayed, Polgar was intent on clothing an idea in the sparsest of language.

The 1920s in Berlin were his most productive period. He was one of the regulars of Jacobsohn's *Schaubühne* (later: *Weltbühne*). By 1933 he had inhaled enough foul Nazi air to return to Vienna. After the *Anschluß*, he left for Zurich, went on to Paris, and finally ended up in Hollywood and New York.

His subjects were diverse. He might be moved to do a satiric piece on the uniform, its powers in war and peace, the absurd privileges it could confer. Or he might write a short piece on "Shylocks Plaidoyer" ("Shylock's Summation Plea"), in which he would jokingly suggest that a portion of the courtroom scene must have been lost. (Shylock, a master of words, schooled in the Talmud, would never have silently accepted Portia's absurd declaration!) Or he might comment on the visit to Vienna of the Moscow Yiddish Theater. His observations were original, though not always profound.

Polgar labeled certain of his attitudes as "Hebraic." Perhaps this meant that he possessed a Jewish sensibility and wit and that certain notions the Germans held sacrosanct struck him as absurd. But he rarely employed specifically Jewish themes and was content with accepting his Jewishness as a fact of life. Like most Jews writing in German, he became Jewish only when he scented anti-Semitism about him. He would then fire every bit of ammunition at the enemy.

Polgar's Jewish interests were rich, compared to those of the versatile **Egon Friedell** (1878–1938), playwright, actor, cultural historian, translator, and amateur philosopher. Friedell's Jewish origin was not widely known, and when he commented on his own Jewishness, or that of others, he did so in a self-deprecatory manner. For one merely born a Jew and for whom this fact had no value, Friedell suffered the ultimate irony. The Jewish label was solely responsible for Nazis' entering his residence after the *Anschluß*, whereupon Friedell hurled himself through the window to a certain death. His *Kulturgeschichte der Neuzeit* (*Cultural History of Modern Times*) (1927–1932), probably his most substantial work, was subjective, witty, and ironic, a stylistic enterprise of note rather than an achievement in history.

Unlike Friedell, **Friedrich Torberg** (1908–1979) was a conscious Jew, addressed Jewish topics, and fitted clearly into the liberal tradition. Before his exile, which eventually took him to Hollywood, Torberg already had to his credit two novels that had gained some attention. One of these, *Der Schüler Gerber hat absolviert* (*Young Gerber Has Graduated*) (1930), told of a teacher's cruelty in the classroom that led to a student's suicide. *Die Mannschaft* (*The Team*) (1935) is probably the only sports novel in the annals of German-Jewish literary history. Torberg uses water sport as a means for a man to rise from purely self-centered concerns to socialization and awareness of others. After *Abschied* (*Farewell*) (1937), a story of first love, Torberg addressed more specifically Jewish subjects.

In 1943, he published *Mein ist die Rache* (*Revenge Is My Domain*). In it, the Orthodox Jewish inmate of a concentration camp keeps preaching to other prisoners that revenge must be left to God alone. When his own life is threatened, however, the hero shoots his tormentor and manages to escape. He now suffers pangs of guilt, since he believes himself responsible for the presumed death of his comrades. The novel touches on such topics as Jewish passivity, personal initiative, leaving to God the task of avenging injustices to Jews, and the Jewish psyche which has been shaped by this attitude. It is evident that Torberg has qualms about this psyche and that he would wish for more firmness and resistance to replace softness and cowardice.

Written toward the end of World War II, *Hier bin ich, mein Vater* (*Here I Am, My Father*) (published in 1948) revolved about the failed life of a young Jewish jazz pianist who has always been morbidly sensitive to anti-Semitic remarks. His abnormal psychology leads him to an anti-Semitic classmate who is now a Nazi mogul. In return for the Nazi's promise to release his father from Dachau, he betrays some of his best friends. In the end, the Jew discovers the truth about himself: From the moment he knew he was a Jew, he had wanted to belong to the other side—that healthy, carefree majority that did not have to be defensive about identity and could direct instead of being directed. In this novel of tragic self-hate that destroys human lives, Torberg achieves a high level of psychological insight.

Lack of naturalness and spontaneity is evident also in his *Golem,* not one of Torberg's better works. As a critic and essayist, Torberg showed a Krausian capacity for hatred, applied especially to communism, for him the ultimate foe.

The Austrian half-Jews **Raoul Auernheimer** (1876–1948) and **Ernst Lothar** (1890–1974) displayed little interest in their partly Jewish background, though it was that background that forced them into exile. Auernheimer wrote mostly *Lustspiele* (comedies). In his memoirs he devoted a chapter to Theodor Herzl, to whom he was related on his mother's side. Like Herzl, he wrote *feuilletons* for the *Neue Freie Presse,* with Austria and Vienna among his favorite subjects.

Lothar, born Müller, was raised as a Catholic and allegedly did not like being reminded of his partly Jewish origins. He wrote novels and directed Reinhardt's theater in the "Josefstadt." His own plays had strong erotic overtones.

• • • • •

Exit: Minor Writers

S everal minor writers escaped late into the Nazi years, while others perished at Auschwitz. Among the latter was the poet **Arthur Silbergleit** (1881–1944), many of whose poems reflected a strong Jewish consciousness. "Die Balalaika," based on his World War I experiences in Eastern Europe, emphasized his abiding respect for Orthodox Jews. A poem on "The Sabbath," written originally with purely spiritual fervor and rewritten in 1935 with Jewish suffering in mind, has been anthologized. His Christian wife had hidden him in the forest, but Silbergleit could not long tolerate the isolation. He returned to her, was quickly caught, and shipped off to Auschwitz, and his wife was informed "with regret" of his demise.

Friedrich Koffka (1881–1951) wrote but a few short plays. In *Kain* (1917) he opposes a sensitive, confused, unproductive Cain to his girl-chasing, heavy-drinking brother Abel. When Kain kills his brother, it is because their attraction-repulsion relationship has become intolerable. Another drama, *Herr Oluf* (n.d.), based on a Norwegian legend, is reminiscent of "Der Erlkönig" ("The Erl-King"). A groom lives so intensely the night before his wedding that he arrives dead in his bride's chamber. For reasons difficult to fathom, Koffka, an exile in London, inserts a scene in which two Yiddish-speaking Jews argue about merchandise to be sold. Whether the scene was included for comic relief or to meet a need to mock the Jewish money connection is difficult to determine.

Victor Hahn (1869–?), a Berlin newspaper editor, wrote historical dramas on Cesare Borgia (1910) and the Empress Eugenie (1932). Clearly he had the nationalist-militarist factions in mind when he denounced any action, however nobly conceived, if it leads to the loss of even one human life. While these plays are forceful, his Moses drama is not; it is too close to biblical narrative to be dramatically effective.

The plays of **Moritz Goldstein** (1880–?) are deeply pessimistic. All characters are selfishly pursuing despicable goals, with parents selling their daughter, the daughter selling herself, and all eager to lay their hands on the money of an old farmhand who has suddenly inherited great wealth.

Walter Meckauer (1889–1966) had published a promising novel, *Die Bücher des Kaisers Wutai* (*The Books of the Emperor Wutai*) (1928), when only a few years later he was forced into exile. Meckauer was never to regain his momentum.

The fiction of the baptized Jew **Wilhelm Speyer** (1887–1952) seldom rose above the level of *Konversationsroman* (conversational novel). But late in life, Speyer recounted the history of a Jewish family in Berlin during the "Year of the Three Emperors." *Das Glück der Andernachs* (*The Happiness of the Andernachs*) (1947) was perhaps his one work of stature.

The physician **Martin Gumpert** (1897–1955) conjured up some hallucinatory images in poetry published during the Expressionist decade but then devoted himself mostly to scientific and philosophic insights derived from his medical practice. This does not by any means exhaust the list of minor writers whose careers were cut short by exile or tragic death in the camps.

Vicky Baum (1880–1960) is remembered for her *Menschen im Hotel* (*Grand Hotel*) (1928) which brought this Ullstein editor instant success in the Anglo-Saxon world. A Hollywood contract followed, but after seven months she was back in Germany. The 1932 presidential election convinced her, however, that she did not wish to raise her children in a country that offered a choice between Hindenburg and Hitler. Before long she was back in the United States, where she never again enjoyed a success comparable to *Grand Hotel*.

Like her friend Vicky Baum, **Gina Kaus** (1894–1985) failed to achieve major status in spite of a prolific production. Her strength lay in creating the erotic tensions that generate psychological suspense. Novels such as *Die Verliebten* (*The Lovers*) (1931) and *Die Schwestern Klee* (*The Klee Sisters*) (1933) reveal a competent craftsman with a special interest in women's causes, social democracy, and the preservation of political freedoms. Though her characters often bear Jewish-sounding names, she rarely identifies them as Jews.

Willy Haas (1891–19?), a literary conversationalist, memorialist, and critic, was skilled in identifying the uniqueness of a writer and his work. After Hitler, he returned to his native Prague and, in 1939, emigrated to

India. In 1947, he returned to Europe to become the critic for *Die Welt*. While incisive in describing the individuality of Hofmannsthal and Brecht, he had a special affinity for Jewish writers such as Werfel and Kafka.

The same holds true for the poet, anthologist, and theater critic **Julius Bab** (1880–1955). He acknowledged his Jewish identity in social and cultural terms and was sometimes harsh toward those who looked upon their Jewishness as a burden. He staunchly defended Heine against his Jewish and Gentile detractors. Jews, he admonished, should be proud rather than apologetic about the great poet.

•　•　•　•　•

The Empty House

T*he Empty House,* the title of an anthology of works by German-Jewish writers, was **Karl Otten**'s appropriate metaphor for the virtual disappearance of Jewish writers from the German scene. This history has not dealt with those writers, born in this century, who were too young to have established a reputation before 1933 and who came into their own after 1945, when the ties between German and Jew had been severed. Few of the writers who came to the fore after the war established domicile on German soil or were writing in the Federal Republic. Several have contributed to the literature of the Holocaust. **Nelly Sachs**, Nobel Prize Laureate, born in the last century, but recognized only late in life, chose to live in Sweden, as did **Peter Weiss**, whose Holocaust docudrama *Die Ermittlung (The Investigation)* (1965) is less well known than his epoch-making *Marat/Sade*. The poet **Paul Celan** (b. 1920 as Paul Antschel) lived in Paris before his tragic end by suicide in 1970. The Austrian-born **Jacov Lind,** who has also interpreted the Nazi atrocities, has made London his home base, as has Nobel Prize Winner **Elias Canetti** (b. 1905), **Erich Fried** (1921–1988), and **Arthur Koestler** (b. 1905) of Austro-Hungarian origin.

Some live in German-speaking countries. **Günther Anders** (b. 1902) has lived in Vienna since his return from exile. **Hans Mayer** (b. 1907) and **Marcel Reich-Ranicki** (b. 1920), respected and feared critics in the manner of old, have lived in Hannover and Hamburg, respectively.

A leftist writer, **Stefan Heym** (b. 1913 as Hellmuth Fliegel) lived in East Germany after many years in the United States and after serving in the American armed forces. The East German regime viewed Heym's work with disfavor and for many years refused to publish it. The communist had his novels published in the Federal Republic.

Jurek Becker, born in 1937, spent his childhood in the Lodz Ghetto and Nazi camps. He is certainly the only major Jewish writer in German who had no direct knowledge of the pre-Hitler years. Becker grew up in East Germany, which gave him some artistic latitude. However, there were also conflicts, and Becker went to live in the Federal Republic. Becker's *Jakob der Lügner* (*Jacob the Liar*) (1969) is one of the neglected masterpieces of Holocaust literature. A ghetto-dweller spreads the fiction that he owns a radio; the latest news says the Russians are advancing, and Jewish liberation may be near. Jacob's lie does not save the ghetto population from deportation to extermination camps, but it offers them solace and hope and makes their horrendous fate a trifle lighter to bear. The book has been called an "optimistic tragedy," hardly an appropriate designation, though it does suggest a measure of wit, inventiveness, and compassion against a backdrop of death and despair. Becker's *Schlaflose Tage* (*Sleepless Days*) (1978) details the many dissatisfactions of an East Berlin schoolteacher with both himself and the authorities. In another Holocaust novel, *Bronsteins Kinder* (*Bronstein's Children*), Becker has a seventeen-year-old East German Jewish youngster rebel against his father, whom he surprises one day in the act of abusing, if not torturing, a former concentration-camp guard. The youngster stands for cold reason, for forgetting the past, for finally laying the Holocaust to rest. The father cannot oblige and is tormented by the son's incapacity to understand and to see the present as an extension of the past.

Also a product entirely of the postwar era is the cabaret poet and satirist **Wolf Biermann** (b. 1936) whose critique of the East German government frequently embroiled him in conflict with the regime. When this *Unbequemer* (*persona non grata*) left for a tour of the Federal Republic in 1976, he was denied readmission to East Germany. Today he lives partly in Hamburg and partly in France.

For that tiny number of authors writing in German and living in a German-speaking country, the decisive experience of their lives has been the Nazi past. Jewish life as such has played a wholly insignificant role. The dilemma of German and Jew has been solved. These Jewish writers no longer aspire to being German, which has lost its halo. But neither are they Jews, for the opportunity to be Jews is circumscribed. They exist. They exist in Germany, but their existence is burdened by memory.

In terms of Jewish writers, since 1945, Germany has indeed been if not an entirely empty house, then at least a sparsely inhabited one. It has been a house haunted by ghosts.

•　•　•　•　•

V

• • • • •

Postscript

The 150-year history of Jewish writers in Germany bears out the contention that this history was not all bad, that Jews and Germans were significantly enriched. It cannot be wholly coincidental that the greatest moment of German literary history—the years 1800–1830 and 1900–1933—were those in which Jewish voices were first heard, and heard most clearly. Nor can it be mere chance that contributions to Jewish thought stemmed from the minds of men and women whose Jewish studies were cross-fertilized by German philosophy. No French or British Jewish writer attained the stature of Heine or Kafka. It would also be difficult to name a Jewish thinker in France or Britain with innovative contributions on the level of Zunz, Cohen, Buber, or Rosenzweig.

Even if Heine, Kafka, Marx, Freud, and others are individual phenomena to be viewed independently of group considerations, there are still enough gifted writers to make the literary record impressive. Whatever their flaws, Börne, Moses Hess, Schnitzler, Broch, Lasker-Schüler, Feuchtwanger, and the Zweigs (Arnold and Stefan) were only a notch below uniqueness. The sheer number of German-Jewish writers during a century and a half adds up to an impressive record of accomplishment.

However, if the relationship was not all bad, it cannot be described as all good. The very fact that German intellectual leaders, from Fichte to Thomas Mann, voiced misgivings at one time or another about the Jewish presence must raise serious doubts. As Alfred D. Low pointed out, German cultural and political life was suffused with anti-Jewish bias and even hostility. With the exception of some noteworthy Judeophiles, German writers from the Enlightenment to the Jews' departure deplored Jewish individuality, character, and influence. They juxtaposed "true German qualities" and the alleged Jewish attributes of materialism, stubbornness, adulation of mind, reason, and wit. Nor was there universal satisfaction on the Jewish side. Emancipation was too long delayed, acceptance too conditional, rejection too arrogant, and the demand for Jews to prove themselves true Germans too persistent and even vicious. This demand led to the somewhat questionable attitude of Jakob Löwenberg: Conceding that the German aversion for Jews was deeply rooted, whether in the home, family, school or church, he nevertheless concluded, "We are Germans and want to remain German."

It is significant that the most vital friendship between a German and a Jewish writer—that of Lessing and Mendelssohn—occurred at the very onset of the cultural nexus. Close and casual friendships did exist even in later years. Yet, on the whole, Jewish writers tended to associate with other Jewish writers, people of often similar backgrounds, tensions, and obsessions, with an implied common struggle. In no manner or form was positive Jewishness a factor in bringing them together. It was the negative factor of living on the periphery, of marginal acceptance. Relationships continued with apostates and even with mockers of Judaism.

The Jewish writers were also united by the generational struggle with their fathers. Among them they perceived an overconcern with "making money," financial security, cultural shabbiness in some instances, and a pathetic craving for *Bildung* in others. The young writers were ungenerous in their understanding of these traits. They ignored the historical basis and proclaimed instead their contempt for the merchant or for such occupations as peddling or cattle and horse trading—almost as though their elders had an inborn fondness for such work. Similarly, they mocked the empty ritual followed by their fathers, a ritual with a meaning long forgotten, if it had ever been known. Most unfortunate of all was the insecurity of many of the sons and the fear that if some allegations about Jews were true, others might be also. They ignored the fact that their own distance from Jewish life prompted non-Jews to consider them—the younger generations—as rootless and shiftless and as meddlers in a life that was not theirs. Some of the newer prejudices which this provoked proved more devastating than the anti-Jewish accusations of old. The perception of undesirable qualities in Jews led, in some writers of the turn of the century, to a self-deprecating stance with a solid measure of self-hate encapsuled within it.

While Jewish writers could be found in all sociopolitical camps in the first half of the nineteenth century, they belonged predominantly to the liberal faction. Later they split their loyalty between liberals and socialists until their departure in the 1930s. There was also a smattering of conservatives and left-wing radicals. At one time or another, nearly all heralded their German identity, surely to distinguish it from their suspect Jewishness. As they progressively imagined themselves more and more secure, several added "world citizen" to their German and Jewish identities. Those we have called "aggressors" were especially prone to don the mantle of world citizenship, while the dwindling number of "apologists" adhered to the liberal credo. Neither side was ever exempt from the generally felt pressure to demonstrate its right to be part of German society.

It would have been unnatural if the writers had not been attracted to movements that afforded them greater opportunity to be human beings, i.e., to define themselves independently of outside pressures. It would have been masochistic to latch on to parties that would circumscribe their freedom as self-defining human beings. Many German conservatives and nationalists would have admitted that in their midst the Jewish future would look even dimmer. The dominant liberal or socialist stance, born partly of self-protective instincts, became another reason for blaming the Jews: they were not German enough or they had not abandoned the last vestiges of their Jewishness.

While self-protection was a factor in their political and social choices, it was decidedly not the only factor. The association with other Jewish writers, already discussed, did not lead to Jewish issues, even obliquely. Jewish writers veered toward liberalism or socialism out of idealism and devotion. Unbeknownst to them, the love of God and Torah had once inspired similar devotion, a trait they had inherited minus God and Torah. They had transferred the intensity of commitment to freedom of speech and the press, or to the welfare of the poor and neglected. The ideals of the French Revolution were the new Torah. To be sure, some believed more in liberty and others in equality and all in fraternity, but if there was a trinity that Jews and apostates alike could worship, it was that of the three revolutionary slogans.

They pursued their goals with an intensity that was seen as non-German, if not shocking. Wit, irony, and satire had not been German cultural staples. Within two decades after their appearance in German letters, the humor of Heine, Börne, and others was impugned as an undesirable French import. Lack of taste and restraint and unbridled enthusiasm were laid at the doorstep of Jewish writers, from Heine and Börne through the Kalisches and Blumenthal, to Kerr, Tucholsky, and Kraus. German observers were mindful only of the immoderate criticism and refused to see the underlying moral earnestness. If they were aware of the writers' single-minded pursuit of a noble goal, they were in doubt about the goal, or they deemed the pursuit too vigorous.

That goal was not always political or social. The writers could be quite as determined in reaching artistic goals: promoting Hauptmann and Ibsen; advancing the new modes of Expressionism; defending the French comedy. Earlier they had displayed a comparable zeal in promoting Goethe, Kant, Schiller, Hegel, and Hebbel. The Jewish writers appeared comfortable in the export-import world of literary commodities; many were content to serve as advance publicity people for new talent they deemed worthy.

Jewish writers did not run interference for great Jewish writers as they did for major Gentile authors. Perhaps there were not enough major Jewish greats in each period, and perhaps, too, opportunity was lacking. Certainly, in Heine's time, there were too few Jewish writers to serve as the vanguard for his talent. Perhaps educated Jewry was secretly proud of his achievement, but publicly there were more prominent Jewish detractors than advocates. Gabriel Riesser and Berthold Auerbach, and others in every generation, assaulted Heine's reputation mercilessly. As for Kafka, he was as noiseless as Heine's impact was noisy, and Max Brod's efforts resulted from personal friendship. Only after World War II, when the world turned Kafkaesque, did Jewish and Gentile writers alike recognize his genius. By then, no advocacy or promotion was needed.

Indeed, except for Heine's lyric cadences and his distinctive way of twisting his satiric stiletto, and except for the haunting quality of Kafka's eerie fantasies, the originality of Jewish writers becomes somewhat problematic. And yet, the erotic "premature" psychoanalytic plays of Schnitzler; the myth-laden work of Hermann Broch; the angry, often venomous, and yet morally consistent diatribes of Karl Kraus; the stylistic innovations and neo-Expressionist novels of Alfred Döblin; the interplay of political and psychological subtleties in the historical fiction of Lion Feuchtwanger; the color and imagery in the lyrics of Else Lasker-Schüler; the tiny jewels of Expressionist poems by writers long forgotten—all represent a level of originality that can hold its own with the more distinguished non-Jewish writers of the times.

Few writers availed themselves of Jewish religious or spiritual sources for their art. The few who did were not, on the whole, among the more gifted. Only Richard Beer-Hofmann and Lion Feuchtwanger were familiar enough with basic texts to employ them with skill. To be sure, there was no dearth of biblical dramas on Saul, David, Salomon and Samson, but most writers kept too closely to the biblical text and produced dramatizations rather than dramas. Beer-Hofmann's *Jacobs Traum* and Feuchtwanger's *Josephus* trilogy and *Jephtha* stand in a class apart as creative interpretations of old texts and sources. Did they have so little regard for the holy texts of their fathers, or was there a subliminal fear that anything too Jewish—too "Talmudic"—would deflate their German-ness in the eyes of demanding Germans?

Also, why did so few Jewish writers make significant use of more accessible aspects of their Jewish experience? Writers, it is said, write about what they know best. Well, Jewish writers had issued from Jewish families, grown up in Jewish homes, often attended religious schools, or experienced the pangs of minority status in Christian schools. Why, except for father-son conflicts, were these experiences used so sparsely?

Why were there not more family chronicles? Holiday scenes that trigger plots in Yiddish and American fiction are conspicuous by their absence in German-Jewish fiction. In one of the few family novels—perhaps the best—Georg Hermann's *Jettchen Gebert,* there is a Christmas scene, but no reference to a Seder or Rosh Hashana or Yom Kippur. Jewishness in this novel is no more than an indefinable Jewish sensibility. Other family novels, mostly of this century, feature women so intent on concealing their Jewish identity as to become caricatures or grotesques. The authors are ostensibly revolted by the families they depict; their intent is to hold up a mirror for other Jews who might be engaged in similarly despicable conduct.

Why was there such neglect of Jewish experience? Was it again the subconscious fear of the German perception? Were Jewish authors troubled by inhibitions about self-revelation to the ever-judging Germans? Had the German perception of Jews so damaged their inner self that it was silenced? Or did the writers believe that Jewish experience was too painful or insignificant for literary utilization? With the exception of a handful of family novels, only the ghetto and historical fiction of the mid-nineteenth century revolved about Jewish life. Coincidentally, much of the historical Jewish fiction of the period came from the pen of rabbis.

In poetry, there was a greater readiness to celebrate the holiness of the Sabbath, memories of the lost land, lamentations over Jewish suffering, and the awe of Yom Kippur. Whether in the lyrics of converts like Heine and Beck, Jewishly committed poets like I. L. Frankl or Arno Nadel, individualistic voices like those of Lasker-Schüler or Gertrud Kolmar, there is evidence of a pulsating Jewish heart. It is also in verse that the first Zionist echoes were heard. In fiction, Zionist characters begin to appear in Schnitzler's *Der Weg ins Freie* and *Professor Bernhardi.* Zionism receives a more pleasant reception from Feuchtwanger's *Die Oppermanns* and in the early novels of Arnold Zweig. There were, of course, works that approximated Zionist publicism, such as the novels and plays of Herzl and Nordau.

In the vast majority of works, Jewish characters are peripheral. This is true of Döblin's *Berlin: Alexanderplatz,* Broch's *Die Schlafwandler,* and Arnold Zweig's *Grischa* cycle, as well as many of the forgotten comedies of the last century. The Jew appears in many guises, as capitalist and socialist, financier and thief, reformer and revolutionary, as apostle of women's rights, workers' rights, human rights. The one time nearly all writers spoke up, almost in unison, was during periods of anti-Semitic activity. Then the aggressors vigorously, and the apologists more gently, heaped blame on the culprits and protested the innocence of Israel.

The majority of Jewish writers professed their solidarity with other oppressed or repressed groups. Heine and Börne criticized slavery in the New World, and a century later Hugo Bettauer devoted a novel to race relations in America. Unjust treatment of the Negroes in the United States is treated extensively in the travel reportages of Holitscher and Roth.

In numerous dramas Jewish playwrights exhibited their solidarity with the aspirations of women and workers. All women writers identified with the emancipatory aspirations of their sex. But, also like other dominated groups, Jews were not above inwardly accepting the oppressors' stereotypes of themselves. Like blacks and colonized peoples in their contacts with whites and colonizers, Jews became unhealthily entangled in a love-hate relationship with Germans. They could briefly love each other, long doubt each other, but never be wholly indifferent to each other.

Moreover, instability marred the lives of many German-Jewish writers. The businessman mentality of the father and the nascent "artist's personality" of the son frequently led to prolonged periods of self-searching and floundering. Resistance to parental pressure in the choice of an occupation was prone to lead to a succession of careers. The *Kaufmann-Dichter* (businessman-poet) syndrome still generated antagonism in such late writers as Kafka, Werfel, Broch, and Feuchtwanger. Where the parent was a physician, as was Schnitzler's father, the ties were friendly and supportive.

Instability manifested itself in restlessness. Jewish writers moved erratically from city to city, often from country to country. Long before the 1930s, Jewish writers, including patriots like Lissauer and Borchardt, chose to live outside the Fatherland. From Heine and Börne through Ludwig Kalisch and Moses Hess, to Tucholsky and Leonhardt, they opted for Paris as a long-term domicile. Their cultural affinities, they claimed, were for Berlin; personal and artistic freedom drew them to Paris.

The number of suicides must be noted. Most occurred, to be sure, in the aftermath of Hitlerism, and many after May 1940, when Germany seemed invincible. (At least six—Eisner, Landauer, Rathenau, Bettauer, Lessing, and Mühsam—were assassinated or murdered in cold blood.) The earlier suicides of Daniel Lessmann and Walter Calé cannot be imputed, in the main, to the duality of German and Jew, but Jewish self-loathing was the dominant factor in the voluntary death of Otto Weininger. Poor mental health afflicted many—from Ludwig Fulda to Carl Sternheim, from Albert Ehrenstein to Else Lasker-Schüler.

As in other countries, Jewish writers in the German linguistic community were mostly city dwellers, and their literary products revealed a predominantly urban and sophisticated character. Even when they were born in an obscure hamlet of Silesia, Posen, or Westphalia, the settings were largely urban. The virtual absence of Jewish village literature cannot be easily explained. Only the ghetto tales of the nineteenth century, the peripheral Jews of Auerbach's *Dorfgeschichten,* and the reminiscences of Jakob Picard remind readers that there were Jews dwelling in the rural areas of Germany.

Aside from these commonalities, the writers revealed a great deal of diversity. Many were in the forefront of the new, the different, and the experimental. But there were others, less noisy and rambunctious, who aspired to other goals with measure, restraint, and a sense of the possible. There were the "aggressors," critical of Germans and their ways, but critical because they loved them best. The same aggressors were equally critical of Jews. But there were also apologists who demanded reason from the Germans and good behavior from Jews. Though the apologists were less critical of Germans than were the aggressors, they were distinctly more protective of Jews. Whether aggressors or apologists, Jewish writers possessed attitudes that were the result of direct or indirect pressures they felt as Jews in Germany.

Neither Jewish writers nor their enemies agreed on characteristics of the Jew. Some saw the Oriental, others the Westerner *par excellence,* some the God-saturated, others the atheist, some the proponents of pure "spirit," others the purveyors of matter. Ernst Lissauer, of "God Punish England" fame, perceived the effects of Judaism in such figures as Jessner, Reinhardt, Tucholsky, and Kraus. Others saw the tragedy of German Jewry in Lissauer. Theodor Lessing wrote Freud an unpleasant letter in which he dubbed psychoanalysis an excrement of the Jewish spirit. Socialists pronounced this same Jewish spirit as parasitic, at least in the economic sphere. Cowardly and submissive to some, Jews were ostensibly belligerent and aggressive to others. Anti-Semites attributed to the Jew those qualities they disliked most in life.

Did most of the writers have a common denominator? Perhaps. There was an ambitious desire to deepen the sense of the truly human. The precise concept of the "truly human" was not always the same, nor did Jewish writers have a monopoly on this quest. But the attempt was both more discernible and more persistent among them than among other writers, and they brought special qualifications to their search. They had been treated as barely human for so long that awareness of what was human was clearer to them and closer to their hearts. Although for centuries treatment of Jews had been little better than that of animals and objects, because of their particular traditions of Torah and Talmud learning, they had cultivated the faculties of the mind to an exceptional degree. These faculties were ready to be applied to the quest for new goals for humankind and for means of attaining them.

These goals were not always those of the Germans. They were acceptable to those whose values were descended from Herder, Goethe, and Schiller. They were unacceptable to those for whom the principles of iron, blood, and power had become the ultimate good. To them the deepened sense of humanity was weakness, a dilution of German substance, a threat to what (in their opinion) was the essence of *Deutschtum.* Without Jews or others becoming aware of this fact, this latter group of Germans had moved to the helm. A Jewish contribution—whatever it was—was not desired, not needed. What some have regarded as the unique contributions of Jews to German life, the Nazis resented keenly and without apology.

Yet this contribution was real, and it centered on the question of how people could become more truly human. Jewish writers in neighboring countries wanted to serve the same goal. But being less pressured and harassed, they felt less of a challenge. They had been under less provocation to show their mettle. Moreover, Germans and Jews had an unwholesome need to compete, for both were latecomers to the world stage. Germans needed to assert themselves with long-established nations in stature and power. Jews needed to compete because they had been excluded for so long from both achievement and human status.

Bibliographies

A. POLITICAL AND SOCIAL WORKS

Adler, H. G. *Die Juden in Deutschland: Von der Aufklärung bis zum National-sozialismus.* München, 1960.

Angress, Werner T. "Juden im politischen Leben der Revolutionszeit." In *Deutsches Judentum in Krieg und Revolution: 1916–1923* ed. Werner E. Mosse and Arnold Pauker, pp. 137–315. Tübingen, 1971.

Bach, Hans. *Jüdische Memoiren aus Drei Jahrhunderten.* Berlin, 1936.

Bato, Ludwig. *Die Juden im alten Wien.* Wien, 1928.

Bauer, Bruno. *Die Judenfrage.* 1843.

Bein, Alex. *Die Judenfrage. Biographie eines Weltproblems.* 2 vols. Stuttgart, 1980.

Berkley, George E. *Vienna and Its Jews: The Tragedy of Success, 1880–1980s.* Lanham, Md., 1988.

Berneri, C. *Le Juif antisémite.* Paris, 1935.

Bernfeld, Simon. *Juden und Judentum im 19. Jahrhundert.* Berlin, 1894.

Bloch, Jochanan. *Das anstößige Volk. Über die weltliche Glaubensgenossenschaft der Juden.* Heidelberg, 1964.

Blumenfeld, Kurt. *Erlebte Judenfrage.* Stuttgart, 1962.

Boehlich, Walter. *Der Berliner Antisemitismusstreit.* 1959.

Borochov, Ber. *Klasse und Nation: Zur Theorie und Praxis des jüdischen Sozialismus.* Berlin, 1932.

Brunner, Constantin. *Der Judenhaß und die Juden.* Berlin, 1918.

Dinse, Helmut. *Die Entwicklung des jüdischen Schrifttums im deutschen Sprachgebiet.* Stuttgart, 1972.

Dohm, Chr. W. von. *Über die bürgerliche Verbesserung der Juden.* Berlin, 1781.

Elbogen, Ismar. *Geschichte der Juden in Deutschland.* Berlin, 1935.

Eloesser, Arthur. *Vom Ghetto nach Europa: Das Judentum im geistigen Leben des 19. Jahrhunderts.* Berlin, 1936.

Fraenkel, Joseph, ed. *The Jews of Austria: Essays on Their Life, History and Destruction.* London, 1967.

Freund, Ismar. *Die Emanzipation der Juden in Preußen.* Unter besonderer Berücksichtigung des Gesetzes vom 11. März 1812. (2 vols.) Berlin, 1912.

Gans, Eduard. *Rückblick auf Personen und Zustände.* Berlin, 1936.

Goldschmidt, Hermann Levin. *Das Vermächtnis des modernen Judentums.* n.p., 1957.

Gutzkow, Karl. *Berliner Erinnerungen.* Friedländer, Paul, ed. Berlin, 1960.

Hitzig, Julius Eduard. *Gelehrtes Berlin im Jahre 1825.* Berlin, 1826.

Katz, Jacob. *Out of the Ghetto: The Social Background of Jewish Emancipation.* Cambridge, 1973.

Klatzkin, Jacob. *Probleme des modernen Judentums.* Berlin, 1930.

Knütte, Hanns-Helmuth. *Die Juden und die deutsche Linke in der Weimarer Republik. 1918–1923.* Düsseldorf, 1971.

Kobler, Franz. *Jüdische Geschichte in Briefen aus Ost und West.* Berlin, 1938.

Kohler, Ruth, and Wolfgang Richter. *Berliner Leben, 1806–1847.*

Lessing, Theodor. *Der jüdische Selbsthaß.* Berlin, 1930.

_____. *Deutschland und seine Juden.* Prag und Berlin, 1933.

Liebeschütz, Hans. *Das Judentum im deutschen Geschichtsbild von Hegel bis Max Weber.* Tübingen, 1970.

Lothar, Ernst. *Das Wunder des Überlebens. Erinnerungen und Ergebnisse.* Hamburg/Wien, 1961.

Lowenthal, Marvin. *The Jews of Germany: A Story of Sixteen Centuries.* Philadelphia, 1936.

Marcus, J. R. *The Rise and Destiny of the German Jew.* Cincinnati, 1934.

Marr, Wilhelm. *Der Sieg des Judentums über das Germanentum: Vom nichtkonfessionellen Standpunkt aus betrachtet.* Bern, 1879.

Melzer, Joseph, ed. *Deutsch-jüdische Schicksal: Wegweiser durch das Schrifttum der letzten 15 Jahre, 1945–1960.* Köln, 1960.

Meyer, Michael A. *The Origins of the Modern Jew: Jewish Identity and European Culture in Germany, 1749–1824.* Detroit, 1967.

Mosse, George L. *Germans and Jews: The Right, the Left and the Search for a "Third Force" in Pre-Nazi Germany.* New York, 1971.

_____. "German Socialists and the Jewish Question in the Weimar Republic." In: *LBY,* London, 1971, pp. 123–151.

_____. "Jewish Emancipation: Between *Bildung* and Respectability." In *The Jewish Response to German Culture,* ed. Jehuda Reinharz and Walter Schatzberg. Hanover and London, 1985.

Spiel, Hilde. *Vienna's Golden Autumn: 1866–1938.* New York and London, 1987.

Stern, Fritz. *Dreams and Delusions.* New York, 1987.

Tietze, Hans. *Die Juden Wiens: Geschichte–Wirtschaft–Kultur.* Wien, 1930.

Toury, Jacob. *Die politischen Orientierungen der Juden in Deutschland: Von Jena bis Weimar.* Tübingen, 1966.

Weltsch, Robert, ed. *Deutsches Judentum: Aufstieg und Krise: Gestalten, Ideen, Werke.* Stuttgart, 1963.

Williams, C. E. *The Broken Eagle: The Politics of Austrian Literature from Empire to Anschluss.* New York, 1975.

Wistrich, Robert S. *Revolutionary Jews from Marx to Trotsky.* New York, 1976.

Wolbe, Eugen. *Geschichte der Juden in Berlin.* Berlin, 1937.

B. CULTURAL AND LITERARY WORKS

Allen, Roy F. *Literary Life in German Expressionism and the Berlin Circles.*

Göppingen, 1974.

Alter, Robert. "Modernism, the Germans and the Jews." *Commentary* (1978).

Baeck, Leo. *Von Moses Mendelssohn zu Franz Rosenzweig: Typen jüdischen Selbstverständnisses in den letzten beiden Jahrhunderten.* Stuttgart, 1958.

Borries, Achim von, ed. *Selbstzeugnisse des deutschen Judentums: 1870–1945.* Frankfurt a/M, 1962.

Eloesser, Arthur. "Literature." In *Juden im deutschen Kulturreich,* ed. Siegmund Kaznelson. Berlin, 1962.

_____. *Vom Ghetto nach Europa: Das Judentum im geistigen Leben des 19. Jahrhunderts.* Berlin, 1936.

Friedenberg, Albert M. "The Jews as German Men of Letters." *Jewish Exponent* (Philadelphia), July 1905.

Furness, R. S. *Expressionism.* London, 1973.

Gay, Peter. *Weimar Culture: The Outsider as Insider.* New York, 1968.

_____. *Freud, Jews and Other Germans: Masters and Victims in Modernist Culture.* New York, 1978.

_____. "Begegnung mit der Moderne: Deutsche Juden in der deutschen Kultur." In *Juden im Wilhelminischen Deutschland 1890–1914,* ed. Werner E. Mosse and Arnold Paucker. Tübingen, 1976.

Geiger, Ludwig. *Die deutsche Literatur und die Juden.* Berlin. 1910.

_____. *Geschichte der Juden in Berlin.* 2 vols. Berlin, 1871.

Gilman, Sander L. *Jewish Self-Hatred: Anti-Semitism and the Hidden Language of the Jews.* Baltimore, 1986.

Goldstein, Moritz. "Deutsch-jüdischer Parnass." *Kunstwart* 25 (1912): 281–95. [Responses to article "Deutschtum und Judentum," *Kunstwart* 25 (1912): 6–15.]

Graupe, Heinz Mosche. *Die Entstehung des modernen Judentums: Geistesgeschichte der deutschen Juden 1650–1942.* Hamburg, 1969.

Greuner, Ruth. *Gegenspieler.* East Berlin, 1969.

Grimm, Günther E., and Hans-Peter Bayerdörfer, eds. *Im Zeichen Hiobs: Jüdische Schriftsteller und deutsche Literatur im 20. Jahrhundert.* Frankfurt, 1986.

Herlitz, Georg. "Three Jewish Historians: Isaak Markus Jost—Heinrich Graetz—Eugen Täubler." *LBY* 9(1864), n.p.

Heselhaus, Clemens. *Deutsche Lyrik der Moderne von Nietzsche bis Ywan Goll.* Düsseldorf, 1961.

Hiller, Kurt. *Leben gegen die Zeit.* Hamburg, 1967.

Kafka, František. *Prager jüdische Autoren* (typed ms.).

Kahn, Lothar. *Mirrors of the Jewish Mind: A Gallery of Portraits of European Writers of Our Time.* New York, 1968.

_____. "Heine's Jewish Writer Friends: Dilemmas of a Generation, 1817–1833." In *The Jewish Response to German Culture,* ed. Jehuda Reinharz and Walter Schatzberg, pp. 121–36. Hanover and London, 1985.

Kahn, Lothar, and Donald D. Hook. "The Impact of Heine on Nineteenth-Century German-Jewish Writers." In *The Jewish Reception of Heinrich Heine,* ed. Mark H. Gelber, 53–65. *Conditio Judaica 1.* Tübingen, 1992.

Kantorowicz, Alfred. "Liquidation der Judenfrage." In *Klärung: 12 Autoren und Politiker über die Judenfrage,* pp. 153–68. Berlin, 1932.

Karpeles, Gustav. *Geschichte der jüdischen Literatur,* Berlin, 1892.

_____. "Salons. Berliner Spaziergänge." In *Literarisches Wanderbuch.* Berlin, 1891.

Kayserling, M. *Die jüdische Literatur von Moses Mendelssohn bis auf die Gegenwart.* Trier, 1896.

_____. *Die jüdischen Frauen in der Geschichte, Literatur und Kunst.* Leipzig, 1879.

Kaznelson, Siegmund, ed. *Juden im deutschen Kulturbereich: Ein Sammelwerk.* Berlin, 1959.

Kobler, Franz, ed. *Juden und Judentum in deutschen Briefen aus drei Jahrhunderten.* Wien, 1935.

Koch, Thilo. *Porträts deutsch-jüdischer Geistesgeschichte.* Köln. 1961.

Kohn, Hans. *Karl, Kraus, Arthur Schnitzler, Otto Weininger: Aus dem jüdischen Wien der Jahrhundertwende.* Tübingen, 1962.

Konut, Adolph. *Die Großmeister des Berliner Humors.* n.p, n.d.

Krojanker, Gustav. *Juden in der deutschen Literatur: Essays über zeitgenössische Schriftsteller.* Berlin, 1922.

Laqueur, Walter. *Weimar: A Cultural History, 1918–1933.* New York, 1975.

Lenz, H. K. *"Judenliteratur und Literaturjuden." Aus Sebastian Brunners Werken dargestellt.* Münster, 1893.

Liebeschütz, Hans. *Von Georg Simmel zu Franz Rosenzweig: Studien zum jüdischen Denken im deutschen Kulturbereich.* Tübingen, 1970.

Liptzin, Solomon. *Germany's Stepchildren.* Philadelphia, 1944.

Lothar, Ernst. *Das deutsche Drama der Gegenwart.* Berlin, 1905.

Marggraff, Hermann. *Deutschlands jüngste Literatur- und Culturepoche.* Leipzig, 1839.

Mendelssohn, Peter de. *S. Fischer und sein Verlag.* Berlin, 1970.

Menzel, Wolfgang. *Denkwürdigkeiten,* ed. Konrad Menzel. Stuttgart, 1877.

Mosse, Werner R., and Arnold Pauker, eds. *Deutsches Judentum in Krieg und Revolution 1916–1923.* Tübingen, 1971.

Nagl, J. W., and J. Zeidler. *Deutsch-österreichische Literaturgeschichte.* Wien, 1899–1937.

Oppler, Friedrich. *Das falsche Tabu: Betrachtungen über das deutsch-jüdische Problem.* Stuttgart, 1966.

Otten, Karl. *Das leere Haus. Prosa jüdischer Dichter,* Stuttgart, 1959.

_____. *Das dichterische Drama des Expressionismus,* n.p., n.d.

Paulsen, Wolfgang. *Expressionismus und Aktivismus.* Strassburg, 1934.

Pazi, Margarita. *Fünf Autoren des Prager Kreises.* Frankfurt, 1878.

Politzer, Heinz. "From Mendelssohn to Kafka: The Jewish Man of Letters in Germany." In *Commentary* 3(1947): 344–51.

Prinz, Joachim. *Wir Juden.* Berlin, 1934.

Prowe-Isenbörger, Ina. *Deutsche Juden: Von Moses Mendelssohn bis Leo Baeck.* Hangelar (bei Bonn), 1962.

Reich-Ranicki, Marcel. *Über Ruhestörer: Juden in der deutschen Literatur.* München, 1973.

Reichmann, Eva G. *Hostages of Civilisation: The Social Sources of National Socialist Anti-Semitism.* Boston, 1951.

Reinharz, Jehuda. "The Zionist Response to Anti-Semitism in the Weimar Republic." In *The Jewish Response to German Culture,* ed. Jehuda Reinharz and Walter Schatzberg. Hanover and London, 1985.

Reisner, Erwin. *Die Juden und das deutsche Reich.* Erlenbach-Zürich and Stuttgart, 1966.

Reissner, Hanns Günter. "Rebellious Dilemma: The Case Histories of Eduard Gans and some of his Partisans." *LBY* (1957).

Röll, Walter, and Hans-Peter Bayerdörfer, eds. *Jüdische Komponenten in der deutschen Literatur.* Akten des 7. Internationalen Germanisten Kongresses, Göttingen, 1985.

Sakheim, Arthur. *Das jüdische Element in der Weltliteratur.* Hamburg, 1924.

Schay, Rudolf. *Von Marx bis Rathenau: Juden in der deutschen Politik.* Berlin, 1929.

Scholem, Gershom. "Jews and Germans." *Commentary,* 42(1966): 31–38.

Schorske, Carl. *Fin-de-siècle Vienna: Politics and Culture.* New York, 1986.

Schühmann, Kurt. *Im Bannkreis von Gesicht und Wirken: Max Brod, Else Lasker-Schüler, Kurt Tucholsky, Alfred Polgar: Vier Vortragsstudien.* München, 1959.

Schultz, Hans-Jürgen, ed. *Juden, Christen, Deutsche.* Stuttgart, 1961.

Simon, Ernst. "Wie jüdisch war das deutsche Judentum?" *Zur Geschichte der Juden im 19. und 20. Jahrhundert,* n.p., n.d.

Soergel, Albert. *Dichtung und Dichter.* Leipzig, 1928.

Sombart, Werner, et al. *Judentaufen.* München, 1912.

Stapel, Wilhelm. "Die literarische Vorherrschaft der Juden in Deutschland 1918–1933." In *Forschungen zur Judenfrage* 1(1937): 165–93.

Sterling, Eleanor. *Judenhaß: Die Anfänge des politischen Antisemitismus in Deutschland, 1815–1850,* n.p., n.d.

Stern, Desider. *Werke von Autoren jüdischer Herkunft in deutscher Sprache: Eine Bio-Bibliographie.* Wien, 1970.

Stern, Guy. *War, Weimar, and Literature.* Philadelphia, 1971.

Straus, H. E., and Ch. Hoffmann. *Juden und Judentum in der Literatur.* München, 1985.

Strauss, Franz Joseph, ed. *Kriegsbriefe gefallener deutscher Juden.* Stuttgart, 1961.

Streckfuss, K. *Über das Verhältnis der Juden zu dem christlichen Staat.* Berlin, 1883.

_____. *Berlin im 19. Jahrhundert.* Berlin, 1879.

Theilhaber, Felix A. *Judenschicksal in 8 Biographien,* Tel Aviv, 1945(?).

Thieme, Karl, ed. *Judenfeindschaft: Darstellung und Analysen.* Frankfurt a/M, 1963.

Tramer, Hans. "Über deutsch-jüdisches Dichtertum: Zur Morphologie des jüdischen Bekenntnisses." *Bulletin des Leo Baeck Instituts* 2/3(1958): 88–103.

_____. "Von deutsch-jüdischem Dichtertum." In *Deutsches Judentum: Aufstieg und Krise: Gestalten, Ideen, Werke,* ed. Robert Weltsch. Stuttgart, 255–70.

_____. "Der Expressionismus. Bemerkungen zum Anteil der Juden an einer Kunstepoche." *Bulletin des Leo Baeck Instituts* 5(1958).

Urzidil, Johannes. "Der lebendige Anteil des jüdischen Prag in der neueren Literatur." *Bulletin des Leo Baeck Instituts* 40(1967): 276–97.

Waxman, Mayer. *A History of Jewish Literature,* vol. IV. New York, 1936.

Wellenworth, G. E., ed. *German Drama between the Wars.* New York, 1972.

Wolfenstein, Alfred. "Das neue Dichtertum der Juden." In *Juden in der deutschen Literatur.* Berlin, 1922.

Zohn, Harry. *Ich bin ein Sohn der deutschen Sprache nur . . .* Vienna, 1986.

_____, trans. *Theodor Herzl: The Complete Diaries.* 4 vols. New York, 1960–1961.

C. WORKS BY AND ABOUT AUTHORS OF SPECIAL INTEREST

This list includes works *by* and *about* writers who are of the first rank or representative of a distinct period of tendency. Information about each citation is as complete as present sources permit.

Key: A = autobiography; B = biography; N = novel; n = novella; D = drama or plays; E = essay or general nonfiction; H = history; L = letters; P = poetry; P = philosophy; R = reportage; citations not labeled may be assumed to be works of fiction.

By Saul Ascher

Ascher, Saul. *Bemerkungen über die bürgerliche Verbesserung der Juden, veranlaßt bei der Frage: Soll der Jude Soldat werden?* Frankfurt a/O, 1788.

_____. *Leviathan, oder über Religion in Rücksicht des Judentums.* Berlin, 1792.

_____. *Eisenmenger der Zweite: nebst einem vorangesetzten Sendschreiben an Herrn Prof. Fichte in Jena.* Berlin, 1794.

_____. *Die Aussöhnung, eine Novelle.* 1803.

_____. *Biographisch-Historische Skizzen.* Berlin, 1810.

_____. *Bagatellen aus dem Gebiet der Poesie, Kritik und Laune.* Leipzig, 1811.

_____. *Die Germanomanie.* Leipzig, 1815.

_____. *Politische Schriften und Novellen.* Leipzig, 1822.

About Saul Ascher

Littmann, Ellen. "Saul Ascher: First Theorist of Progressive Judaism." *LBY* 6(1961):107–21.

Stern-Täubler, Selma. "Der literarische Kampf um die Emanzipation in den Jahren 1816–1820 und seine ideologischen and soziologischen Voraussetzungen." *Hebrew Union College Annual* 23(1950–1951), part 2.

By Berthold Auerbach

Auerbach, Berthold. *Judentum und die neueste Literatur* (E). *Kritischer Versuch.* Stuttgart, 1836.

_____. *Spinoza. Ein historischer Roman* (N). 2 vols. Stuttgart, 1837, 1887.

_____. *Dichter und Kaufmann. Ein Lebensgemälde* (N). 2 vols. Stuttgart, 1840.

_____. *Gesammelte Schriften.* Stuttgart, 1863–1864, 1911.

_____. *Waldfried. Roman.* 3 vols. Stuttgart, 1874.

_____. *Nach dreißig Jahren. Neue Dorfgeschichten.* 3 vols. Stuttgart, 1876.

_____. *Sämtliche Schwarzwälder Dorfgeschichten.* 10 vols. Stuttgart, 1884.

About Berthold Auerbach

Bettelheim, Anton. *Berthold Auerbach.* Stuttgart, 1907.

_____. "Berthold Auerbach." In *Die deutsche Literatur und die Juden,* ed. Ludwig Geiger, pp. 231–49. 1910.

Pazi, M. "Berthold Auerbach and Moritz Hartmann." *LBY* 18(1973):201–16.

Sorkin, David. "The Invisible Community: Emancipation, Secular Culture and Jewish Identity in the Writings of Berthold Auerbach." In *The Jewish Response to German Culture,* ed. Jehuda Reinharz and Walter Schatzberg, pp. 100–119. Hanover and London, 1985.

Zwick, M. J. *Berthold Auerbach.* Stuttgart, 1933.

By Karl Isidor Beck

Beck, Karl Isidor. *Nächte. Gepanzerte Lieder.* Leipzig, 1838.

_____. *König Saul* (D). Leipzig, 1840–1841.

_____. *Stille Lieder* (P). Leipzig, 1840.

_____. *Lieder vom armen Mann* (P). Leipzig, 1846.

_____. *Still und Bewegt* (P). 1870.

About Karl Isidor Beck

Liptzin, Sol. *Lyric Pioneers of Modern Germany.* New York, 1938.

Nelbin, Heinrich. *Aus Karl Becks dichterischer Frühzeit.* Leipzig, 1908.

Thiel, Ernst. *Karl Becks literarische Entwicklung.* Breslau, 1938.

Toury, Jacob. "Moritz Saphir and Karl Beck: Zwei vormärzliche Literaten Osterreichs." In *Juden im Vormärz und in der Revolution von 1848,* ed. Walter Grab and Julius Schoeps. Stuttgart-Bonn, 1983.

By Michael Beer

Beer, Michael. *Klytemnestra* (D). Leipzig, 1823.

_____. *Die Bräute von Arragonien* (D). Leipzig, 1823.

_____. *Der Paria* (D). 1826.

_____. *Struensee* (D). Stuttgart, 1829.

_____. *Sämtliche Werke von Michael Beer.* ed. Eduard von Schenk. Leipzig, 1835.

_____. *Michael Beers Briefwechsel* (L). ed. Eduard von Schenk. Leipzig, 1837.

About Michael Beer

Kahn, Lothar. "Michael Beer—1800–1833." *LBY* 12(1967):149–60.
Manz, Gustav. F. *Michael Beers Jugend and dichterische Entwicklung bis zum Paria.* (diss.) Freiburg im Breisgau, 1891.

By Richard Beer-Hofmann

Beer-Hofmann, Richard. *Novellen.* 1892.
———. *Der Tod Georges* (N). Berlin, 1900.
———. *Der Graf von Charolais* (D). Berlin, 1904.
———. "Schlaflied für Mirjam" (P). 1919.
———. *Der junge David.* 1933.
———. *Gesammelte Werke.* Frankfurt a/M, 1964.
———. *Die Historie von König David* (D). Eine Trilogie.

By Walter Benjamin

Benjamin, Walter. *Einbahnstraße* (P, A). Berlin, 1928.
———. *Deutsche Menschen, eine Folge von Briefen* (P, L). Luzern, 1936.
———. *Berliner Kindheit um Neunzehnhundert* (A). Frankfurt a/M, 1950; 1966.
———. *Illuminationen* (P). Frankfurt, 1960.
———. *Illuminations.* Trans. Harry Zohn. New York, 1968, 1969; London, 1970, 1973.
———. *Städtebilder* (E, R). Frankfurt, 1963.
———. *Briefe,* ed. Gershom Scholem and Th. Adorno. 2 vols. 1966.
———. *Charles Baudelaire—Ein Lyriker im Zeitalter des Hochkapitalismus* (E). Frankfurt, 1969; trans. Harry Zohn. London, 1973.
———. *Reflections: Essays, Aphorisms, Autobiographical Writings,* ed. Peter Demetz. (Selected by Hannah Arendt) New York, 1978.
———. *Schriften,* ed. Theodor Adorno. 2 vols.
———. *Gesammelte Schriften,* ed. Rolf Tiedemeyer and H. Schweppenhäuser. Frankfurt, n.d.

About Walter Benjamin

Alter, Robert. "On Walter Benjamin." *Commentary* 48(1969):86–93.
German Critique 17(1979) (special Walter Benjamin issue).
Scholem, Gershom. *Walter Benjamin: The Story of a Friendship.* trans. Harry Zohn. Philadelphia, 1981.
Stüssi, Anna. *Erinnerung an die Zukunft: Walter Benjamins "Berliner Kindheit um Neunzehnhundert."* Göttingen, 1977.
Tiedemann, Rolf. *Studien zur Philosophie Walter Benjamins. Frankfurter Beiträge zur Soziologie* 16(1965).
Witte, Berndt. *Walter Benjamin: Der Intellektuelle als Kritiker. Untersuchungen zu seinem Frühwerk.* Stuttgart, 1976.

Wohlfahrth, Irving. "Sur quelques motifs juifs chez Walter Benjamin." *Revue d'Esthetique* 1(1981):141–62.

By Oskar Blumenthal

Blumenthal, Oskar. *Der Probepfeil* (D). 1882.

_____. *Die große Glocke* (D). 1887.

_____. *Großstadtluft* (D). 1891.

_____. *Im Weißen Rössel* (D). 1898.

_____. *Die Fee Caprice* (D). 1905.

_____. *Satirische Gänge* (n, E). 1905.

_____. *Nachdenkliche Geschichten* (n). 1914.

About Oskar Blumenthal

Lothar, Rudolf. *Das deutsche Drama der Gegenwart.* Berlin, 1905.

By Ludwig Börne

Börne, Ludwig. *Berliner Briefe,* ed. L. Geiger. 1828; 1897.

_____. *Briefe aus Paris.* 1830; 1833.

_____. *Menzel, der Franzosenfresser.* 1838.

_____. *Briefwechsel des jungen Börne und der Henriette Herz,* ed. L. Geiger. Oldenburg, 1905.

_____. *Werke,* ed. Ludwig Geiger. 12 vols. Berlin, 1911f.

_____. *Sämtliche Schriften.* ed. Inge and Peter Rippman. 5 vols. Düsseldorf, 1964.

About Ludwig Börne

Das Judenthum in Börnes Schriften (Anthology). Prag, ohne Jahr, 1852?

Gutzkow, Karl. *Börnes Leben.* Hamburg, 1840.

Heine, Heinrich. *Heine über L. Börne.* Hamburg, 1840.

Holzmann, M. *L. Börne. Sein Leben und sein Wirken.* Berlin, 1888.

Marcuse, Ludwig. *Revolutionär und Patriot: Das Leben Ludwig Börnes,* n.p., n.d.

Ras, G. *Börne und Heine als politische Schriftsteller.* 1927.

Weber, Johannes. *Libertin und Charakter: Heinrich Heine und Ludwig Börne im Werturteil deutscher Literaturgeschichtsschreibung 1840–1918.* Heidelberg, 1984.

By Hermann Broch

Broch, Hermann. *Die Schlafwandler. Romantrilogie* (N). Zürich, 1931–1932; (single volumes) Frankfurt, 1969–1970.

_____. *Die unbekannte Größe* (N). Berlin, 1933; Zürich, 1961.

_____. *Der Tod des Vergil* (P). Zürich and New York, 1945.

_____. *Die Schuldlosen* (N). Zürich, 1950.

_____. *Gesammelte Werke.* 10 vols. Zürich, 1950–1959.

_____. *Der Versucher* (N). Zürich, 1953; Frankfurt, 1969.

About Hermann Broch

Durzak, Manfred, ed. *Hermann Broch. Perspektiven der Forschung.* München, 1972.

Koebner, Thomas. *Herman Broch und sein Werk.* Bern, 1965.

Koopmann, Helmut. *Der Klassisch-moderne Roman in Deutschland: Thomas Mann, Alfred Döblin, Hermann Broch.* Stuttgart, 1983.

Krapoth, Hermann. *Dichtung und Philosophie. Eine Studie zum Werk Hermann Brochs.* Bonn, 1971.

Lützeler, Paul Michael. *Hermann Broch. Ethik und Politik: Studien zu seinem Frühwerk und zur Romantrilogie "Die Schlafwandler."* München, 1973.

Schlant, Ernestine. *Die Philosophie Hermann Brochs.* Bern and München, 1971.

By Max Brod

Brod, Max. *Arnold Beer: Das Schicksal eines Juden* (N). Berlin, 1912.

_____. *Eine Königin Esther* (D). Berlin, 1915.

_____. *Kampf um die Wahrheit (Trilogie)* (N). I. *Tycho Brahes Weg zu Gott.* Leipzig, 1915. II. *Reubeni. Fürst der Juden.* München, 1925.

_____. *Im Kampf um das Judentum* (E). Wien, 1920.

_____. *Das gelobte Land* (E). München, 1921.

_____. *Heidentum, Christentum, Judentum* (E). München, 1922.

_____. *Jüdinnen* (N). München, 1922.

_____. *Die Frau, die nicht enttäuscht* (N). Amsterdam, 1934.

_____. *Heinrich Heine: The Artist in Revolt* (B). Amsterdam, 1934.

_____. *Rassentheorie und Judentum* (E). Prag, 1934.

_____. *Franz Kafka* (B). Berlin, 1936.

_____. *Diesseits und Jenseits* (E). Winterthur, 1947.

_____. *Unambo, Roman aus dem jüdisch-arabischen Krieg* (N). Zürich, 1949.

_____. *Jugend im Nebel* (N). Berlin, 1959.

_____. *Streitbares Leben* (A). München, 1960.

_____. *Die Rosenkoralle; ein Prager Roman* (N). Berlin, 1961.

_____. *Der Prager Kreis* (E, A). Stuttgart, Berlin, Köln, Mainz, 1966.

About Max Brod

Gold, Hugo, ed. *Max Brod: Ein Gedenkbuch. 1884–1968.* Tel Aviv, 1969.

Gronemeyer, Horst, and Werner Kayser. *Max Brod, 1884–1984,* ed. Margarita Pazi. Bern and New York, 1987.

Pazi, Margarita. *Max Brod: Werk und Persönlichkeit.* Bonn, 1970.

Wessling, Berndt W. *Max Brod: Ein Portrait.* Stuttgart, 1969.

By Ferdinand Bruckner (Theodor Tagger)

Bruckner, Ferdinand. *Das neue Geschlecht* (E). 1917.

_____. *Der Herr in den Nebeln* (P). 1917.

_____. *Krankheit der Jugend* (D). 1928.

_____. *Verbrecher* (D). 1928.

_____. *Die Kreatur* (D). 1930.

_____. *Elizabeth von England* (D). 1930.

_____. *Timon* (D). 1932.

_____. *Die Marquise von O* (D). 1933.

_____. *Die Rassen* (D). 1934.

About Ferdinand Bruckner

Lehfeld, Christine. *Der Dramatiker Ferdinand Bruckner.* Göppingen, 1975.

By Martin Buber

Buber, Martin. *Ich und du* (P). 1923; Heidelberg, 1962.

_____. *Israel und Palästina* (E). Zürich, 1950.

_____. *Begegnung* (A). Stuttgart, 1960.

_____. *Werke.* 3 vols. Zürich, 1962–1964.

_____. *Gesammelte Aufsätze und Reden.* Köln, 1963.

_____. *Briefwechsel aus sieben Jahrzehnten.* 3 vols. Heidelberg, 1972.

_____. *Die Erzählungen der Chassidim.* Zürich, n.d.

_____. *Der Jude und sein Judentum* (E).

About Martin Buber

Friedmann, M., ed. *Martin Buber and the Theatre.* New York, 1969.

Friedmann, Maurice. *Martin Buber's Life and Works.* 3 vols. 1984.

Oliver, Roy Martin Buber. *Der Wanderer und der Weg.* Heidelberg, 1968.

Paquet, Alfons. "Martin Buber." In *Juden in der deutschen Literatur,* ed. C. Krojanker, 1922.

Schilpp, P. A., and M. Friedmann, eds. *Martin Buber.* Stuttgart, 1963.

By Jakob Julius David

David, Jakob Julius. *Das Höferecht* (n). 1885.

_____. *Am Wege sterben* (N). 1900.

_____. *Troika* (n). 1901.

_____. *Der Übergang* (N). 1903.

_____. *Die Hanna* (n). 1904.

_____. *Gesammelte Werke.* München, 1908.

About Jakob Julius David

Kloos, Hans. *Jakob Julius David als Novellist.* 1930.

By Alfred Döblin

Döblin, Alfred. *Die Ermordung einer Butterblume* (n). Berlin, 1913.
_____. *Die drei Sprünge des Wang-lun*(N). Berlin, 1915.
_____. *1918* (trilogy) (N). 1918.
_____. *Der deutsche Maskenball* (E). Berlin, 1921. (pseud. Linke Poot)
_____. *Berge, Meere und Giganten* (N). Berlin, 1924.
_____. *Reise in Polen* (E, R). Berlin, 1926.
_____. *Alfred Döblin im Buch, zu Haus, auf der Straße,* with Oskar Loerke (A). Berlin, 1928.
_____. *Berlin: Alexanderplatz* (N). Berlin, 1929.
_____. *Unser Dasein* (E). 1933; Olten und Freiburg i/Br., 1964.
_____. *Jüdische Erneuerung* (E). Amsterdam, 1933.
_____. *Babylonische Wanderung* (N). Amsterdam, 1934.
_____. *Flucht und Sammlung des Judenvolkes* (H). Amsterdam, 1935.
_____. *Schicksalsreise: Bericht und Erkenntnis* (E, A). Frankfurt a/M, 1949.
_____. *Hamlet oder die lange Nacht nimmt ein Ende* (N). München, 1956.

About Alfred Döblin

Busch, Arnold. *Faust und Faschismus. Thomas Manns 'Doktor Faustus' und Alfred Döblins 'November 1918' als exilliterarische Auseinandersetzung mit Deutschland.* Frankfurt, 1984.
Kahn, Lothar. "Alfred Döblin." *Mirrors of the Jewish Mind.* New York, 1968.
Links, Roland. *Alfred Döblin.* München, 1981.
Peitz, Wolfgang. *Alfred Döblin Bibliographie 1905–1966.* Freiburg i/Br., 1968.
Schuster, Ingrid, and Ingrid Bode. *Alfred Döblin im Spiegel der zeitgenössischen Kritik.* Bern, 1976.
Weyemberg, Roussart. *Alfred Döblin.* Bonn, 1969.

By Lion Feuchtwanger

Feuchtwanger, Lion. *H. Heines Rabbi von Bacherach* (E). 1907 (fragment); Frankfurt, 1985.
_____. *Jud Süß* (N). München, 1917.
_____. *Thomas Wendt (1918)* (D). 1919.
_____. *Die häßliche Herzogin* (N). Berlin, 1923.
_____. *Jud Süß* (N). München, 1925.
_____. *Erfolg* (N). Berlin, 1930.
_____. *Josephus Trilogie: I. Der jüdische Krieg* (N). Berlin, 1932. II. *Die Söhne* (N). Amsterdam, 1935. III. *Der Tag wird kommen* (or *Das gelobte Land*) (N). Stockholm, 1941.

_____. *Geschwister Oppenheim (Geschwister Oppermann)* (N). Amsterdam, 1933.

_____. *Der falsche Nero* (N). Amsterdam, 1936.

_____. *Moskau 1937* (E, R). 1937.

_____. *Exil* (N). Amsterdam, 1940.

_____. *Der Teufel in Frankreich (Unholdes Frankreich).* 1942.

_____. *Waffen für Amerika* (N). 2 vols., (incl. *Füchse im Weinberg*). Amsterdam, 1947–1948.

_____. *Goya oder der arge Weg der Erkenntnis* (N). Frankfurt, 1951.

_____. *Raquel. Die Jüdin von Toledo* (N). Hamburg, 1955.

_____. *Centum Opuscula: Eine Auswahl,* ed. Wolfgang Berndt (E, A). Rudolstadt, 1956.

_____. *Jefta und seine Tochter* (N). Hamburg, 1957.

_____. *Gesammelte Werke.* 12 vols. Berlin (East) and Weimar, 1965–1974.

About Lion Feuchtwanger

Jeske, Wolfgang, and Peter Zahn. *Lion Feuchtwanger oder der arge Weg der Erkenntnis.* Stuttgart, 1984.

Kahn, Lothar. *Insight and Action: The Life and Work of Lion Feuchtwanger.* Rutherford, N.J., and London, 1975–1976.

Köpke, Wulf. *Lion Feuchtwanger.* München, 1983.

Modick, Klaus. *Lion Feuchtwanger im Kontext der zwanziger Jahre: Autonomie und Sachlichkeit.* Königstein/Ts., 1981.

Pischel, Joseph. *Lion Feuchtwanger: Versuch über Leben und Werk.* Frankfurt a/M, 1984.

Spalek, John M., ed. *Lion Feuchtwanger: The Man, His Ideas, His Work.* Los Angeles, 1972.

Sternburg, Wilhelm von. *Lion Feuchtwanger: ein deutsches Schriftstellerleben.* Königstein, Ts, 1984.

Wolff, Rudolf, ed. *Lion Feuchtwanger: Werk und Wirkung.* Bonn, 1984.

Yuill, W. E. "Lion Feuchtwanger." In *German Men of Letters,* ed. Alex Nathan, 3:179–206. London, 1964.

By A. L. Frankl

Frankl, A. L. *Elegien* (P). Wien, 1842.

_____. *Rachel* (P). Wien, 1842.

_____. *Zur Geschichte der Juden in Wien* (H). Wien, 1853.

_____. *Libanon* (P). 1855.

_____. *Nach Jerusalem* (P, R). 2 vols. Wien, 1858–1860.

_____. *Ahnenbilder* (P). Wien, 1864.

_____. *Gesammelte poetische Werke.* 3 vols. Wien, 1880.

About A. L. Frankl

Wolee, E. *Ludwig August Frankl, der Dichter und Menschenfreund.*

By Karl Emil Franzos

Franzos, Karl Emil. *Juden von Barnow* (N). 1877.

_____. *Skizzen aus Halb-Asien* (Kulturbilder) (R, E). 4 vols. Leipzig, 1877 f.

_____. *Moschko von Parma* (N). Stuttgart, 1880.

_____. *Aus der großen Ebene* (R, E). 1888 f.

_____. *Judith Trachtenberg* (N). Breslau, 1890.

_____, ed. *Die Geschichte des Erstlings-Werkes* (incl. his own *Juden von Barnow*), 1894.

_____. *Der Pojaz* (N). Stuttgart, 1905.

About Karl Emil Franzos

Geiger, Ludwig. "Karl Emil Franzos." In *Die Juden in der deutschen Literatur,* pp. 250–304. Berlin, n.d.

Gelber, Mark. "Ethnic Pluralism and Germanization in the Works of Karl Emil Franzos," *The German Quarterly* 56(1983):376–85.

Hermand, Jost. "Karl Emil Franzos—Der Pojaz." In *Unbequeme Literatur,* pp. 112–27. n.p., 1965.

Lim, Jong Dae. *Das Leben und das Werk des Schriftstellers Karl Emil Franzos* (diss.). 1982.

Sommer, Fred. *'Halb-Asien': German Nationalism and the Eastern European Works of Emil Franzos.* Stuttgart, 1984.

By Ephraim Frisch

Frisch, Ephraim. *Das Verlöbnis* (N). Berlin, 1902.

_____. *Von der Kunst des Theaters* (E in dialogue). 1910.

_____. *Zenobi* (N). 1927. (also in Otten, Karl. *Das leere Haus* [A])

_____. *Gog und Magog* (N fragment). Privatdruck, Zürich, 1943.

_____. *Zum Verständnis des Geistigen* (E), ed. Guy Stern. Heidelberg, 1963.

About Ephraim Frisch

Stern, Guy. *War, Weimar and Literature. The Story of the 'Neue Merkur' 1914–1925.* University Park and London, 1971.

By Ywan (or Ivan) Goll (Isaac Lang)

Goll, Ywan. *Lothringische Volkslieder* (P). 1912.

_____. *Requiem für die Gefallenen von Europa* (P). 1917.

_____. *Der neue Orpheus* (D). 1918.

_____. *Noemi* (D). 1919.

_____. *Methusalem oder der ewige Bürger* (D). 1920.

_____. *Die Eurokokke* (P). 1927.

_____. *Der Miteuropäer* (N). 1928.

_____. *Stimmen der Völker* (A). 1938.

_____. *Dichtungen, Lyrik, Prosa, Drama*, ed. Richard Exner. 1959.

_____. *Dichtungen*, ed. Claire Goll. Darmstadt, 1960.

_____. *Claire-Iwan Goll. Briefe.* Mainz and Berlin, 1966.

_____. *Sodom, Berlin* (N). Berlin, 1985.

About Ywan Goll

Berg, Phyllis. *Jüdische Themen und das Hiob Schicksal im Werke Yvan Golls.* Ph.D. diss. Univ. of Cincinnati, 1976.

Mennemeier, F. N. *Modernes Neues Drama I. 1910–1933.* München, 1973. pp. 166–187.

Parmee, Margaret. *Ivan Goll: The Development of His Poetic Themes and Their Imagery.* Bonn, 1981.

Phillips, James. *Yvan Goll and Bilingual Poetry.* Stuttgart, 1984.

By Friedrich Gundolf

Gundolf, Friedrich. *Cäsar in der deutschen Literatur.* 1904.

_____. *Shakespeare und der deutsche Geist.* 1911; Düsseldorf, 1959.

_____. *Stefan George in unserer Zeit.* 1913.

_____. *George.* Berlin, 1920–1921.

_____. *Stephan George–Friedrich Gundolf Briefwechsel.* Düsseldorf, 1962.

_____. *Friedrich Gundolf Briefe—Neue Folge.* Amsterdam, 1965.

About Friedrich Gundolf

Schmitz, Victor. *Gundolf.*

By Maximilian Harden

Harden, Maximilian. *Apostata* (E). 2 vols. 1892.

_____. *Literatur und Theater.* 1896.

_____. *Krieg und Friede* (E). 2 vols. 1918.

_____. *Köpfe* (E). 3 vols. 1924.

_____. *Köpfe, Porträts, Briefe und Dokumente.* 1963.

About Maximilian Harden

Frank, Walter. *Höre Israel—Harden, Rathenau und die moderne Judenfrage.* Hamburg, 1959.

Gottgetreu, Erich. *Maximilian Harden: Ways and Errors of a Publicist. LBY* (1962):215–246.

Hellige, Hans Dieter, ed. *Walther Rathenau–Maximilian Harden: Briefwechsel.*

München, 1983.

Weller, Uwe. *Maximilian Harden und die Zukunft.* Bremen, 1970.

Young, Harry F. *Maximilian Harden.* Münster, 1970.

_____. *Maximilian Harden—Censor Germaniae.* The Hague, 1959.

By Moritz Hartmann

Hartmann, Moritz. *Kelch und Schwert* (P). 1845.

_____. *Reimchronik des Pfaffen Maurizius.* Frankfurt, 1849.

_____. *Moritz Hartmanns Gesammelte Werke,* ed. L. Bamberger and W. Vollmer. Stuttgart, 1874.

_____. *Revolutionäre Erinnerungen* (A). 1919.

_____. *Bruchstücke revolutionärer Erinnerungen.* In *Demokratische Studien,* ed. Ludwig Walesrode, vol. 2.

_____. *Novellen* (n).

About Moritz Hartmann

Pazi, Margarita. "Berthold Auerbach and Moritz Hartmann—Two Jewish Writers of the Nineteenth Century." *LBY* 18(1973):201–18.

Wittner, Otto, ed. *Briefe aus dem Vormärz.*

Wolkan, Rudolph, ed. *Briefe von Moritz Hartmann.* Wien, 1921.

By Moritz Heimann

Heimann, Moritz. *Prosaische Schriften.* 5 vols., incl. *Jüdische Kunst* (E), *Die Geschichte des Rabbi Nachman* (n), *Die Sagen der Juden* (L), *Born Judas* (L). Berlin, 1918.

_____. *Die Wahrheit liegt nicht in der Mitte* (E). Frankfurt, 1966.

_____. *Kritische Schriften.* Zürich, 1969.

_____. *Novellen.* Berlin.

_____. *Das Weib des Akiba* (D).

About Moritz Heimann

Bab, Julius. "Moritz Heimann." In *Juden in der deutschen Literatur,* ed. G. Krojanker. Frankfurt, 1922.

Reich-Ranicki, Marcel. "Der Kritiker Moritz Heimann."

By Heinrich Heine

Heine, Heinrich. *Sämtliche Werke,* ed. A. Strodtmann. 21 vols. 1861–1869; ed. E. Elster. 7 vols. Leipzig, 1887–1890 (New ed. Leipzig, 1925); ed. O. Walzel. Leipzig, 1911–1920; ed. F. Strich. 10 vols. München, 1925.

_____. *Heinrich Heine: Briefe,* ed. Friedrich Hirth. 6 vols. Mainz, 1950–1951.

_____. *Sämtliche Schriften,* ed. Klaus Briegleb, et al. 6 vols. Müchen, 1968–1976.

About Heinrich Heine

The literature about Heine is entirely too copious. Only the tiniest fraction of recommended works is given below:

Bieber, Hugo, ed. *Heinrich Heine, Gespräche: Briefe, Tagebücher, Berichte seiner Zeitgenossen.* Berlin, 1926.

Brod, Max. *Heinrich Heine.* Wien, 1934.

Hirth, F. *Heinrich Heine. Bausteine zu einer Biographie.* Mainz, 1950.

Kircher, Hartmut. *Heinrich Heine und das Judentum.* Bonn, 1971.

Löwenthal, E. *Studien zu Heines Reisebildern.* Berlin, 1922.

Marcuse, Ludwig. *Heine: Melancholiker, Streiter in Marx, Epikureer.* Rothenburg ob der Tauber, 1970.

Prawer, S. *Heine: Buch der Lieder.* London, 1960.

_____. *Heine's Jewish Comedy.* Oxford, 1983.

Rose, William. *Heinrich Heine: Two Studies of His Thought and Feeling.* Oxford, 1956.

Rosenthal, Ludwig. *Heinrich Heine als Jude.* Frankfurt and Berlin, 1973.

Sammons, Jeffrey L. *Heinrich Heine: A Modern Biography.* Princeton, 1979.

Seifert, Siegfried, ed. *Heine Bibliographie 1954–1964.* Berlin and Weimar, 1968.

Strodtmann, A. *Heine Leben und Werke,* 3d ed. 2 vols. Hamburg, 1884.

Wilhelm, Gottfield, and Eberhard Galley. *Heine Bibliographie.* 2 vols. Weimar, 1960.

By Moses Hess

Hess, Moses. *Die heilige Geschichte der Menschleit* (E). 1837.

_____. *Rom und Jerusalem* (E). 1862, and 11 other editions.

_____. *Ausgewählte Schriften.* Köln, 1962.

About Moses Hess

Alvineri, Shlomo. "Socialism and Nationalism in Moses Hess." In *Judentum in der Krise,* ed. Jochanan Bloch. Göttingen, 1966.

Silberner, Edmund. *Moses Hess.* Leiden, 1966.

By Ludwig Jacobowsky

Jacobowsky, Ludwig. *Funken* (P). 1890.

_____. *Satan lachte* (P). 1898.

_____. *Werther der Jude* (N). Dresden and Leipzig, 1899.

_____. *Leuchtende Tage* (P). 1900.

_____. *Diyab der Narr* (P). Berlin, n.d.

About Ludwig Jacobowsky

Bauschinger, Sigrid. "Zur Literatur der Jahrhundertwende. Der Nachlaß von

Ludwig Jacobowsky."

Friedrich, H. *Ludwig Jacobowsky. Ein modernes Dichterbild.* 1901.

Stern, Fred B. *Briefe aus dem Nachlaß von Ludwig Jacobowsky.* 2 vols. Heidelberg, 1974.

_____. *Ludwig Jacobowsky: Persönlichkeit und Werk eines Dichters.* Darmstadt, 1966.

By Franz Kafka

Kafka, Franz. *Die Verwandlung* (n). Leipzig, 1915.

_____. *Das Urteil* (n). Leipzig, 1916.

_____. *In der Strafkolonie* (n). Leipzig, 1919.

_____. *Der Prozeß* (N). Berlin, 1925.

_____. *Das Schloß* (N). München, 1926.

_____. *Amerika* (N). München, 1927.

_____. *Beim Bau der chinesischen Mauer* (n). Berlin, 1931.

_____. *Gesammelte Werke.* Frankfurt, 1951.

_____. *Tagebücher* (A). Frankfurt, 1951.

_____. *Briefe an Milena* (L), ed. Willy Haas. Frankfurt, 1952.

_____. *Briefe 1902–1924.* Frankfurt, 1958.

_____. *Sämtliche Erzählungen,* ed. Paul Raabe, Frankfurt, 1970.

About Franz Kafka

As with Heine, the bibliography *about* Kafka is vast. A few particularly useful references are indicated below:

Brod, Max. *Über Franz Kafka* (contains *Franz Kafka, eine Biographie*). 1936, 1954.

Canetti, Elias. *Kafka's Other Trial: The Letters to Felice.* London and New York, 1974.

Flores, Angel. *The Kafka Debate.* New York, 1976.

Gray, Ronald, ed. *Kafka: A Collection of Critical Essays.* 1962.

Greenberg, Clement. "The Jewishness of Franz Kafka." *Art and Culture.* Boston, 1961.

Haymen, Ronald. *Kafka: A Biography.* New York, 1982.

Heller, Erich. "The World of Franz Kafka." *The Disinherited Mind.* Cambridge, 1952.

Pawel, Ernst. *The Nightmare of Reason: A Life of Franz Kafka.* New York, 1984.

Politzer, Heinz. *Franz Kafka: Parable and Paradox.* Ithaca, 1962.

Robertson, Ritchie. *Kafka: Judaism, Politics and Literature.* Oxford, 1985.

Sokel, Walter H. "Franz Kafka as a Jew." *LBY* 18(1973).

Weltsch, Felix. "The Rise and Fall of the Jewish-German Symbiosis: The Case of Franz Kafka." *LBY* (1956).

By David Kalisch

Kalisch, David. *Lustspiele* (D). Berlin, 1852.
_____. *Berliner Leierkasten* (couplets) 3 vols. Berlin, 1859.
_____. *Lustige Werke von David Kalisch* (5 Hefte). 1870.

About David Kalisch

Hermann, Georg. *Das Berliner Lokalstück*. Berlin, 1920.
Ring, Max. *D. Kalisch*. 1872.
Schulz, Klaus. *Kladderadatsch*. n.d.

By Alfred Kerr

Kerr, Alfred. *Das neue Drama*. 1905.
_____. *Die Harfe* (P). 1917.
_____. *Gesammelte Schriften in zwei Reihen*. 1917, 1920.
_____. *Die Welt im Licht* (E). 2 vols. 1920 (reed. by F. Luft, Köln, 1961).
_____. *New York und London—Stätten des Geschicks* (R). 1923.
_____. *Yankeeland* (R). 1925.
_____. *Was wird aus Deutschlands Theater?* (C). 1930.
_____. *Die Diktatur des Hausknechts* (S). Brüssels, 1934.
_____. *Melodien* (P). Paris, 1938.

About Alfred Kerr

Blass, Ernst. "Alfred Kerr." In *Juden in der deutschen Literatur,* ed. Gustave
     Krojanker. 1922.
Chapiro, Joseph. *Für Alfred Kerr: Ein Buch der Freundschaft*. Berlin, 1928.
Hiller, Kurt. "Bekenntnis zu Alfred Kerr." *Köpfe und Tröpfe.*
Kühnert, Hanno. "Noch immer in der Emigration." *Die Zeit,* March 29, 1985.

By Gertrud Kolmar

Kolmar, Gertrud. *Versband* (P). Berlin, 1917.
_____. *Preußische Wappen* (P). Berlin, 1934.
_____. *Die Frau und die Tiere*. 1938.
_____. *Welten* (P). ed. Hermann Kasack. Hamburg, 1947.
_____. *Gertrud Kolmar: Das lyrische Werk*. Heidelberg, 1955.
_____. *Susanna* (n). In *Das leer Haus,* ed. Karl Otten. Stuttgart, 1959.
_____. *Eine Mutter* (n). München, 1965.
_____. *Briefe an die Schwester Hilde*. München, 1970.
_____. *Dark Soliloquy: Selected Poems by Gertrud Kolmar*. New York, 1975.

About Gertrud Kolmar

Byland, Hans. *Zu den Gedichten Gertrud Kolmars.* Bamberg, 1971.
Eben, Michael C. "Gertrud Kolmar: An Appraisal." *German Life and Letters* (New Series) 37(1984):197–210.

By Leopold Kompert

Kompert, Leopold. *Aus dem Ghetto* (n). 1848.
_____. *Böhmische Juden* (n). 1851.
_____. *Am Pfluge* (N). 2 vols. 1855.
_____. *Neue Geschichten aus dem Ghetto* (n). 2 vols. 1860.
_____. *Geschichten einer Gasse* (n). 2 vols. 1865.
_____. *Zwischen Ruinen* (N). 3 vols. 1875.
_____. *Franzi und Heine: Geschichten zweier Wiener Kinder* (N). 1881.
_____. *Leopold Komperts sämtliche Werke.* 10 vols. Leipzig, 1906.

About Leopold Kompert

Amann, Paul. *Leopold Komperts literarische Anfänge. Prager Studien* 5(1907).
Kahn, Lothar. "Karl Emil Franzos and Ludwig Kompert: Tradition and Modernity in the German Ghetto Novel." *Judaism* 28(1979).
Muller, Joel. "Ludwig Kompert als jüdischer Geschichtsschreiber" (Vortrag). Frankfurt a/M, n.d.
Steinthal, H. "Leopold Kompert." In *Über Juden und Judentum,* ed. Gustav Karpeles. Berlin, 1925.

By Karl Kraus

Krause, Karl. *Die demolirte Literatur* (E). Wien, 1897.
_____. *Eine Krone für Zion* (E). Wien, 1898.
_____. *Sittlichkeit und Kriminalität* (E). Wien, 1908.
_____. *Die chinesische Mauer* (E). München, 1910.
_____. *Heine und die Folgen* (E). München, 1910.
_____. *Weltgericht.* 2 vols. Leipzig, 1919.
_____. *Die letzten Tage der Menschheit* (D). Wien, Leipzig, 1922.
_____. *Werke,* ed. Heinrich Frischer. 14 vols. München, 1952–1967.
_____. *Frühe Schriften* ed. J. J. Braakenburg. 2 vols. München, 1979.
_____. *Worte in Versen* (P). 9 vols. Leipzig and Wien.
_____. *Literatur und Lüge* (E).

About Karl Kraus

Benjamin, Walter. "Karl Kraus." *Illuminationen.* Frankfurt, 1961.
Field, Frank. *The Last Days of Mankind: Karl Kraus and his Vienna.* London,

1967.

Grimstad, Kari. *Masks of the Prophet. The Theatrical World of Karl Kraus.* Toronto, 1982.

Heller, Erich. "Karl Kraus." *The Disinherited Mind.* Cambridge, 1952.

Kraft, Werner. *Karl Kraus—Beiträge zum Verständnis seines Werkes.* Salzburg, 1956.

Liegler, Leopold. *Karl Kraus und sein Werk.* Wien, 1920.

Pfabigan, Alfred. *Karl Kraus und der Sozialismus. Eine politische Biographie.* Wien, 1976.

Scheu, Robert. *Karl Kraus.* Wien, 1909.

Timms, Edward. *Karl Kraus: Apocalyptic Satirist.* New Haven, 1986.

Zohn, Harry. *Karl Kraus.* New York, 1971.

By Moses Ephraim Kuh

Kuh, Moses Ephraim. *Hinterlassene Gedichte,* ed. K. W. Rambler. Zürich, 1792.

_____. *Epigramme des Dichters Kuh,* ed. Th. Seemann. Dresden, 1872.

About Moses Ephraim Kuh

Bauer, S. "Moses Ephraim Kuh." In *Gallerie der berühmtesten Dichter des 18. Jahrhunderts.* Leipzig, 1805.

Galliner, Arthur. "Ephraim Kuh. Ein jüdisch-deutscher Dichter der Aufklärungszeit." *Bulletin, LBI.*

Hirschfeld, Moses. *Das Leben des Dichters Kuh.* In *Moses Ephraim Kuh. Hinterlassene Gedichte.* 1792.

Kayserling, M. *Der Dichter Ephraim Kuh. Ein Beitrag zur Geschichte der Literatur.* Berlin, 1864.

By Gustav Landauer

Landauer, Gustav. *Der Todesprediger* (N). Dresden, 1893.

_____. *Macht und Mächte* (n). Köln, 1903.

_____. "Ostjuden und deutsches Reich." *Der Jude* 1(1916/17):433–37.

_____. *Der werdende Mensch. Aufsätze über Leben und Schriften* (E). Potsdam, 1921.

_____. *Gustav Landauer: Sein Lebensgang in Briefen* (L). 2 vols. Frankfurt, 1929.

_____. *Aufruf zum Sozialismus,* ed. Heinz-Joachim Heydorn. Frankfurt, 1967.

_____. "Gustav Landauer. Zwang und Befreiung" (Eine Auswahl aus seinem Werk). *Philosophisches and Literaturhistorisches.* Köln.

About Gustav Landauer

Breines, Paul. "The Jew as Revolutionary. The Case of Gustav Landauer." *LBY* 12(1967):75–84.

Kalz, Wolf. *Gustav Landauer: Kultursozialist und Anarchist.* Meisenheim a/Glau,

1967.

Lunn, Eugene. *Prophet of Community: The Romantic Socialism of Gustav Landauer.* Berkeley, 1973.

Maurer, Charles B. *Call to Revolution: The Mystical Anarchism of Gustav Landauer.* Detroit, 1971.

Schmolze, Gerhard. "Biblische Hoffnung im deutschen Zusammenbruch 1918–19. Kurt Eisner und Gustav Landauer in der Münchner Revolution." *Emuna* 4(1969).

_____. *Revolution und Räterepublik in München.* Düsseldorf, 1969.

By Else Lasker-Schüler

Lasker-Schüler, Else. *Der siebente Tag* (P). 1905.

_____. *Das Peter Hille Buch* (P). 1906.

_____. *Die Nächte Tino von Bagdads* (n). 1907.

_____. *Die Wupper* (D). 1909.

_____. *Mein Herz* (N). Berlin, 1912.

_____. *Hebräische Balladen* (P). 1913.

_____. *Der Prinz von Theben* (n). 1914.

_____. *Die gesammelten Gedichte.* 1917.

_____. *Der Wunderrabbiner von Barcelona* (n). 1921.

_____. *Styx* (P). 1922.

_____. *Theben* (D). 1923.

_____. *Arthur Aronymus. Die Geschichte meines Vaters* (D). Berlin, 1932.

_____. *Verse und Prosa aus dem Nachlaß,* ed. Werner Kraft. München, 1961.

_____. *Gesammelte Werke in drei Bänden.* München, 1962.

_____. *Sämtliche Gedichte.* München, 1966.

About Else Lasker-Schüler

Cohn, Hans. *Else Lasker-Schüler. The Broken World.* Cambridge, 1974.

Guder, Gotthold. *Else Lasker-Schüler.* Siegen, 1966.

Hessing, Jakob. *Else Lasker-Schüler. Biographie einer deutsch-jüdischen Dichterin.* Karlsruhe, 1985.

Kraft, Werner. *Else Lasker-Schüler. Eine Einführung in ihr Werk und eine Auswahl.* Wiesbaden, 1951.

Mennemeier, F. N. "On Else Lasker-Schüler." *Modernes Deutsches Drama, 1910–1933,* pp. 134–46. München, 1972.

Wallmann, Jürgen P. *Else Lasker-Schüler.* Mühlacker, 1966.

Wiener, Meir. "Else Lasker-Schüler." In *Juden in der deutschen Literatur,* ed. G. Krojanker. 1922.

By Ferdinand Lassalle

Lassalle, Ferdinand. *Philosophie Heraklits* (P). 1857.

_____. *Franz von Sickingen* (D). 1859.

_____. *Arbeiterlesebuch.* 1860.

_____. *System der erworbenen Rechte.* 1862.

_____. *Gesammelte Reden und Schriften.* 12 vols. 1919.

_____. *Ferdinand Lassalle. Auswahl.* Wien, 1964, 1966.

About Ferdinand Lassalle

Bein, Alex. "Lassalle als Verteidiger Geigers und der jüdische Lehr- und Leseverein in Breslau." 9(1966):330–41.

Friederici, Hans Jürgen. *Ferdinand Lassalle. Eine politische Biographie.* Berlin (East), 1985.

Karpeles, Gustav. "Ferdinand Lassalle." In *Heinrich Heines Leben,* 259. Leipzig, 1889.

Na'aman, Shlomo. *Ferdinand Lassalle, Deutscher und Jude.* 1968.

Oncken, Hermann. *Lassalle. Zwischen Marx und Bismarck. Eine politische Biographie* (new ed.), ed. Felix Hirsch. Stuttgart, 1966.

Schrokauer, Alfred. *Lassalle.* 1928.

By Fanny Lewald

Lewald, Fanny. *Clementine* (N). 1842.

_____. *Jenny* (N). 1843.

_____. *Diogena. Roman von Iduna Gräfin H . . . H.* Leipzig, 1848.

_____. *Adele* (N). Braunschweig, 1855.

_____. *Meine Lebensgeschichte* (A). 1861–1863.

_____. *Der dritte Stand. Novellistisches Zeitbild* (N). Berlin, 1862.

_____. *Ein armes Mädchen* (N). Berlin, 1862.

_____. *Gesammelte Novellen* (n). Berlin, 1862.

_____. *Gesammelte Werke.* 12 vols. Berlin, 1871.

_____. *Clementine* (n). Berlin, 1872.

_____. *Jenny* (N). Berlin, 1872.

_____. *Stella* (N). 2 vols. Leipzig, 1884.

_____. *Die Familie Darner* (N). 3 vols. Berlin, 1887.

_____. *Erinnerungen aus dem Jahre 1848* (A), ed. Friedrich Schaefer. Frankfurt, 1969.

_____. *Diogena. Roman von Iduna Gräfin H . . . H* (N). Leipzig, 1848.

_____. "Erinnerungen an Heinrich Heine." *Illustrierte deutsche Monatshefte.* n.p., 1886.

About Fanny Lewald

Drewitz, Ingeborg. *Berliner Salons.* Berlin, 1965.

Pazi, M. "Fanny Lewald: Das Echo der Revolution von 1848 in ihren Schriften." In *Juden im Vormärz und in der Revolution von 1848,* ed. W. Crab and J. H. Schoeps. Stuttgart and Bonn, 1983.

Steinhauer, Marielouise. *Fanny Lewald—Die deutsche George Sand.* 1937.

By Ernst Lissauer

Lissauer, Ernst. *Der Acker* (P). 1907.
_____. *Der Strom* (P). 1912.
_____. *Yorick* (D). 1921.
_____. *Das Weib des Jeptha* (D). 1928.
_____. *Luther und Thomas Münzer* (D). 1929.
_____. *Die Steine reden* (P). 1936.
_____. *Zeitenwende* (P). 1936, 1956.

About Ernst Lissauer

Bab, Julius. "Ernst Lissauer." *Deutsche Kriegslyrik*. Stettin, 1920.
Brand, Guido R. *Ernst Lissauer*. Stuttgart, 1927.

By Fritz Mauthner

Mauthner, Fritz. *Nach berühmtem Muster* (parodies). 1879.
_____. *Der neue Ahasver. Roman aus Jung-Berlin* (N). 2 vols. Dresden. 1882.
_____. *Xantippe* (N). Dresden, 1888.
_____. *Zehn Geschichten* (n). Berlin, 1891.
_____. *Hypatia. Roman aus dem Altertum*. Stuttgart, 1892.
_____. *Die Geisterseher. Humoristischer Roman* (N). Berlin, 1894.
_____. *Die bunte Reihe. Berliner Roman* (N). Berlin, 1896.
_____. *Wörterbuch der Philosophie: neue Beiträge zu einer Kritik der Sprache* (P). 2 vols. 1910.
_____. *Prager Jugendjahre* (A). 1918; Frankfurt, 1960.
_____. *Ausgewählte Schriften*. 6 vols. Stuttgart and Berlin, 1919.
_____. *Der Atheismus und seine Geschichte im Abendlande*. 4 vols. 1920–1923.
_____. *Beiträge zu einer Kritik der Sprache: Sprache und Psychologie* (P). Stuttgart, 1981.

About Fritz Mauthner

Bab, Julius. "Fritz Mauthner." *Über den Tag hinaus*. 1960.
Betz, Frederick, and Jörg Thunecke. "Fritz Mauthners Berliner Jahre 1876–1984: Erinnerungen des Buddha vom Bodensee." In *Jahrbuch für Brandenburgische Landesgeschichte*, vol. 35. Spandau, 1984. 137–61.
Eisen, W. *Fritz Mauthners Kritik der Sprache*. 1929.
Knappstein, T. *Fritz Mauthner: der Mann und sein Werk*. 1926.
Weiler, Gershon. "Fritz Mauthner: A Study in Jewish Self-Rejection." *LBY* 8(1963).
_____. "Fritz Mauthner as a Historian." *Studies in the Philosophy of History* 4(1964).

By Alfred Mombert

Mombert, Alfred. *Tag und Nacht* (P). 1894.
_____. *Der Glühende* (P). 1896.
_____. *Die Schöpfung* (P). 1897.
_____. *Der Denker* (P). 1901.
_____. *Die Blüte des Chaos* (P). 1905.
_____. *Musik der Welt* (P). 1915.
_____. *Der Held der Erde* (P). 1919.
_____. *Atair* (P). 1925.
_____. *Aigla,* I and II (P). 1929–31.
_____. *Briefe* (1893–1942).
_____. *Sfaira der Alte* (myth). 1936, 1958.
_____. *Dichtungen.* 3 vols. München, 1972.

About Alfred Mombert

Benz, R. *Der Dichter Alfred Mombert.* 1947.
Buber, Martin. "Der Dichter Alfred Mombert." In *Juden in der deutschen Literatur,* ed. G. Krojanker. 1922.

By Salomon Hermann Mosenthal

Mosenthal, Salomon Hermann. *Die Sklaven* (D). 1847.
_____. *Cäcilia von Albano* (D). 1849.
_____. *Deborah* (D). Budapest, 1849.
_____. *Isabella Orsini* (D). 1870.
_____. *Die Sirene* (D). 1875.
_____. *Der Sonnenwendhof* (D). 1875.
_____. *Bilder aus dem jüdischen Familienleben* (n). 1878.
_____. *Gesammelte Werke.* 6 vols. Stuttgart and Leipzig, 1878.

By Arno Nadel

Nadel, Arno. *Aus vorletzten und letzten Gründen* (P and aphorisms). 1909.
_____. *Cagliostro und die Halsbandgeschichte* (D). 1913.
_____. *Um dieses alles* (P). 1914.
_____. *Adam* (D). 1917.
_____. *Das Jahr der Juden* (P). 1920.
_____. *Der Sündenfall* (D). 1920.
_____. *Rot und glühend ist das Auge des Juden* (P). 1920.
_____. *Der Ton* (P). 1921.
_____. *Heiliges Proletariat* (P). 1924.
_____. *Drei Augen-Blicke* (n). 1932.
_____. *Für Brigitte und alle Welt* (N). 1932.
_____. *Das Leben des Dichters* (P). 1935.

_____. *Der weissagende Dionysos* (P). Heidelberg, 1959.

About Arno Nadel

Isolani, Gertrud. "On Arno Nadel." *Briefe, Gespräche, Begegnungen.* Köln, 1985.
Kemp, Friedhelm. "Arno Nadel (1878–1943)." *Neue Zürcher Zeitung* (Zürich).
    October 4, 1958.

By Alfred Neumann

Neumann, Alfred. *Die Lieder vom Lächeln und der Not.* (P). 1917.
_____. *Die Brüder* (N). 1924.
_____. *Der Patriot* (n). 1925.
_____. *Der Teufel* (N). 1926; Amsterdam, 1935.
_____. *König Haber* (n). 1926; München, 1968.
_____. *Neuer Cäsar* (N). 1934.
_____. *Leben der Christine von Schweden.* 1936.
_____. *Es waren ihrer sechs* (N). Stockholm, 1945.
_____. *Der Patriot—König Haber.* Ebenhausen, 1968.

About Alfred Neumann

Kesten, Hermann. "Alfred Neumann." *Meine Freunde die Poeten.* München,
    1959.

By Robert Neumann

Neumann, Robert. *Gedichte.* 1919.
_____. *Die Pest von Lianora* (n). 1927.
_____. *Mit fremden Federn* (parodies). 1927.
_____. *Jagd auf Menschen und Gespenster* (E). 1928.
_____. *Sintflut* (N). 1929.
_____. *Blinde Passagiere* (N). 1931.
_____. *Karriere* (n). 1931.
_____. *Die Nacht* (N). 1932.
_____. *Zaharoff* (biography). 1934.
_____. *An den Wassern von Babylon* (N). Oxford, 1939.
_____. *Ein leichtes Leben* (A). 1963.

About Robert Newmann

Robert Neumann. Stimmen der Freude. Prepared by Kurt Desch Verlag.
    München–Wien. 1957.
Scheck, Ulrich. *Die Prosa Robert Neumanns; mit einem bibliographischen Anhang.*
    Berlin–Bern, 1985.

By Max Nordau

Nordau, Max. *Aus dem wahren Milliardenlande* (R, E). 1878.
_____. *Vom Kreml zur Alhambra* (R). 1879.
_____. *Die neuen Journalisten,* with Ferdinand Gross (D). 1880.
_____. *Paris unter der dritten Republik* (E, R). 1880.
_____. *Der Krieg der Millionen* (D). 1881.
_____. *Die konventionellen Lügen der Kulturmenschheit* (E, C). 1883.
_____. *Die Krankheit des Jahrhunderts* (N). 1887.
_____. *Entartung* (E). 1892.
_____. *Seelenanalysen* (n). 1892.
_____. *Das Recht zu lieben* (D). 1894.
_____. *Doktor Kohn* (D). 1898.
_____. *Von Kunst und Künstlern* (E). 1908.

About Max Nordau

Ben-Horin, Meir. *Max Nordau: Philosopher of Human Solidarity.* London, 1956.
_____. "Reconsidering Max Nordau." *Herzl Yearbook.* New York, 1960.
Fischer, Jens Malte. "Entartete Kunst—zu einer Geschichte eines Begriffs." *Merkur* 38(1984):346–52.
Rosenthal, Jakob. "Max Nordau—Kritiker einer Epoche." *Aufbau,* Jan. 12, 1973.
Schaf, Rafael. "A Forgotten Critic and Non-Conformist." *Jewish Quarterly* (London)1973:28.

By Ludwig Philippson

Philippson, Ludwig. *Die Juden: ihre Bestrebungen und ihre Denuncianten.* Magdeburg, 1838.
_____. *Gesammelte Dichtungen.* Leipzig, 1857.
_____. *Sepphoris und Rom. Ein historischer Roman aus dem 4. Jahrhundert.* Berlin, 1866.
_____. *Jacob Tirado. Geschichtlicher Roman aus der zweiten Hälfte des 16. Jahrhunderts.* Leipzig, 1867.
_____. *An den Strömen durch drei Jahrhunderte* (H, N). Leipzig, 1872.
_____. *Gesammelte Schriften.* Breslau, 1891.
_____. *Novellenbuch* (N). Breslau, 1892.

About Ludwig Philippson

Eliav, Mordechai. "Philippsons Allgemeine Zeitung des Judentums und Eretz Israel." *LBI Bulletin* 12(1969):155–82.
Kahn, Lothar. "Neglected Nineteenth-Century German-Jewish Historical Fiction." In *Identity and Ethos,* ed. Mark H. Gelber. New York and Bern, 1986.

By Jakob Picard

Picard, Jakob. *Der Gezeichnete. Jüdische Geschichten aus einem Jahrhundert.*
　　Berlin, 1936.
_____. *Childhood in the Village* (A). *LBY* 4(1959).
_____. "Vergeltung" (N). *Deutsche Rundschau* 87(1961):161–72.
_____. *Die alte Lehre. Geschichten und Anekdoten.* n.p., n.d.

About Jakob Picard

Pinthus, Kurt. "Ein Stiller im Lande. Zum 75. Geburtstag Jakob Picards am 11.
　　Januar." *Aufbau* (New York), Jan. 10, 1958.

By Alfred Polgar

Polgar, Alfred. *Der Quell des Übels* (N). 1908.
_____. *Goethe,* with Egon Friedell. 1908, 1926.
_____. *Soldatenleben im Frieden,* with Egon Friedell (D). 1910.
_____. *Hiob* (N). 1912.
_____. *Gestern und heute* (n). 1922.
_____. *Ja und nein.* 1926–27; Reinbek, 1956.
_____. *Bei dieser Gelegenheit* (sketches). 1930.
_____. *Die Defraudanten* (D). 1931.
_____. *Auswahl.* Reinbek, 1968.
_____. *Kleine Schriften,* ed. M. Reich-Ranicki. 4 vols. Reinbek, 1984.

About Alfred Polgar

Greuner, Ruth. "Alfred Polgar: Epitaph auf einen Dichter." *Gegenspieler.* East
　　Berlin, 1969.
Weinzierl, Ulrich. *Alfred Polgar. Eine Biographie.* Wien, 1985.

By Gabriel Riesser

Riesser, Gabriel. *Verteidigung der bürgerlichen Gleichstellung der Juden gegen die
　　Einwürfe des Herrn Paulus* (H). Altona, 1831.
_____. *Börne und die Juden* (E). Altenburg: Hochbuchdr., 1832.
_____. *Jüdische Briefe.* Berlin, 1840.
_____. *Stellung der Juden in Preußen* (E). n.p., 1842.
_____. *Ein Wort über die Zukunft Deutschlands* (E). n.p., 1848.
_____. *Gesammelte Schriften,* ed. M. Isler. 4 vols. Frankfurt a/M., 1867–68.

About Gabriel Riesser

Feiner, J. *Gabriel Riessers Leben und Wirken.* Leipzig, 1911.

Friedländer, F. *Das Leben Gabriel Riessers.* Berlin, 1926.
Geiger, Ludwig. "Gabriel Riesser." *Die deutsche Literatur und die Juden*, pp. 212–30. 1910.
Rinott, Moshe. "Gabriel Riesser—Fighter for Jewish Emancipation." *LBY* 7(1962).
Seifensieder, Jakob. *Gabriel Riesser, ein deutscher Mann jüdischen Glaubens.* Frankfurt a/M, 1920.

By Julius Rodenberg

Rodenberg, Julius. *Lieder* (P). Hannover, 1854.
_____. *Pariser Bilderbuch* (R). Braunschweig, 1856.
_____. *Alltagsleben in London* (R). Berlin, 1860.
_____. *Die neue Sündflut* (N). Berlin, 1865.
_____. *Erinnerungen aus der Jugendzeit* (A). 2 vols. Berlin, 1899–1901.
_____. *Von Gottes Sulamit* (D). Berlin, 1899.
_____. *Aus der Kindheit* (A). Berlin, 1902.

About Julius Rodenberg

Haacke, W. *Julius Rodenberg und die "Deutsche Rundschau."*
_____. *Julius Rodenberg. Aus seinen Tagebüchern.* Berlin, 1919.
Maync, H. *Julius Rodenberg.* 1925.
Reuter, Hans-Heinrich. *Theodor Fontane. Briefe an Rodenberg.* East Berlin, 1969.
Spiero, H. *Julius Rodenberg.* 1921.

By Joseph Roth

Roth, Joseph. *Das Spinnennetz* (N). 1923; Köln, 1967.
_____. *Die Rebellion* (N). 1924; Amsterdam and München, 1962.
_____. *Hotel Savoy* (N). 1924.
_____. *Juden auf der Wanderschaft* (E). 1926–27.
_____. *Die Flucht ohne Ende* (N). 1927.
_____. *Hiob* (N). 1930; Frankfurt, 1969.
_____. *Panoptikum* (E). 1930.
_____. *Der Antichrist* (E). 1934.
_____. *Tarabas. Ein Gast auf dieser Erde* (N). 1934.
_____. *Die hundert Tage* (N). Amsterdam, 1936.
_____. *Kapuzinergruft.* 1938; Amsterdam, 1950.
_____. *Die Legende vom heiligen Trinker* (n). Amsterdam, 1939.
_____. *Romane, Erzählungen, Aufsätze.* Köln, 1964.
_____. *Radetzkymarsch* (N). Köln, 1965.
_____. *Werke*, ed. H. Kensten. 2 vols. Köln, 1975.
_____. *Zwischen Lemberg und Paris.*

About Joseph Roth

Bönig, Hansjürgen. *Joseph Roth's "Radetzkymarsch."* München, n.d.
Bronsen, David. *Joseph Roth.* Köln, 1974.
Kesten, Hermann. *Meine Freunde die Poeten.* 1960.
Linden, Hermann. *Joseph Roth. Leben und Werk. Ein Gedächtnisbuch.* Amsterdam and Köln, 1949.

By Felix Salten

Salten, Felix. *Der Gemeine* (D). 1901.
_____. *Die Gedenktafel der Prinzessin Anna* (N). 1902.
_____. *Die kleine Veronika* (N). 1903.
_____. *Das Buch der Könige.* 1905.
_____. *Wiener Adel.* 1905.
_____. *Olga Frohgemut* (N). 1910.
_____. *Bambi. Eine Lebensgeschichte aus dem Wilde* (N). 1923; Wien, 1952, 1965.
_____. *Geister der Zeit* (E). 1924.
_____. *Neue Menschen auf alter Erde* (E, R). 1925.
_____. *Simson* (N). 1928.

About Felix Salten

Weinzierl, Ulrich. "Typische Wiener Feuilletonisten? Am Beispiel Salten, Blei, Friedell, Polgar und Anton Kuh." *Literatur und Kritik* 191–92(1985):72–86.
"Zum 100. Geburtstag von Felix Salten am 6. September. Versuch eines Porträts." *Das neue Israel* (Zürich) 22(1969):179–85.

By Hugo Salus

Salus, Hugo. *Gedichte.* 1898.
_____. *Neue Gedichte.* 1899.
_____. *Ehefrühling* (P). 1900.
_____. *Susanna im Bade* (D). 1901.
_____. *Neue Garben* (P). 1904.
_____. *Novellen des Lyrikers* (n). 1904.
_____. *Die Blumenschale* (P). 1907.
_____. *Römische Komödie* (D). 1909.
_____. *Glockenklang* (P). 1911.
_____. *Nachdenkliche Geschichten* (n). 1914.
_____. *Die Beschau. Eine Ghettogeschichte.* Wien, 1920.
_____. *Der schöne David des Michelangelo* (n). 1922.
_____. *Helle Träume* (P). 1924.
_____. *Seelen und Sinne* (n). (n.d.)

About Hugo Salus

Moses, J. *Die Lösung der Judenfrage.* 1907.
Tichy, Frantisek R. "Jüdische Thematik bei Hugo Salus." *Zeitschrift für Geschichte der Juden.* 1966.

By Moritz Gottlieb Saphir

Saphir, Moritz Gottlieb. *Poetische Erstlinge* (P). 1821.
_____. *Der getötete und dennoch lebende M. G. Saphir* (H). 1822.
_____. *Conditorei des Jokus* (H). 1828.
_____. *Gesammelte Werke.* 4 vols. 1832.
_____. *Neueste Schriften.* 3 vols. 1832.
_____. *Humoristische Glasperlen.* 1833.
_____. *Humoristische Abende.* 1853.
_____. *Humoristisches Album für den Weihnachtsbaum.* 1854.
_____. *Pariser Briefe* (H, E). 1856.
_____. *M. G. Saphirs Schriften. Gesamtausgabe.* 26 vols. 1875–88.

About Moritz Gottlieb Saphir

Bato, Ludwig Yomtov. "Moritz Gottlieb Saphir, 1795–1858." In *LBI Bulletin* 5(1958):28–29.
Kahn, Lothar. "Moritz Gottlieb Saphir." *LBY* 20(1975):247–57.

By Arthur Schnitzler

Schnitzler, Arthur. *Anatol* (D). 1893.
_____. *Sterben* (n). 1894; trans. Harry Zohn. New York, 1977.
_____. *Der grüne Kakadu* (D). 1898.
_____. *Der Schleier der Beatrice* (D). 1899.
_____. *Der blinde Geronimo und sein Bruder* (N). 1900.
_____. *Leutnant Gustl* (N). 1901.
_____. *Der einsame Weg* (D). 1903.
_____. *Der Weg ins Freie* (N). 1907.
_____. *Komtesse Mizzi* (D). 1907.
_____. *Der junge Medardus* (D). 1909.
_____. *Das weite Land* (D). 1910.
_____. *Professor Bernhardi* (D). 1912.
_____. *Dr. Gräsler, Badearzt* (N). 1917.
_____. *Fräulein Else* (N). 1924.
_____. *Therese* (N). 1928.
_____. *Arthur Schnitzler—Otto Brahm Briefwechsel,* ed. Oskar Seidlin. 1953.
_____. *Georg Brandes—Arthur Schnitzler Briefwechsel,* ed. Kurt Bergel. Bern, 1956.
_____. *Gesammelte Werke. Die erzählenden Schriften.* Frankfurt a/M, 1961.

_____. *Die dramatischen Werke*. 2 vols. (*Das Wort: Dramatisches Fragment*), 1966.

_____. *Erzählungen* (n). Frankfurt a/M., 1966.

_____. *Jugend in Wien* (A), ed. Therese Nickl and Heinrich Schnitzler. Wien, 1968.

_____. *Liebelei, Reigen*. Frankfurt a/M., 1968.

About Arthur Schnitzler

Beharriell, F. J. "Schnitzler, Freuds Doppelgänger." *Literatur und Kritik* 19(1967):546–55.

Fritsche, Alfred. *Dekadenz im Werke Arthur Schnitzlers*. Bern, 1974.

Gaisbauer, Adolf. "Der historische Hintergrund von Arthur Schnitzlers 'Professor Bernhardi' Stück." *LBI Bulletin* 50(1974):113–63.

Liptzin, Sol. *Arthur Schnitzler*. New York, 1932.

Rey, W. H. *Arthur Schnitzler. Die späte Prosa als Gipfel seines Schaffens*. Berlin, 1968.

Urbach, Reinhard. *Arthur Schnitzler*. New York, 1973.

Willehad, Paul Eckert. "Arthur Schnitzler und das Wiener Judentum." *Emuna* 8(1973).

By Anna Seghers

Seghers, Anna. *Aufstand der Fischer von St. Barbara* (N). 1920, 1938, 1951, 1958.

_____. *Auf dem Wege zur amerikanischen Botschaft* (n). 1930.

_____. *Die Gefährten* (N). 1932, 1959.

_____. *Der Kopflohn* (N). 1933.

_____. *Der Weg durch den Februar* (N). 1935.

_____. *Die Rettung* (N). 1937, 1947.

_____. *Transit* (N). 1941.

_____. *Das siebte Kreuz* (N). 1942.

_____. *Der Ausflug der toten Mädchen* (n). 1946, 1948, 1950.

_____. *Die Toten bleiben jung* (N). 1949.

_____. *Der Mann und sein Name* (n). 1952.

_____. *Frieden der Welt*. Ansprachen und Aufsätze, 1953.

_____. *Die große Veränderung und unsere Literatur* (E). 1956.

_____. *Ausgewählte Erzählungen*. Reinbek, 1968.

_____. *Werke*. 10 vols. Darmstadt, 1977.

About Anna Seghers

Batt, Kurt. *Anna Seghers. Versuch über Entwicklung und Werke*. Frankfurt, 1973.

Cernyak, Susan E. *Anna Seghers: Between Judaism and Communism*. (diss.). 1978.

Diessen, Juge. *Seghers Studien. Interpretationen von Werken aus den Jahren 1925–1935*. East Berlin, n.d.

Gruss, Noe. "Die Dissertation der Nelly Reiling; der Jude und jüdische Motive bei Rembrandt." *Tribüne* 23(1984):143–44.

Jay, Martin. "Anna Seghers and the Weimar Left." *Midstream* 20(1974):42–50.

Neugebauer, Heinz. *Anna Seghers.* East Berlin, 1978.

Sauer, Klaus. *Anna Seghers.* München, 1978.

By Carl Sternheim

Sternheim, Carl. *Die Hose* (D). 1911.

_____. *Der Snob* (D). 1914.

_____. *Perleberg* (D). 1917.

_____. *Die Marquise von Arcis* (D). 1919.

_____. *Berlin oder Juste-Milieu* (C). 1920.

_____. *Europa* (N). 2 vols. 1920.

_____. *Fairfax* (N). 1921.

_____. *Manon Lescaut* (D). 1921.

_____. *Aus dem bürgerlichen Heldenleben.* 1922.

_____. *J. P. Morgan* (sketch). 1930.

_____. *Aut Caesar, aut Nihil* (E). 1931.

_____. *Gesammelte Werke* ed. Wilhelm Elmrich. 8 vols. Neuwied, 1969.

_____. *Bürger Schippel* (D). 1920.

About Carl Sternheim

Budde, Bernhard. *Über die Wahrheit und über die Lüge des radikalen, antibürgerlichen Individualismus; eine Studie zum erzählerischen und essayistischen Werk Carl Sternheims.* Frankfurt, 1983.

Karasek, Hellmutch. *Carl Sternheim.* 1969.

Nagel, Ivan. "Der Dramatiker Carl Sternheim." *Neue Rundschau* 75(1964):477–82.

Sebald, Winfried G. *Carl Sternheim—Kritiker und Opfer der Wilhelminischen Ära.* Stuttgart, 1969.

Zweig, Arnold. "Versuch über Sternheim." In *Juden in der deutschen Literatur,* ed. G. Krojanker. 1922.

By Ludwig Strauss

Strauss, Ludwig. *Der Mittler* (N). 1916.

_____. *Die Opfer des Kaisers* (P). 1918.

_____. *Ostjüdische Liebeslieder* (P). Berlin, 1920.

_____. *Der Weg* (P). 1921.

_____. *Ruf aus der Zeit* (P). 1927.

_____. *Der Reiter* (n). 1929.

_____. *Ein jüdisches Lesebuch.* 1933.

_____. *Jüdische Volkslieder* (anth., P). Berlin, 1935.

_____. *Land Israel* (P). 1935.

_____. *Gedichte aus den Jahren 1933–1941.* 1941.

_____. *Heimliche Gegenwart* (P). 1952.

_____. *Wintersaat* (E). Zürich, 1953.

_____. *Fahrt und Erfahrung* (documentary sketches). Heidelberg, 1959.

_____. *Dichtungen und Schriften.* München, 1963.

About Ludwig Strauss

Kraft, Werner. "On Ludwig Strauss." *Dichtungen und Schriften,* pp. 795–810.

By Ernst Toller

Toller, Ernst. *Die Wandlung* (D). 1919.

_____. *Der Tag des Proletariats* (P). 1920.

_____. *Requiem der ermordeten Brüder* (P). 1920.

_____. *Masse Mensch* (D). 1921.

_____. *Die Maschinenstürmer* (D). 1922.

_____. *Hinkemann* (D). 1922.

_____. *Das Schwalbenbuch* (P). 1923.

_____. *Der entfesselte Wotan* (D). 1923.

_____. *Hoppla, wir leben!* (D). 1927.

_____. *Justiz* (A). 1927.

_____. *Quer durch. Reisebilder und Reden* (R, E). 1930.

_____. *Verbrüderung* (P). 1930.

_____. *Wunder in Amerika,* with Hermann Kesten (D). 1931.

_____. *Jugend in Deutschland* (A). 1933.

_____. *Briefe aus dem Gefängnis* (L). 1935.

_____. *Die blinde Göttin* (D). 1935.

_____. *Prosa, Briefe, Dramen, Gedichte.* Reinbek, 1961.

About Ernst Toller

Benson, Renate. *German Expressionist Drama: Ernst Toller und Georg Kaiser.* London, 1984.

Dorst, Tankred. *Toller.* Frankfurt, 1969.

Kaiser, H., ed. *Die Dichter des sozialen Humanismus: Porträts.* München, 1960.

Kesten, Hermann. "Ernst Toller." *Meine Freunde die Poeten,* pp. 153–67.

Rühle, Jürgen. "Die Schriftsteller und der Kommunismus." *Literatur and Revolution.* Köln–Berlin, 1960.

Singer, Paul. *Ernst Toller.* 1934.

Spalek, John M. *Ernst Toller and His Critics: A Bibliography.* Charlottesville, Va., 1968.

Unger, Wilhelm. "Für die Revolution ohne Terror und Blut." *Emuna* 44(1969): 186–87.

Wagner, Geoffrey. "Ernst Toller." *The Chicago Jewish Forum* 18(1960):239–44.

Willibrand, W. A. *Ernst Toller, Product of Two Revolutions.* 1941.

By Kurt Tucholsky

Tucholsky, Kurt. *Rheinsberg, ein Bilderbuch für Verliebte.* 1912.
_____. *Der Zeitsparer* (pseud. Ignaz Wrobel). 1914.
_____. *Fromme Gesänge* (P). 1919.
_____. *Ein Pyrenäenbuch* (travel book). 1927.
_____. *Das Lächeln der Mona Lisa.* 1929.
_____. *Deutschland, Deutschland über alles* (picture book). 1929, 1964; trans. A. Halley, ed. Harry Zohn, 1972; trans. John Heartfield, 1973.
_____. *Träumereien an Preußischen Kaminen* (pseud. Peter Panter). 1930.
_____. *Lerne lachen ohne zu weinen.* 1931.
_____. *Schloß Gripsholm* (n). 1931; trans. Michael Hofmann, London, 1985.
_____. *Gesammelte Werke,* ed. Mary Gerold-Tucholsky and Fritz J. Radatz. 3 vols. Reinbek, 1960.
_____. *Ausgewählte Briefe* (1913–1935). 1962.
_____. *Politische Briefe.* 1969.

About Kurt Tucholsky

Doerfel, Marianne. *Kurt Tucholsky.* Stuttgart, 1969.
Mayer, Hans. "Kurt Tucholsky, der pessimistische Aufklärer." *Zur deutschen Literatur der Zeit.* Reinbek, 1967.
Mehring, Walter. *Kurt Tucholsky.* Berlin, 1985.
Prescher, Hans. *Kurt Tucholsky.* 1968.
Schulz, Klaus-Peter. *Tucholsky.* 1959.
Zohn, Harry, ed. *Germany? Germany: A Kurt Tucholsky Reader,* trans. H. Zohn, K. F. Ross, and L. Golden. Manchester, 1990.
_____. *The World is a Comedy: A Kurt Tucholsky Anthology,* trans. H. Zohn. Cambridge, 1957.
Zohn, Harry, and Karl F. Ross, eds. *What If . . . ?: Satirical Writings of Kurt Tucholsky,* trans. H. Zohn and K. F. Ross. New York, 1968–69.

By Rahel Varnhagen von Ense

Briefwechsel mit August Varnhagen von Ense (mostly correspondence). München, 1957.
Gesammelte Werke, eds. K. Feilchenfeldt Uwe Schweikert and Rahel Steiner. 10 vols. München, 1983.
Briefwechsel mit Alexander von der Marwitz (mostly correspondence). München, n.d.

About Rahel Varnhagen von Ense

Arendt, Hanna. *Rahel Varnhagen. Lebensgeschichte einer deutschen Jüdin aus der Romantik.* Frankfurt–Berlin, 1974 (with selected letters); New York, 1974.
Feilchenfeldt, Konrad. "Die Anfänge des Kults um Rahel Varnhagen und seine

Kritiker." In *Juden im Vormärz und in der Revolution von 1848,* ed. W. Grab and Julius H. Schoeps. Stuttgart–Bonn, 1983.

Isselstein, Ursula. "Rahel und Brentano. Analyse einer mißglückten Freundschaft." *Jahrbuch des Freien Deutschen Hochstifts.* Tübingen, 1985.

T. H. M. (Theodore Mundt). "Rahel und ihre Zeit." *Charaktere und Literatur.* n.p., n.d.

By Jakob Wassermann

Wassermann, Jakob. *Die Juden von Zirndorf* (N). 1897.

———. *Caspar Hauser oder die Trägheit des Herzens* (N). 1908. Frankfurt, 1969.

———. *Das Gänsemännchen* (N). Munich, 1915.

———. *Christian Wahnschaffe* (N). Munich, 1919.

———. *Der Fall Maurizius* (N). Munich, 1928; 1961.

———. *Etzel Andergast.* Munich, 1931; 1961.

———. *Mein Weg als Deutscher und als Jude* (A). Munich, 1933.

———. *Selbstbetrachtungen* (A, E). Munich, 1933.

———. *Joseph Kerkhovens dritte Existenz* (N). Munich, 1961.

About Jakob Wassermann

Bing, Siegmund. *Jakob Wassermann.* Berlin, 1933.

Blankenagel, J. C. *The Writings of Jakob Wassermann.* n.p., 1942.

Karlweis, M. *Jakob Wassermann.* 1935.

Poeschel, Erwin. "Jakob Wassermann." In *Juden in der deutschen Literatur,* ed. G. Krojanker. 1922.

Shaked, Gershon. "The Wassermann Case." *Hebrew University Studies in Literature and the Arts* 13(1985):98–117.

Stengel-Marchan, Birgit. "Das tragische Paradox der Assimilation—der Fall Wassermann." In *Juden und Judentum in der Literatur,* ed. H. E. Straus and Christhard Hoffmann. München, 1985.

By Otto Weininger

Weininger, Otto. *Geschlecht und Charakter* (E, P). Wien, 1903.

———. *Über die letzten Dinge* (P). Nachlaß, 1904.

———. *Genie und Verbrechen* (E, P). Graz, 1962.

About Otto Weininger

Abrahamsen, David. *The Mind and Death of a Genius.* New York, n.d.

Baum, Oskar. "Otto Weininger." In *Juden in der deutschen Literatur,* ed. Gustav Krojanker. 1922.

Dallago, Carl. *Otto Weininger und sein Werk.* 1912.

Le Rider, Jacques. *Der Fall Otto Weininger: Wurzeln des Antifeminismus und Antisemitismus.* Wien, 1985.

Le Rider, Jacques, and Norbert Leser, eds. *Otto Weininger: Werk und Wirkung*. Wien, 1984.

Susman, Margaret. "Ein Frühvollendeter." *Gestalten und Kreise*. Zürich, 1954.

Swoboda, Hermann. *Otto Weiningers Tod*. 1923.

Thaler, Leopold. *Weiningers Weltanschauung*. 1935.

By Franz Carl Weiskopf

Weiskopf, Franz Carl. *Lissy oder die Versuchung* (N). 1937; East Berlin, 1969.

_____. *Vor einem neuen Tag* (N). 1944.

_____. *Das Himmelfahrtskommando* (N). 1945; East Berlin, 1967.

_____. *Abschied vom Frieden* (N). 1950.

_____. *Kinder ihrer Zeit* (N). n.d.

About Franz Carl Weiskopf

Gallmeister, Petra. *Die historischen Romane von Franz Carl Weiskopf 'Abschied vom Frieden' und 'Inmitten des Stroms'*. Frankfurt, 1983.

Hiebel, Irmfried. *F. C. Weiskopf: Schriftsteller und Kritiker*. East Berlin, 1973.

Reimann, Paul. *Von Herder bis Kisch. Studien zur Geschichte der deutsch-österreichisch-tschechischen Literaturbeziehungen*. East Berlin, 1961.

By Ernst Weiss

Weiss, Ernst. *Die Galeere* (N). 1913.

_____. *Franziska* (N). 1915.

_____. *Der Kampf* (N). 1916.

_____. *Tiere in Ketten* (N). 1918, 1922.

_____. *Tanja* (D). 1920.

_____. *Versöhnungsfest* (P). 1920.

_____. *Daniel* (N). 1924.

_____. *Boetus von Orlamunde* (N). 1927.

_____. *Das Unverlierbare* (E). 1928.

_____. *Georg Letham, Arzt und Mörder* (N). 1931.

_____. *Die Herznaht* (n). Amsterdam, 1934.

_____. *Der arme Verschwender* (N). Amsterdam, 1936.

_____. *Der Verführer*. Zürich, 1937.

_____. *Ich, der Augenzeuge* (N). Nachlaß. 1963.

_____. *Gesammelte Werke*, eds. P. Engel and M. Voker. 16 vols. Frankfurt, 1982.

About Ernst Weiss

Engel, Paul, ed. *Ernst Weiss*. Frankfurt, 1982.

Kesten, Hermann. "Ernst Weiss." *Meine Freunde die Poeten*. 1960.

Pazi, Margarita. "Das Problem des Bösen und der Willensfreiheit bei Max Brod, Ernst Weiss und Franz Kafka." *Modern Austrian Literature* 18(1985):63–81.

Wondrak, Eduard. *Einiges über den Arzt und Schriftsteller Ernst Weiss.* München, 1968.

By Franz Werfel

Werfel, Franz. *Der Besuch aus dem Elysium* (D). 1911.
_____. *Der Weltfreund* (P). 1911–12.
_____. *Wir sind!* (P). 1913.
_____. *Einander* (P). 1914.
_____. *Gesänge aus den drei Reichen* (P). 1914.
_____. *Nicht der Mörder, der Ermordete ist schuldig* (N). 1915.
_____. *Der Gerichtstag* (P). 1916.
_____. *Die Mittagsgöttin* (D). 1917.
_____. *Spiegelmensch* (D). 1920.
_____. *Bockgesang* (D). 1921.
_____. *Juarez und Maximilian* (D). 1924.
_____. *Paulus unter den Juden* (D). 1925.
_____. *Gesammelte Gedichte.* 1927.
_____. *Der Abituriententag* (N). 1928.
_____. *Gesammelte Dramen.* 1928.
_____. *Barbara oder die Frömmigkeit* (N). 1929.
_____. *Die Geschwister von Neapel* (N). 1931.
_____. *Können wir ohne Gottesglauben leben?* (E, speech). 1932.
_____. *Die vierzig Tage des Musa Dagh* (N). 1933; Frankfurt, 1965.
_____. *Der Weg der Verheißung* (D). 1935.
_____. *Jeremias. Höret die Stimme* (N). 1937; 1956; Frankfurt, 1966.
_____. *Der veruntreute Himmel* (N). 1939.
_____. *Das Lied der Bernadette* (N). 1941; 1962.
_____. *Die wahre Geschichte vom wiederhergestellten Kreuz* (N). 1942.
_____. *Jacobowsky und der Oberst* (D). 1945.
_____. *Stern der Ungeborenen* (N). 1946; Frankfurt, 1967.
_____. *Zwischen Oben und Unten* (E). 1946; 1969.
_____. *Gesammelte Werke.* 6 vols. Frankfurt, 1948–67.

About Franz Werfel

Braselmann, Werner. *Franz Werfel: Dichtung und Deutung.* n.p., n.d.
Jungk, Peter. *Franz Werfel: Eine Lebensgeschichte.* Frankfurt, 1987.
Kayser, Rudolf. "Franz Werfel." In *Juden in der deutschen Literatur,* ed. Gustav Krojanker. 1922.
Specht, Richard. *Franz Werfel.* Wien, 1926.
Zahn, Leopold. *Franz Werfel.* n.d.

By Alfred Wolfenstein

Wolfenstein, Alfred. *Die gottlosen Jahre* (P). 1914.

_____. *Die Freundschaft* (P). 1917.

_____. *Die Nackten* (P). 1917.

_____. *Der Lebendige* (n). 1918.

_____. *Menschlicher Kämpfer* (P). 1919.

_____. *Sturm auf den Tod* (D). 1921.

_____. *Der Mann* (D). 1922.

_____. *Jüdische Wesen und neue Dichtung* (E). 1922.

_____. *Der Flügelmann* (P). 1924.

_____. *Unter den Sternen* (n). 1924.

_____. *Bäume in den Himmel* (D). 1926.

_____. *Die Celestina* (D). 1926.

_____. *Die Nacht vor dem Beil* (D). 1929.

_____. *Die gefährlichen Engel* (n). 1937.

_____. *Ausgewählte Werke.* 1955.

_____. *Werke,* ed. Günther Holz. 3 vols. Mainz, 1984–85.

About Alfred Wolfenstein

Fischer, Peter. *Alfred Wolfenstein. Zur Literatur des Expressionismus.* München, 1968.

_____. "Alfred Wolfenstein." *Expressionismus und verehrende Kunst.* n.p., 1968.

Mumm, Carl, ed. *Alfred Wolfenstein: Einführung in sein Werk und eine Auswahl.* Wiesbaden, 1955.

Petersen, Klaus. *'Die Gruppe 1925'. Geschichte und Soziologie einer Schriftstellervereinigung.* Heidelberg, 1981.

By Karl Wolfskehl

Wolfskehl, Karl. *Ulais* (P). 1897.

_____. *Gesammelte Dichtungen* (P). 1903.

_____. *Der Umkreis* (P). 1927.

_____. *Bild und Gesetz.* 1930.

_____. *Die Stimme spricht* (P). 1934.

_____. *An die Deutschen* (P). 1947.

_____. *Hiob oder die vier Spiegel* (P). 1950.

_____. *Sang aus dem Exil.* Heidelberg, 1950.

_____. *Zehn Jahre Exil, Briefe 1938–1948,* ed. Margot Ruben. Heidelberg, 1959.

_____. *Gesammelte Werke,* ed. Margot Ruben and Claus Victor Bock. 2 vols. Hamburg, 1960.

_____. *Karl Wolfskehl: Briefe und Aufsätze, München 1925–1933,* ed. Margot Ruben. Hamburg, 1966.

_____. *Kalon bekawod namir—Aus Schmach wird Ehr.* Nachlaß, n.d.

About Karl Wolfskehl

Bowert, Ruth. *Die Prosa Karl Wolfkehls: Grundzüge seines Denkens und seiner*

Ausdrucksform (diss.). 1965, n.p.

Euler, Walter, and Hans Rolf Rompetz. *Karl Wolfskehl (Gedenkbuch)*. Darmstadt, 1966.

Grimm, Gunter. *Die Hiob-Dichtung Karl Wolfskehls*. Bonn, 1972.

Hoffmann, Theodor. *Das religiöse Spätwerk Karl Wolfkehls* (diss.). Wien, 1957.

Klussmann, Paul Gerhard, ed. *Karl-Wolfskehl-Kolloquium* Bonn, 1978; Amsterdam, 1983.

Landau, Erwin. *Karl Wolfskehl* (diss.). n.p., 1928.

Schloesser, Manfred, ed. *Laßt das Wort stehn! Karl Wolfskehl Bibliographie*. Darmstadt, 1969.

Susman, Margarete. *Gestalten und Kreise*. Zürich, 1954.

By Arnold Zweig

Zweig, Arnold. *Vorfrühling* (N). 1908.

_____. *Aufzeichnung über eine Familie Klopfer* (n). 1911.

_____. *Novellen um Claudia* (N). 1912.

_____. *Abigail und Nabal* (D). 1913.

_____. *Ritualmord in Ungarn* (D). 1914.

_____. *Das ostjüdische Antlitz* (E, n). 1920.

_____. *Entwicklung und Aufruhr* (P). 1921.

_____. *Gerufene Schatten* (n). 1923.

_____. *Das neue Kanaan* (E). 1925.

_____. *Die Umkehr des Abtrünnigen* (D). 1925.

_____. *Lessing, Kleist, Büchner* (B, E). 1925.

_____. *Der Regenbogen* (n). 1926.

_____. *Caliban oder Politik und Leidenschaft* (E). 1927.

_____. *Der Streit um den Sergeanten Grischa* (N). 1927.

_____. *Juden auf der deutschen Bühne* (E). 1927.

_____. *Herkunft und Zukunft* (E). 1928.

_____. *Pont und Anna* (N). 1928.

_____. *Junge Frau von 1914* (N). 1931.

_____. *Knaben und Männer* (n). 1931.

_____. *Mädchen und Frauen* (n). 1931.

_____. *De Vriendt kehrt heim* (N). 1932.

_____. *Bilanz der deutschen Judenheit* (E). 1933.

_____. *Spielzeug der Zeit* (n). 1933.

_____. *Erziehung vor Verdun* (N). 1934.

_____. *Einsetzung eines Königs* (N). 1937.

_____. *Versunkene Tage* (N). 1938.

_____. *Das Beil von Wandsbek* (N). 1943.

_____. *Bonaparte in Jaffa* (D). 1949.

_____. *Feuerpause* (N). 1954.

_____. *Soldatenspiele* (D). 1956.

_____. *Die Zeit ist reif* (N). 1957.

_____. *Dramen.* 1963.

_____. *Sigmund Freud-Arnold Zweig/Briefwechsel.* Frankfurt, 1968.

_____. *Der große Krieg der Weißen Männer* (N). 1969.

(Many of Zweig's earlier and nearly all of his later works were published or republished in East Berlin.)

About Arnold Zweig

Goldstein, Moritz. "Arnold Zweig." In *Juden in der deutschen Literatur,* ed. Gustav Krojanker. 1922.

Gottgetreu, Erich. "Arnold Zweigs Wanderung von Berlin nach Berlin." *Emuna* 4(1969):7–14.

Kahn, Lothar. "Arnold Zweig: From Zionism to Marxism." *Mirrors of the Jewish Mind.* 1968.

Kamnitzer, Heinz. *Der Tod des Dichters* (A). East Berlin, 1981.

Pfeiler, W. K. *War and the German Mind.* 1941.

Voigtländer, Annie, ed. *Welt und Wirkung eines Romans.* (Zu Arnold Zweig's *Der Streit um den Sergeanten Grischa).* East Berlin, 1969.

von Hofe, Harold, ed. *Lion Feuchtwanger–Arnold Zweig Briefwechsel 1933–1958.* 2 vols. East Berlin, 1984.

Wolf, Arie. *Arnold Zweigs Ostjudenbild. LBI Bulletin* (1984).

Wolf, Gerhard. "Zum Briefwechsel Louis Fürnberg–Arnold Zweig." *Weimarer Beiträge* 13(1967):355–70.

By Stefan Zweig

Zweig, Stefan. *Silberne Saiten* (P). 1901.

_____. *Die Liebe der Erika Ewald* (n). 1904.

_____. *Tersites* (D). 1907.

_____. *Der verwandelte Komödiant* (D). 1913.

_____. *Das Herz Europas* (E). 1918.

_____. *Jeremias* (D). 1918.

_____. *Drei Meister* (E). 1920.

_____. *Fahrten* (E). 1920.

_____. *Amok* (n). 1922.

_____. *Brief einer Unbekannten* (N). 1922.

_____. *Die gesammelten Gedichte* (P). 1924.

_____. *Angst* (n). 1925.

_____. *Der Kampf mit dem Dämon* (E). 1925.

_____. *Verwirrung der Gefühle* (n). 1926.

_____. *Die unsichtbare Sammlung* (E). 1927.

_____. *Begegnungen mit Menschen, Büchern, Städten* (A, R). 1937.

_____. *Schachnovelle* (n). 1943.

_____. *Sternstunden der Menschheit* (N). 1943.

_____. *Die Welt von gestern* (A). 1944.

_____. *Der begrabene Leuchter* (n). 1963.

_____. *Unbekannte Briefe aus der Emigration an eine Freundin* (L, A). 1964.

_____. *Buchmendel* (n). n.d.

_____. *Die Legende der dritten Taube.* n.d.

_____. *"Rachel rechtet mit Gott"* (legend). n.d.

Also biographies of Joseph Fouche (1929, 1952) and Marie Antoinette (called biographical novels), Erasmus, Maria Stuart, Magellan (1938), and others; monographs on *Gesammelte Werke in Einzelbänden,* ed. Knut Beck. Frankfurt, 1983.

About Stefan Zweig

Allday, Elizabeth. *Stefan Zweig: A Critical Biography.* London, 1972.

Arens, Hans. *Stefan Zweig, der große Europäer.* München, 1960.

Fitzbauer, Erich, ed. *Spiegelungen einer schöpferischen Persönlichkeit.* (Erste Sonderpublikation der S. Zweig Gesellschaft.) Vienna, 1959.

LBI Bulletin, 63. (Stefan Zweig Symposium at Beer Sheva, Königstein, Ts., 1982).

Leftwich, Joseph. "Stefan Zweig and the World of Yesterday." *LBY,* (1958):81–100.

Liptzin, Sol. *Germany's Stepchildren.* 1944.

Prater, Donald A. *European of Yesterday. A Biography of Stefan Zweig.* Oxford, 1972.

Relgis, Eugen. "Stefan Zweig and Judaism." *Jewish Affairs* (South Africa) 11(1956).

Rieger, E. *Stefan Zweig.* 1928.

Romains, Jules. *Stefan Zweig, Great European.* 1941.

Zech, Paul. *Stefan Zweig.* 1943.

Zohn, Harry. "Stefan Zweig, Bericht und Bekenntnis." *Wiener Juden in der deutschen Literatur.* Tel Aviv, 1964.

Zohn, Harry, and W. H. McClain. "Stefan Zweig and Romain Rolland." *Germanic Review* 28(1953).

INDEXES

NAME INDEX

313

SUBJECT INDEX

TITLE INDEX